David Frankfurter is Assistant Professor of History and Religious Studies at the University of New Hampshire. He is the author of *Elijah in Upper Egypt: The Apocalypse of Elijah and Early Egyptian Christianity*.

# RELIGION IN ROMAN EGYPT

# ·RELIGION IN· ROMAN EGYPT

ASSIMILATION AND RESISTANCE

# DAVID FRANKFURTER

·PRINCETON UNIVERSITY PRESS·

PRINCETON, NEW JERSEY

COPYRIGHT © 1998 BY PRINCETON UNIVERSITY PRESS

PUBLISHED BY PRINCETON UNIVERSITY PRESS, 41 WILLIAM STREET,

PRINCETON, NEW JERSEY 08540

IN THE UNITED KINGDOM: PRINCETON UNIVERSITY PRESS, CHICHESTER, WEST SUSSEX

ALL RIGHTS RESERVED

LIBRARY OF CONGRESS CATALOGING-IN-PUBLICATION DATA

FRANKFURTER, DAVID, 1961–

RELIGION IN ROMAN EGYPT : ASSIMILATION AND RESISTANCE / DAVID

FRANKFURTER.

P.   CM.

INCLUDES BIBLIOGAPHICAL REFERENCES AND INDEX.

ISBN 0-691-02685-8 (CL : ALK. PAPER)

1. EGYPT—RELIGION—332 B.C.–640 A.D.   2. CHRISTIANITY AND OTHER

RELIGIONS—EGYPTIAN.   I. TITLE.

BL2455.F73   1998

200′.932′09015—DC21   97-49576   CIP

THIS BOOK HAS BEEN COMPOSED IN SABON TYPEFACE

TITLE PAGE ILLUSTRATION: ARMORED, MOUNTED HORUS SPEARING CROCODILE.
SANDSTONE. H: 49.1 CM. W: 32 CM. D: 7.8 CM. PARIS, LOUVRE E.4850. COURTESY OF
THE LOUVRE.

PRINCETON UNIVERSITY PRESS BOOKS ARE PRINTED ON ACID-FREE PAPER

AND MEET THE GUIDELINES

FOR PERMANENCE AND DURABILITY OF THE COMMITTEE ON PRODUCTION

GUIDELINES FOR BOOK LONGEVITY OF THE COUNCIL ON LIBRARY RESOURCES

HTTP://PUP.PRINCETON.EDU

PRINTED IN THE UNITED STATES OF AMERICA

3   5   7   9   10   8   6   4   2

DEDICATED TO THE MEMORY OF

*Alexander Moritz Frankfurter*

1963–1993

HOW COULD WE SING THE LORD'S SONG

IN A FOREIGN LAND?

—PS 137

# CONTENTS

*A section of plates follows chapter 2.*

# ACKNOWLEDGMENTS

THIS BOOK began with a footnote, briefly compiling some evidence for Egyptian priests' activity in the later Roman period, only to burgeon into a rapidly consuming interest in the vitality of Egyptian religion in a period when most scholars assumed its decay. But the interest would never have come to such fruition if not for a summer stipend from the National Endowment for the Humanities (1992), a two-year Historical Studies fellowship at the Institute for Advanced Study (1993–95), and the continuing interest, encouragement, and critical gifts of Glen Bowersock, John Baines, John Gager, and Peter Brown.

In assembling a book so rooted in Egyptology I am extraordinarily grateful to Terry Wilfong, Janet Johnson, Dorothy Thompson, and the late Evasio DeMarcellis for their generous aid and advice (and I hold them in no way responsible for what lingering errors there may be). Others have been generous with bibliographical advice, advance copies of publications, or lively discussion, and I am delighted to acknowledge the various assistances of Jan Assmann, Roger Bagnall, Heike Behlmer, David Brakke, Ted Brock, Stephen Emmel, Richard Jasnow, Sarah Iles Johnston, László Kákosy, Olaf Kaper, Joseph Manning, Richard and Sally Price, Jan Quaegebeur, Albert Raboteau, James Tait, and Deborah Winslow. For their invaluable help in procuring illustrations I thank Robin Meador-Woodruff of the Kelsey Museum of Archaeology, Krisztina Bóka Di Cave of the Budapest Museum of Fine Arts, Helen Whitehouse of the Ashmolean Museum (Oxford), Mervat Seif el-Din of the Greco-Roman Museum of Alexandria, Marie-Hélène Rutschowscaya of the Louvre (Paris), Anne Minault-Gout of the Institut Français d'Archéologie orientale in Cairo, Yvonne Markowitz of Boston's Museum of Fine Arts (for drafting a fine sketch of a Bes amulet), and Juliette Rogers for smoothing epistolary communications abroad.

A preliminary form of chapters 5 and 6 was delivered to the Seminar on Magic at the School of Historical Studies (Institute for Advanced Study) in December 1994, since published in *Envisioning Magic: A Princeton Seminar and Symposium,* edited by Peter Schäfer and Hans G. Kippenberg (Leiden: Brill, 1997), 115–35. Chapter 7 was delivered in an earlier form as the 1995 Davis Lecture in Early Christianity at the Ohio State University, and I remain grateful for the invitation and the conversations the lecture developed. Funds for some final production costs were generously granted by Marilyn Hoskyn, Dean of the College of Liberal Arts of the University of New Hampshire, and Burt Feintuch, Center for the Humanities at the University of New Hampshire. I am also indebted to Alan K.

Bowman for providing me with his map of Roman Egypt and to Chris Brest for adjusting it to my needs.

For my family, of course, Roman Egyptian religion has remained the esoteric study that kept me strangely obsessed late into many nights and weekends, and I gratefully acknowledge their patience. It is my son Raphael's special gift to have imagined, at three years old, a "kid's Egypt" that he could visit while his father was off studying temples.

# ABBREVIATIONS

| | |
|---|---|
| Aelian, *De nat. animal.* | *De natura animalium* |
| *AJP* | *American Journal of Philology* |
| *AnBoll* | *Analecta Bollandiana* |
| *ANCL* | *Ante-Nicene Christian Library* |
| *ANF* | *Ante-Nicene Fathers* |
| *ANRW* | *Austieg und Niedergang der römischen Welt,* ed. W. Haase and H. Temporini (Berlin, 1974– ) |
| *AOH* | *Acta Orientalia Hungaricae* |
| *Apophth.Pat.* | *Apophthegmata Patrum* |
| *Archiv* | *Archiv für Papyrusforschung* |
| *ASAE* | *Annales du Service des Antiquités de l'Égypte* |
| *Ascl.* | *Asclepius* |
| ASP | American Studies in Papyrology |
| *ASSR* | *Archives des sciences sociales des religions* |
| Athanasius, *V.Ant.* | *Vita Antonii* |
| *Ep.* | *Epistuli* |
| *BACE* | *Bulletin of the Australian Centre for Egyptology* |
| *BASP* | *Bulletin of the American Society of Papyrologists* |
| *BCH* | *Bulletin de corréspondance hellénique* |
| *BES* | *Bulletin of the Egyptological Seminar* |
| *BGU* | *Ägyptische Urkunden aus den königlichen [/staatlichen] Museen zu Berlin, Griechische Urkunden* |
| *BICS* | *Bulletin of the Institute for Classical Studies* |
| *BIE* | *Bulletin de l'institut d'Égypte* |
| *BIFAO* | *Bulletin de l'institut français d'archéologie orientale* |
| *BJRL* | *Bulletin of the John Rylands Library* |
| BJS | Brown Judaic Studies |
| *BSAA* | *Bulletin de la société archéologique d'Alexandrie* |
| *BSAC* | *Bulletin de la société d'archéologie copte* |
| *BSE* | *Bulletin de la société égyptologique* |
| *BSFE* | *Bulletin de la société française d'égyptologie* |
| *CdÉ* | *Chronique d'Égypte* |
| *CAH* | *Cambridge Ancient History* |

| | |
|---|---|
| *C.H.* | *Corpus Hermeticum* |
| *CIG* | *Corpus Inscriptionum Graecarum*, ed. A. Boeckh (Vienna, 1828–77) |
| Clement, *Strom.* | *Stromateis* |
| *Paed.* | *Paedogogos* |
| *Protrept.* | *Protrepticos* |
| *CP* | *Classical Philology* |
| *CPJ* | *Corpus Papyrorum Iudaicarum*, ed. V. Tcherikover and A. Fuks (Cambridge, 1957–64) |
| *CPR* | *Corpus Papyrorum Raineri* 1– (Vienna, 1895– ) |
| CRINT | Compendia Rerum Iudaicarum ad Novum Testamentum |
| CSCO | Corpus Scriptorum Christianorum Orientalium |
| CSS | Cistercian Studies Series |
| *DACL* | *Dictionnaire de l'archéologie chrétienne et de liturgie* (Paris, 1907–53) |
| *DOP* | *Dumbarton Oaks Papers* |
| EPRO | Études préliminaires aux religions orientales dans l'Empire Romain (continued by RGRW) |
| *ERE* | *Encyclopedia of Religion and Ethics*, ed. J. Hastings (New York, 1911) |
| Eunapius, *V.P.* | *Vita Philosophorum* |
| Eusebius, *H.E.* | *Historia Ecclesiastica* |
| *GM* | *Göttinger Miszellen* |
| *GRBS* | *Greek, Roman, and Byzantine Studies* |
| *HAHR* | *Hispanic American Historical Review* |
| HDR | Harvard Dissertations in Religion |
| *Hist. Mon.* | *Historia monachorum in Aegypto* |
| *HTR* | *Harvard Theological Review* |
| *HUCA* | *Hebrew Union College Annual* |
| *ICS* | *Illinois Classical Studies* |
| *IESS* | *International Encyclopedia of the Social Sciences*, ed. D. Sills (New York, 1968) |
| IDemPhilae | *Catalogue of the Demotic Graffiti of the Dodecaschoenus* 1, ed. F. Griffith (Oxford, 1937) |
| *IGAkoris* | *Inscriptions grecques et latines d'Akôris*, ed. É. Bernand (Cairo, 1985) |
| IGFayyum 1–3 | *Recueil des inscriptions grecques du Fayoum,* |

ed. É. Bernand, 1 (Leiden, 1975); 2–3 (Cairo, 1981)

| | |
|---|---|
| IGPhilae | *Les inscriptions grecques et latines de Philae* 1–2, ed. É. Bernand (Paris, 1969) |
| JAARTS | *Journal of the American Academy of Religion Thematic Studies* |
| JAC | *Jahrbuch für Antike und Christentum* |
| JAOS | *Journal of the American Oriental Society* |
| JARCE | *Journal of the American Research Center in Egypt* |
| JCS | *Journal of Coptic Studies* |
| JEA | *Journal of Egyptian Archaeology* |
| JECS | *Journal of Early Christian Studies* |
| Jerome, *V.Hil.* | *Vita Hilarionis* |
| JHS | *Journal of Hellenic Studies* |
| JJP | *Journal of Juristic Papyrology* |
| JJS | *Journal of Jewish Studies* |
| JNES | *Journal of Near Eastern Studies* |
| JRA | *Journal of Roman Archaeology* |
| JRAf | *Journal of Religion in Africa* |
| JRS | *Journal of Roman Studies* |
| JSSEA | *Journal of the Society for the Study of Egyptian Antiquities* |
| JTS | *Journal of Theological Studies* |
| LCL | Loeb Classical Library |
| Leipoldt 1–4 | Johannes Leipoldt, *Sinuthii archimandritae vita et opera omnia* 1 & 3–4 CSCO 41–42, 73 (Paris, 1906–13) |
| *LexÄg* | *Lexikon der Ägyptologie* 1–6, ed. W. Helck and E. Otto (Wiesbaden, 1972– ) |
| *MDAIK* | *Mitteilungen des deutschen archäologischen Institut, Abteilung Kairo* |
| MIFAO | Mémoires publiées par les membres de l'institut français d'archéologie orientale |
| MPN | Mitteilungen aus der Papyrussammlung der Nationalbibliothek, Vienna |
| NHC I–XIII | Nag Hammadi Codex I–XIII |
| *NHLE* | *The Nag Hammadi Library in English*, ed. J. Robinson (San Francisco, 1988) |
| NHS | Nag Hammadi Studies |
| *NPNF* | *Nicene and Post-Nicene Fathers* |
| OLA | Orientalia Lovaniensia Analecta |
| *OLP* | *Orientalia Lovaniensia Periodica* |

OMRO

*Oudheidkundige Mededeelingen uit het Rijksmuseum van Oudheden te Leiden*

O.Theb.

*Theban Ostraca*, ed. A. H. Gardiner, H. Thompson, and J. G. Milne (London, 1913)

OTP

*The Old Testament Pseudepigrapha* 1–2, ed. J. Charlesworth (Garden City, N.Y., 1983–85)

OUCA

Oxford University Committee for Archaeology

PAPS

*Proceedings of the American Philosophical Society*

P.Athens

*Papyri Societatis Archaeologicae Atheniensis,* ed. G. A. Petropoulos (Athens, 1939)

P.Fayyum

*Fayûm Towns and Their Papyri,* ed. B. P. Grenfell, A. S. Hunt, and D. G. Hogarth (London, 1900)

PG

*Patrologia Graeca,* ed. J. P. Migne (Paris, 1857–66)

P.Giss.

*Griechische Papyri im Museum des oberhessischen Geschichtsvereins zu Giessen* (Leipzig/Berlin, 1910–12)

P.Grenfell I–II

I = *An Alexandrian Erotic Fragment and Other Greek Papyri,* ed. B. P. Grenfell (Oxford, 1896); II = *New Classical Fragments and Other Greek and Latin Papyri,* ed. B. P. Grenfell and A. S. Hunt (Oxford, 1896)

PDM xiv, lxi

*Papyri Demoticae Magicae*

P.Köln I–VII

*Kölner Papyri,* ed. B. Kramer et al. (Opladen, 1976– )

PGM I–CXXX

*Papyri Graecae Magicae* (I–LXXI), ed. K. Preisendanz (Stuttgart, 1973–74); *The Greek Magical Papyri in Translation* (I–CXXX), ed. H. D. Betz (Chicago, 1986)

P.Heid.

*Veröffentlichungen aus der Heidelberger Papyrussammlung*

PL

*Patrologia Latina,* ed. J. P. Migne (Paris, 1841–64)

P.Lond. I–

*Greek Papyri in the British Museum* (London)

P.Lugd.-Bat.

*Papyrologica Lugduno-Batava* (Leiden)

P-M 1–7

*Topographical Bibliography of Ancient Egyptian Hieroglyphical Texts, Reliefs and*

|  |  |
|---|---|
|  | *Paintings* 1–7, ed. B. Porter and R. L. B. Moss (Oxford, 1927– ) |
| *P.Merton* I–III | *A Descriptive Catalogue of the Greek Papyri in the Collection of Wilfred Merton,* ed. H. I. Bell et al. (London, 1948–67) |
| *P.Mich.* | *Michigan Papyri* |
| *P.Mil.Vogl.* I–VII | *Papiri della Università degli Studi di Milano* (Milan, 1937–81) |
| PO | *Patrologia Orientalis* |
| *P.Oslo* | *Papyri Osloenses,* ed. S. Eitrem and L. Amundsen (Oslo, 1925–36) |
| *P.Oxy* I– | *The Oxyrhynchus Papyri* (London, 1898– ) |
| *P.Ross.Georg.* | *Papyri russischer und georgischer Sammlungen* (Tiflis) |
| *P.Sakaon* | *The Archive of Aurelius Sakaon,* ed. G. M. Parássoglou (Bonn, 1978) |
| PSBA | *Proceedings of the Society for Biblical Archaeology* |
| PSI | *Papyri grece e latini* (Florence, 1912– ) |
| *P.Sta.Xyla.* | *The Byzantine Papyri of the Greek Papyrological Society* 1–, ed. B. G. Mandilaras (Athens, 1993) |
| *P.Strasb.* | *Griechische Papyrus der kaiserlichen Universitäts- und Landesbibliothek zu Strasburg* (Leipzig) |
| *P.Tebtunis* | *The Tebtunis Papyri* (London) |
| *P. Turner* | *Papyri Greek and Egyptian in Honour of Eric Gardner Turner,* ed. P. Parsons et al. (London, 1981) |
| Plutarch, *De Iside* | *De Iside et Osiride* |
| RdÉ | *Revue d'Égyptologie* |
| REAug | *Revue des études augustiniennes* |
| RevPhil | *Revue de philologie* |
| RGRW | Religions of the Graeco-Roman World |
| RHR | *Revue d'histoire des religions* |
| ROC | *Revue de l'orient chrétien* |
| RSO | *Rivista degli studi orientali* |
| Rufinus, *H.E.* | *Historia Ecclesiastica* |
| SAOC | Studies in Ancient Oriental Civilization |
| SB | *Sammelbuch griechischer Urkunden aus Ägypten* |
| SC | Sources chrétiennes |
| SCO | *Studi classici et orientali* |

| | |
|---|---|
| SJLA | Studies in Judaism in Late Antiquity |
| Socrates, *H.E.* | *Historica Ecclesiastica* |
| Sozomen, *H.E.* | *Historia Ecclesiastica* |
| *SPP* | *Studien zur Palaeographie und Papyruskunde*, ed. C. Wessely (Leipzig, 1901–24) |
| *Suppl. Mag.* | *Supplementum Magicum*, ed. R. Daniel and F. Maltomini (Opladen, 1990–92) |
| *TPAPA* | *Transactions and Proceedings of the American Philological Association* |
| TU | Texte und Untersuchungen |
| *VigChr* | *Vigiliae Christianae* |
| W.Chr. | L. Mitteis and U. Wilcken, *Grundzüge und Chrestomathie der Papryuskunde* (Leipzig/Berlin, 1912) |
| YCS | *Yale Classical Studies* |
| Zachariah, *V.Sev.* | Zachariah of Mytilene, *Life of Severus* |
| ZÄS | *Zeitschrift für ägyptische Sprache und Altertumskunde* |
| ZPE | *Zeitschrift für Papyrologie und Epigraphik* |

# RELIGION IN ROMAN EGYPT

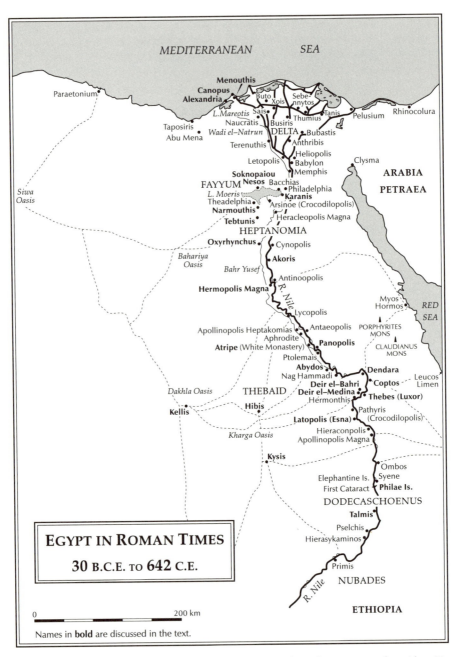

MEDITERRANEAN SEA

Paraetonium

Menouthis
Canopus
Alexandria
L.Mareotis
Taposiris
Abu Mena
Wadi el–Natrun
Naucratis
Terenuthis
Buto
Xois
Sais
Busiris
DELTA
Sebennytos
Thumius
Tanis
Pelusium
Rhinocolura
Anthribis
Bubastis
Heliopolis
Babylon
Memphis
Letopolis
Clysma

ARABIA
PETRAEA

Siwa
Oasis

Soknopaiou
FAYYUM    Nesos    Bacchias
L. Moeris      Philadelphia
Theadelphia    Karanis
Narmouthis   Arsinoe (Crocodilopolis)
Tebtunis    Heracleopolis Magna

HEPTANOMIA

Oxyrhynchus    Cynopolis

Bahariya
Oasis

Akoris

Bahr Yusef    Antinoopolis

Hermopolis Magna    R. Nile
Lycopolis

Myos
Hormos    RED
SEA

PORPHYRITES
MONS

Apollinopolis Heptakomias    Antaeopolis
Aphrodite
Atripe (White Monastery)    Panopolis
Ptolemais
Abydos
Nag Hammadi    Dendara
Deir el–Bahri    Coptos
Deir el–Medina    Thebes (Luxor)
Hermonthis    Pathyris
Latopolis (Esna)    (Crocodilopolis)
Hieraconpolis
Apollinopolis Magna

CLAUDIANUS
MONS

Leucos
Limen

Dakhla Oasis

THEBAID

Hibis

Kellis

Kharga Oasis

Kysis

Ombos
Elephantine Is.    Syene
First Cataract    Philae Is.

DODECASCHOENUS

Talmis
Pselchis
Hierasykaminos

Primis    NUBADES

R. Nile

ETHIOPIA

EGYPT IN ROMAN TIMES
30 B.C.E. TO 642 C.E.

0          200 km

Names in **bold** are discussed in the text.

Egypt in Roman Times, 30 B.C.E. to 642 C.E. Map by Chris Brest, after Alan K. Bowman, *Egypt after the Pharaohs.*

# OVERTURE

## THE ARMOR OF HORUS

IN BRONZE, in terra-cotta and stone, in graffiti and paint, the gods of Egypt began to appear in armor. They brandished swords and shields; they rode horses. They radiated victory over invisible forces of evil, even from a meter's height, frightening demons from wall niches. They were, to be sure, those gods long popular for their powers to protect. Anubis the dog-headed god, Bes the leonine dwarf-god, and especially Horus, ever the avenger of Osiris and destroyer of demonic animals, the very expression of royal protection, came out of workshops decked in the equipment of the Roman military (see pls. 1, 14).

And in this form the gods persevered. Still in the fourth century an Egyptian of some means commissioned a relief for a window in his house or his local temple that would project the god Horus's ancient powers of vengeance and expulsion, but now according to the image of a victorious emperor. Thus he rides, in the famous Louvre relief reproduced on the jacket of this book, a falcon-headed warrior with breastplate and cape, pulling back the reins of his horse with one hand while impaling a demonic crocodile with the other.

The armored gods change with these new trappings of imperial authority; but all the while they retain functions essential to any sacred image of victorious power: to protect the household or sacred place according to the most basic traditions of warding off evil and certainly also to celebrate the timeless power of an ancient god. Coptic art historians have long seen a clear line of development between the armored Horus (and like gods) and the images of the great Coptic Christian military "rider-saints" like Saint George and Saint Sissinios produced in the sixth and later centuries. The connection is not merely form but what the images conveyed in the cosmos: apotropeia, repulsion, victory over chaos and misfortune. So it is with the obscure Saint Sissinios, portrayed on a chapel wall in the sixth-century monastery of Bawit astride a horse, with spear and shield in hand, repelling all the demonic forces that the painter could muster in his or her imagination: a scorpion, a snake, an ibis, two figures with animal bodies, and a voluptuous demon of concupiscence, through whom Sissinios drives his spear.

The armor, the posture, the triumph of this ancient image preserve the practical meaning of Horus through the end of the pharaohs, the decline of the temples, and the ascendancy of Christianity. And thus religion in its most basic and most traditional aspects, in its devotion to everyday safety and conservative allegiance to the image of divine victory, also continues by reasserting itself in ever new idioms and legends.[1]

[1] *Louvre Armored Horus* (Paris, Louvre, inv. X5130): Clermont-Ganneau 1876; Pierre M. Du Bourguet, *The Art of the Copts* (New York: Crown, 1971), 89, 98; Suzanne Lewis, "The Iconography of the Coptic Horseman in Byzantine Egypt," *JARCE* 10 (1973):27–63, esp. 55. *Bawit St. Sissinios:* J. Clédat, *Le monastère et la nécropole de Baouît,* MIFAO 12 (Cairo: IFAO, 1904), 80–81, pls. 55–56; Paul Perdrizet, *Negotium Perambulans in Tenebris: Études de démonologie gréco-orientale* (Strasbourg: Istra, 1922); Van der Vliet 1991:232–33. Similar Coptic images discussed in Michailidis 1950:91–101 and Barb 1964:12–16. In general on armored gods in Roman Egypt, see R. Paribeni, "Divinita' straniere in Abito militare romano," *BSAA* 13 (1910):177–83; Loukianoff 1936; Ernst H. Kantorowicz, "Gods in Uniform," *PAPS* 105 (1961):368–93; Suzanne Lewis, "The Iconography of the Coptic Horseman in Byzantine Egypt," *JARCE* 10 (1973):27–63; Grenier 1978; Dunand 1979:81–82; Nachtergael 1988:16 (#17). Armored Bes figures in Perdrizet 1921, 1:46–47, 2:XLI; Nachtergael 1988:16; Dunand 1990:38–39, ##30–33; and Török 1995, #119 (on horseback). A prominent graffito in the Kalabscha temple of Mandulis portrays an imperial (armored and caped) figure on horseback who is crowned with the feather-headdress of Amun by a winged being and who spears a barbarian (Castiglione 1970:99–101, figs. 7–8; identified as the fifth-century C.E. Meroitic king Silko in Trigger 1978:116–17). The image of a mounted Horus is only known from Roman sources: Plutarch, *De Iside* 19 (358C); *PDM* xiv.1219–20 = P.Lond./Leiden xxxiii, 1–2. Military and rider gods became popular throughout the empire, often with regional characteristics: Delatte/Derchain 1964:261–64; Sarah Iles Johnston, "Riders in the Sky: Cavalier Gods and Theurgic Salvation in the Second Century A.D.," *CP* 87 (1992):303–21.

# 1

## SCOPE AND METHOD

### 1.1 Introduction

A S MUCH as this book concerns Egyptian religion in its later phases (roughly 100 to 600 C.E.), it is a study in cultural resilience, and it draws comparatively upon other such studies in order to answer the question, How does an established culture preserve its religious ways despite multiple pressures and traumas? And how indeed should one conceptualize "religion" so that meaningful answers might be found?

Roman Egypt has always held an ironic place in ancient history. With temples crumbling and hieroglyphs nearly forgotten and yet with startling evidence for the progression of Christianity, it has provided church historians (like their fourth-century forebears) with a convenient vantage point for watching the "twilight of paganism" and the rise of a complex ecclesiastical establishment. At the same time, with numerous examples of symbols preserved from ancient tradition in Egyptian Christian literature and art, the Coptic Christianity that was consolidated in the fourth and fifth centuries offers a rich deposit of "pagan survivals," proving either the error of the postapostolic church (to some Protestant eyes) or the authenticating legacy of the pharaohs in the contemporary Coptic church. For even the most objective scholar Roman Egypt has served as a crucible for proving, or at least illustrating, one's deepest assumptions about religious truth and religious change, and it is therefore a daunting task to cover this well-mapped ground without promoting one or another hackneyed presupposition about the rise of the church or the decline of "paganism."

But several factors together beg for a reassessment of late Egyptian religion, whether in decline or in transformation, and I would name principally the ongoing publication of materials—literary, documentary, archaeological—from Egypt under Roman and Christian rule, an increasingly sophisticated anthropology of transitional cultures and popular religions, and the flowering of anthropologically informed studies of late antique religions and cultures.

Much of this book seeks to reframe the scope and context of "religion" as it should pertain to late antique cultures. I argue that religion in Roman Egypt should be understood first as a local, collective endeavor to negotiate fertility, safety, health, misfortune, identity, and collective solidarity. Understood in this way, the various historical ideologies that bound together many locales and regions within a single institutional framework (like the various royal systems of classical and Ptolemaic Egypt or Christianity itself) appear in complementary relations, if not outright tension, with local religion, akin to Redfield's heuristic notion of a "great tradition" in dialectic with a "little tradition." The belief-systems that characterized these institutions are neither distinctive of, nor irrelevant veneers upon, general piety in village and city. They provide, rather, idioms through which local religions and cultures can articulate their worlds.

And indeed some of these idioms become precisely the means by which native religious traditions are maintained, particularly in the public arena (the village festival, the regional oracle) but also in the icons of the domestic altar and the promotional literature of the priestly hierarchy. As the royal ideology had from earliest times allowed the promotion of regional gods, so Hellenism and its literary, representational, and mythological idioms brought native religious traditions into new scopes of authority and meaning, and so also did Christianity's various idioms allow the redefinition and continuation of many kinds of religious practice. In this sense the subtitle, "Assimilation and Resistance," is meant to challenge the simplistic notion of "pagans" deliberately fighting off Christian encroachment. While there are diverse examples of such conflicts, a culture's resistance to conversion or religious decline often amounts to a complex process of embracing new idioms and ideologies in order to reinterpret them, to indigenize them. And following upon Egyptian culture's profound assimilation of Hellenism, the native encounter with Christianity must be seen as part of such a complex process.[1]

This book asks the reader to begin thinking about Egyptian religion within a local and domestic context, that context often described as rural or popular, rather than from the vantage point of some crumbling hypostyle of the New Kingdom or half-buried Ozymandias, compared to whose lost grandeur practically anything might look "in decline." And indeed, the evidence for native religion in Egypt after the middle of the fourth century C.E. reflects this local and domestic sphere of piety rather than the elaborate and centralized temple cults of classical Egypt. There was, I argue, a progressive centrifugal tendency from regional centers toward local and domestic practice during the Roman period; but this tendency should be seen as a retrenchment of the basic spheres of reli-

---

[1] Fowden 1986 and Bowersock 1990 have been the most important contributors to this nuanced view of Hellenism.

gious practice rather than a decline of religion itself. Paralleled as it is in many other historical cultures seeking to maintain some symbolic continuity in the face of various traumas, a centrifugal tendency of popular piety can show the strength and resilience of local culture, not popular anxieties in search of a broader ideology.

To approach the transformation of Egyptian religion in this way requires somewhat of a new paradigm, as I argue in chapter 1. One reason for departing from the "decline of paganism/triumph of Christianity" model is that Egypt itself was different from other Mediterranean cultures that underwent great social and political changes in the Roman period. Religious systems and hierarchies in Egypt, for example, were entrenched in society, displayed in temples, and experienced in rhythms of the environment like the Nile's annual surge. The native religious idioms—the central symbolism of kingship, the conventions of sacred representation, the gods themselves—had long dominated the interpretation of rulers, Ptolemaic and Roman, and the very deployment of "Hellenism" in culture. They were not nearly as subject to the ideologies of the rulers as other Mediterranean religions.

As a further component of our new paradigm, one must set oneself loose from a weighty theological legacy that assumes Christianity's ideological significance to ordinary people, especially in the countryside, such that it could simply replace traditional worldviews. Indeed, one must reject a concept of Christianity's uniformity altogether, except as an ideal in Coptic sermons. One must look at Christianization, as it were, from the bottom up, considering how the new leaders and ideas might be received by people practicing religious forms of great antiquity. Most of all, one must get beyond the notion that religions actually die, taking seriously the anthropology of small communities in dynamic relationship with ever-changing great traditions.

Following this agenda of looking at religious institutions "from the outside in," chapter 2 discusses that axis of local and regional piety, the temple, stressing the ways in which people could interact with and, indeed, maintain institutions of such particular exclusivity. And temples in the third and later centuries (as in earlier times) do function within those essential religious contexts of fertility, healing, and safety, their priests meeting these concerns explicitly in temple ritual. So also through festivals and various organized and spontaneous demonstrations of support for the temple institution we can see Egyptian religion as a dynamic social system, not a floundering set of superstitions dependent upon the priestly purses. Even in the fifth century, when I focus in on a particular case of local religious patronage, we can see the strength of local self-determination in maintaining tradition.

Chapters 3 and 4 conceptualize religion according to concentric spheres of practice, authority, and identity, each of which is dominated by one or more gods or cults. The largest sphere would be the pan-Mediterranean, that ecumenical ideal for divinity and religious society introduced at the beginning of the Hellenistic period, following which we find the transregional cult, the regional cult, the interlocal, the local, and —leaping over the various cultic districts typical of towns and cities— the domestic. Realities were doubtless much more complex, as they have been in the Spanish and African areas in which this approach to religion has proven itself: inevitably, alliances, rivalries, ideologies, and inter-lopers (new oracles, prophets, immigrants) cut across the concentricity or at least complicate the nature of authority one might find in a particular sphere.[2] However, the concentric scheme provides an invaluable model for understanding both the nature of Egyptian religion in its static phases and the parameters of its change. Thus, while chapter 3 emphasizes the local and even centrifugal scopes of religious practice through late antiquity, chapter 4 discusses centripetal tendencies: oracle cults as regional or transregional centers, and their transformation or legacy in new religious "centers."

Chapter 3 in fact argues that religion in Roman Egypt was essentially a localized phenomenon, neither a pan-Mediterranean "paganism" nor a monolithic "Egyptian paganism." The Hellenistic forms in which one finds the Egyptian gods and goddesses (not only in Egypt but throughout the Roman world) represent not a tendency toward impossibly dislocated or otiose deities, as has sometimes been argued, but rather new idioms by which various priesthoods and local communities could articulate the powers and virtues of their particular deities. Finally, a variety of evidence for the continuity of domestic religious practices in late antique Egypt can, viewed comparatively, illustrate the ways in which cultures can maintain binding traditions when temples and public space no longer provide effective venues for religious practice.

The phenomenon of the Egyptian oracle is the subject of chapter 4. Based in temples and usually part of the temples' festival processions, the oracle was traditionally the major context in which a community or communities interacted with the temple, its god and priests. In the Greco-Roman period the oracles of certain temples also became the dominant form of a regional or transregional piety, drawing pilgrims from afar. This discussion fills out the scope in which a "popular" piety should be viewed: essentially local but with broader spheres as well. Indeed, since it is this religious dimension that underwent distinctive transformations in the Roman period it provides a context for certain early forms of Christianity, such as the rise of holy men and Christian pilgrimage shrines.

Chapters 5 and 6 cover the vicissitudes of the Egyptian priesthood, its

---

2 For example, Turner 1974; Werbner (ed.) 1977; Christian 1981; Werbner 1989.

literary and ritual functions, into late antiquity. Egypt's temples not only represented the religious infrastructure but also had stood as the axes of Egyptian religion for millennia, distinguishing Egyptian culture from other ancient Mediterranean religions in which priesthoods were neither so ancient nor so institutionalized or socially distinct. But it was precisely this institution that most directly suffered under Roman economic and, subsequently, religious edicts. Still, we find a variety of routes that Egyptian priests took to maintain their traditions, roles, and social authority. They consolidated their roles as ritual experts in a broad Mediterranean culture that upheld the *magos* as the epitome of Oriental wisdom, as we see in chapter 5. Using Greek and Hellenistic literary conventions and the synthetic writing system Coptic, they reinterpreted ancient legends, spells, and other traditions of the "House of Life," the temple scriptorium, for an outsider's culture anxious to plumb its hitherto illegible secrets (ch. 6). In both cases we can follow priestly traditions assimilated by Christian institutions.

Chapter 7 returns to the problem of Christianization that hangs over this entire book. Posed afresh the question becomes, What made Christianity appealing if Egyptian religion could continue in so many domains? I discuss three ways in which people found the Christian movements and their representatives attractive. But I make the point that, in the end, everyday and local realities governed the assimilation of Christianity, often to the point of producing rather vivid recollections of pre-Christian tradition.

This book admittedly covers less than its title might be construed as advertising. Even if not including basic introductions to gods, temples, and priesthoods in their Roman guise, the topic "Religion in Roman Egypt" should properly cover the complex mortuary cults, the veneration of the emperor, cults unique to Alexandria, the life and fortunes of those cults exclusively Greek, Syrian, Jewish, or of Asia Minor, and the complex, schismatic history of Christianity, a topic itself requiring coverage of Gnosticism and that hybrid movement that dominated the rural missions through the fourth century, Manichaeism.

Even while alluding to most of these topics in limited contexts, however, my purpose here is not to stress Egypt's religious eclecticism, a somewhat worn topic that can be found in numerous books on the religious life of the Greco-Roman period. Nor is there space for a more basic introduction to the official infrastructure—the ranks and functions and calendars of priests, the layout of temples—than is absolutely necessary, for the focus is on the religious life of ordinary people in their communities.[3]

Other topics are neglected on more specific grounds. The cult of the

[3] Otto 1905/8 is still the basic resource on these issues, but good introductions can be found in Milne 1924 and Sauneron 1960a.

Roman emperor, which was promoted throughout the empire with increasing anxiety and pomp, touched Egypt proper (without Alexandria) almost exclusively in Egyptian terms: that is, the emperor was revered in pharaonic terms (not worshiped: he is portrayed like the pharaoh offering *to* the gods), his image stood in many temples among the "associated gods [*sunnaoi theoi*]" to receive the customary priestly devotions and in the occasional exclusive shrine that was visited and served almost entirely by Greco-Roman constituents. Coins portraying emperors with divine iconography circulated among some citizens. But the sporadic presence of the emperor cult, even more rarely as a distinct "religion," seems to have had little effect on local or popular Egyptian piety.[4]

It is not the entire history of Christianity in Egypt that is relevant to "Egyptian religion," but only those streams that in one way or another give voice to or grow in dialectic with aspects of traditional religion.[5] So also Manichaeism, increasingly well-documented in its spread throughout Egypt from the third century on, nevertheless reveals a discrete society, albeit with an active mission in Coptic.[6] The distinctive religious history of Alexandria, while certainly continuous with religion in Egypt proper, has tended to be given the dominant voice for the whole extended region because of the city's prominence in the works of ancient historians. In this book Alexandria tends to stand for the "intellectual pagan" subculture of Sosipatra, Antoninus, Hypatia, and their chronicler Eunapius.

It is partly for reasons of space and repetition that I have left out a full discussion of mortuary practice, whose vivid continuity throughout the Roman and Coptic periods has been voluminously documented since the nineteenth century with necropolis excavations, mummies, mortuary texts and their analogues in Coptic apocrypha, and the epigraphy and iconography of grave stelae.[7] But it is also because mortuary practices and beliefs in general are so historically resilient, so impervious to the vicissitudes of ideology, so intertwined with the self-definition of family and community, that their continuity in Egypt through the Roman period

---

[4] See Milne 1924:214–16; Jean-Claude Grenier, "L'Empereur et le Pharaon," *ANRW* II.18.5 (1995):3181–94; Heinz Heinen, "Vorstufen und Anfänge des Herrscherkultes im römischen Ägypten," *ANRW* II.18.5 (1995):3144–80; and Eleanor G. Huzar, "Emperor-Worship in Julio-Claudian Egypt," *ANRW* II.18.5 (1995):3092–3143. Glare (1993) connects a decline in funding for temples with an increased commitment to "civic temples" associated with the emperor cult.

[5] Cf. Pearson/Goehring (eds.) 1986; Griggs 1990.

[6] See now Lieu 1994:61–105, and I. M. F. Gardiner and S. N. C. Lieu, "From Narmouthis (Medinet Madi) to Kellis (Ismant el-Kharab): Manichaean Documents from Roman Egypt," *JRS* 86 (1996):146–69.

[7] In general, see D'Auria et al. 1992; Françoise Dunand, "Pratiques et croyances funéraires en Égypte romaine," *ANRW* II.18.5 (1995):3216–3315; with Baumeister 1972 on Christian continuities.

says little in and of itself about the broader spectrum of piety analyzed in this book.

What remains are the local and regional religious traditions of the land and its temples, followed by the interconnections this native religion forged with both the civic religion and "intellectual paganism" of the cities and the institutions of Christianization.

## 1.2 The Problem of Egypt in Its Mediterranean Context

The tendency among historians has been to put Egypt (and Egyptian materials) at the center of the broadest cultural changes in the Mediterranean world over the Hellenistic and Roman periods. And this concept of a "great metamorphosis" has had much influence on the way Egyptian materials have been interpreted. Often what has attracted students to the Greco-Roman period and late antiquity has been the notion and the conviction that key aspects of classical culture were in the process of metamorphosis *toward* Christianity. But at what point does our fascination with change and its implications begin to govern our grasp of an enormous range of materials?

There has, for example, developed a catalogue of cultural motifs alleged to be distinctive of the Greco-Roman period, like an individualism in crisis, a lapse into magic, a scurrying to oracles, a veritable bazaar of foreign wizards—in essence, an all-pervading superstition that either culminates in, or is vanquished and unified with, the victory of Christianity. Scholars have bent this image of the late antique mentality alternately toward downfall, like Gibbon, or awakening, as in Sir Harold Bell's unabashed triumphalism:

> Later paganism at its best has a singular attractiveness. It died with a kind of mellow splendour, like a beautiful sunset, but dying it was. It had been conquered by the truer and finer religion, for which it had itself prepared the way, a religion which at last brought the solution of problems which paganism had posed but to which it had found no answer.[8]

Trying to capture the mood of this liminal period in less cataclysmic (if equally spiritual) terms, other scholars have spoken of a "failure of nerve," a pervasive anxiety, a "cosmic paranoia," and a preference for an "active religion."[9] The intermediary aspect of the Roman period continues to be the issue—how Christianity was *reached*.

[8] Bell 1953:105.

[9] Respectively: Gilbert Murray, *Five Stages of Greek Religion,* 3rd ed. (Garden City: Doubleday, 1955), ch. 4; Dodds 1965; Jonathan Z. Smith, "Birth Upside Down or Right Side Up?" (Smith 1978:147–71); and Potter 1994, ch. 1.

To illustrate these great changes scholars continue to draw upon the same eclectic set of sources—the same lives of holy men, the same inscriptions, the same novels and historiographies, the same papyri, the same Mithraea—all plucked haphazardly from many Mediterranean and Near Eastern lands and from more than five centuries of Mediterranean history. Even new sources tend to be assimilated to the same zeitgeist built out of the older sources. For example, an Egyptian oracle book preserved in multiple manuscript fragments is still quoted for its questions about everyday fate—"Am I to find what is lost? Am I to recover from my illness? Am I to be reconciled with my masters? Shall I have a baby?"[10]—as if to reveal that in this period no one could leave the house without deference to some charlatan's advice. And the preface of a first-century herbal attributed to one Thessalos of Tralles, describing the author's private epiphany in a chamber in Thebes, has been commonly invoked to express the decadent state of the old Egyptian religion: a crumbling Thebes in whose shadows aged priests pander hybrid religious experiences and magic to Greco-Roman youth.[11]

Indeed, the images of change coming from classicists, church historians, and Roman historians are remarkably repetitive. But these are fields primed to see the Roman and late antique periods according to the starkest conceivable contrasts: the classical world, the Christian empire, and that interregnum in which somehow the first must become the other. The alternative perspective is one that subsumes the Roman period within the broader historical evolution of a single country or region. Does the Age of Anxiety then actually break down into much more complex *regional* developments due to distinctly unspiritual causes?

This is the case with Egypt. This trove of papyrological witnesses to an alleged decline in reason, rise in superstition, and bastardizations of noble Homeric divinities actually reveals a quite different picture if one appreciates the Roman evidence in light of continuing Egyptian traditions. What if we were to approach Roman Egypt by assuming the persistence of religious needs and consequent resilience of religion itself? What if we regarded new developments and innovations as potential vehicles of continuity and religious revitalization?

By this approach the old edifices of anxiety or spiritual decline begin to fall away. Materials on religious festivals in Egypt, which continue through the fourth century, prove that the temple cult was not a "rickety formalism" or "near-ghetto" but rather the dynamic center of religious activities that had continued for centuries, even millennia, the ritualiza-

---

[10] *Sortes Astrampsychi* qq. 40, 42, 46–47 = *P.Oxy* XII.1477, i, 1, 3, 7–8. Standard editions in Browne 1974, 1983. See below, 4.4.1.

[11] Ed. Friederich 1968. See Smith 1978a and compare Fritz Graf, "The Magician's Initiation," *Helios* 21 (1994):161–77. See below, 5.3.3.

tion of environment and society.[12] That general Hellenistic pursuit of the urbane Greek divinities, immortalizing mysteries, or pantheistic saviors turns into a series of potential idioms for an Egyptian local religiosity that continued with astounding resilience well into the Byzantine period. The well-documented oracle cults continue archaic temple practices for communicating divine decisions.[13] A preoccupation with attaining personal revelation and epiphanies distinguishes not a putative individualism (or "active religion") of the Roman period but long and well-established Egyptian divination procedures among the priesthoods. The priesthoods themselves cease to appear as greedy anachronisms in a world embracing personal piety, becoming instead authoritative extensions of local religious solidarity. The popular wizardry for which Egypt was renowned in the Roman era and that seems to be well documented in the voluminous "magical" papyri becomes merely the traditional ritual expertise of the official priesthood.

Behind all these reassessments of the old historians' truisms we find notable continuities of the classical Egypt of the Egyptologists: traditional festival practices, healing rites, fertility beliefs, the "magical" services and even literary pursuits of the priesthoods. Thus a third-century lament for Egypt bereft of its gods, its temples crumbling, its sacred voices silenced, signals not the gloom of a proper "pagan" beholding the inevitable advance of Christianity (or the destruction of the Serapeum), but rather one of several late forms of an archaic literature of "chaos-description," once invoked as contrasts to the ordering effect of the king's accession.[14] And this Egyptian lament is not alone in prompting such misinterpretations on the part of historians:

> It was similarly believed by an older generation of Norse literature scholars that the theme of *Götterdämmerung* reflected native anxieties about the encroachment and expected victory of Christ over the old gods. But this theme too was found upon more thorough (and less triumphalist) investigation to be much older than Christianity.[15]

If we then depart from such macroscopic perspectives on the Roman Empire that seem perennially to emphasize Christianization as some kind of end point and return to the dynamics of the specific culture and its internal processes and traditions, what do we find?

[12] The quoted phrases are Roger Bagnall's (1993:268, 324).

[13] A point well emphasized for the whole empire pre-250 by Lane Fox 1986:204–61, esp. 213.

[14] *Ascl.* 24, on whose Egyptian literary context (*pace* Athanassiadi 1993a:15–16) see Mahé 1982:47–113; Frankfurter 1993:183–94; and below, 6.2.

[15] A. T. van Holten, quoted by Gottfried Oosterwal in *Current Anthropology* 12 (1971):33.

For all its firsthand documentation of a broad late antique mentality and for all the attention it receives from Greco-Roman authors, Egypt and Egyptian culture were in fact quite uncharacteristic of the Roman world. Administered in unique fashion by the Romans, a culture allowed to appropriate reverence for the emperor into its own iconography and religious idioms, bearing no traces of that Babel of self-styled wizards and conjurers whose dominance of other religious landscapes is so well captured in ancient authors like Celsus and Lucian, Egypt in almost every way stands apart from the rest of the Mediterranean and Near Eastern worlds.

The reason for this difference in Roman views, of course, is the antiquity of the culture; but what does this mean? First, it means an economy based for millennia on the predictable annual cycle of Nile surges, around which crystallized both archaic social rhythms and equally archaic religious practices and mythology.[16] Second, it means a continuously functioning, literate temple culture that was able to maintain religious practices, traditions, and ideologies even at the local level with varying degrees of centralization and yet little overall formal change over several millennia, a stark contrast to the comparatively briefer or less unilinear histories of Greece, Palestine, and Asia Minor with their great vicissitudes of religious centralization. And third, responding to this antiquity and this deep linkage of priests and temples with the culture, Romans—both emperors and authors—developed a vivid exoticism that combined (in often conflicting or alternating sentiments) a fascination with Egyptian "wisdom"—its priests, traditions, lifestyles, ideologies of kingship; a wariness and often outright fear of the popular power of these priesthoods that translated into both repressive and capitulatory measures; an insatiable hunger for the land's produce; and a disgust for the indigenous people, their piety and habits.[17]

Many of the apparent changes in the religious culture of Roman Egypt seem much less striking when traced back to earlier periods: written oracle requests, for example, so well-attested from the Greco-Roman period, derive from the New Kingdom. In Egypt the major religious changes occur, first, through Hellenism, its new settlements and its idioms, especially as they defined new contexts for priestly traditions and ritual expertise (e.g., providing a niche for dispensing ancient wisdom and

[16] See Bonneau 1964, 1995.

[17] On the ideology of Roman administration of Egyptian religion, see Milne 1924:120–26, 286–89; Glare 1993; and Kákosy 1995:2900–2931. On the character of Roman views toward Egypt and Egyptian religion, see in general Smelik/Hemelrijk 1984:1920–81. Further on positive appraisals of Egypt as an exotic land of Oriental wisdom: Festugière 1950, 1:17–44; Geffcken 1978:6, 26, 133; Iversen 1961:38–56; Froidefond 1971; Hengel 1974:212–13; Joly 1982. Further on Egypt as a land of uncouth and violent peasants: Reinhold 1980 and Bertrand 1988.

"magic" to urban youth), and second, through the economic decline of the religious infrastructure—the temple cults—in the third and fourth centuries due to Roman administrative pressures. This decline stimulated compensatory developments in priestly and temple functions and probably encouraged competitive religious systems.

In countless respects, then, Egypt's various contributions to the image of religious novelty, anxiety, superstition, spiritual longing, individualism, or fruitlessness recede from distinguishing a distinctive spiritual current of the Greco-Roman period and fall into an ancient line of development, in which temples had risen and fallen continually and sages had repeatedly lamented the impiety and religious breakdown of their times. We cannot, to be sure, thus obliterate the sense that cultures changed in the Hellenistic and Roman periods; but we can assess the changes in their Egyptian cultural context.

## 1.3 Tracing the Continuity of Egyptian Religion in Late Antiquity

### 1.3.1 Sources

A variety of materials serve the reconstruction of Egyptian religion in the Roman period. Large collections of crudely molded terra-cotta figurines, lamps, and jugs illustrate popular, especially domestic, religious life in this period: the most accessible deities, the most important concerns (see pls. 1, 7–9, 13–15); and both the craft and some of the actual forms continue into Christian workshops (pl. 18).[18] Papyri offer abbreviated, often enigmatic, but extraordinarily intimate documentation of priests pursuing their tasks, ordinary people preparing for festivals, supplicants requesting the guidance of a god.[19] Papyri and inscriptions, both formal dedications and informal graffiti, which commonly illustrate the extent of people's devotion to a cult through the dedication of structures or votive statuary, often provide exact dates.[20] Caches or archives of papyri, particularly when found in connection with a properly excavated

[18] See Dunand 1976, 1979, 1984, 1990; Nachtergael 1985, 1988; Török 1993, 1995.

[19] The variety of papyrological publications is immense, and matters pertaining to religion appear throughout the Oxyrhynchus papyri (*P.Oxy*), Berlin papyri (*BGU*), London papyri (*P.Lond.*), and Florence papyri (*PSI*), among others. For overviews of such material, see Ulrich Wilcken, *Grundzüge und Chrestomathie der Papyruskunde* 1, 2 (Leipzig and Berlin: Teubner, 1912); Zucker 1956; with some new data collected in Quaegebeur Clarysse/ Van Maele 1985 and Bagnall 1993:264–67. Among more recent documents of native religious practice in the fourth century should be mentioned Borkowski 1990 and Łajtar 1991 (others to be dealt with in the course of this study).

[20] Among the most important collections of inscriptions illustrating religion in Roman Egypt are Griffith 1937 and the extensive oeuvre of Étienne Bernand.

archaeological site, offer the fullest picture of religious life in a particular area. Historians have thus been well served by towns like Karanis, Soknopaiou Nesos, Tebtunis, and several other remains of Egyptian culture in the Fayyum; by the city of Oxyrhynchus with its huge deposits of papyri still being published; by the oasis towns of Kysis and Kellis (the latter which is still revealing new materials); and perhaps most of all by the Upper Egyptian city of Panopolis, whose various papyrus archives document many aspects of religious and priestly life through the fourth century, after which we are blessed with the direct testimony of the fifth-century Abbot Shenoute of Atripe.[21]

Shenoute is only the most acerbic and prolific of a number of Christian authors who described continuing native religion in various degrees of detail and polemical *topoi*: Paphnutius (fifth century), Zachariah of Mytilene (sixth century), the anonymous biographers of Pachomius (fourth century), Moses of Abydos (fifth century), Makarios of Tkôw (fifth century), the anonymous compilers of the *Historia Monachorum in Aegypto* (fourth century), and the *Apophthegmata Patrum* (fourth to fifth centuries), and the imperial historians Rufinus (fourth century), Sozomen, and Socrates Scholasticus (fifth century).[22] Somewhat less biased reports of

[21] *Fayyum towns:* For example, Gilliam 1947 (Soknobraisis); Boak (ed.) 1933; Gazda 1978, (ed.) 1983 (Karanis); Rübsam 1974:162–66 (Soknopaiou Nesos). *Oxyrhynchus:* Whitehorne 1995. *Kellis* (temple of Toutou and Tapshay): Guy Wagner, "Inscriptions grecques des Oasis de Dakhleh et Baharieh découvertes par le Dr. Ahmed Fakhry," *BIFAO* 73 (1973):177–80; Hope et al. 1989:10–15; Kaper 1991:64–66; Hope 1994; and Colin Hope, "The Excavations at Ismant El-Kharab in 1995: A Brief Report," *BACE* 6 (1995):51–58; Kaper 1997. *Kysis* (temple of Isis and Serapis): Vernus 1979; Wagner 1987:176–78; Reddé 1990; Dunand 1991a:246. *Panopolis:* Maspero 1914; Welles 1946; Browne 1977; Willis 1978, 1979; Fowden 1986:120–26, 173–74; Borkowski 1990; and Heike Behlmer, "Staat, Kirche und Gesellschaft im spätantiken Panopolis," in *Quaerentes Scientiam: Festgabe für Wolfhart Westendorf,* ed. by H. Behlmer (Göttingen, 1994), 13–26. *Shenoute:* Besa, *Life of Shenoute* 83 (ed. Leipoldt 1:41), with Shenoute's sermon "Only I Tell Everyone Who Dwells in This Village" (ed. Leipoldt 3:86–90, #26), on whose history see Emmel 1993:994–95. Further references to native religion in "The Lord Thundered" (ed. Amélineau 1909:379–83), on which see Emmel 1993:889–92, 1264–65; Acephalous Work A4 (ed. Bentley Layton, "Two Unpublished Shenute Fragments *Against Kronos,*" *JCS* 2 [1992]:122–31), on which see Emmel 1993:522, 1007; and Acephalous Work A26 (tr. Behlmer 1993, 1996a), on which see Emmel 1993:555–56, 1003. Also on Shenoute, see Barns 1964; Thissen 1992/93; and Van der Vliet 1993.

[22] *Paphnutius:* Vatican ms. ed. Émile Amélineau, "Voyage d'un moine égyptien dans le désert," *Recueil de travaux* 6 (1885):166–94; London ms. ed. Budge 1915:432–95, tr. Vivian 1993; *Zachariah of Mytilene: Life of Severus,* ed. and tr. Kugener 1907, also in A. Bernand 1970:207–13; *Pachomius:* tr. Veilleux 1980; *Moses of Abydos:* ed. Amélineau 1888/95:680–706 and Till 1936:46–81; *Makarios of Tkôw:* Ps-Dioscorus of Alexandria, *A Panegyric on Makarios* 5, ed. D. W. Johnson 1980; *Historia Monachorum:* ed. Festugière 1971, tr. Russell 1981; *Apophthegmata Patrum:* PG 65:76–440 (alphabetical); ed. Nau 1907, 1908, 1909, 1912, 1913 (anonymous); *Rufinus:* extension of Eusebius of Caesarea, *Historia Ecclesiastica,* PL 21; *Sozomen: Historia Ecclesiastica,* PG 67:843–1630, tr. Hart-

earlier Egyptian religious culture appear in the Roman historians and "intellectual pagan" writers like Dio, Strabo, Plutarch, Eunapius, and Ammianus Marcellinus.

Finally, there are fictionalized and didactic tracts, often datable only to the most general span of decades or centuries, which illustrate the religious interests of the literate in Roman and Coptic Egypt: cult propaganda and oracles; satires and novels like Lucian's *Philopseudes*, Heliodorus's *Aethiopica*, and Apuleius's *Metamorphoses*; Hermetic instructions and revelations; the by-now enormous corpus of ritual or "magical" texts; and diverse narratives about late antique Egypt included in such texts as Thessalos of Tralles's *De virtutibus herbarum* and the *Recognitions* of Pseudo-Clement.[23]

## 1.3.2 Interpretation

Egypt gives evidence, paradoxically, both for Christianity's rapid establishment in the fourth century and for the idiosyncratic and incomplete state of the land's "conversion" by the time of the Arab conquest. One certainly assumes that the empire changed fairly rapidly to Christianity in the century following Constantine's embrace of the creed. Whatever "conversion" should mean in such instances—and it most certainly did not mean an emotional or psychological "dying to the old" for the vast majority—a fair (if not by any means scientifically random) sampling of papyri from the fourth century has shown a quite large proportion of people giving their children biblical and Christian names by the end of the fourth century.[24] This observation seems to support the general profile of a Christian "triumph" over the course of the fourth century. But to assess what this means for religion as a whole one must balance such

---

ranft, *NPNF* 2:179–427; *Socrates: Historia Ecclesiastica*, PG 67:28–842, tr. Zenos, *NPNF* 2:1–178.

[23] Cult propaganda and oracles: see below, 4.1–3. Hermetica: ed. Festugière 1950, Mahé 1982; tr. W. Scott 1924/36 (cf. Brian Copenhaver, *Hermetica* [Cambridge: Cambridge University Press, 1992]). Ritual and "magical" texts: ed. Preisendanz 1973/74; Griffith/Thompson 1904, 1905; J. Johnson 1975, 1977; R. W. Daniel and F. Maltomini, *Supplementum Magicum* (Opladen: Westdeutscher Verlag, 1990, 1992); Kropp 1930/31; tr. Betz (ed.) 1986; Meyer/Smith (eds.) 1994; and *Sortes Astrampsychi* (sources discussed below, 4.4.1). Thessalos of Tralles: ed. Friederich 1968; tr. Festugière 1939. Ps-Clement, *Recognitions* (1.1–5): ed. Bernhard Rehm (Berlin: Akademie-Verlag, 1965), 6–9; tr. Thomas Smith, *ANF* 8:77–78.

[24] Roger S. Bagnall, "Religious Conversion and Onomastic Change," *BASP* 19 (1982):105–24; "Conversion and Onomastics: A Reply," *ZPE* 69 (1987):243–50; and 1993:279n.115, 280n.121, answering important challenges by Ewa Wipszycka ("La valeur de l'onomastique pour l'histoire de la christianisation de l'Égypte: A propos d'une étude de R. S. Bagnall," *ZPE* 62 [1986]:173–81 and 1988:119–22, 164–65). See also Peter Van Minnen, "The Roots of Egyptian Christianity," *Archiv* 40 (1994):73n.22.

naming tendencies as one finds in certain towns against the large and diverse body of evidence for continuing native cultic piety through the fifth century and later.

If one combs through the archaeological and literary evidence from the eastern Mediterranean world, one finds that native religions continued in most areas with quite wide appeal up to and in some areas beyond the Muslim conquest. Greece, Asia Minor, Syria, and Palestine all reveal the slow and halting process of Christianization at the local level, a process often completed through violence or else through considerable compromise on the bishops' part toward local religious practices.[25] And Egypt, which of all Mediterranean cultures offers the most extensive material on the antiquity, spread, subcultures, and political establishment of Christianity in a single land from the first century on, offers no different a picture of the survival of native cults.[26]

Indeed, if one were to plot them on a map of Egypt the continuing traditional cults for which we have evidence would represent virtually every major region of Egypt—a compelling argument for the resilience of even more undocumented temples (see the frontispiece of this book). Priests record their visits and cultic services at the temple of Akoris through the late fourth century and at the great Isis temple of Philae through the fifth century.[27] Pilgrims' inscriptions as well as the Roman historian Ammianus Marcellinus attest to the phenomenal success of an oracle cult at the Osiris temple of Abydos during the fourth century, only brought to a halt in 359 and then only because its archives revealed questions the emperor deemed subversive. Throughout the fifth century the temple was still popularly viewed as the dwelling of the god Bes, and some nearby cults continued with priesthoods.[28] Out in the Kharga and

[25] See Walter E. Kaegi, "The Fifth-Century Twilight of Byzantine Paganism," *Classica et Mediaevalia* 27 (1966):243–75; Van Dam 1985; Trombley 1985 and 1993/94 (with my cautionary remarks in *Bryn Mawr Classical Review* 5 [1994]:640–42); Gregory 1986; Frankfurter 1990:177–79; Chuvin 1990; Whitby 1991; Cameron 1993:69–71, 141–42; and MacMullen 1997.

[26] See résumés of data by Roger Rémondon, "L'Égypte et la suprême résistance au Christianisme (Vè-VIIè. siècles)," *BIFAO* 51 (1952):63–78; Kákosy 1984, 1995; Wipszycka 1988.

[27] *Akoris* (temple of Ammon and Sobek): Lefebvre 1921; É. Bernand 1988, esp. xxi–xxv, with Worp 1989:137 on the fourth-century inscriptions. *Philae* (temple of Isis): graffiti with dates from or after the reign of Diocletian include IDemPhilae 159, 240, 259, 332, 364, 366, 369–72, 376, 436, 450, ed. Griffith 1937; IGPhilae 188–99, ed. É. Bernand 1969b, 2:217–51; Priscus fr. 27 (ed. Blockley 1981/82, 2:322); Procopius, *Wars* 1.19.35–37; Paphnutius, *Histories of the Monks of Upper Egypt* 31–36, ed. Budge 1915:445–47; with discussions by Wilcken 1901:396–407; Spiegelberg 1924; Munier 1938:41–42; É. Bernand 1969b, 2:242–45; Burkhardt 1984; Vivian 1993:54–69; Kákosy 1995:2444–46.

[28] Memnon graffiti and commentary in Perdrizet/Lefebvre 1919; Ammianus 19.12.3–6. On the fifth-century continuity of Bes traditions at Abydos, see *Life of Moses of Abydos*

Dakhla oases the central temples of Kellis and Kysis were functioning well into the fourth century. The *Vita* and sermons of Shenoute of Atripe describe his battles with native piety in the region of his monastery; and an otherwise fantastic life of a contemporary, Makarios of Tkôw, gives a credible description of traditional local religion (surrounding a god obscurely named "Kothos") at the time of his own crusades.[29] Eunapius, Rufinus, and Zachariah of Mytilene all describe a fairly thriving cult center within fifty kilometers of Alexandria that could only be replaced—forcibly—near the end of the fifth century.[30] A great number of papyri and inscriptions make reference to priests, festivals, and temple operations through the fourth century. And in the middle of the fourth century an anonymous Syrian merchant visiting Alexandria gathered the following about the regions up the Nile that he was not himself able to visit:

> [Here the people are] eminently reverent towards the gods. At no other place are the mysteries of the gods thus celebrated as they were from ancient times through today. . . . For truly there we know that the gods have lived and still live.
>
> . . . [In Egypt] the worshippers offer the gods most particularly representations [*historias*]. And there are all sorts of sacred objects and temples decorated in every manner; they are full of sacred custodians, priests, attendants, diviners, *adoratores* and the best holy men. Everything is done according to custom. And thus you find the altars always illuminated with fire and full of sacrifices and incense, the altar cloths emitting divine odors as much as the aromatic-filled censers.[31]

How should we balance these various testimonies against the even more extensive images of an entrenched and even multiform Christian institution in fourth-century Egypt?[32] The perspective increasingly em-

---

(above, n. 22), with discussions in Kákosy 1966a; Coquin 1986; Wipszycka 1988:155–56; Kákosy 1995:2943–44, 2980–82.

[29] Makarius of Tkôw: D. W. Johnson 1980. On evidence for native piety continuing under Shenoute's successor Besa, see below, 7.3.

[30] Eunapius, *V.P.* 6.9.17; Epiphanius, *De fide* 12.1–4 (in A. Bernand 1970:199–201); Rufinus, *H.E.* 26–27; Zachariah of Mytilene, *V. Severus* (in A. Bernand 1970:202–5, 207–13); Sophronius of Jerusalem (in A. Bernand 1970:214–17). See discussions by Thelamon 1981:207–43 and, on dating the end of the Isis cult in Menouthis, Duchesne 1910:10–12; Herzog 1939; Kákosy 1984:68–69; Wipszycka 1988:138–42; Kákosy 1995:2941–43. Further evidence for Isis cults in the third and fourth centuries discussed in Dunand 1981:139–43.

[31] *Expositio totius mundi et gentium* 34, 36, ed. Jean Rougé, SC 124 (Paris: Éditions du Cerf, 1966), 168–69, 172–75 (the use of *historias* here is still an enigma in scholarship). These images of Egyptian temple cult are unclear, reflecting the author's own relative unfamiliarity with the subject (see ibid., 31–32, 266–67).

[32] The extent of Christian institutions in Egypt during this period has been amply documented (and somewhat overstated) by Annick Martin ("L'Église et la khôra égyp-

braced by historians of late antiquity and taken in this book argues the collective nature of religion in late antique rural cultures, that it was not individuals but small societies—entire villages—that embraced or rejected Christianization or responded to its imperial or monastic agents and thus that "conversion" was by necessity a slow and patchwork process, dependent upon the singular charisma of a motivated bishop or abbot rather than some putative "pagan decline" or "spiritual vacuum."[33]

### 1.3.3 Christian Witnesses to Native Religion

Some scholars have sought to redress the balance of evidence by negating the value of Christian hagiographical sources as witnesses to ongoing native religion.[34] These sources, the argument goes, are so dominated by the agenda of extolling their main characters that the background in which they set these characters becomes a parade of dramatic foils drawn either from whole cloth or from biblical typological tradition.

For example, the *Vitae* of Shenoute and his ally Makarios manifestly portray them as new versions of the prophet Elijah, an identification apparently often made for charismatic Christian figures of this period. Dramatic encounters between Christian leaders and "pagans" in these texts thus tend to recall the biblical story of Elijah and the priests of Ba'l (1 Kings 18), leading to the common if premature conclusion that all such religious clashes in Coptic literature were drawn up entirely to reenact this story.[35] Athanasius in his *Life of Antony* and Shenoute in his sermons depend rhetorically upon caricatures of a "paganism" populated with Greek gods (inverted as demons) to such a degree that their capability to reflect contemporaneous native religious practices might also fall into doubt.[36] The anonymous biographer of Makarios of Tkôw asserts that local temples engaged in the ritual sacrifice of Christian children, a broad motif of ancient novels, which made a specialty of imagining cannibalistic races, and of ancient religious polemic as well.[37] One can in-

---

tienne au IVè. siècle," *REAug* 25 [1979]:3–26); Philip Rousseau, *Pachomius: The Making of a Community in Fourth-Century Egypt* (Berkeley: University of California Press, 1985), ch. 1; Griggs 1990; Bagnall 1993:278–309.

[33] Argued most compellingly in MacMullen 1984, 1997, and, for Egypt, Wipszycka 1988. See also Brown 1982, 1995; Cameron 1993:69–71, 141–42.

[34] For example, Bagnall 1988:292–93.

[35] See Frankfurter 1993:65–74.

[36] Cf. Van der Vliet 1993:110–12.

[37] See Arthur Darby Nock, "Greek Novels and Egyptian Religion" (Nock 1972, 1:169–75); Winkler 1980; Van der Vliet 1993:108n.45; and Andrew McGowan, "Eating People: Accusations of Cannibalism against Christians in the Second Century," *JECS* 2 (1994):413–42.

deed wonder whether such encounters between Christian saint and "pagan" are memories, albeit imprecise, or dramatic motifs based on literary
typology and caricature, just as ideological competitors within Christianity tended to be castigated as "Manichees," "Gnostics," "Arians," or
other grossly anachronistic categories.[38]

But battle with native religion actually does not occur so widely or
consistently in late antique hagiography that one can designate it as a
literary motif in its own right. Sometimes the native religious institution
is described merely as part of an ascetic's personal background. Particularly outside Egypt the native religion is depicted as a more inchoate
world of folk healers with whom the saint or the saint cult is in competition.[39] Coptic hagiographers do indeed cast their heroes as new Elijahs
or Daniels in their dramatic encounters with native priests and cults:
Makarios of Tkôw can even call down fire from heaven upon the temple
of "Kothos." But the Elianic references cluster around just these dramatic
dénouements, the actual battles (or thaumaturgical displays) that eradicate the native cults—the fire from heaven, the miraculous floods—and
tend not to control the descriptions of the cults themselves.

What stand out distinctly from the biblical typologies and rhetorical
caricatures are the details of these cults, which conform to no literary
tradition. For example, despite the allegations of child sacrifice (which
are easily recognized as ahistorical), the temple of "Kothos" and its
priesthood in the story of Makarios of Tkôw are credibly described as the
cultic center of a piety based normally in house shrines, which the author
describes in detail. Thus the priesthood in the story inspires the protective
instincts of local people *against* Makarios and his monks, a striking
contrast to the sentiments of Elijah's audience in 1 Kings 18 and to the
widespread motif of conversion narratives in which populaces would rise
up against their temples and the "pagan élite" who controlled them. In
the story of the monk Moses of Abydos, who does battle with a "demon"
named Bes in an Egyptian temple, the anonymous author explicitly invokes Elijah and Daniel but gives credible information about native piety
that could depend on no literary sources: the specific ranks of Egyptian
priests he encounters, local concern for temples, and the name and iconography of "Bes," who was one of the most popular deities among
ordinary Egyptians of the Roman period.[40] Even Shenoute breaks out of

---

[38] On a "standard vocabulary of denigration" used in late antique Christian circles, see
Robert Markus, *The End of Ancient Christianity* (Cambridge: Cambridge University Press,
1990), 48.

[39] Monks' backgrounds in temple priesthood: for example, *Apophth.Pat.* (anon.) 190.
World of folk healers: *Life of St. Theodore of Sykeon* 35–38 (tr. Dawes/Baynes 1977:112–
15); Gregory of Tours, *Miracles of St. Martin* 27; with Flint 1991:59–84.

[40] See Kákosy 1966a; Wipszycka 1988:156.

polemical caricature occasionally to give a "demon's" local name (Min, Petbe, Shai—all gods otherwise attested in the third and later centuries) or a detail of popular religious piety (figurines, amulets) of which we have an immense corpus for the Roman period.[41] Besa's description of a village's attempt to repel Shenoute and his monks using ritual substances conforms to what we know of official execration rites practiced in Egyptian temples from ancient times.[42]

It is not difficult to perceive historically authentic reflections of native religious practice in Coptic (or, for that matter, Greek, Syriac, and Latin) hagiography even while admitting the genre's dependence on biblical typology, literary caricature, and an overall ideological agenda that steers the author away from historical precision and toward a self-contained and fantastic world of the saint's exaltation. To discover these authentic details one must begin with the documentary evidence, to be alert for credible details in literary texts. One must bring a familiarity with the literary workings of typology, caricature, and motif in late antique literature: how these techniques, in the process of directing the audiences' attention toward typological meaning, actually leave spaces for details to be authentic—"'imaginary gardens with real toads in them,'" as the poet Marianne Moore put it.[43] One must keep in mind that the effectiveness of any hagiographical text within an area like Egypt or Syria or Asia Minor—what impels its transmission, copying, and natural links with oral tradition—depends on its recognizability, the verisimilitude of the setting against which the saint operates and performs.

Finally, one can never push the historicity of details further than the texts warrant: Makarios's battle with "Kothos" can function as no more than a general portrait of a fifth-century cult as these must have still existed in the countryside at the time of the writer; the chronological sequence of Shenoute's crusades on nearby villages and their cults is vague, even if it could only span part of the abbot's own lifetime; while Zachariah of Mytilene's eyewitness account of the destruction of the Isis temple at Menouthis can be dated quite precisely, around 484 C.E.[44]

---

41 *Min:* "Only I Tell Everyone Who Dwells in This Village" (ed. Leipoldt 3:89.12–14), on which see Emmel 1994. *Petbe:* "The Lord Thundered," p. 55 (ed. Amélineau 1909:383–84). *Shai:* ibid., p. 45 (ed. Amélineau 1909:379), on which see Quaegebeur 1975:39. In general, see Van der Vliet 1993:113–15.

42 Besa, *Life of Shenoute* 83, on whose details compare Ritner 1993, ch. 4.

43 Marianne Moore, "Poetry" (1921).

44 On the historical interpretation of such sources, see Evelyne Patlagean, "Ancient Byzantine Hagiography and Social History," in *Saints and Their Cults,* ed. by S. Wilson (Cambridge: Cambridge University Press, 1983), 101–21; Wipszycka 1988:123–24, 145, 149, 157; Whitby 1991:113–14; Bowersock 1994; and the model application of such methods to Rufinus in Thelamon 1981.

## 1.4 Pressures and Traumas of the Late Empire

The denial of the value of hagiographical sources as witnesses to continuing traditional piety stems from the inability of many scholars to reconcile such testimony with the pressures to which Egyptian traditional religion seems to have been subject in the later Roman period.

Of those pressures that have been proposed, the least likely is the notion that it died naturally of internal causes: spiritual dissatisfaction, psychological rootlessness, the focus on but never the salvation of the individual. This image of a "paganism" that merely prepares the way for Christian conversion, receiving its best statement at the end of Sir Harold Bell's 1952 Forwood Lectures quoted above, still lives on in newer attempts to explain the success of the Christian institution.[45] It is a wishful notion of religious evolution, and its strongly teleological overtones reflect its basis in ideology rather than data—the ideology of religious triumphalism or, in the post-Enlightenment tradition of James Frazer, intellectual triumphalism.

But how does one square the evidence for continuing traditional piety with the economic pressures on temples under Roman administration, especially during the third century, and with the explicit proscriptions of the imperial edicts against native religions during the fourth and subsequent centuries?

### 1.4.1 Edicts

We may begin with the latter pressure, for while the procession of edicts collected within the Theodosian law code of 438 C.E. certainly reflects a concerted hostility to native cults and popular piety, that same procession ironically provides vivid evidence for the *continuity* of these same cults and practices and the imperium's general failure at coercing people from their traditions.[46] Edicts of 392 and 435 detail a thriving popular piety (16.10.12, 25). An edict of 382 actually preserves the temple's function as the axis of religious festivals (16.10.8). Priests are still performing diverse temple services, including divination, in the late fourth century, as edicts of 385 and 391 seek meticulously to proscribe such cultic leadership (16.10.9, 11). An edict of 399 asserts that "even now the worship of a vain superstition is being paid to idols," while another of the same year, trying to encourage the peaceful demolition of rural temples, makes clear that they still ground traditional piety (16.10.18, 16). Traditional priests still carry considerable civic authority in 416,

---

[45] Bell 1953:105. Cf. Gregory 1986:233; Bagnall 1993:322–24.
[46] See Whitby 1991:114–19; Trombley 1993/94, 1:3–35.

when an edict tries to prevent them from roles in imperial service (16.10.21). And as late as 386 the holder of the imperial office of High Priest of all Egypt had to be someone

> who has *not* withdrawn from the cult of the temples by his observance of Christianity. Indeed . . . it is illicit for the temples and the customary rites of the temples to belong to the care of those persons whose conscience is imbued with the true doctrine of divine religion.[47]

The religious edicts themselves were relatively impotent, however, for they were engaged in proscribing a "paganism" that only slightly overlapped with the traditional religions as they were practiced throughout the many regions of the Mediterranean world. They focused above all on "sacrifice," an issue of elevated debate in intellectual circles of the time and perhaps a sore point in Christian institutional memory as it was cultivated in the public reading of martyrologies.[48] But one must remember that public sacrificial rites like those enjoined under Decius in a previous imperial attempt at pan-Mediterranean religious conformity— "to sacrifice [*thuein*] and pour libations [*spendein*] and taste the sacrificial offering [*geuesthai*]"—were a series of gestures not in any way distinctive of Egyptian religion. No doubt they would have seemed quite odd to Aurelia Ammonous, local priestess of the crocodile-god Sobek, who was also called to prove her pan-Mediterranean religious conformity in 250.[49] Egyptian records of popular temple "offerings" return constantly to the votive figurine or object, occasionally to the setting of foodstuffs by a domestic image. Terra-cotta figurines, which tend to idealize the temple cult and its processions for domestic value, occasionally portray libations, the offering of agricultural produce, and festival foods, but not animal offerings. The public aspect, indeed the dramatic apex, of the priestly cult as it appears both in temple reliefs and in the Roman author Apuleius's *Metamorphoses* is the glorious procession of the god's image out of the temple—not some bloody tauroctany.[50]

---

[47] *Codex Theodosianus* 12.1.112. All translations from Clyde Pharr, *The Theodosian Code and Novels and the Sirmondian Constitutions* (Princeton, N.J.: Princeton University Press, 1952).

[48] It is also an issue of immense complexity in anthropology and history of religions: see, for example, Th. P. Van Baaren, "Theoretical Speculations on Sacrifice," *Numen* 11 (1964):1–12.

[49] Knipfing 1923, esp. 364–65 (Aurelia Ammonous), and now *P.Oxy* LVIII.3929.

[50] On popular "offerings [*anathēmata*]" to temples, see esp. *P.Oxy* XII.1449 (213–17 c.e.); on popular foodstuff offerings, the terra-cotta discussed by Castiglione 1957 and Török 1995:33–34 (pl. 13 ; ...is volume), as well as Török 1995, ##14, 146; on priestly libations in public cult, see Török 1995, ##145, 147, 161–62 and Perpillou-Thomas 1993:211–12. On festival foods, see Török 1995:119 (#159); Perpillou-Thomas 1993:190–214; and below, 2.4. In general on Egyptian "sacrifice," articles by Gertie En-

At the same time it would be difficult to apply the wording of the edicts to the sacred butchery that Plutarch describes in local festivals. The act of (blood-)sacrifice played a minor role in local religion in its normal realm of affairs (bound up as it was with everyday and life-cycle issues of health, fertility, and safety) and only one, exclusive aspect of priestly service in Egypt. When we find, for example, a group of men practicing traditional sacrifice in mid-fourth-century Egypt, it is quite clearly an imitation of a priestly service; it involves a substantial group of people who make pilgrimage to a holy place and hold a feast; and the killing of the animal has a quite clear mythic significance.[51]

Animal offerings may have constituted a most public form of individual participation in some established traditional cults, primarily Roman transplants like the emperor cult or the Dioscuri; and those members of the élite for whom public gesture was important for status would then have found themselves constricted in those places where edicts were enforceable.[52] But from a local Egyptian perspective the edicts' obsessive proscriptions against sacrifices would seem rather arbitrary, theoretical—occasionally hurtful and oppressive, but not catastrophic.[53]

Even less pertinent to ancient Mediterranean religious practice and yet far more entrenched in the imperial *mentalité* were the edicts against that complex of sins encompassing political divination and sorcery, which were issued repeatedly into the fifth century. "One can readily see what was targeted" in such legislation, Pierre Chuvin has observed: "the political dangers of a science capable of indicating, however obscurely, who would succeed a reigning emperor and when. This had nothing to do with persecuting pagans."[54] Indeed, one can trace the same fear of mantic subversion to the beginning of the empire, inspiring at various times imperial inquisitions, sorcery and "magic" trials, edicts like those of Decius and Valerian that imposed general religious requirements on all citizens, and direct attempts to intervene in traditional divination practices. Continuing a judicial theme launched already under Augustus, for

---

glund and Jan Bergman, in *Gifts to the Gods: Proceedings of the Uppsala Symposium 1985*, Boreas 15, ed. by Tullia Linders and Gullög Nordquist (Uppsala: Uppsala University, 1987), 31–42 (Bergman), 57–66 (Englund); and Baines 1991:180–83.

[51] Łajtar 1991:66–69. For Plutarch on blood "sacrifices" in Egypt, see *De Iside* 8 (354A), 31 (363A–C), 50 ((371D), 61 (375E). See also Perpillou-Thomas 1993:201–3 on animal sacrifices in Egyptian religion.

[52] Cf. Brown 1992:19–20.

[53] See R. Turcan, "Les motivations de l'intolérance chrétienne et la fin du mithraicisme au IVè. siècle ap. J-C," in *Proceedings of the VIth Congress of the International Federation of the Societies of Classical Studies*, vol. 2, ed. by J. Harmatta (Budapest: Adakémiai Kiadó, 1984), 209–26; Limberis 1994:20–24; Bradbury 1994:129–32; MacMullen 1997:42–43; *pace* Harl 1990.

[54] Chuvin 1990:40.

example, an edict of 199 C.E. proscribed (or sought to proscribe) local Egyptian oracles, and the renowned Bes oracle of Abydos was shut down in 359 after its archives revealed inquiries of a political nature. This last case in particular shows the overriding fear of political subversion, since a prominent Alexandrian devotee of Bes was interrogated not for his "heathen" practices but for his possible use of the oracle cult for political purposes.[55] Such interventions were bound to fail because they regarded native practices that were part of total religious systems instead as secretive manipulations of illegitimate power for purposes of subversion. Proscriptions, accusations, inquisitions all had an arbitrary, ideologically motivated character that could have little sustained effect in the country or the city.

To the extent that they were even meant to be enforced—and there is good reason to believe their function was throughout largely symbolic—the Theodosian laws could only be as effective as the instruments of their enforcement, the local governors and their forces. But provincial governors inevitably found the task of persecuting traditional piety expensive and highly disruptive, particularly in regions of poverty or volatility.[56] One finds, especially in Egypt, that the vanguard in destroying native religion consisted of the holy men, the charismatic bishops, and the monks that followed them. And, generally partaking in the same culture as the devotees of temples and traditional images, these forces cared little for the nuances or even the existence of the imperial codes, instead rampaging freely and homicidally throughout the countryside with the distinct sensation of extirpating demons. "Antipaganism" in this mode be-

---

[55] Ammianus 19.12.12, and in general on the closure of the Abydos Bes oracle 19.12.3–6. On Augustus's own decree against traditional oracles as subversive, see Cassius Dio 56.25.5 On the motivations for sorcery and "magic" trials in the later empire, see Ramsay MacMullen, *Enemies of the Roman Order: Treason, Unrest, and Alienation in the Empire* (Cambridge, Mass.: Harvard University Press, 1966; repr. London and New York: Routledge, 1992), ch. 4; idem 1984:96; Peter Brown, "Sorcery, Demons, and the Rise of Christianity from Late Antiquity into the Middle Ages," in Douglas (ed.) 1970:17–45; Franziska E. Shlosser, "Pagans into Magicians," *Byzantinoslavica* 52 (1991):49–53; Kákosy 1995:2924–25, 2929, 2935 (compare earlier attempts to appreciate these ideological themes by Jules Maurice, "La terreur de la Magie au IVè. siècle," *Revue historique de droit français et étranger* 6 [1927]:108–20, and Clyde Pharr, "The Interdiction of Magic in Roman Law," *TPAPA* 63 [1932]:269–95). The ideological basis for the third-century religious edicts outlined by G. E. M. de Ste. Croix ("Why Were the Early Christians Persecuted?" in *Studies in Ancient Society,* ed. by M. Finley [London and Boston: Routledge, 1974], 210–49) provides an analogous example of the imperium's concern to legislate religion out of a fear of the destabilizing potential of covert religions. On P.Coll.Youtie I.30 = P.Yale 299 (the 199 edict against oracles), see Parássoglou 1976; Rea 1977; and Ritner 1993:217–20.

[56] On the function and enforcement of the codes, see Milne 1924:95; Barnes 1987:324–25, 331–33; Cameron 1993:74–75; and esp. Bradbury 1994:132–39.

comes a kind of native iconoclastic movement whose religious and social roots are perhaps more accurately sought in studies of comparable cases in modern societies, than in putative or professed links with scripture or laws (as I shall explore further in ch. 6).[57]

The imperial religious edicts had only a marginal effect on the traditional practice of religion in the late empire, certainly contributing an atmosphere of persecution and eroding the civil authority of cults and their personnel, but hardly affecting local practice in village or city. Indeed, an edict of 423 levels strict penalties against any Christians who, like the Coptic monks, ransacked the homes (and, by extension, private shrines) of "pagans who are living quietly and attempting nothing disorderly or contrary to the law" (16.10.24).

### 1.4.2 Impoverishment of Temples and Domesticization of Religious Practice

A far more compelling proposition for the crippling of Egyptian religion over the course of the Roman Empire has focused on the economic state of its infrastructure.[58] Augustus's Egyptian program consisted of placing a Roman official as "High Priest of Alexandria and Egypt" and consolidating priestly authority, tradition, lifestyle, and economic livelihood according to a *Gnomon,* or manual, of an imperial administrative office, the *Idios Logos.* The religious infrastructure was thus more closely monitored in Egypt than in any other province, a fact quite visible in the outpouring of official papyri concerning circumcision, temple landholdings and inventories, and oaths of priestly office, delivered in Greek for Roman administrative purposes.[59]

Reined in tightly to the imperial economy through their dependence on stipends, with only a fraction of the landholdings they had enjoyed under the Ptolemies, the temples of Egypt were doomed to follow the empire's downward spiral in the various economic catastrophes of the third century. Where the munificence of Augustus and the first-century emperors appears in temples throughout Egypt, the effects of the third-century crisis on the temple infrastructure are rather stark: a drastic decline in building dedications and other inscriptions.[60] Temples, at least the major ones, seem to be in a state of progressive ruin, dwindling vestiges of pha-

---

[57] Fowden 1978; Van Dam 1985; Frend 1990. Soldiers were often assigned to temple demolition projects: see Eusebius, *Life of Constantine* 3.55–57 and Nautin 1967:25–26 on the mutilation of the Isis temple of Philae.

[58] As proposed by Otto 1905/8, 1:404–5, and Bagnall 1988.

[59] Milne 1924:286–89; Lewis 1983:91–94; and now Glare 1993.

[60] Bagnall 1988 and Jean-Claude Golvin, "Enceintes et portes monumentales des temples de Thèbes," in Vleeming (ed.) 1995:40–41. On building programs under Augustus and his successors, see Kákosy 1995:2907–17.

raonic and Ptolemaic patronage. What effect would this economic cause have upon the local religious practices and piety? Roger Bagnall has offered a compelling scenario:

> The end of any vital existence for most village temples stripped away the literate and respected leadership class the priesthood had long provided and no doubt eliminated to a large degree the ritual occasions that lent the village a sense of itself as a community. Even spatially it is hard to imagine that abandoned and decaying temples, whether in the center of villages or integrated on the periphery, did not depress the ability to perceive the village as something more than a collection of houses.[61]

This vision of local religion itself pulled down through general economic decline is given all the more weight in its echo of Libanius's famous testimony to the emperor Theodosius:

> Temples are the soul of the countryside: they mark the beginning of its settlement, and have been passed down through many generations to the men of today. In them the farming communities rest their hopes for husbands, wives, children, for their oxen and the soil they sow and plant. An estate that has suffered [a temple's deliberate demolition] has lost the inspiration of the peasantry together with their hopes, for they believe that their labour will be in vain once they are robbed of the gods who direct their labours to their due end.[62]

Thus as the axis of piety wobbles, so wobbles the commitment. But is infrastructure religion, properly conceived? To be sure, no historian of religions would deny the importance of the temple and its cult as a critical center in the social lives and cosmos of people in a region in just the ways Libanius describes. Egyptian culture, however, had watched temples rise and fall for millennia, and its scribes had used the image of abandoned shrines as a literary trope. Viewed over the long term, the third century's dwindling temples hardly amounted to a unique and final catastrophe, and certainly no Egyptian proposed this interpretation until, in a very limited context, the Alexandrian Eunapius in the late fourth century.[63]

In addition, there are abundant examples across cultures of "religion"—

---

61 Bagnall 1993:315.

62 Libanius, *Or.* 30.9–10, tr. Norman, LCL, 2:109–11.

63 Eunapius, *V.P.* 6.9.17 (471), 10.11 (472). I owe this point, seldom brought up in discussions of religious "decline," to Martin Goodman (*Mission and Conversion: Proselytizing in the Religious History of the Roman Empire* [Oxford: Clarendon, 1994], 26–27). Fowden has similarly argued against interpretations of the Hermetic Asclepius as evidence for pessimism in late antique Egypt (1986:38–44). For an early (Middle Kingdom) example of abandoned shrines as tropes to highlight the integrating power of kingship, see *Admonitions of Ipuwer* 6, 5–15, tr. Lichtheim 1973/80, 1.155.

practice, belief, social relations, festal observance—continuing by various means in the face of gross trauma to cultic infrastructures: one thinks of Judaism after 70 C.E., Mesoamerica after the sixteenth century, and the diverse Islamized cultures of the Middle East, Africa, and Asia. To conceptualize religion as it continues in these circumstances requires a particularly nuanced sense of popular and local religion, of the active contribution of local people to temples and their cults, and of the integrating functions these temple-centered activities played in life, rather than people's passive, vicarious dependence upon cults. Indeed, religion in ancient and peasant societies is nothing if not the active negotiation of life, integrally bound up with subsistence, procreation, and location. And it is this kind of piety, in which the temple is the symbolic or projected center, not the alleged "passive" piety that might continue or die with temples, that we find still continuing in the fifth century, according to an anonymous Coptic homily whose author wanted to channel these active sentiments toward the Christian cult of martyrs:

> [T]here are among us today those who worship the "poetic" forms of demons—(forms) contrived from the beginning in their deceitfulness and deluding people as healing cults; . . .
>
> . . . some of them practice abominations in city and village. For it is said that some of them ablute their children in polluted water and water from the arena, from the theater, and moreover they pour all over themselves water with incantations (spoken over it), and they break their clay pots claiming it repels the evil eye. Some tie amulets on their children, hand-crafted by men—those (men) who provide a place for the dwelling of demons—while others anoint themselves with oil that is evil and incantations and such things that they tie on their heads and necks.[64]

In this late witness to continuing native piety, full-fledged cults operated by priests make up a minor part of the preacher's complaint. The phrase "poetic forms of demons" certainly refers to Egyptian deities with their traditional names, but it is their healing powers that apparently draw people. Even more frustrating to the preacher is the vast range of private rites to protect—rites that in fact vividly recall classical Egyptian priestly tradition.[65] We catch a glimpse here of a native piety focused upon issues of health and protection and at the same time fully equipped by tradition and by the many sacred points in the environment to cope with these issues.[66] It is not a "magic," a state of mundane superstition

---

[64] Ps-Athanasius, Homily on Virgin, ed. Lefort 1958:35–36 (ms. pp. 92, 95).

[65] See Goyon 1981 (apotropaic ablutions) and Ritner 1993:144–53 (magical breaking of pots).

[66] See esp. Baines 1987:83–94. On popular religion as oriented toward the resolution of everyday dangers, see also Christian 1981:20–31, 175–76.

or some decayed version of a pristine paganism, by which people now occupy their lives, but rather the autochthonous piety that had always existed, rooted in the immediate environment and its features and cycles, mediating between everyday needs and the traditions fundamental to collective self-definition. Just such a regional piety, we now know, also continued in the sixteenth-century Andes despite Spanish destruction of the great Inca cults that had overlain and integrated this piety.[67]

With the decline of the major centers, then, the axis of religious practice spins out at two levels: (1) to regional prophets who embraced a broader and more absolutist ideology of piety than local cults required or encompassed (a subject to which we return in more detail in 4.5); and (2) *centrifugally* from the main national or regional temples, first to the village and its dynamic interplay of shrine and village society, and finally to the household, the mainstay cross-culturally of traditional practice, festival observance, the miniaturized vision of cult and its dramas, and resistance to the trends and pressures of the public space (the subject of 3.6).[68] As Egyptian Christianity accommodates these indigenous religious dynamics, it also becomes assimilated by them. And thus it is the religion of the village, the local community, that ultimately can continue in late antique Egypt, rather than some ahistorically abstract Christianity.

This dynamic character of Egyptian popular religion can be used as a basis for observing the continuity throughout the Roman period and into Coptic culture of important religious traditions, not as "pagan survivals" but as the organizing phenomena of local religious culture, the substance of accessible power. People respond to the decline of temples, therefore, by establishing or moving their attentions to new loci—oracle cults, prophetic figures, or simply the chief local image or stela that had always served as the local axis and could be celebrated with minimal priestly services. Priests respond to the decline of the infrastructure by shifting their realm of primary authority from temple cult to a locally circumscribed role of ritual expert or to an itinerant mode connected to the culture and needs of Roman Hellenism. Viewed from the standpoint of Egyptian history, these "shifts in the locus of the holy," as Peter Brown once signaled the late antique transformation, are not the death-gasps of a crumbling culture but natural occurrences in a succession of religious vicissitudes stretching back over considerable time.[69]

---

[67] MacCormack 1991:145–48, 181–204; and see also 148–49, 155, on the character of Inca overlay.

[68] See MacMullen 1997:61–64 and esp. Harry O. Maier, "Religious Dissent, Heresy and Households in Late Antiquity," *VigChr* 49 (1995):49–63, on the character of domestic space in guarding religious practice.

[69] Brown 1975.

### 1.4.3 The Dynamics of Local Christianization

For many this notion of religious continuity is challenged by the popularization of Christianity itself over the fourth, fifth, and sixth centuries. At what point must one draw the curtain on Egyptian religion? Traditional historians of the church and the Roman Empire, whose notions of "conversion" imply some kind of mental shift and rebirth that precludes any continuity with preceding worldview and practice, would say that the demographic increase of "Christians," however defined, spelled the concomitant erasure of traditional beliefs and practices. Many Egyptologists, on the other hand, would insist that Coptic Christianity represented essentially an Egyptianizing, a cultural absorption, of a Christian cosmos and rite little different from the many other historical incidences of religious adoption. Our elevation of local and popular religion in this study would impel the Egyptologist's perspective. But it requires some nuance to be convincing.

Was Christianity, for example, an ideology or an idiom as it penetrated the culture of Egypt in the fourth and fifth centuries? The Christian streams that emerge initially in the fourth-century cities and countryside are by no means mere idioms. Those streams from Alexandria (including Gnostic) stem from concerted cosmological systematizing, while the often millennialist versions in the countryside, including the Melitians and other Jewish-Christian groups that exalted martyrdom and otherworldly communion, were maintaining high social and cosmic boundaries against the world. In these cases one must talk of a Christian sectarian *ideology:* a sociopolitical and cosmological worldview that actively rejects the dominant culture in its religious practices and sacred places. At the same time, one need only look at the overwhelming Egyptian legacy in a violently sectarian, martyrdom-oriented text like the *Apocalypse of Elijah* (third century) to realize that millennialist sectarianism can often serve to revitalize a traditional worldview under a new idiom.[70]

Even in the early fourth century there were those whose allegiance to Christianity lay not in the embracing of an ideology but in the sense of participating in an organization supremely versed in the acquisition and dispensing of sacred power. Just as Egyptian priests carried a particular charisma by virtue of their scribal abilities—their acquaintance with sacred books, their training in the use of myth and writing for practical efficacy—so also the popular fascination with Christians and their organization invariably lay in their thaumaturgical reputations, their iconography of the miraculous, and, perhaps most of all, their sacred texts. From biblical fragments used as amulets (a practice continued from Jews)

---

[70] Frankfurter 1993:127–40, 159–238; 1994a.

to the increasing number of Christian spells, the literary materials themselves testify to a steady relationship between the liturgical or lectionary corpus and the dispensing of efficacious power. So even in its most "textual" or official aspects Christianity appeared and functioned as a most powerful system for safeguarding everyday life, much as had the temple institution.[71]

As one leaves the "official" world for the Christianity of the countryside these "magical" elements become more pervasive, even dominant, in the mutual relationship of populace and shrine. The cult of the holy man or woman addressed everyday crises directly, much like a temple's oracle, while Christian oracle shrines were themselves in place by the fifth century.[72] Countless chapels built within temples maintained popular respect and awe for these places, and the sermons presented at their installation often assert their continuing sacrality by virtue of their Christianization.[73] Between the ritual services offered by monks and diverse ecclesiastical functionaries on the one hand, and the network of pilgrimage shrines and "reactivated" holy sites on the other, one gets the distinct sense of a religious organization specifically devoted to the mediation of supernatural power for everyday needs and crises. In this case it is not an ideology that the Christian institutions bring to the local level but rather an idiom for the understanding of sacred power and its points of access.

This process of Christianizing sacred power as it was perennially sought in relation to everyday needs has been exactingly detailed for the western part of the empire in Valerie Flint's *Rise of Magic in Early Medieval Europe*. But rather than a "rise of magic," the Egyptian (and for that matter all other regions') evidence shows the very determining character of local religion—the dynamic assertion of these basic needs and traditions upon the new institution and the cosmos it proffers. What begins as an ideology with overwhelming ramifications for social behavior evolves into an accommodating institution and finally, in the context of local and popular religion, into the indigenous appropriation of a new idiom for the essential mainstays of native tradition and its sense of accessible

---

[71] See below, 7.1, and more generally MacMullen 1984, ch. 3.

[72] Brown 1982, and below, 4.5. On Christian oracle shrines, see MacCoull 1991; and papyrological evidence in Meyer/Smith (eds.) 1994, ##30–35, 65; Papini 1985; Papaconstantinou 1994; and below, 4.4.3.

[73] Sermons: *PG* 77:1105, presented at the fifth-century installation of the incubation cult of Saints Cyrus and John on the location of a previous Isis cult (see below, 4.3.1); and Shenoute, acephalous work A6, pp. 3–4, 13–14 (ed. Young 1981; quoted at beginning of chapter), on which see Emmel 1993:1005, 1182. On the Christianization of Egyptian temples, see Jullien 1902; O'Leary 1938:53–55; Piankoff 1958/60; Nautin 1967; Coquin 1972.

power. And from the very beginning Christian evangelism excelled at addressing precisely this local need for accessible power.

## 1.5 Examining Native Religions: From the Pan-Mediterranean to the Local

We have come, then, to a method that places utmost significance in the data for popular and local religion. To comprehend the persistence of native religions or to reconstruct the process of Christianization one can no longer allow the field of inquiry to extend to the entire Mediterranean world, as if a monolithic Christianity and "paganism" might be faced off in a uniform struggle around the Roman Empire. Regional studies of native religious persistence in late antique Greece, Anatolia, Gaza, Syria, and Egypt have illustrated how difficult it is to make broad geographical generalizations about the decline of native religions. The life of native religions exists in the village and the region, not in a synthetic "paganism"; and regional studies of religious transformation consistently point up the actual fallacy of depending on such pan-Mediterranean "-isms" for understanding any particular religious phenomena.[74] The term "paganism" itself, it has been aptly observed, has historically covered

> just a collection of ethnic polytheisms, whatever was not Judaism or Christianity, but given a name by the lazy cunning of Christian apologists, who could then use their most salacious material to discredit all their opponents at one go.[75]

To buy into such a category is thus to render oneself immediately imprecise, subject far more than is commonly thought to the worldview of ancient polemicists. One notices a tendency even among otherwise critical scholars to slip easily from using "pagan" to allowing the outspokenly conservative intellectuals of the period like the emperor Julian or the biographer Eunapius to represent traditional religions as a monolithic body, thus creating a pagan*ism* out of an idiosyncratic and élite minority.[76] Even if formulations like "traditional rural Syrian religion" or "native religion in the Thebaid" appear awkward and even unfocused in themselves, they bring one that much closer to the realities, the life-contexts of ancient religious life: local identity and cosmos, traditional

---

[74] See Beaujeu 1976; Frankfurter 1990.

[75] Fowden, review of Lane Fox 1986, *JRS* 78 (1988):176, with similar remarks by John Matthews, *The Roman Empire of Ammianus* (Baltimore: Johns Hopkins University Press, 1989), 425–26.

[76] For example, Barnes 1987:329–30; Gregory 1986; Harl 1990; Trombley 1993/94. On the culture of such "intellectual pagans," see Maspero 1914; Geffcken 1978:126–90; Cameron 1965; Fowden 1986, ch. 7; Athanassiadi 1993a.

practice, the negotiation of life and misfortune in the context of regional society and economy.

The shift of focus toward the regional and local requires also a shift of emphasis from the belief-system, the "-ism," to the component religious phenomena that orient sacrality and tradition in the culture: practices, places, institutions, and offices or social roles. With Egypt, especially Roman Egypt, the seductiveness of the strange theologies of Amun, Isis and Osiris, Horus, Re, and the rest might easily lead one to research the status of belief in such gods as a gauge of the religion's vitality. It is a subject, to be sure, that fascinated our most valuable ethnographer of the period, Plutarch, and that has dominated most of the last century's hunt for "pagan survivals." But the modern lure of belief-systems must be tempered with that oft-stated anthropological principle that religion for most people in history has been a matter of practice, not intellection—that the belief-systems themselves arise out of evolving practices.[77] And practices tend to be the heritage, the defining gestures, of specific groups in specific places.

The effectiveness of analyzing religions in their local or regional contexts has emerged particularly clearly in anthropological studies of both contemporary and past cultures, particularly those in the tradition of Robert Redfield.[78] These approaches to religion reveal the degree to which even the particular landscape, the society's geophysical environment, shapes belief and practice. Within (or at least in the context of) local religion one can accommodate and highlight the important continuities in religious practice between socioeconomic classes, a problem that previous constructions of "popular religion" have been unable to negotiate.[79] Across local religions can sweep, in Roman Egypt as much as in modern Africa, prophet movements and their lasting cults, which establish whole new dimensions and rituals for understanding the local cosmos and the broader world in which it participates.[80] And in cultures deeply penetrated by textuality and books even while remaining predominantly illiterate, Redfield's heuristic notion of a great tradition in perpetual dialectic with a little or local tradition remains an important model for taking apart the relations of shrines and temples, local priests and high (or central) priests, everyday rituals ("magic") and festival liturgy, text and amulet, village and cultural center, and so on.[81]

---

[77] See Geertz 1973:213–18, and well argued for antiquity by Phillips 1986:2697–2711.

[78] In particular, Redfield 1941, 1956; Marriott 1955; J. Scott 1977. Compare also Emmanuel Le Roy Ladurie, *Montaillou: The Promised Land of Error,* tr. by Barbara Bray (New York: Braziller, 1978), chs. 17–19, 21; Christian 1981; MacCormack 1991; with C. Stewart 1991 and Hart 1992 on contemporary Greece.

[79] See Brown 1981:12–22.

[80] Cf. Werbner (ed.) 1977; D. H. Johnson 1992, 1994; Ranger 1993:72–76.

[81] Redfield 1956; Marriott 1955; J. Scott 1977. It should be noted that Redfield's binary

Local religious traditions tend to dominate the form that any great tradition might take, particularly in late antiquity. And like pharaonic Egypt itself, with its elaborate temple ideologies and concerted focus on kingship, the Roman Empire was host to multiple great traditions, attempts to create or assert a sense of ideological, pan-Mediterranean unity, often undergirded with myths. These unifying discourses included not only Christianity but also Hellenism, Manichaeism, and, most recently proposed, an imperial legalism that focused all sacred and mantic charisma on the Roman emperor.[82] Each could, in its delineation of social boundary, provide a context in which autonomous, delocalized societies could form: the quasi-sectarian "intellectual pagans" and the ecclesiastical cabals of Antioch, Rome, Alexandria, and other cities, or the similarly urban and literate culture in which the power of the emperor was felt in its most religious sense.

But these same discourses exerted upon local cultures no more than idioms for native traditions to be articulated and asserted. Hellenism offered the idiom of the god Aion for the Nubian god Mandulis to function as an attractive pilgrimage and oracle point for Roman tourists, and it offered an iconographic style for traditional Egyptian gods to gain more "dimension" in terra-cotta form.[83] Christianity and its ascetic displays provided the opportunity for new assertions of local religious leadership. Prophetic figures who might naturally have arisen in the disintegrated times of the late third and fourth centuries, as they have in modern Sudan, now roughly shared a discourse of demonology, iconoclasm, and a millennialist incarnation of supernatural powers.[84]

Manichaeism, the most explicitly ecumenical religious movement of the late empire, now seems to have worked closely with the religions into whose languages the Manichaean texts were translated, often manifestly extending traditional belief-systems and nomenclature.[85] And, to the

---

model does not reify two distinct worlds of great and little tradition, but rather functions heuristically for the purpose of examining the dialectic between the two spheres.

[82] See Averil Cameron, *Christianity and the Rhetoric of Empire: The Development of Christian Discourse*, Sather Classical Lectures 55 (Berkeley: University of California Press, 1991) on Christianity; Bowersock 1990 on Hellenism; Fögen 1993 on imperial legalism; and Beaujeu 1976 on local/great tradition interplay in Gaul.

[83] *Mandulis:* Nock 1972a and Bowersock 1990:22–28. *Terra-cotta iconography:* Dunand 1979:13–16, 62–70, 150–58.

[84] Cf. D. H. Johnson 1994 and Goody 1975 on analogous dynamics in African regional cults. The Syrian Saint Symeon the Elder, whose innovation of pillar-standing as an ascetic act once made him the favorite example of dramatic repudiations of a "pagan" past, actually built his initially *regional* charisma upon a religious symbolism traditional to the region, the pillar itself. What therefore began as a quite *recognizable* ritual or iconographic tradition in its local context quickly captivated the empire and Western Europe as an ascetic display (see Frankfurter 1990).

[85] See Peter Brown, "The Diffusion of Manichaeism in the Roman Empire," in *Religion and Society in the Age of Saint Augustine* (London: Faber & Faber, 1972), 94–118; Jes P.

degree that an emperor-based civic religion arose in the fourth century and effectively installed new categories of religious identity and holiness based on imperial law and the person of the emperor, this religion does not seem to have displaced local religious traditions beyond the cities and their literary cultures, especially in rural Egypt, where imperial control of traditional culture was minimal and whose documents show persisting native tradition far more than rising emperor cults. Indeed, in the most striking example of imperial "replacement" of an Egyptian cult—Diocletian's conversion of the Luxor Amun temple into an imperial audience hall—the motivations seem to have lain in the desire to assimilate the emperor's divine person to the Egyptian high-god.[86]

One can hardly deny such a complex of pan-Mediterranean religious ideologies in the later Roman Empire; moreover, these ideologies clearly gave rise to various subcultures. But these subcultures were an autonomous, minority social phenomenon—not proof of a historical "paganism" existing apart from the native religions of various regions. The vast majority of villages, towns, and regions that embraced these pan-Mediterranean ideologies found in them, rather, opportunities to express local culture. The task must then be to shift our questions and analysis to this local context, to examine native religions (both centralizing cult and popular practice), Christianities, and (it is to be hoped) even Judaisms and Manichaeisms, all as regional phenomena, to consider apparent novelties of the Roman period in terms of the history of religions of a particular region.[87] By attending to the full range of data for indigenous religion, by recalling ancient religions' emphasis on praxis and tradition (over ideology and belief-system), and by deliberately avoiding such misleading categories as "pagan" except in critically delimited circumstances, we can approach a certain degree of precision in the history of religions.

Asmussen, *Manichaean Literature*, Persian Heritage Series 22 (Delmar, N.Y.: Scholars' Facsimiles and Reprints, 1975), 37–43; Richard Lim, "Unity and Diversity among Western Manichaeans: A Reconsideration of Mani's *Sancta Ecclesia*," *REAug* 35 (1989):231–50; Lieu 1994, ch. 2. I am much indebted to Jason BeDuhn's paper, "The Cross-Cultural Unity of Manichaeism: Problems and Prospects," presented at the annual meeting of the Society for Biblical Literature, 1993.

[86] On the development of an imperial religion, see Fögen 1993, borne out partly by Limberis 1994, for late antique Constantinople and Glare 1993 for early Roman Egypt. On the Luxor Roman sanctuary, see Idi Kalavrezou-Maxeiner, "The Imperial Chamber at Luxor," *DOP* 29 (1975):225–51. Kákosy (1995:2929) describes Diocletian's attraction to Egyptian lore and symbolism.

[87] Cf. Frankfurter 1990, 1994a.

# 2

## RELIGION AND TEMPLES

IF THERE WERE ever a land in which the sacred was truly marked off and rigidly separated from a profane outside world, as scholars used to propose as a general fact of religion, it would be Egypt. So much of what we know went on in Egyptian religion—the dressing and procession of images, the presentation of offerings, the chanting of prayers and curses—took place within a precinct restricted to *waab* ("pure") priests that a historian might well surmise that the religion of the outer populace, to the extent that it existed, took place in an entirely separate world. Conversely, some historians have concluded that these segregated rites themselves so constituted Egyptian religion as a whole that without them (or with the temples' economic demise) no religion was possible.

But there has always been evidence for a popular piety around Egyptian temples. In this chapter, using evidence from the Roman period, I demonstrate the interplay between populace and temple not only in the context of ritual but also socially (festivals and associations) and economically (patronage). The resulting picture of Egyptian religion shows people who are, as communities, very much responsible for their own religious practice and piety, not to the degree that they would not feel the effect of a lapse in festival processions of the god's official image through the streets, but in the sense that in their "active" piety people could readily continue life-sustaining rites and traditions, retrench with respect to major community rites, or find new centers of piety.

### 2.1 The Distribution of Powers: Fertility

Marcus Aurelius Apollonios, hierophant, to the [priestess-]basket-carrier of [the village of] Nesmeimis, greeting. Please go to [the village of] Sinkepha to the temple of [Isis-]Demeter, to perform the customary sacrifices for our lords the emperors and their victory, for the rise of the Nile and increase of crops, and for favourable conditions of climate. I pray that you fare well. [*P.Oxy* XXXVI.2782]

This letter is from the second or third century C.E. and reflects a phenomenon both common and important in Roman Egypt: the unstaffed local shrine dependent upon the scheduled appearances of priests for its official cult.[1] What is particularly notable, however, is the characterization of this occasional cult's purposes: to be sure, the fortune of the emperor, but even more the fertility of the landscape as the goddess Isis was supposed to provide this from her shrine. (Indeed, it is tempting to take the priestess's "basket-bearing" function [*kalatēphoros*] as a dramatization of the agrarian Isis-Demeter, who is portrayed carrying a cornucopia or basket in other shrines and figurines to represent her powers of fertility.)[2]

In an agricultural economy like Roman Egypt's it is not surprising to find terrestrial fertility a major focus of both temple cult and the popular relationship to the temple cult. The temple of Kysis at the south end of the Kharga oasis, built for a predominantly agricultural society in the late first century C.E., was dedicated to "Isis who rejoices in the abundant fields"; and a second-century priestly inscription renews the praises in invoking Isis as "life-bearing [*pheresbios*]" in her capacity of providing grain, fruit, and wine—an image of the goddess reflected in hymns throughout Greco-Roman Egypt.[3] Outfitted with "external" altars accessible to the multitude who visited from around the oasis (and, by the oil residues on them, evidently well-used), the temple of Kysis seems to have functioned as a major center for the understanding and transference of fertility for a number of villages.[4]

The temple of Khnum at Esna-Latopolis, with imperial cartouches extending through the reign of Decius, evidently enjoyed enough prosperity through the mid-third century to operate its cult in full splendor. In its festival calendar, which itself dates from no earlier than the late first century C.E., there is described an annual procession of the cult image of the god Heka ("cosmic power," here identified as the son of the main temple-god, Khnum) through the countryside after the Nile's inundation,

[1] See Gallo 1992:121–23 and Dunand 1981:143–45 on one such shrine excavated.

[2] See Solmsen 1979:9–11, 24–25; Dunand 1979:65–67; 1981:136–39. The use of Demeter here instead of Isis or Thermouthis may be a self-conscious claim to the status of Greek gods. Lewis (1986:86) notes the tendency in papyri for priests of local gods to identify themselves in connection with Greek gods. In the Ptolemaic period the Egyptian shrines at Karnak are recorded with Greek divinities' names (see Jan Quaegebeur, "Les appellations grecques des temples de Karnak," *OLP* 6/7 [1975/76]:463–78, esp. 474: a shrine of the goddess Ipet designated a Dēmētrion). László Török proposes a dissociation of the Demeter cult from that of Isis during the Roman period; but his evidence, terra-cotta figurines, might also prove increasing synthesis (Török 1995:21, 41–42, ##29, 31). Bonneau (1971:57, 62) proposed the Nile cult as the context of this papyrus.

[3] IGDoush I–II, ed. Wagner 1987:48–51 w/comm. 335–36. Compare Isidorus, Hymns to Isis I.8–14; II (early first century B.C.E.), ed. Vanderlip 1972, and Philae Isis-Hymn III, tr. and comm. Louis V. Žabkar, *Hymns to Isis in Her Temple at Philae* (Hanover and London: Brandeis University Press, 1988), 39–45 (early Ptolemaic).

[4] Vernus 1979:12. Further on the fertility aspects of oasis gods, see Kaper 1997:156–57.

to be enthroned at the sanctuary of Pi-Neter. The hymn for this procession manifestly identifies Heka as the power behind crops, the producer and nourisher of all vegetation.[5]

This kind of rite was hardly unique to Esna and demonstrates that, alongside a ritual cycle exclusive to the priesthood and to the temples' inner courts, temples would actively serve the needs of farmers, infusing the fields with the very sacred power that "lived" in the temples. Temples would thus be popularly regarded as repositories of such power for the sake of the landscape and fields, much as Libanius described: "In them the farming communities rest their hopes for husbands, wives, children, for their oxen and the soil they sow and plant."[6] In actively penetrating the countryside with the images of gods the temples involved themselves intimately with a basic concern of popular culture, according to a calendar of festivals and processions. The fact that such processions adhered to calendrical cycles does not so much set up some sort of "temple hegemony" as integrate the natural cycles of the Nile Valley with the temple, the local "center" of sacred power, and with the worldview that the temple epitomized.

By the Roman period such traditional forms of administering the fertilizing power of the temple-gods were often supplemented locally with more "open" shrines. Thus in Thebes, outside the main temple of Luxor, stands a small mud-brick shrine dedicated in the early second century to Serapis and his accompanying images and holding a large statue of Isis-Thermouthis (see pl. 2). Although other temples were still being built or refurbished in the more traditional manner that excluded the sacred images from the eyes of devotees, the structure of the Luxor shrine allowed for devotees to be separated from this central icon of popular agricultural fertility only by front doors, which were ritually opened by a priest at certain times; and offerings might be made immediately in front of the shrine. Exterior niches and a basin provided for continual access to sacred images and to consecrated water. The shrine has parallels in the Thebaid (an Iseion at Deir el-Medina), the Delta (Ras el-Soda), and mining villages along the eastern highways (Mons Porphyrites and Mons Claudianus), altogether showing an extensive popular cult of Isis during the Roman period, in which local access to her fertilizing capacity did not always depend on festivals and processions.[7]

---

[5] I. Esna 341, 8, tr. Sauneron 1962a:35, on which see ibid., 29–35, 381–82; Kákosy 1995:3023–24. On Roman munificence at Esna, see *P-M* 6:110–18, with Grenier 1988:61–63 (cartouche of Alexander Severus).

[6] Libanius, *Or.* 30.10, tr. Norman, LCL, 2:109.

[7] In general on Luxor Isis shrine (actually labeled a *serapeion* in dedicatory inscription): Leclant 1951 and Jean-Claude Golvin, Sayyed 'Abd el-Hamid, Guy Wagner, and Françoise

On the other side of the temple procession and the traditional Egyptian reliefs and inscriptions that record it lay a popular iconography and deployment of icons that together illustrate an overwhelming concern for fertility in field as well as in herd and womb. Terra-cotta statues of Isis, her agricultural avatar Isis-Thermouthis, Harpocrates bearing a pot or cornucopia (or an enlarged phallus), and related figures that evoked these gods' processions, produced en masse from the first through early fourth centuries and either displayed in special wall niches or (more rarely) presented to temples *ex voto*, bear witness to such popular interests in directing sacred power especially toward agricultural production (see pls. 7–9). The far more skillfully crafted images that were found in Roman Karanis (used through the beginning of the fourth century) show similar interests: images of Isis associated with the local god Sobek, two images specifically of Isis-Thermouthis, and images erected in village granaries. The Hellenizing iconography of all these Isis figures implies not a different constituency from the participants in traditional temple processions but a distinctively syncretistic popular piety in the Roman period, when Greco-Roman crafts, making up a large portion of domestic religious iconography, now provided a principal medium for indigenous religious ideas, such that the ancient temples were now supplemented by shrines with icons in the Hellenistic style. The result is a kind of *interpretatio aegyptiaca,* an indigenization of alien iconography to bring new significance to traditional images of supernatural power.[8]

In at least one pocket of Egypt such a fertility cult of Isis persisted into the fifth century C.E., as a regional "ultimate appeal" for women's maternity in the western Delta. The temple of Isis at Menouthis, although just about twenty kilometers from Alexandria, seems to have easily resisted the Christianity in power there. Along with another distinct Isis cult in the neighboring town of Canopus, the Menouthis temple had established an incubation cult by the early Roman period: one would spend the night

Dunand, "Le petit Sarapieion romain de Louqsor," *BIFAO* 81 (1981):115–48. On exterior niches: Golvin/Abd el-Hamid 1981:123–24; Dunand 1981:145. On the nature of the shrine's "open" layout: Dunand 1981:143–46, comparing the Luxor shrine to the Isis temple at Deir el-Shelwit, on the west bank of Thebes (see *P-M* 2.530–32 and Christine M. Zivie, *Le temple de Deir Chelouit* 4 [Cairo: IFAO, 1992], esp. 93–94). On similar shrines of same period: Dunand 1981:139–43, 148; *P-M* 2.407 (Deir el-Medina); Adriani 1935/39 (Ras el-Soda); David Meredith, "Eastern Desert of Egypt: Notes on Inscriptions," *CdÉ* 28 (1953):126–31, and Theodor Kraus, Josef Röder, and Wolfgang Müller-Wiener, "Mons Claudianus—Mons Porphyrites," *MDAIK* 22 (1967):172–82 (Mons Porphyrites), 125 (Mons Claudianus).

8 Quaegebeur 1983a:316, 318–23. On the nature of Hellenism in terra-cotta medium: Dunand 1979:150–58 and Török 1995:20–22. On terra-cotta figurines: Dunand 1979:60–67, 105–8; 1984:26–27; cf. 1979:73–77 and Török 1995:20–21 on Harpocrates figure. On Karanis figures: Gazda 1978:12–15 (compare Isis figurines found in the main temple of Kellis, in Hope 1994).

in the temple to receive a dream revelation from Isis, which would then be interpreted by an attending priest. And while the cult of Isis at Canopus seems to have ended around 389 (when the great Serapis temple of Alexandria fell to a Christian mob), that of Menouthis continued for another century. For one Zachariah of Mytilene, recounting a Christian raid on Menouthis in 484 in which he took part, describes an Isis cult and temple there (which subsequently fell in the raid). And it was this temple, Zachariah describes, which had gained a reputation among Alexandrian intellectuals for assuring maternal conception. Indeed, so important was this particular promise that, in Zachariah's narrative, when it failed for one person the Menouthis priest sent him to another village to receive a baby from the priestess there, suggesting a kind of priestly network in the western Delta region.[9]

One must assume the existence of other temple cults that pertained directly to regional fertility. Near Hermopolis the local god Osiris of Hasro might still be expected to bring a woman her husband's attentions and impregnation in about 100 C.E.[10] In Oxyrhynchus the temple of the (maternal) fertility goddess Taweret still required eight guards at the end of the third century, more than the Serapeum and the Iseum, and at least two guards in the mid-fourth century, most of whom were posted inside the precinct, presumably to oversee popular devotions.[11] So also the "birth-temples" of Philae and Dendara, two particularly resilient temple centers, must have been popularly interpreted as fonts of accessible power of the same sort, since Christians' peculiar mutilation of all the images of the god Bes, high up in the Roman birth-temple at Dendara, suggests their awareness of a popular attraction to the place for maternal success and protection (as represented by the Bes image; see pl. 22).[12]

Such evidence of the fertility processions of a major cult like Esna's, or of local temples and popular icons that focused on the fertility powers of Isis or Horus (bearing a cornucopia, exposing a breast, or, as at Kysis, invoked epigraphically as produce-bringer), all from the second and later centuries, serve quite vividly to flesh out Libanius's words about the temple's function. But even more than grounding such passionate oratory in the realities of Egyptian religion, such materials undergird a more subtle point in Libanius's same defense of temples—the mutual participation of temple and peasant worlds: "Temples are the soul of the countryside"

[9] Zachariah of Mytilene, V. Severus, in A. Bernand 1970:211, with Wipszycka 1988:138–42. On the practice of incubation for conception in classical Egypt, see Pinch 1993:223. See fuller discussion below, 4.3.

[10] P. Schmidt, ed. Satzinger 1975.

[11] W.Chr. 474 = P.Oxy 43v iv, 12 (295 C.E.); P.Oxy XIV.1627 (342 C.E.). On the state of this cult in the Roman era, see Quaegebeur et al. 1985:224–30 and Whitehorne 1995:3080–82.

[12] Cf. Daumas 1958:140–43.

insofar as "they mark the beginning of its settlement, and have been passed down through many generations to the men of today."[13] Through their cults the temples organized the agricultural cycle. And in the popular iconography and minor shrines one can observe not a private religion on the part of devotees but the active endeavor on the part of peasants to participate in and even to appropriate the temples' supernatural powers into everyday life.

## 2.2 The Cult of the Nile as a Popular and an Institutional Phenomenon

The rites around the Nile's surge display a different dynamic of persistence: not the resilience of traditional temple religion (although this too occurred) so much as a popular ritual tradition bound up so inescapably with the rhythms of the agricultural cycle that neither priestly nor imperial nor, ultimately, Christian institutions could alter its cultural significance.

In a culture dependent economically on the annual swell of the river, Egyptians up and down the Nile had perennially symbolized their connection with this phenomenon, vital to fertility and success, through various rituals of anticipation and of celebration. Those rites that anticipated the surge, consisting of appeals and invocations, were fixed astronomically; whereas celebrations took place when the river attained a certain height, or gave its "sign"—hence the festival's name in Roman times, *sēmasia*.

But where the Romans inferred a kind of national religion out of this consistency in reverence throughout Egypt, in fact both these sets of rites differed considerably from region to region and from temple to temple. The chief differences concerned the deity responsible for invoking the surge or from whose powers the Nile was an extension, and to what extent the king himself was celebrated in connection with the Nile. Underlying these differences is the subtle interplay between temple religion and popular tradition. As part of a continual process throughout much of Egyptian history, the different temples (from whom we receive our early documentation of the cults of the Nile) seem to have appropriated these popular, local traditions and centralized them in their own precincts. Popular appeals for the surge, for example, became systematized as a function of the temple-god, who would process out annually to the bank of the Nile to make his or her appeal in utmost pomp, a focus and elevation of popular sentiment. And in the Dakhla oasis, over two hundred

---

[13] Libanius, *Or.* 30.9, tr. Norman, LCL, 2:109.

kilometers west of the Nile, temple inscriptions still acclaimed the Nile surge and its powers of fecundity as the source of local irrigation.[14]

This systematization of popular tradition is a phenomenon hardly un- usual in the history of religions and, indeed, basic to the very activity of priesthoods. In Egypt it appears most vividly in the construction of Nilometers in temple precincts. These small structures (often consisting only of staircases down to water level) allowed the measuring and re- cording of each surge; and included as they were within the purview of the temple, Nilometers immediately focused the observation and "con- trol" of the surge on the priesthood. Indeed, the Nilometer allowed priests a mantic authority over each coming inundation and over all that inundation might correspond to in the realms of kingship and social or- der, as an oracular papyrus of the third century reveals: a low surge is connected to wars, multiple kings, and social chaos (*P.Oxy* XXXI.2554).

Ptolemies and Romans gave the cults an iconography on coins and terra-cotta images and a ludic dimension, with extravagant festivals over which presided civil authorities. It was a thoroughgoing attempt to ap- propriate into Hellenistic or imperial idiom what would have appeared to the authorities the most essential and "national" of popular Egyptian ritual traditions. Through this Hellenistic idiom we gain vivid, if ideal- ized, pictures of Nile rites continuing in the Roman period: a prayer cop- ied in the late third or early fourth century C.E., for example, describes how "men standing at the river mouth invoke the beloved water of divine Nile, and children singing all together the annual hymn in prayer invite you to manifest yourself most perfect. . . . [W]ith your current raise yourself before the altar for your sacrifices."[15]

One of the singular developments in Egyptian religion under Roman administration was the addition of new priestly or quasi-priestly offices, and the "national" character of Nile cults must have offered some incen- tive to expand their festal hierarchy. Thus prefects often presided over the rites, and some towns even included such novel offices as a "high priest of the most holy Nile."[16] But priestly authority over the Nile rites was idiosyncratic. The Soknobraisis priesthood explained their normal

[14] See in general Morenz 1973:78, 150–51, 302n.38, 317n.52; Bonneau 1964, 1971; and on Dahkla fertility beliefs, Kaper 1997, ch. 6. Romans were not the first to idealize a pan-Egyptian devotion to the Nile, for Egyptian poets had long (since the Middle Kingdom) used the hymn to the Nile as a literary form and model, extolling the river's beneficence to all Egypt. See Lichtheim 1973/80, 1:204–10.

[15] On a waxed tablet in the Louvre: inv. MNE-911, ll.9–13, 24–25, ed. and tr. Raffaella Cribiore, "A Hymn to the Nile," *ZPE* 106 (1995):97–106. On the development of the Nile cult under the Ptolemies and Romans, see Bonneau 1964:390–93; 1995:3207–15.

[16] *P.Wisc.* 9.4 (Oxyrhynchus 183 C.E.), ed. P. J. Sijpestein, *The Wisconsin Papyri* (Leiden: Brill, 1967).

cultic activities to the local Roman authorities in 171 C.E. as serving "also
the full rise of the most holy Nile" (P.Yale 349),[17] and when some unknown priests were still registering the inundation at the temple of
Akōris as late as the fifth century they most likely held general functions.
Akōris indeed provides important evidence for the resilience of the traditional Nile cult, for although the inscriptions recording the priests' visits
are sparse and irregular after the reign of Diocletian, they certainly bespeak an intention of maintaining local ritual. The latest inscription reflects the "sign" of the *sēmasia* festival, which "rose according to the
sacred mark" (i.e., the high-water point on the Nilometer).[18]

Nile rites consisted in their most basic form of the procession of a local
god's bark shrine to the river's bank in order that the god might convince
the river to bring an abundant inundation. Thus the festival was still
practiced in fourth-century Hermopolis (just south of Akōris), according
to a Christian source:

> There was a huge temple in one of the villages which housed a very famous
> idol, though in reality this image was nothing but a wooden statue. The
> priests together with the people, working themselves up into a bacchic
> frenzy, used to carry it in procession through the villages, no doubt perform-
> ing the ceremony to ensure the flooding of the Nile.[19]

This popular enthusiasm (a detail we cannot simply ascribe to Christian typology) points to the intense local concern with which the Nile
surge was regarded, still in the fourth century. Indeed, there were also
Nile rites practiced apart from the temple institution, in which villagers
simply congregated on the riverbank and sang, prayed, and made offerings according to local custom. What the Nile prayer above described in
the extravagant terms of men and children arrayed on the banks singing
appears in the biography of the fourth-century abbot Pachomius as a
simple family rite, an extension of domestic ritual, addressed to the local
gods: "As a child his parents took him with them somewhere on the river

---

17 P. Yale 349 = Gilliam 1947, #19, ll.25–26. See also Gilliam 1947:253–54n. ad loc.

18 IGAkoris 41, ed. É. Bernand 1988:58 (= Lefebvre 1921, #13). Cf. IGPhilae 187 (ed.
É. Bernand 1969b, 2:214–17), also demonstrating the late Roman practice of the Nile cult.
On *sēmasia*, see Bonneau 1971:58–59, and in general on Akōris: Lefebvre 1921; É. Bernand 1988, esp. xxi–xxv on the character of the cult; Bonneau 1964:391–92; Worp
1989:137. In general on the functions of priests in Nile rites, see Bonneau 1964:382–83,
386–87. P.Mich. inv. 5794 (unpubl.), 5795 (ed. O. Pearl, *TPAPA* 87 [1956]:51–59), and
5796 (unpubl.) form part of a mid-second-century C.E. archive of a Nilometer priest,
recovered from Karanis, to be published by Traianos Gagos and Terry Wilfong.

19 *Hist. Mon.* 8.25 (ed. Festugière 1971:56), tr. Russell 1981:73–74. In general on Nile
processions, see Bonneau 1964:393–98.

to sacrifice to those [creatures] that are in the waters."[20] In both types of Nile cult, the temple procession and the popular rites, one traditionally implored not the Nile per se but the local god to bring the surge.[21]

But the importance, even inevitability, of the tradition of appealing for the Nile's surge and the institutions or idioms through which these appeals were conveyed always lay in some disjunction. As the divinity of the Nile cannot properly be understood through Roman images of a god "Neilos," so also the cults' centralization in temples and their processions did not determine their resilience over time.[22] Nile cults should be understood as tradition in its deepest sense: as community-sustaining ritual patterns that inevitably determine those local activities sponsored by any "great" or institutional religion. Thus we may also understand why veneration for the Nile flood constitutes one of the best documented "survivals" in Coptic culture, for it was a tradition too intertwined with a popular economic mentality, and yet sufficiently independent of official religion, to be effectively eliminated as "pagan."[23]

Recast as the beneficent manifestation of the power of Michael, or Christ, or one or another of the saints, or even a divine element in itself (an effluence from paradise), the supernatural Nile was one of the chief features of the cultural landscape determining the shape of Christianity. We would be hard-pressed, for example, to label either "pagan" or "Christian" a Nile festival in 424 Oxyrhynchus or, in the sixth century, a prayer "for the festival marking the rising of the most sacred Nile, the festival with its sacred rites of abundance," when Aristainetos reports the Nile's *heortē* still celebrated throughout Egypt with feasting and traditional hymns.[24] It would likewise be in the context of such a popular tradition, independent of temple or priestly authority or identifiable gods, that ritual power over the Nile's surge might become part of the supernatural virtue of a Christian abbot. Shenoute of Atripe's biography promotes the abbot alone as master of the flood through vision and inter-

---

[20] *V. Pachomii* Bohairic Life (SBo) 4, tr. Veilleux 1980:25.

[21] See Bonneau 1964:398–401. The liturgical category of "Hymns to the Nile" belongs to a different order of rite, celebrating the actual event of the surge: Bonneau 1964:405–10.

[22] Such Hellenized images of Neilos found in Egyptian contexts, then, should be understood as occasional expressions, not determiners, of local Nile cult belief, like the mass-produced Catholic saint images employed to represent traditional Loas in Haitian voudou. On an example of such a Neilos, see Gazda (ed.) 1983:42, fig. 73.

[23] Lewis 1983:94–95.

[24] *P.Oxy* XLIII.3148; *P.Lond.* lit. 239 (on which see Bonneau 1964:410–13); Aristainetos in Pseudo-Nonnos, *Mythological Scholia* 27, ed. Nimmo Smith, Corpus Christianorum Series Graeca 27, 203, tr. Sebastian Brock, *The Syriac Version of the Pseudo-Nonnos Mythological Scholia* (Cambridge: Cambridge University Press, 1971), 145–46 (with Syriac and Armenian texts).

cession (102–4, 122); by his directive an island floods permanently (86); and well after his death Shenoute was still being invoked to cause the Nile's rise "to [its] full measure" and thereby to "multiply the harvests of the earth." Indeed, a heavenly vision attributed to him clarifies the abbot's intercessory powers with the surge, for in the vision he beholds the very angel in charge of the river.[25]

The Nile festivals thus on the one hand show a disjunction between communities' ritual traditions and temples' tendencies to centralize and systematize. But on the other hand they demonstrate the strength of basic, fertility-oriented local traditions to affect the structure and calendar of temple practices, to convey to Roman administrative eyes the semblance of a "national" religious practice that might be developed to extravagant proportions, and to present to new ideologies like Christianity an inevitable fact of cultural practice that might be rearticulated but never obliterated.

## 2.3 Healing Cults as a Nexus of Temple and Popular Piety

There were as well a range of ritual means of appropriating powers of the temple for immediate healing and ongoing health, from those rites administered largely by priests to those practiced exclusively by laity. Every case represents the continual involvement of regional populations in the life of the temple through a sense of necessity and need for "center" in the resolution of misfortune.[26]

Many temples in the Greco-Roman period opened considerable medical facilities that combined herbal and "magical" substances with incubation oracles. Whereas the full significance of the oracle will be addressed in the following chapter, one must note that alongside graffiti declaring pilgrims' devotions (*proskunēmata*) to the "speaking" god at major Roman pilgrimage cults like Abydos and Deir el-Bahri are nu-

---

[25] Appeal to Shenoute: Stud. Pal. XV.250a–b, ed. and tr. Leslie S. B. MacCoull, "*Stud. Pal.* XV 250ab: A Monophysite Trishagion for the Nile Flood," *JTS* 40 (1989):130–32. See also ibid., 132–35 and Bonneau 1964:435–37. Vision of "angel of the waters": "Apocalypse of Shenoute," ed. Leipoldt 4, #182, on which see Gérard Roquet, "L'Ange des eaux et le dieu de la crue selon Chenouté: Sur un fragment copte des visions de l'*Apocalypsis Sinuthii*," *Apocrypha* 4 (1993):83–99. In general on post-third-century transformations of the Nile cult, see Alfred Hermann, "Der Nil und die Christen," *JAC* 2 (1959):30–69, and Bonneau 1964:421–39. The Christianization of Nile rites did not constitute a "desacralization" (*pace* Danielle Bonneau, "Continuité et discontinuité notionale dans la terminologie religieuse du Nil, d'après la documentation grecque," *Mélanges Étienne Bernand,* Annales littéraires de l'Université de Besançon 444, ed. by N. Fick and J.-C. Carrière [Paris: Les Belles Lettres, 1991], 23–35; cf. Bagnall 1993:270), for even when occasionally demonized the river remained sacred in the context of attitude and ritual.

[26] See in general Malaise 1987.

merous graffiti requesting healing of ailments.[27] At Kysis, numerous small gold *ex voto* medallions portraying both Isis and the Apis bull suggest that the town's temple answered a variety of requests of which health probably comprised a large fraction, altogether inspiring such conviction on devotees' parts that they would offer such expensive objects. At Dendara a mud-brick sanatorium with separate rooms for patients was erected in the temple precinct of Hathor during the first century C.E. The process of "healing" here evidently combined incubation with both devotion to the icons that stood in each room's niche and the consumption of water that passed over a central stela covered with healing-related spells (see pl. 22). The temple of Isis at Menouthis was such a major source of maternity and health in the western Delta during the fifth century that it could only be replaced by a Christian healing cult, of Saints John and Cyrus.[28] Such evidence of healing cults within or in the precincts of temples shows the extent of interplay between popular expectations of healing power from the temple on the one hand, and on the other the priesthoods' own responsiveness to these expectations through the redirection of space or erection of structures specifically for healing.

Beyond these centralized "cults" of healing existed an even broader form of therapeutic interaction with temples through iconography: the healing stelae. A large corpus of stelae exists from the Late and Greco-Roman periods showing the god Horus as a child standing on crocodiles and holding hostile animals in his hands, his head surmounted by a "Bes" face. Best exemplified in the Metternich stela, a mid-fourth-century B.C.E. monument in the Metropolitan Museum bedecked with hieroglyphic spells, these "Horus-*cippi*" were produced in sizes ranging from several centimeters to over a meter in height (see pls. 4–6). Associated with them are stelae that present amalgamations of divine power focused on other figures, like the dwarf-god Bes (pl. 12) or the sphinx-god Tutu. The enormity of the corpus of these stelae among Egyptian collections suggests that they were among the most important religious images in Egyptian popular religion of the Greco-Roman period.[29]

The religious value of such images lay both in their peculiar conglomeration of aggressive or victorious images, which rendered them apo-

[27] *Abydos:* Perdrizet/Lefebvre 1919:xv–xvi; *Deir el-Bahri:* Bataille 1951:xix–xxiii.

[28] *Kysis:* Reddé 1992:62; *Dendara:* Daumas 1957; *Menouthis:* see discussion below, 4.3.1.

[29] Sauneron 1960b; Daressy 1903:36–37, ##9428–29. In general on Horus-*cippi*, see Daressy 1903; Pierre Lacau, "Les statues 'guérisseuses' dans l'ancienne Égypte," *Académie des inscriptions et belles-lettres, Commission de la fondation Piot, Monuments et Mémoires* 25 (1921/22):189–209; Keith C. Seele, "Horus on the Crocodiles," *JNES* 6 (1947):43–52; Jelínková-Reymond 1956; László Kákosy, "Some Problems of the Magical Healing Statues," in Roccati/Siliotti (eds.) 1987:171–86; Ritner 1989; Sternberg-El Hotabi 1994.

tropaic of demons and dangerous fauna, and in the spells inscribed on their sides, backs, and bases, which command the retreat of, or describe the victory of diverse gods over, venoms, poisons, and other illnesses. In this way, by analogy to divine acts, the larger stelae often specifically functioned to *cure* such ailments, but in a peculiar way: water poured over the stelae would absorb and transfer the power in the spells to those who drank or applied it. This principle of contagion is, of course, fairly widespread in the ancient world and in traditional cultures: one notes the widespread late antique dissemination of blessed liquids from Christian pilgrimage shrines and in contemporary Sudan the preparation of healing liquids by washing Qur'anic verses off paper. In Egypt, however, the principle had been long institutionalized and centralized: some stelae and statue bases are actually equipped with depressions for the water to pool and be collected after passing over the hieroglyphs.[30]

Classical Egyptian examples of the larger stelae make clear that a patron would endow the manufacture and erection of a healing or apotropaic stela for a place of public access like a temple courtyard; thus the patron would be continually remembered through visitors' perennial rites of charging water.[31] Beyond this essentially do-it-yourself facility, however, some temples developed whole buildings devoted to the charging and dispensing of healing water: at Karnak, a chapel of the Late Period (712–332 B.C.E.), whose walls were entirely covered with healing-spells and probably contained a healing image; and Dendara's sanatorium, whose hydraulic system distributed water that had passed over a large stela inscribed with healing-spells (and probably originally surmounted by a statue of a healing god). It must also have been for such a function of distributing "charged" water that the small Roman era shrine outside the great temple of Luxor provided an external basin.[32]

Other stelae and statues erected in public places may have functioned more for civic or domestic protection than for healing per se: one finds

[30] On spells: Moret 1915; Jelínková-Reymond 1956; Adolf Klasens, *A Magical Statue Base (Socle Behague) in the Museum of Antiquities at Leiden* (Leiden: Brill, 1952); Ritner 1992; Borghouts 1978, ##87–88, 90–91, 93–95, 114, 118, 123, 139–46. On contagion (water) rites: Goyon 1981:147–50; Ritner 1993:106–10, with late antique and contemporary Sudanese parallels described in Vikan 1982:10–27 and El-Tom 1985.

[31] On patronage, László Kákosy, "New Studies in Magical Healing Statues," *Annales Universitatis Scientiarum Budapestinensis, Sectio Classica* 9–10 (1982–85):57–62; Ritner 1989:104–7; 1992:500–501. An inscription on an apotropaic stela of the god Tutu from Coptos (209/10 C.E.) attributes its establishment to an "association of the great god Tout-ou" (Cairo Museum #JE 37538, in Guéraud 1935:5 = Sauneron 1960b, #29).

[32] Luxor Isis shrine: see Dunand 1981:145. Karnak chapel: Claude Traunecker, "Une chapelle de magie guérisseuse sur le parvis du temple de Mout á Karnak," *JARCE* 20 (1985):65–92; Dendara sanatorium: Daumas 1957.

numerous large images of the protective gods Bes and Tutu. Yet in their popular accessibility and often physical centrality such images no doubt played a diversity of roles in the lives of people. A large stela of early Hellenistic workmanship with an apotropaic image of the god Bes in the Brooklyn Museum, for example, apparently hung above a font for sacred water.[33]

The general picture of ritual as it pertained to the Horus-*cippi* and associated stelae and statues, therefore, suggests a comparatively minor priestly role beyond iconographic design and a considerable private role for supplicant or pilgrim. Even the monumental healing statues and shrines erected by temples were apparently designated for independent popular use (although one must assume their occasional incorporation with priestly healing rites). Establishments like Dendara's are therefore most important in showing, not the exclusiveness or bureaucracy of healing ritual in Greco-Roman Egypt, but how a priesthood might systematize a principal mode of popular piety. Publicly erected or accessible images were thus a basic part of the religious landscape in Roman Egypt; and as an autochthonous ritual tradition essentially independent of temple cult, the veneration of healing stelae and statues could continue in local culture despite the utter demise of local temples.[34]

This is undoubtedly the context of the "healing cults [*ehentherapia*]" that a Coptic preacher dismissed as demonic trickery in his promotion of the cult of saints.[35] With no indication of a priesthood or official cult and in the context of the popular apotropaic rites mentioned subsequently we can assume no more than that people practiced such "cults" in a private or popular sense, with no apparent priestly mediation—much in the way one might be apt to steal a strip of "linen cloth . . . from a marble statue of Harpocrates in any temple," as a third- or fourth-century ritual spell instructs.[36] And it is in this context of popular accessibility that we should take seriously an account that goes back to the earliest (Sahidic) version of Besa's *Life of Shenoute*: that in Panopolis or a neighboring village a large statue of the fertility-god Min stood in the marketplace and was widely viewed as protective. Although framing the power of the statue in purely demonic and malevolent terms, Besa's account accords with the evidence for healing and apotropaic statues in Egyptian village

[33] Brooklyn 37.229 (unpubl.); cf. Cairo ##JE 9428–29 in Daressy 1903, where the same "winged Bes" functioned like a Horus-*cippus*.

[34] See Traunecker 1979 and Sadek 1987:72–76 on New Kingdom Egypt, and Ramsay MacMullen, *Paganism in the Roman Empire* (New Haven, Conn., and London: Yale University Press, 1981), 31–32, on the Roman period in general.

[35] Pseudo-Athanasius, Homily on the Virgin Mary, p. 92, ed. Lefort 1958:35, quoted above, 1.4.2.

[36] PGM IV.1073–74.

life: the spirit (or *Ba*) of the god that dwells in this statue, along with associate-gods, actually declares their combined power to guard the village, and his "words" carry the power of "magic" to cure illnesses and infirmities.[37]

It would not have been unusual, nor even unique to Egypt, that ancient figures like this Min might continue to attract private ritual for centuries after the figure had lost its cultic significance, its association with priestly processions—a great tradition. Even in the thirteenth century a legend remained about an Isis *lactans* (or so it indeed seems) erected in the middle of a city, and the function it served:

> In the centre of the city [the antediluvian king Surid] erected the statue of a woman seated with a child in her lap as if she were suckling him. Any woman who, afflicted by a disease in her body, rubbed the (corresponding part of) the body of that statue, recovered her former state. In a likewise manner, if her milk diminished and she rubbed its breast, then it increased. And in the same manner, if she wanted that her husband feel affection towards her, she rubbed its face with good oil and told it: Make this and this. If her menstruation decreased and she became afraid of this, she rubbed it under its knees. If anything afflicted her son, she did the same to (its) son, and he recovered. If her delivery was difficult, she rubbed the head of (its) son and it became easy. In the same manner, it made deflowering easier for the virgin. If the adulteress put her hand on it, she (started) to tremble so that she renounced her dissolute life. The acts associated with the night had to be performed during the night and the acts associated with the daytime had to be performed in daytime. . . . In some of the books of the Copts (it is claimed) that it was found after the Flood and that they used it and worshipped it. Her picture can be found in every temple in Egypt, represented in colours.[38]

Presented as a "charter myth" about the foundational acts of the king Surid and the prototypical city he established, this legend probably arose

---

[37] *Life of Shenoute* (Ar.), tr. Amélineau 1888/95:439–40; cf. Besa, *Life of Shenoute* (Sa) frgs. 8–9, ed. Amélineau 1888/95:644–47. The episode seems to have belonged to that section of the more complete *Life of Shenoute* (Bo) that focused on conflicts with local religion (81–88). On the originality of the Sahidic life, see D. Bell 1983:2–3. Van der Vliet (1993:102) and Emmel (1994) offer good grounds for identifying the figure as the god Min.

[38] Tr. Sándor Fodor, "Traces of the Isis Cult in an Arabic Love Spell from Egypt," in *The Intellectual Heritage of Egypt: Studies Presented to László Kákosy*, Studia Aegyptiaca 14, ed. by U. Luft (Budapest: La chaire d'Égyptologie, 1992), 185, with useful commentary on 186–87. On the potential for such traditions to continue in Muslim Egypt, see also Ulrich Haarman, "Medieval Muslim Perceptions of Pharaonic Egypt," in Loprieno (ed.) 1996:612, 621. Compare similar reports from eleventh-century Georgia, discussed in Trombley 1985:349–52.

to comprehend a living tradition in Egyptian villages where such images still stood or lay. It would be incorrect to regard such phenomena as broken-down folk customs utterly disconnected from their earlier meanings. In this local Isis image, for example, the appeal to the "son's" illness in order to cure sympathetically the illness of one's real child would require oral formulas that would have been little different from those used in classical Egypt, appealing to the child Horus's successful cures in order to effect cures in this world.[39]

At a further extreme from the priest-enacted rite or procession would lie those forms of popular piety enacted "spontaneously"—apart from those established or approved by temple officials—and yet toward the temple as a sacred place. The chief evidence for this kind of spontaneous ritual consists of the gouges made by pilgrims and supplicants as they rubbed sand from the walls and columns of temples (see pl. 21). The geographical extent of these gouges and the duration of the practice, from the New Kingdom through the fifth century C.E. (and even to recent times), confirm the importance of this practice in religious devotion toward the Egyptian temple.[40] The use of the dust should be compared to that of *hnana*, the mixture of holy oil with dust gathered from the environs of living or enshrined saints in Christian Syria: medicinal drinks and salves, protection when carried or applied to walls, and fertility when imbibed or sown in the ground.[41] What the phenomenon assumes, and therefore points to, is the tremendous power of the place from which it is scraped, that this same power might be carried contagiously through the temple's parts. The pilgrim gouges reflect a perspective on temples altogether nonpriestly, which understands and "appropriates" the temple in relationship to popular needs for contagious power in all aspects of life.

One could imagine this practice leading to the gross mutilation of temples, but the distribution of pilgrim gouges tends to concentrate in certain areas of temple precincts: outer corners of buildings, hypostyle pillars, and certain hieroglyphs and divine faces on outside walls (see pl. 3).[42] These choices reflect, on the one hand, those areas that would have been accessible to lay supplicants and pilgrims (or, by the same token, beyond the supervision of priests), and on the other hand a tendency to organize

[39] Most representative spells are on the Metternich stela: see examples in Borghouts 1978, ##69, 90–94.

[40] See esp. Traunecker 1987, esp. 226–28 on datable examples; Nautin 1967:33 on continuity of the practice at Philae. Gouges in the ruins of the church built in the sacred precinct of Dendara offer a striking example of the continuity of popular practice.

[41] On efficacious substances carried from healing shrines in late antiquity, see Vikan 1982:24–31. *Hnana* is a term used with some precision in the Syriac Life of Saint Simeon the Stylite.

[42] See Traunecker 1987:224–26.

sacred objects, structures, and places in terms of more and less powerful spots: not only images, which had always carried special power in Egyptian religious tradition, but also corners, pillars, and often that section of the temple's rear wall that abutted the holiest part of the sanctuary within.[43]

## 2.4 Temple Festivals in Egyptian Life

The religious festival in Roman Egypt constitutes particularly important evidence for the life of native religion, since it is in the festival that the temple and the social and physical environment enter into most intimate interaction through, on the one hand, the appearance of the gods' images outside the temple, and on the other hand, the enthusiasm of the audience toward the temple, its symbols and officials.

In its most basic historical sense the Egyptian religious festival encompasses the public appearance of a divine image that has been normally housed and ritually maintained within the temple confines by priests, and its procession along a traditional route, often accompanied by ritual acclamations and hymns.[44] But it is essential to approach the phenomenon of the festival in its broadest context and with some attention to parallel examples from other societies, such as the processions of saints in rural Christianities. Cross-culturally one can observe festivals as carrying similar functions: the display of symbols that define a locale, region, or broader social entity; through the enthusiasm of festival participation the rearticulation and celebration of social solidarity along lines defined by adherence to the festival and its symbols; the rearticulation of social and cosmic order through the ritual symbolizing or enactment of disorder; the social articulation of time through coordination with a festival calendar; the sanctification of the natural (i.e., agricultural) cycle through coordination with mythology; the integration of a great or priestly tradition with little or local traditions and experience; a concrete dispensing of power for personal and domestic needs from divine images, priests' gestures and prayers, and such substances as might be scattered during pro-

---

[43] See Traunecker 1987:233–35 and Murnane 1983:219 (with Daumas 1969:70–71) on Dendara. Since the New Kingdom the rear walls of temples were often outfitted with shrines to accommodate and focus popular (or unofficial) piety: see Wagner/Quaegebeur 1973:54–58; Sadek 1987:46; Traunecker 1979 (Karnak); Malaise 1987:73–75; and Pinch 1993:337.

[44] See Fairman 1954:182–203; C. J. Bleeker, *Egyptian Festivals: Enactments of Religious Renewal,* Numen Supplements 13 (Leiden: Brill, 1967); Perpillou-Thomas 1993:xiv, 216–18.

cession; and a safe or opportune time for personal access to deities or spirits.[45]

All such functions assume a thorough integration of priestly and popular constituencies and interests and, in many cases, the integral participation of ordinary villagers in ritual activities. Of course, it is important to recognize the existence of different dimensions of festival in local communities. Just as Easter, Saint Patrick's or Saint Antony's Day, and Labor Day involve varying scopes of public activity, social or familial interaction, solemnity, and position in the annual cycle of a contemporary secularized society, so we must expect diverse festival types in Roman Egypt, from those primarily domestic, to those primarily local, to those involving the pilgrimage and congregation of several villages (or entire regions) at a large temple. In each case the festival will involve different degrees of interaction between priesthood and populace.[46]

From such general observations we may now survey the documentary data on festivals during the Roman period, which extends from the vivid pictures of local celebrations preserved in Plutarch's *De Iside et Osiride* to idiosyncratic allusions to festival activities in papyri of the fourth century and a sermon of the fifth.

Plutarch's descriptions, whether first- or secondhand, are most valuable in showing the active participation of festival-goers in processions and other collective ritual activities in various Roman Egyptian locales. The mourning rites for the body of Osiris conclude with a night procession to the riverbank, where priests pour water into a special box; at the precise moment "a shout goes up from those assembled, 'Osiris has been found!'"[47] Thus a full assembly participates in the drama.

Often the focal act of these festivals consisted in the symbolic participation in a mythic drama in which the priests were engaged. For example, the full body of worshipers would eat honey and figs at a festival of Thoth and cry out, "Sweet is the truth" (378B, 68). Whether these foods were taken in awesome formality or spontaneity, and whether the slogan was chanted in unison at one point or shouted as a greeting throughout

[45] On social and religious aspects of festivals in local religion, see J. Scott 1977:22; Wolf 1966:97–99; Turner 1974; Christian 1981:112–20; and Jeanine Fribourg, "Les rues de la ville: Scène du religieux," *ASSR* 73 (1991):51–62. On social aspects of temples and festivals in Egypt in particular, see Fairman 1954:201–3; Baines 1991:180–82. For the Roman period, Bonneau 1974; Perpillou-Thomas 1993:265–76, 282–83; Frankfurter 1992:213–14; and MacMullen 1997:36–44.

[46] Cf. R. W. Scribner, "Cosmic Order and Daily Life: Sacred and Secular in Pre-Industrial German Society," in *Popular Culture and Popular Movements in Reformation Germany* (London: Hambledon, 1987), 2–6.

[47] Plutarch, *De Iside* 39 (366F), on which see Griffiths 1970:452–53. Cf. 7 (353D), 17 (357E), 29–30 (362E–F), 68 (378B).

the day, it is obvious that these rites of Thoth penetrated the very lives and conduct of people during the festival. The numerous terra-cotta images of the toddler Harpocrates delightedly stirring a pot seem to reflect the preparation of some festival food in his honor: like the contemporary Japanese festival for the infant Buddha this *Harpocrateia* may have involved the distribution of festival sweets to children in particular. Festivals of ritual execration against the demonic god Seth-Typhon would include, in Busiris and Lycopolis, the making (and eating?) of cakes with a bound ass stamped on them (362F, 30); and in Edfu, the site of the great temple where priests would reenact Horus's defeat of Seth-Typhon,

> it is customary for everyone throughout the town to eat of a crocodile; and on one day, after hunting as many as they can and killing them, they throw them out right opposite the temple.[48]

If we can imagine a variety of sentiments among the participants (an awed or mournful silence, a carnivalesque gladness, a collective and focused hostility) and a variety of postures (moving as a crowd along the procession, or standing still and chanting in response to priestly utterances), we can at least see the local audiences of processions in every case playing an active part in the extramural functions of the temple.[49] Indeed, the collective hunts and feasts that Plutarch records for early Roman Egypt are not so different from traditional Christian festivals both medieval and contemporary, with their sacred processions, periods of "antistructure" and mock warfare, and slogans and symbolic foods peculiar to the day.[50]

That local populations in Roman Egypt sought earnestly to render festivals more than just ephemeral spectator events is shown particularly by the large corpus of terra-cotta altars and figurines evidently mass-produced during the Roman period (first to fourth centuries) for domestic display (see pls. 7–9, 13–16). Lamps portraying Isis of Pharos above her lighthouse in the Greco-Roman Museum of Alexandria would most likely have been lit in connection with her festival. Among the figurines (found throughout Egypt) are many bearing miniature shrines, dancing, or playing musical instruments. A particularly large number portraying

---

[48] Plutarch, *De Iside* 50 (371D), tr. Griffiths 1970:199; cf. ibid., 493 and Herodotus 2.69. *Sweets at Harpocraeteia:* See Török 1995:119 (#159), with additional images in Dunand 1979, ##134–87 (cf. ibid., 74–75), and on Japanese Buddhist parallel: Taitetsu Uno, "Buddhist Cultic Life in East Asia," in *Buddhism and Asian History,* ed. by J. Kitagawa and M. Cummings (New York: Macmillan, 1989), 319.

[49] See also Fairman 1954:165–203.

[50] The collective "devouring" of a bound Seth might also be plausibly compared to the eating of "ears of Haman," the archenemy of the Jews in the Book of Esther, on the carnivalesque Jewish holiday of Purim.

priestesses of Isis suggest that these cultic roles and their ritual contexts had enough importance to the populace that they would carry them into their homes (or, occasionally, tombs).[51]

But what kind of meaning would a priestess or any cultic functionary have projected to people through the medium of these figurines? A clue is found in the fact that many of the female cult figures are presented nude, an unlikely mode of ritual dress in Egypt but symbolic—in both Greek and Egyptian art—of powers of fertility. Indeed, it has been proposed that the image of the priestess (or, less often, priest), shrine-bearer, dancer, or musician would project—and therefore regularly invoke—the powers immanent in the ritual procession itself on the day it is carried out. That is, through the figurine the powers of the procession might be kept in an accessible form beyond the temporal limits set by the temple for the procession. Placed in domestic space—an altar, a niche—these figures would bring the temple's procession and all it signified into a state of accessibility, a miniaturization that would articulate the relationship between domestic altar and temple altar throughout and beyond the festival.[52]

The very types of festivals and processions associated with temples of the Roman period suggest the strong influence of popular needs. The attention to local fields demonstrated by the cults of Khnum of Esna and Isis of Kysis through the third century and the continuing importance of Nile rituals throughout late antiquity may be expanded with details from Dendara's festival calendar during the second century C.E. according to a papyrus document in Heidelberg.[53] Among the four festivals mentioned, an *Isia*, a *Rhodophoria*, a *Bēsia*, and one "for Typhon" or "Typhonian figures" [*typhōniois*], the latter two are unique and must reflect particularly local, popular interests: Bes as a god of childbirth who may have achieved some prominence in Dendara during the Roman period; and Seth-Typhon, usually the object of ritual execration along the Nile, but still venerated as an apotropaic god in Roman temples out in the Dakhla oasis and perhaps celebrated in this case for similar purposes.[54] In providing these festivals (or the sacred image processions that focused the festivals) Dendara's priesthoods were responding to local needs and reflecting local custom. One may thereby take the perspective that festivals

[51] Dunand 1979, esp. 93–105 on cultic figures; Dunand 1984. On lamps of Isis of Pharos, cf. Dunand 1976; Tranh Tam Tinh 1986:360–61.

[52] Dunand 1979:100–102.

[53] *P.Heid.* inv. 1818, in Youtie 1973.

[54] On Bes, see Perpillou-Thomas 1993:73–74 and below, 3.5.2. On Seth-Typhon, see Youtie 1973:189–92; Perpillou-Thomas 1993:150; Te Velde 1977:140n.1; Griffiths 1970:407–8; and for another interpretation of this festival, Frankfurter 1993:166. See further below, 3.5.2; 4.3.

were not dramatic productions that priests staged for local audiences coming for entertainment or passive reception, but moments of interaction between the religious symbols preserved within the temples and a populace without, in need of the concrete power of those symbols and accustomed to the traditional social interaction of the festival.

The papyrus record documents festivals both local and national through the second and third centuries, with scattered evidence extending into the fourth century and Nile rites continuing beyond that. Third-century letters show the function of religious festivals in marking time and establishing contexts for social reunion: "Be sure, dear," writes Petosiris to Serenia from Oxyrhynchus in the late third or early fourth century, "to come up on the 20th for the birthday festival of the god, and let me know whether you are coming by boat or by donkey, in order that we may send for you accordingly. Take care not to forget!" Another from the third century refers to a house lease made informally from one Isis festival to the next.[55]

National festivals continue through the fourth century. The Serapia (festival of the god Serapis) is documented up and down the Nile Valley as late as 315. Richly attested by sixteen papyri of the second and third centuries, the Amesysia, a celebration of the birth of Isis unique to the Roman era (but continuing earlier festivals of the same event), achieved particular prominence throughout Egypt as an occasion of reunion, the exchange of gifts, and probably the celebration of Isis's fertilizing powers. Its more ancient sister festival, the Isia, commemorating Isis's discovery and reconstitution of the corpse of Osiris, is also attested as late as the early fourth century in a list of sacrificial materials.[56]

Local festivals tend to appear in papyri less often, perhaps because their circumscribed and often exclusively rural functions did not require correspondence with remote family members; nor would they have entailed as much financial record-keeping, since they would have operated with less financial outlay by the community and would not have been in competition with other places holding the same festival.[57] Yet the Heidelberg papyrus does reflect such local festivals in Dendara (Typhon, Bes); and the Fayyum festival of Sobek is well attested for the second

[55] *P. Mich.* inv. 1355 = SB XIV.12182; see Herbert C. Youtie, "P.Mich. inv. 1355 verso: *apo amesusiōn mesri amesusiōn*," *ZPE* 30 (1978):186–90. Petosiris to Serenia: *P.Oxy* I.112 (cf. *P.Oxy* XIV.1666; LIX.3991). In general on papyri and festivals, see Perpillou-Thomas 1993.

[56] *Isia: P.Oxy* XXXVI.2797, on which see Perpillou-Thomas 1993:39, 206, and in general, 94–100. *Serapia: P.Strasb.* IV.559 (315), with third-century papyri: *P.Strasb.* IV.635; P.Giss. I.40, ii, 20; *BGU* II.362, xii, 16; *P.Oxy* XXXI.2586; *SB* V.7336; *Amesysia:* Bonneau 1974, with additional documentation in Perpillou-Thomas 1993:66–71.

[57] Cf. Perpillou-Thomas 1993:271–73.

century C.E.[58] A traditional celebration of "the birth of the greatest god Kronos" still held in late-third-century Oxyrhynchus, while replete with Hellenistic spectacles like Homeric recitation, probably masks an indigenous festival for either the crocodile-god Sobek or the popular spirit of vengeance and protection Petbe, who is otherwise well attested for the later Roman period.[59]

A festival mentioned in one fourth- and several sixth- and seventh-century papyri only in terms of its location, the Hermopolite village of Thynis (or the village's eponymous god), seems to have exercised considerable attraction well through the Byzantine period. The large donations of wine it received by custom and one landlord's expectation that his tenant should provide him with a mule to get there illustrate the central importance played by this festival in the regional calendar.[60] Even in an era when the archaic discourse of the local god was no longer appropriate, the festival itself, presumably with vestigial religious symbolism, could function in broader social terms (perhaps as a harvest celebration) and quite evidently as an opportunity for patronage and prestige.[61]

Beyond the perpetual social functions of festivals that are reflected in these later materials one can also see evidence for the continuity of specific religious practices. Orders to supply honey and honey-cakes for a festival in fourth-century Oxyrhynchus suggest the preparation of specific festival foods (whose ritual functions Plutarch had described two centuries earlier).[62] A list of payments made to participants in the Oxyrhynchus Serapia during the late third century includes one for "gifts to the dog-headed one [*kynopou*]," apparently referring to a priest wearing a mask of the god Anubis.[63] Processional masks were traditional aspects of Egyptian festivals; and the Roman author Apuleius refers to the appearance of such an Anubis priest in a procession of the Roman Isis

[58] *SPP* XXII.183, 25 (Soknopaiou Nesos, ca. 138 C.E.); *SPP* XXII.117, 23 (Soknopaiou Nesos? 149–50); P.Mil.Vogl. III.145, 12 (Tebtunis, 152 C.E.); *P.Ross.Georg.* II.41, 89 (Fayyum, second century). See Perpillou-Thomas 1993:140–44.

[59] *P.Oxy* VII.1025, 13–15. The local character of this festival is evident in the following wording: "in our hometown festival [ . . . *en tē patrōa hē[mōn] heortē*]" (13). See Perpillou-Thomas 1993:107–9 and IGFayyum 3:217 (Kronos = Sobek); Quaegebeur 1983b:51–54 (Kronos elsewhere as Petbe); and in general on the alternatives, Pettazzoni 1949:288–98. On Petbe in Roman Egypt, see below, 3.4.3.

[60] References to wine donations: *CPR* V.26, 469, 799; *P.Lond.* III.1036, 8–9; 1056; *P.Sta.Xyla.* inv. 0/154, 7–11. Supply of mules: *P.Lugd.-Bat.* III.16, 16.

[61] See, in general, Wegener in *P.Lugd.-Bat.* 3:78 and Basil G. Mandilaras, "The Feast of Thynis—*En heortē Thyneōs*," *Tyche* 6 (1991):113–16 (attempting to argue the festival's originally Christian nature).

[62] *P.Oxy* XLVIII.3406, 9–11. See Perpillou-Thomas 1993:190–91 on the ritual use of honey and 190–201 generally on festival cakes and breads mentioned in papyri. Compare Török 1995:119 on the preparation of "Harpocrates food."

[63] *SB* V.7336, 24, ed. Wormald 1929.

cult.[64] But set among Homerists and actors in a festival celebrating an essentially Hellenistic god, the appearance of Anubis functioned to root the Serapia in the traditions of Osiris, in which Anubis figured largely. Thus it would have been a nod to the indigenous Egyptian populace of (or visitors to) Oxyrhynchus, for whom such traditional Egyptian symbols were vital.[65] That this figure was additionally to receive "gifts [*xenia*]" during the course of the procession suggests that his presence had great significance for many observers, probably to assure benefits in the afterlife.

## 2.5 The Evolution of Religious Festivals

### 2.5.1 Spectacle Culture

The same papyrus also gives a close sense of the way religious festivals were evolving in late Roman Egypt. The Serapia includes a comedian, two Homerists, dancers, and athletes. During the same period (late third century) the sponsors of the essentially local Kronos festival invite an actor and Homerist to attend "according to your custom in participating in festivals [*sunpanēgurizein*]."[66] It is clear that, at least in a city like Oxyrhynchus, festivals were increasingly presented as "spectacles," staged civic events for purposes of entertainment and, on the face of it, with no more sacrality than a carnival.[67]

Does the development of such civic spectacles constitute a diminution of the public aspect of temple cults—a decline in Egyptian religion itself? Over the Roman period festivals in Oxyrhynchus came increasingly to be designated by the term *panēgyris*, rather than the traditional *heortes*. The latter word had always carried a religious, temple-based cast, while *panēguris* implied an affiliation with the gymnasium, and therefore roots in Hellenistic cultural traditions.[68] Thus in an Oxyrhynchite invitation of 323 *panēguris* might connote an élite world of social comportment quite separate from that of Egyptian religion: "Custom just as much as the distinguished character of the *panēguris* requires that [the athletes] should do their utmost in the gymnastic display" (*P.Oxy* I.42, 3–5). It is as if the professional performers—athletes, poets—were expected to carry a kind of piety toward their festival roles equivalent to that of tem-

---

[64] Apuleius, *Metamorphoses* 11.11. See esp. Wormald 1929:242; Griffiths 1975:217–18; and below, 5.1.1.

[65] Perpillou-Thomas 1993:134–35.

[66] *P.Oxy* VII.1025, 6–12.

[67] W. L. Westermann, "Entertainment in the Villages of Graeco-Roman Egypt," *JEA* 18 (1932):16–27.

[68] Françoise Perpillou-Thomas, "La panégyrie au gymnase d'Oxyrhynchos (IIᵉ–IVᵉ s. après J.-C.)," *CdÉ* 61 (1986):303–12.

ple priests in procession. Such sentiments may represent not a secularization of festivals but a developing view of (or longing for) a Hellenistic "tradition" to which such performers should conform in order to render the spectacles sacred. We see, in fact, an evolving popular sense that the arena might be an outlet for sacred power. The fifth-century Coptic homily cited above specifically criticizes people who "ablute their children in 'polluted' water and water from the arena, from the theater," apparently attributing to these substances an apotropaic or otherwise powerfully contagious function.[69] The image of the athlete is thereby appropriated as an accessible locus of power akin to the Horus-*cippi* discussed above. In this way it is difficult to speak of a complete change in religious mentality with the rise of the circus and other types of Hellenistic spectacle; rather, it shows a multiplication of contexts in which "power" might be accessible.

Even if *panēgures* were indeed beginning to carry a kind of piety based on Hellenistic mores and gymnasium culture, its use to designate the festival of the Nile in 424 suggests that it could not have reflected a strict separation between Egyptian religious festivals and gymnasium-based spectacles.[70] Even earlier, in the late second century, its designation of a celebration of victory over the Jews (during the revolt of 116–17) would also have covered the inclusion of traditional Egyptian elements, in this case the ancient religious discourse of victory over impure foreigners.[71]

Far from signifying a Hellenistic leaching of traditional religious sentiment and symbolism, so Robin Lane Fox has argued, the increasing affiliation of spectacles with the festival calendar points to "an underlying sense of community and a wish to show prominent vigour in pagan civic life," all under the aegis of the traditional gods and their priesthoods.[72] Thus the church father Epiphanius's rich, if disapproving, picture of festivals at a diversity of Egyptian shrines during the fourth century illustrates the complementary relationship of spectacle with the basic religious authority of the temple:

> If I described the orgies of Memphis and Heliopolis, where the tambourine and the flute capture hearts, and the dancing girls, and the triennial festivals of Batheia and Menouthis where women abandon their modesty and their customary state, to what verbal pretensions and to what drawn-out style should I resort to express the number that is truly inexpressible? If even I

[69] Ps-Athanasius, Homily on the Virgin, ed. Lefort 1958:36 (ms. p. 95). See esp. Van der Vliet 1991:225–28.

[70] P.Oxy XLIII.3148.

[71] CPJ 450, on which see Frankfurter 1992, esp. 213–15; cf. Françoise Perpillou-Thomas, "La panégyrie au gymnase d'Oxyrhynchos (IIᵉ–IVᵉ s. après J.-C.)," CdÉ 61 (1986):307–8.

[72] Lane Fox 1986:579, and 578–82 generally.

were to make an extraordinary effort I would not reach the end of this enumeration—as it is said, "young girls innumerable!" The sanctuaries of Saïs, of Pelusis, of Boubastis, of Abydos, and of Antinoë; the mysteries there, those of Pharbetos, those in honor of the ram of Mendes, as well as those in Bousiris, all those in Sebennytos, and in Diospolis; ceremonies [*teletas*] performed just as much in the name of Seth, that is, Typhon, as the one for Tithrambos, indigenized [*hermēneuomenēn*] Hekate; others sacrifice to Senephty, others to Thermouthis, others to Isis.[73]

Epiphanius inevitably exaggerates the extent of "immoralities" occurring around him.[74] But here his sense of the geography of festival life in Egypt and its connection with temples and indigenous gods (including the otherwise hardly attested celebrations of Seth) speaks of more than rhetorical stereotype or dependence on classical authors.

Spectacles and performers of the Hellenistic idiom spanned the range of festivals, creating on the one hand an extensive fund of artists in circuit around Egypt and on the other hand a catalogue of opportunities for improving one's local events and thus drawing ever larger crowds. Indeed, the very existence of spectacles and the payment lists that record them reveals the immense opportunities for individual patronage of a sort both highly public and—when one considers the contribution of gifts for the Anubis priest—assured of blessed returns.[75]

The rise of spectacles, then, speaks more of interfestival competition and opportunities for civic patronage than a decline in native piety. They reflect the increasing competitiveness often observed of late antique culture along with a commitment to promoting one's locale in the distinctively ecumenical terms of Hellenism: that is, maintaining a stance at the same time rooted in a place and its traditions and participating in the wide world of spectacles.

### 2.5.2 Decline of Major Festivals

The papyri also show an undeniable drop in festival documentation after the third century, and the idiosyncrasies of papyrus caches can only par-

---

[73] Epiphanius, *De fides* 12.1–4 (ed. K. Holl, *Epiphanius* 3, Die griechischen christlichen Schriftsteller 37 [Berlin: Akademie-Verlag, 1933; repr. Berlin, 1985], 511), in A. Bernand 1970:199–200.

[74] Besides the "antistructure" natural to any festival, religious festivals do provide traditional opportunities for sexual drama, since pilgrimages bring together youth from quite parochial communities with the chance of meeting others. An Indian folksong about a religious festival at a temple in Rajasthan celebrates precisely this aspect (Kumar 1984:25n.9).

[75] See Lewis 1983:148–51; Perpillou-Thomas 1993:223–26, 273–76; and Bonneau 1964:419–20, 1971:62–64 on spectacles in Nile rites; and Wolf 1966:79–80 on cross-cultural aspects of festival patronage.

tially account for that drop. The Amesysia, for example, which seems only to have gained prominence in the Roman period and is abundantly documented through the third century, does not appear thereafter. Danielle Bonneau attributed this phenomenon to a putative "disaffection for Isiac cults, particularly in their indigenous Egyptian manifestations."[76] But this proposition rests on a dichotomy of "Hellenized" and "indigenous" Egyptian religion that, if the media of Egyptian religion we have surveyed so far are any indication, cannot possibly reflect social and iconographic realities of later Roman Egypt (especially in the case of an Isis festival unattested before the first century C.E.).[77] If the Amesysia in fact dwindled at the end of the third century it must be due to specific social and economic factors that would have affected the staging of festivals of such national popularity.

By the late third century two factors were operating against such festivals: on the one hand, the financial straits of the temples themselves, which would have limited the staffing of processions and the magnificence of the divine images; and on the other hand, a diminishment in the very competitiveness that spurred patronage. "Public cults," Robin Lane Fox observed,

> were occasions for winning esteem through generosity and, indirectly, for confirming the social order of a city through "consensual pageantry," largely financed by the notables themselves. During the third century, self-advertisement and rivalry with fellow townsmen lost some of its appeal. . . . [L]ocal families in the ranks of potential councillors found themselves encumbered ever more with the duties and requirements of Imperial rule. The expense and bother of these tasks diminished the impulse to compete in "voluntary munificence" before fellow townsmen. . . . Where only one or two families found themselves left in social isolation as the richest notables in a town, there was less need for them to be seen to compete and to spend freely in asserting their own eminence.[78]

Of course, such economic factors only affect the external trappings of the festival—the "spectacles." If one understands the festival itself as an inevitable and necessary aspect of social life according to the functions outlined above, then such factors must pertain not to the festivals' disappearance—which would be doubtful, as the festival of Thynis suggests—but to its shift or transformation. And one such shift is immediately apparent for the public life of Egyptian cities in the fourth and later centuries: the rise of the circus. The circus offered an opportunity

[76] Bonneau 1984/85:369–70. Bagnall (1993:267) stretches this conclusion even further.

[77] See Dunand 1979:150–60; Quaegebeur 1983a:318–23; Bowersock 1990.

[78] Lane Fox 1986:582–83.

not only for the collective rituals of enthusiastic "antistructure" and transregional identity typical of traditional religious festivals, but also for the Hellenistic cultural spectacles that had been added increasingly to Egyptian religious festivals in the cities during the Roman period.[79]

The rise of the circus may, of course, explain the situation of festivals in that well-scrutinized crucible for generalizations, Oxyrhynchus; but it does not pertain significantly to the countryside. For the peasant culture of third- and fourth-century Egypt the decline in festivals of national popularity and intertown competition (according to the papyrus record) probably reflects, as a general result of the third-century crisis, a centrifugal shift in the locus and scope of religious celebrations (and therefore of religious identity) to regional or village-based cults and their occasional processions. The fundamental importance of such local cult festivals is clear in the documentation for celebrations of Sobek, Bes, Typhon, and the elusive "Kronos," along with Plutarch's own regionally sensitive descriptions of Egyptian religion in the early Roman period. This evidence makes it doubtful that there would have been a previous (e.g., Ptolemaic) centripetal shift *away* from such local cults and their festivals, and *toward* the spectacular cult festivals in the cities. The local festivals had continued throughout.

### 2.5.3 The Resilience of Parochial Festivals

Festivals marked social time, wove it with the ecological cycles so foundational to Egyptian culture, and occasionally preserved archaic holidays as socially binding events even when "original" rites had been forgotten and new ones predominated.[80] Both the local scope of activity and identity in peasant life and the pressing everyday concerns about misfortune would have impelled traditional festival practices to continue well past the fourth century as an active concern of villages. And if used critically, Christian materials confirm this continuity. The fourth-century biographers of Pachomius remembered, for example, that the abbot's parents customarily gave offerings to the *Lates*-fish, sacred to the region of Esna-Latopolis, apparently in hopes of a beneficent Nile surge (late third century):

> As a child his parents took him with them somewhere on the river to sacrifice to those [creatures] that are in the waters. When those [creatures] raised their eyes in the water, they saw the boy, took fright and fled away. Then the one who was presiding over the sacrifice shouted, "Chase the en-

[79] On the circus in late antique Egyptian civic life, see Bagnall 1993:104–5.

[80] See Bonneau 1995:3213 on Nile rites fixed to days outside the agricultural or meteorological calendar.

emy of the gods out of here, so that they will cease to be angry with us, for because of him they do not come up."[81]

Although the Pachomian biographies tended increasingly to render this memory as a caricature of an official "paganism," its simple form essentially describes family participation in the festival rites of a local deity.[82] Interestingly, this was the same area through which the processions of Khnum passed during his festivals at the temple of Esna. One can hardly assume from the silence of the Coptic text that these processions no longer occurred; but the evidence of a local cult in addition to that of Khnum does offer an important nuance to the character of piety in Roman Esna-Latopolis.

In such local contexts even specific deities or powers—the "poetic forms of demons," in the words of the Coptic Mary homily—might be invoked during festivals, as Shenoute demonstrates in his fifth-century sermon on native religion in the region of Panopolis:

> Woe to any man or woman who gives thanks to demons, saying that "To-day is the worship of *Šai,* or *šai* of the village or *šai* of the home," while burning lamps for empty things and offering incense in the name of phantoms.[83]

The passage refers to some kind of local festival and its domestic rites: a particular day is singled out for ritual activity, one "gives thanks [*šp hmot*]," and one performs obligatory rituals with domestic paraphernalia. Indeed, the paraphernalia recalls not only the many terra-cotta lamps and incense burners extant from Roman Egypt but also Herodotus's description of an ancient domestic "festival of lamps [*hortēs luchnokaiēs*]" in Saïs, where "on the night of the sacrifices everybody burns a great number of lights in the open air round the houses; . . . and even the Egyptians who cannot attend it mark the night of the sacrifice by lighting lamps."[84] The god Shai ("fate"), once the Egyptian origin of the civic god of Alexandria (Agathos Daemon), would at this time have designated a local spirit popularly supplicated for protection and prosperity.[85] As reflected in Shenoute's homily, the Shais of the home and village constitute the typical local

[81] *V.Pachomius* SBo 4, tr. Veilleux 1980:25.

[82] Compare on same episode G 3a (Veilleux 1980:299), and in general Van der Vliet 1993:115–16. See also above, 2.2.

[83] Shenoute, Discourses 4: The Lord Thundered (codex DU), p. 45, ed. Amélineau 1909:379. On the reconstruction of this sermon, see Emmel 1993:889–92, 1264–65.

[84] Herodotus 2.62.1–2, tr. by Aubrey de Sélincourt, *Herodotus: The Histories,* rev. by A. R. Burn (Harmondsworth: Penguin, 1972), 153. *P.Athens* 60 (early Hellenistic) instructs its recipient to "light a lamp for the shrines." Further on the ritual use of lamps in the Roman period, see Dunand 1976.

[85] Quaegebeur 1975:160–66 and see also 39 on the Coptic passage; Crum 1939:544, s.v. *šai;* Van der Vliet 1993:114–15; *šai* is still an aspect of Antoninus Pius's supernatural beneficence: Grenier 1988:59–61.

and domestic spirits propitiated in peasant cultures.[86] Such details, then, presented in the context of a sermon to the folk of Atripe, provide important historical evidence for the continuity of festivals for deities of essentially local relevance outside the main cities well into the Coptic period.

To Shenoute's witness of popular festival rites in the region of Panopolis can be added late evidence for local processions, such as the "Nile" procession accompanied by an enthusiastic crowd in fourth-century Hermopolis, complete with priest and wooden statue of the god, and even the substantial cache of wooden theriomorphic icons of the sort carried in festival processions, uncovered at the closing of the shrine of Isis of Menouthis according to Zachariah of Mytilene (ca. 484).[87] It would thus seem that over the course of the fourth and fifth centuries Egyptian religion became increasingly a local phenomenon, the festivals tending to encompass smaller social units and to evoke more localized identities, symbols, and needs: the celebrations of Bes or Typhonian powers held at Dendara as part of an official calendar with national gods, for example, or the later Roman festival of Thynis.

But even this tendency toward the parochial could only have been geographically idiosyncratic. Roman authorities continued to elevate the Nile cult to an official status, systematizing an essentially diverse and popular tradition with imperial trappings. In addition, a need to seek out "most powerful" places seems to have continued to pull at many people, and not only in the important sphere of oracles to be dealt with in the next chapter. Throughout much of the fourth century a small guild of ironworkers sought out the intrinsic holiness of the temple of Hatshepsut at Deir el-Bahri, a good twenty kilometers from their homes in Hermonthis, to leave their testimonial devotions on the walls and to immolate donkeys as part of the traditional New Year festival of the overcoming of Seth.[88] The cult of Isis at Philae, which hosted an annual pilgrimage of the Nubian Blemmyes, was evidently the site of festivals into the sixth century (despite the existence of a Christian outpost there from about the late fourth century), since festivals were the occasion for the pilgrimages themselves.[89] One may be right in suspecting that this cult or its festivals would not have lasted so long were it not for the involvement of the Blemmyes, a particularly strong people whose peace-

---

[86] See J. Scott 1977:22–24; Meeks 1971.

[87] *Hist. Mon.* 8.25–26 (see above, 2.2). Zachariah, *V.Severus*, in A. Bernand 1970, 1:211. Wooden images and their shrines and accoutrements make up second-century C.E. temple inventories in Soknopaiou Nesos (*BGU* III.2217, 2218) and Bacchias (P.Yale 378, 379 = Gilliam #7 [1947:230–33]).

[88] Łajtar 1991.

[89] IGPhilae 188–99 (ed. É. Bernand 1969b, 2:217–51); Priscus fr. 27 (ed. Blockley 1981/82, 2:322); Procopius *Wars* 1.19.35–37; in general, see Wilcken 1901:396–407; É. Bernand 1969b, 2:242–45; Burkhardt 1984; Vivian 1993:54–69.

fulness had long been solicited by Greco-Roman rulers even to the point of indulging their "paganism."[90] But their patronage of, allegiance to, and even staffing of the cult of Isis at Philae only underline the role of local piety and commitment in maintaining native cults in the face of an evaporated imperial munificence, religious edicts, and, at this time, even sporadic persecutions.

Thus temples played an active role in popular piety beyond the temporal and spatial confines of the priestly cults. Indeed, much of the popular piety that focused on temples seems to have been carried out continually on the periphery. Such evidence certainly militates against the notion that the temple as local or regional "axis" would die with the diminishment of the priesthood. On the contrary, it offers the basis for assuming a local inclination to maintain aspects of the temple—rituals as well as structures—and to continue to interact with it as a local source of supernatural power.

Of course, evidence for types of ongoing "popular" ritual in the temple precinct hardly gainsays the importance of the official cult in local life, particularly as we have seen it in the cases of the Esna processions and the ubiquitous (if only seasonal) Nile cults. But to view the official cults thus from the peasant perspective—in terms of a procession's concrete effects on fertility or a priest's application of temple mythology for healing and protection—allows for an interactionist model of Egyptian religion rather than a passive or vicarious one, for in these contexts people actively and anxiously seek out, focus upon, and participate in temple activities, albeit presided over by priests.[91]

## 2.6 Local Support of Temples

How did communities maintain their temples, especially when financial support was thrown back upon the proceeds and distribution of local taxation? If the triumphalist view of late antique Egypt imagined communities rapidly losing interest in the crumbling hulks of once-great temples and seeking more exotic forms of salvation, four types of evidence

---

[90] Bagnall 1993:147; and on the politics of Roman support of shrines honored by Blemmyes, see Castiglione 1970; Török 1989; Robert T. Updegraff, "The Blemmyes I: The Rise of the Blemmyes and the Roman Withdrawal from Nubia under Diocletian," *ANRW* II.10.1 (1988):68–76, 88–90.

[91] *Pace* David Potter, review of *Pagans and Christians*, by Robin Lane Fox, *JRA* 1 (1988):208–12; Bagnall 1988:294–95. Potter subsequently clarified "active" religion as the search for "new" knowledge and experience through revelation as opposed to the normative interaction with local cult (1994:4–15), an echo of Max Weber's idealized notion of "prophecy." But since most novelty, innovation, and revelation in antiquity was gained and expressed through the rites of traditional cults, the categories "active" and "passive" are essentially imaginary.

actually suggest the deep commitment of local people to the ongoing presence of the temple and its cult. The actual militant defense of temples against intruders represents the most enthusiastic form of religious self-determination in local society, while continuing patronage at the local level reflects a kind of solidarity among economic classes focused on the religion. In between (as it were) we find various groups and societies formed around the promotion and continuity of their local cults.

### 2.6.1 Popular Defense of Temples

The history of regional uprisings during the Ptolemaic period suggests that local allegiances to temples could in theory translate into actual mobilizations in defense of the sacred places, structures, or images that defined communities.[92] The actual instruments of mobilization—priests, seers, oracles—will be addressed in 5.1.2. But the evidence for the mobilizations themselves shows that local or regional allegiance to shrines implied a form of latent identity that could be consolidated under the right circumstances.[93] Roman authors, often by virtue of their contempt for Egyptian religion, describe interregion disputes wherein, according to a late antique Egyptian observer, "the same animals which some cities think it right to worship and revere are in other cities held in small esteem; and this . . . is the reason why the cities of Egypt are wont to make war on one another."[94] In these cases both the sacred animals husbanded by priesthoods and those animals ritually execrated and sacrificed functioned as symbols of the priestly cult and a broader religious allegiance among the festival participants, particularly during the animals' dramatic appearances at festivals. The allegiance or animosity that particular villages held toward particular animals thus intrinsically signified their allegiance to the local cults themselves.[95]

The accounts are almost entirely from a Roman perspective that viewed such disputes as a kind of Egyptian tribalism.[96] And yet the consistency of the theme across many authors, often grounded in important local facts, allows for some basis in historical events even if wildly exaggerated in some cases. Plutarch describes, for example, how

---

[92] See Préaux 1936.

[93] On the concept of "latent identities" that might be activated through circumstance or use of ideology, see Lincoln 1989 and Geertz 1973.

[94] *Ascl.* 37, tr. W. Scott 1924/36, 1:361. That the Egyptian author of the Asclepius should give such a Roman, exoticising view of cultic disputes illustrates the extent of priestly Hellenization (see below, 5.2).

[95] So Traunecker on divergent attitudes toward crocodiles within the Coptite nome: "[L]es rivalités existaient surtout entre cultes et non pas entre provinces" (1984:222).

[96] See Smelik/Hemelrijk 1984:1965–66; Whitehorne 1995:3059–60, 3090–91; and below, 5.2.1.

in our time the Oxyrhynchites, when the Cynopolitans ate the oxyrhynchus fish, seized a dog and after offering it in sacrifice, devoured it as sacrificial meat; as a result they went to war and treated each other maliciously until they were later punished and separated by the Romans.[97]

Juvenal describes another such conflict occurring at a regional festival in Upper Egypt attended by inhabitants of Dendara and Ombos:

Between [these two peoples] there burns an ancient and long-cherished feud and undying hatred, whose wounds are not to be healed. Each people is filled with fury against the other because each hates its neighbours' Gods, deeming that none can be held as deities save its own. So when one of these peoples held a feast, the chiefs and leaders [*primoribus ac ducibus*] of their enemy thought good to seize the occasion, so that their foe might not enjoy a glad and merry day, with the delight of grand banquets, with tables set out at every temple and every crossway. . . . On the one side were men dancing to a swarthy piper, . . . ; on the other side, a ravenous hate. First come loud words, as preludes to the fray: these serve as a trumpet-call to their hot passions; then shout answering shout, they charge.[98]

The ensuing satire of the "epic" battle has little historical value, but the general details of the narrative conform to others' accounts of similar events.[99] It has been suggested that the symbolic point of contention here was the crocodile which, according to Aelian, was ritually execrated in Dendara while venerated in nearby towns like Coptos and Ombos.[100] Such a conflict of attitudes apparently operated throughout Egypt, for villages up and down the Nile worshiped the crocodile as sacred to the god Sobek in his multiple forms, while others cursed and sacrificed it as a "Sethian" abomination—Apollinopolis Magna (Edfu) even held massive ritual slaughters of crocodiles.[101] But if the crocodile simply signified the god Seth at Dendara, and given that Dendara like many places in the Roman period held ceremonies and festivals for the ritual execration of Seth, a more likely trigger may have been the fact that Ombos had long been a place in which Seth was worshiped. We know from the Heidelberg festival papyrus that Dendara held a *Tuphonia*, a festival either to placate

[97] Plutarch, *De Iside* 72, tr. Griffiths 1970:233.

[98] Juvenal, *Satire* 15.33–52, tr. Ramsay, LCL, 291–93. On the identification of Juvenal's "Ombos," see Griffiths 1970:17n.2.

[99] See Smelik/Hemelrijk 1984:1965–67.

[100] Aelian, *De natur. animal.* 10.24. See, in general, Traunecker 1984.

[101] Herodotus, *Hist.* 2.69; Aelian, *De natur. animal.* 10.24; Plutarch, *De Iside* 50. Plutarch may be referring to a popular (extratemple) ritual version of the priestly rites expelling Seth (such as often exist in religious festivals to correspond to official liturgies). However, Edfu temple inscriptions do emphasize the spearing of crocodiles as part of the priestly drama: Émile Chassinat, *Le Temple d'Edfou* 4 (Cairo: IFAO, 1929), 211–213; and Griffiths 1970:493.

malicious powers under Seth (it is designated in the dative plural: *tuphōniois*) or to execrate and slaughter Seth in effigy; and this may have been the point of departure for Juvenal's scenario.[102]

People might also mobilize defensively against larger or more alien threats than neighboring villages. In 117 C.E. a Roman army consisting largely of Egyptian conscripts achieved a singular victory in Memphis against a massive Jewish messianic holy war apparently prone to destroy temples; and at this period there is reason to assume a correlation between the concentration of Egyptian forces in Memphis, the holiness of this city's buildings, and the victory itself.[103] Diodorus Siculus himself watched a mob almost lynch a Roman who had killed a cat (sacred to Bubastis). Aelian mentions a regional uprising somewhere in the Thebaid against Romans after the killing of a dog (sacred to Anubis).[104] All such examples imply at the very least—and even allowing a good measure of stereotype—that Egyptian local cultures were hardly passive in their religious involvement with temples and temple traditions. To the extent that the sacred animals extended the function and power of the temple cult into the environment, Egyptian cultures were sufficiently identified with the cults that they might mobilize for their protection.

Coptic hagiographies describing figures and events of the fourth and fifth centuries also reflect situations of local defense of temples facing catastrophe, although in these cases at the instigation of Christians. In Paphnuti's account of Christians on fifth-century Philae, for example, it is "an old woman who lived close by the temple" who informs the high priest about the robbery of a sacred falcon image at the hands of Apa Macedonius and two new converts. Her crime is so great in the eyes of the Philae Christians (and the narrative's audience) that her tongue is cursed useless.[105]

When Shenoute embarks on a crusade against the local religion of the village of Plewit the villagers attempt to repel him with traditional curse-spells:

> [W]hen the pagans came to know of [Shenoute's crusade], they went and dug in the place which led to the village and buried some [magical] potions [*pharmagia*] [which they had made] according to their books because they wanted to hinder him on the road. Our father Apa Shenoute mounted his donkey, but when he began to ride down the road, as soon as the donkey

---

102 *P.Heid.* (above, 2.4). On Seth at Naqada, see John Baines and Jaromir Málek, *Atlas of Ancient Egypt* (New York: Facts on File, 1980), 111; and for documentation of a Seth cult in second-century Egypt, Gallo 1992:128–29. See also Griffiths 1970:490; Traunecker 1984:221–22; and Te Velde 1977:140n.1 on the interpretation of *Tuphōnia*.

103 Frankfurter 1992, esp. 218–19 on the implications of *CPJ* 439.

104 Diodorus 1.83.8–9; Aelian, *De nat. animal.* 11.27.

105 Paphnuti, *Histories of the Monks of Upper Egypt* 35–36, tr. Vivian 1993:88–89.

came to a place where the potions had been buried, it would stand still and dig with its hoofs. Straightaway the potions would be exposed and my father would say to the servant: "Pick them up so that you can hang them round their necks."[106]

The indication "made according to books [Copt. *katanoujōm*]" would signify the traditional binding rites, extant in ritual papyri, generally devoted to repelling military, cosmic, and animal enemies and encompassing both oral utterances and the preparation of figures in papyrus or clay to represent the feared "enemy."[107] As Besa's account implies, Coptic Christians viewed such "magic" as singularly efficacious: it is Shenoute's own intention to turn it back on the villagers by hanging the objects around their necks! To the extent that the story reflects a historical incident, the hand of a traditional priest (being singularly capable of owning, reading, and interpreting such books) would have been required to prepare these curse-spells for the villagers.[108] But in its general recollection the story suggests that the cohesive religious life of small villages—as this was symbolized in its sacred images and shrines—often could galvanize a defensive "movement" against monks who sought to destroy that religion. Indeed, Besa (and Shenoute in his own sermon on the event) never indicates that Plewit was won over to Christ, only that the abbot successfully ransacked the temple and destroyed their images.

The most vivid description of the popular defense of temples in resisting Christianization appears in the *Panegyric on Makarios of Tkôw*. As Makarios and his disciples prepare to move against the temple of "Kothos" the god himself cries out to the people to expel the Christians.

> And when they heard these things from the demon, they came out with rakes in their hands. And their wives too went up on the roof and threw stones down upon us. They said to him: "You are Makarios of Tkôw, the evildoer. What have you come to search for in this place? Our god has already told us about your hatred for him. Get away from us. What is your business with us?"[109]

Makarios enters the temple regardless but is overpowered by a large number of priests, and he is then tied up with two other monks to be sacrificed. At this point a company of monks under Besa (Shenoute's assistant and biographer) breaks in and rescues them. The dramatic nar-

[106] Besa, *Life of Shenoute* 83–84, ed. Leipoldt 1:41, tr. D. Bell 1983:66.

[107] Sauneron 1966:45–49; Ritner 1993, ch. 4.

[108] See below, 5.1.3; 6.4. Shenoute himself reports "books of magic" subsequently taken from the Plewit temple: Leipoldt 3:89, #26.

[109] *Panegyric* 5.5, ed. and tr. D. W. Johnson 1980, 1:31–32, 2:24, ms. M609. Ms. Ham. B substitutes "rods, swords, spears, and axes" for M609's "rakes" as the villagers' weaponry.

rative, reminiscent of the near-demise of heroes in Greco-Roman novels, does indeed make it difficult to tell at what point historical recollection merges with utter literary fantasy. But the general view of popular resistance is quite likely based on actual incidents of attempted Christianization of villages. The notion of a lay populace in allegiance to the "pagan" priesthood and thus actively opposed to the spiritually righteous hero actually represents a vivid divergence from common hagiographical *topoi*, as I have noted, for these tend by biblical paradigm and populist conceit to claim peasants' acclaim for the Christians, not the traditional leaders.[110]

Incidences of local mobilization in defense of traditional institutions became increasingly widespread in the late antique world, especially the Near East, as the imperium began to encourage the outright demolition of local cults at the end of the fourth century. One bishop unleashed a tremendous popular backlash when he tried to have the local temple of Gaza dismantled. Another was lynched as he oversaw an attack on an important temple in Apamea in Syria.[111] And ultimately it is not a strange response on the part of the local community, even if it should challenge notions of Christianity's intrinsic appeal to late antique people. The anthropologist James Scott has attributed these tendencies toward defensive solidarity to the very nature of the little or local tradition as epitomized in (but not limited to) the village:

> First, the village is a local system of action—of status, influence, and authority—which is to some degree isolated from the outside. Second, it thereby constitutes a distinct sphere of perception and information—of political meaning—that is also set apart from the wider society. Finally, it is a unit of moral obligation (i.e. intense social sanctions) which tends to exclude outsiders. Localism in these senses not only differentiates the village from the world of external elites above it but also, to some extent, from other villages, each of which is a distinctive social sphere.[112]

### 2.6.2 Popular Allegiance

This rallying-round the native temples appears also in other kinds of sources. One papyrus carries the complaint of a man who has been left behind with his wife to guard an unnamed temple in early-fourth-century Theadelphia (Fayyum) after the village was abandoned. While he clearly implies some official status (or required civic duty) to his post there, his devotion to the job (when "every day they drag me from the temple") also suggests a more fundamental allegiance to the temple's continuity.

[110] See above, 1.3.3.

[111] Porphyry of Gaza: Van Dam 1985:12–13, 16. Marcellus at Apamea: Sozomen, *H.E.* 7.15.

[112] J. Scott 1977:213.

Both this and another papyrus from mid-fourth-century Oxyrhynchus indeed suggest that the guarding of native temples in the fourth century constituted an important, if light, civic duty (*leitourgia*) for citizens even of higher ranks: the Theadelphia correspondent complains that there are "neither public officials nor chief inspectors [*arkhephodoi*] to keep guard along with me" as if he could expect them.[113]

Thus the popular support of temples might come in an official guise through the system of civic duties or "liturgies," allowing both town councils and liturgists to express allegiance actively. A less formal type of support might arise as the temple and its rites became a regional rallying-point, particularly for some newly formed constituency. This is what happened at the cult of Isis at Menouthis in the late fourth century, as the Alexandrian philosopher-seer Antoninus brought his disciples to the temple's portico, revering it as a symbol of tradition and morality in a declining world.[114] Such "intellectual pagans," devotees of traditional piety bound to the cultural world of the Alexandrian academy, were engaged over the course of the fourth century in synthesizing a "pagan-*ism*," an actual ideology for traditional adherence, whose transcendent overtones might form an effective antidote to the increasing popularity of Christianity. Their choice of the Menouthis temple as a rallying-point communicated not only their traditionalist views of an Egyptian religious and moral center but also a kind of élite nostalgia for the local rural cult as it could not possibly have continued in Alexandria (and with which not all of them could possibly have had acquaintance).[115]

This same constituency provided powerful supporters and patrons for certain Egyptian temples. For in fact Antoninus's reverence was quite typical of a series of charismatic intellectuals and clairvoyants of traditional allegiance who came to renown in late antique Alexandria and Panopolis.[116] Both the author of the *Panegyric on Makarios,* who names the high priest of Kothos "Homer," and Shenoute, who consistently aims his polemical sermons against the most cultured and literate local adherents of the old religion, imply the existence of some type of "élite," Hellenizing constituency among the principal supporters of the temples (often including the priests themselves).[117]

---

[113] *P.Sakaon* 93, 6–7; *P.Oxy* XIV.1627.

[114] Eunapius, *V.P.* 6.9.17 (470–71).

[115] See Herzog 1939; Thelamon 1981:226–29; Athanassiadi 1993a:7–10, 13–14.

[116] Eunapius, *V.P.* 6.9.17, 10.6–11; Zachariah of Mytilene, *V. Sev.* in A. Bernand 1970:207–8, on Asklepiodotos and implying a larger circle of "pagan philosophers"; and in general Fowden 1982:52–54. See also below, 4.4.2.

[117] On Shenoute, see Van der Vliet 1993:102–4. The figures Horapollo, Heraiskos, and Asklepiades (the latter two according to Damaskios) reflect precisely this restricted constituency of priests devoted as much to the cultured syntheses afforded by Hellenism as to temple ritual; see Damascius, *V. Isidori Reliquiae* (ed. Zintzen) fr. 174, on which see Fowden 1982:46–47; Maspero 1914; and below, 5.2.2.

### 2.6.3 Local Religious Associations

A third context in which people would have actively supported temples and their rituals consists in the various religious "associations [*sunodoi*]" known best from the Ptolemaic and early Roman periods. It was generally priests who gathered in such associations, but these were local priests, including shrine-bearers (*pastophoroi*) and other minor ritual functionaries. Hence the associations could offer a measure of continuing religious solidarity to villagers already involved to varying degrees in the functioning of the temple.[118] A second-century roster of a *sunodos* at Deir el-Bahri consists entirely of Egyptian names even though Greek was the customary language for devotions by this time. So also self-proclaimed *sunodoi* were organized around exclusively Egyptian gods like Tutu in the third-century towns of Coptos and Kellis; for the funerary-god Anubis in Narmouthis (Fayyum); and for the obscure folk-god Mestasytmis somewhere in the Fayyum. Such examples show the assimilation of Hellenism for corporate self-conception even in the most indigenous Egyptian contexts. One would certainly imagine some such association contributing labor and financial support to the burial of the last Buchis bulls in Hermonthis, recorded in Egyptian on funerary stelae through 340 C.E. by priests deeply committed to traditional ways.[119]

By the end of the third century these *sunodoi* may not have been the only form of associating in honor of the god. In the Thebaid it is a corporation [*plēthos*] of ironworkers who make annual pilgrimage from Hermonthis to the temple of Hatshepsut at Deir el-Bahri during the fourth century for a ritual banquet and sacrifice, functions traditional to the religious associations.[120] At this time *sunodoi* devoted to Isis were active in the same area; and inscriptions from Philae and Talmis report the doings of associations (both *sunodoi* and *klineis*) of priests of the Blemmye god Mandulis that were still active in the fifth century.[121]

The religious aspect of the Hermonthis "corporation" suggests that other such local trade guilds contributed to the maintenance of religious tradition and ritual in Roman Egypt. And indeed we find a particularly well-documented example of such a guild in Kysis (Kharga oasis): a mortuary guild (*nekrotophoi*), whose activities in late-third- and early-

---

[118] Otto 1905/8, 1:125–33; Arthur Darby Nock, Colin Roberts, and Theodore C. Skeat, "The Gild of Zeus Hypsistos," in Nock 1972, 2:414–43, esp. 438–40; Muszynski 1977; Quaegebeur 1984.

[119] Deir el-Bahri: O.*Theb.* 142 (see Bataille 1951:xv–xvii on Hellenizing Egyptian culture in Thebes). Coptos: Cairo Mus. #JE 37538, in Guéraud 1935:5 = Sauneron 1960b, #29. Kellis: Hussein/Wagner 1994, esp. 111. Narmouthis: IGFayyum 3.171. Mestasytmis: IGFayyum 3.215; Wagner/Quaegebeur 1973. Hermonthis: Grenier 1983.

[120] Łajtar 1991, esp. 56, 64–66 on the sense and function of *plēthos*.

[121] Thebaid: Dunand 1981:140–41. Philae-Talmis: IGPhilae 199, 5, on which see É. Bernand 1969b, 2:250; Wilcken 1901:407–19; Muszynski 1977:160–62.

fourth-century Kysis appear in both an archive of correspondence (in Greek) and examples of their craft, excavated from the Kysis necropolis (active into the fifth century).[122]

The Kysis mortuary guild was responsible not only for the transportation of corpses (as the term *nekrotophoi,* "corpse-bearer," signifies) but also for mummification, a task once performed by the *tarikheuteis*-priests, and some degree of mortuary ritual, if we may judge from the sometimes elaborate burials.[123] The necropolis excavations have revealed the guild's considerable skill in preparing bodies in accordance with traditional Egyptian mortuary practice and with a great range of funeral "grades"—from one that included encasing the head and feet in gold to the most rudimentary burial.[124]

The Kysis guild seems to have served other towns in the region as well, but their archives report additional mortuary guilds operating in towns of the Kharga oasis. So also in the Siwa oasis a first-century C.E. inscription documents a group called *nekrostolisteis.* This term derives from the priestly rank of stolist, the adorner of divine images, and probably implies, if not the participation or supervision of such priests, a tradition or self-definition of past affiliation with stolist-priests.[125] In this way the professional mortuary guilds may not have differed significantly from other religious associations.

In what ways would mortuary guilds have contributed to the maintenance of traditional Egyptian religion? The mortuary cult was both central to domestic religion and family solidarity and a key point at which the Egyptian great tradition of the god Osiris and a complex afterlife mythology was assimilated into the local, domestic sphere of religion. Whereas in many parts of Egypt the mortuary cult had (or would) become largely the responsibility of the family, the existence of a large and established guild in Kysis implies an institutional context for mortuary tradition to continue, even if outside the service of the main temple. And later it would be such guilds or the craftspeople associated with them who would maintain through Christianization traditional iconography on grave stelae, terminology and beliefs in epitaphs, and rituals in mummification.[126]

---

[122] Papyri: *P.Grenfell* II.68–78; *SB* 7206; on which Wagner 1987:350–55; and in general Bataille 1952:238–39; Derda 1991:27–31. Necropolis: Dunand 1982, 1985, 1992.

[123] See Bataille 1952:261–64 (on *tarikheutei*) and, on functions of guild at Kysis, Dunand 1985; Wagner 1987:354; Derda 1991:28.

[124] Dunand 1982, 1985, 1992.

[125] Rémondon 1951:159–61; Derda 1991:21–22.

[126] See Nabil Selim Atalla, *Coptic Art 2: Sculpture-Architecture* (Cairo: Lehnert and Landrock, n.d.), 44–45, on examples of traditional mortuary idiom in fourth-century stelae in Coptic Museum, Cairo. Epitaphs: Alexandre Badawy, "La persistance de l'idéologie et du formulaire païens dans les épitaphes coptes," *BSAC* 10 (1944):1–26. Coptic mummification: Scott-Moncrieff 1913:25–27; Bataille 1952:198; Baumeister 1972:51–86; D'Auria et al. 1992:201–15. In general on Egyptian continuities in Coptic funerary tradi-

## 2.6.4 Local Patronage

Such religious associations provided more than just ritual "support" for temples. They also provided a context for financial patronage and munificence that in the late third and early fourth centuries would have augmented the declining civic or imperial funds significantly. And such patronage would likewise have come from "intellectual pagans" anxious to prove their traditional allegiance. Indeed, the inscriptional evidence reveals a time when popular patronage, or reliance on popular patronage, was far more central to the upkeep of temples than in Ptolemaic or pharaonic times.[127]

Thus in the early second century one Alinē writes that she has built a "shrine [topos]" for the Dioscuri in Apollinopolis Heptakomia.[128] At roughly the same time the "inhabitants of Kysis" provide the portal for their new temple of Isis and Serapis. In 180 the temple of Petesouchos and Pnepheros at Karanis is erected from civic funds; and ten years later it is restored by a local patron, Apollonios. Also in second-century Fayyum someone dedicates pavement and statues for a shrine in Narmouthis, while in Theadelphia a legionary reconstructs a whole temple (hieron) of Amun. Similar donations are documented through the third century around Egypt: in the eastern desert a temple for Serapis and Isis of Senskis; in the Kharga oasis a pavement for the temple of Hibis; in the Dakhla oasis a statue to the Tutu temple of Kellis. Ptolemaios, priest of Amun and associated gods in Madamud, near Luxor, doubtless won some additional reward for his temple when he dedicated a statue to the nome strategos.[129] And on a pillar of the first century C.E. a landowner

---

tion, see Krause 1983. On the shift in the Greco-Roman era to family-centered mortuary rites, see Derda 1991:28, with *P.Leipzig* 30 = W.Chr. 500 and Diodorus 1.93.1. On domestic entombment, ibid., 1.91.7 and 92.6; Athanasius, *V.Ant.* 90; *Ep.* 41; H. R. Hall, "Death and Disposal of the Dead (Egyptian)," *ERE* 4 (1911):459, 462; John Gwyn Griffiths, "Xenophon of Ephesus on Isis and Alexandria," in *Hommages à Maarten J. Vermaseren,* vol. 1, EPRO 68, ed. by M. de Boer and T. Edridge (Leiden: Brill, 1978), 433–37; Baumeister 1972:56–57. Since lector-priests (ḥry.w ḥḥb) often functioned as embalmers at least through the early Roman period, temple traditions could have had an established link and means for continuing through mortuary ritual (see Didier Devauchelle, "Notes sur l'administration funéraire égyptienne à l'époque gréco-romaine," *BIFAO* 87 [1987]:141–60, esp. 148, 153).

127 Nock 1972b:571.

128 P.Giss. 20 = W.Chr. 94.

129 Apollinopolis Heptakomia: P.Giss. 20 = W.Chr. 94. Karanis: *SB* VIII.10168–10169 = IGFayyum 1.88–89 = É. Bernand 1984, ##27–28. Narmouthis: IGFayyum 3.170. Theadelphia: IGFayyum 2.124. Senskis: *SB* V.8384 = É. Bernand 1984, #29. Hibis: IG-Hibis 5–6 = Winlock et al. 1941, 1:37–38, 2:45–48. Kellis: Hussein/Wagner 1984. Madamud: É. Bernand 1992, #32. On private and communal donations in the Roman period, see É. Bernand 1984:83–84.

in Panopolis boasts that he not only built a garden for the city god, Min, but also

> feasts twice yearly the entire people of Pan[-Min] the mountain-dwelling at the solemn banquets of Phoebus (= Horus?) by inviting two men, leaders, according to class, as well as priestly classes and companions in strife, up to a hundred, twice each year at the festival of Pan.[130]

From a statistical point of view such patronage clearly peaks in the second century and all but vanishes from the epigraphical record by the middle of the third, but one cannot extrapolate anything more from this evidence than the most general reflection of economic hardships. By the second century the common use of mud-brick for shrines meant that the architectural elements donated—the very insignia of patronage—often consisted merely of the lintel or architrave. The shrines themselves could be easily erected and maintained by local devotees.[131] In this way the continuity of a local shrine could be assured with minimum private patronage supplemented by community hands.

By the public nature of patrons' inscriptions we would assume that prestige was a major benefit of patronage. Thus also in second- and third-century Kysis a magnificent gold crown bearing images of Serapis and Isis, evidently used in religious processions, would have been the headgear not of a high priest (who had to maintain a bare head) but of an illustrious patron or beneficent official.[132] But the reasons for civic munificence were probably much more concrete than simple prestige, for such contributions to temples usually came about in exchange for some perceived supernatural beneficence. Alinē, for example, builds the Dioscuri's shrine after receiving an oracle to this effect; and indeed, oracle "services" could earn temples considerable income. Local Roman administrators in the late-third-century oases and small-scale patrons throughout the Fayyum dedicated statues "in thanks for beneficence [ep' agathōi]," and one in Narmouthis "for the deliverance [sōtērias] of his son and for beneficence."[133] Temples profited equally from smaller gifts presented ex voto: a large image of a foot on a pedestal that one Isidorus donated to the temple of Ras el-Soda after he recovered from a chariot race accident in the second

[130] Cairo JE 26903, cat. 9267, iv.1–5, ed. É. Bernand 1969a:442–62 (see commentary, 456–59, and Welles 1946).

[131] See, on shrine construction, A. J. Spencer, Brick Architecture in Ancient Egypt (Warminster: Aris & Phillips, 1979), 77–82, 140–41; É. Bernand 1984:82. Note esp. the simplicity of the Luxor Isis shrine, on which Golvin/'Abd el-Hamid 1981:117–18.

[132] Reddé 1992:51–52.

[133] Kellis (Dakhla) inscription of Aurelios Ophellianos, ed. Hussein/Wagner 1994; Qasr el Ghoueita (Kharga), ed. Guy Wagner, "Une dédicace grecque de la Grande Oasis," in Mélanges Pierre Lévêque, Centre de Recherches d'Histoire Ancienne 96, pt. 4, ed. by M.-M. Mactoux and E. Geny (Besançon: Annales Littéraires de l'Université de Besançon, 1990), 419–22. Narmouthis inscription: IGFayum III.184. Further inscriptions ep' agathōi in Fayyum: IGFayyum II.124, III.170.

century, and the numerous gold plaquettes portraying the Apis bull and other divinities that were received in the temple of Kysis (second through fourth centuries) in exchange for some kind of supernatural benefits.[134]

The livelihood of temples, at least the smaller, local or regional temples, thrived specifically upon local patronage and donations, and in this way reflected popular interest and allegiance. And for the devotees patronage and donation brought with it not only prestige (for the most public acts or monuments) but also a sense of ritual exchange and salvific bond with the deity. We might in the same vein understand the inclusion of the temple guard among the required public services of certain towns from the second through the fourth centuries. The civic protection of the temples—central features of villages and cities—would have offered people a certain security and orientation; and for this reason some town councils sought to ensure their functional existence.[135]

In such ways as defensive mobilization and popular patronage many temples received the active support of communities, not simply their religious participation. Why some temples like those described in Coptic sources managed to continue into the fifth and sixth centuries while others were abandoned comes down by necessity to regional variation, even to the relative appeal of one temple in a region over another, that perennial shifting of influence, authority, and appeal that had long characterized Egyptian religion.

And even when we focus upon the cult centers for which we have some direct evidence we miss a far more widespread phenomenon essential to regional religious continuity, the unstaffed local shrine that could continue almost entirely dependent on local support: Isis shrines like the one excavated at Luxor, which could function with one or two priests (pl. 2), and those of the crocodile-god Sobek serviced by priests of the towns of Narmuthis or Soknopaiou Nesos.[136] Here we return to the letter of Marcus Aurelius Apollonios to the basket-carrying priestess of Nesmeimis, instructing her to perform a diversity of rituals at another small village's shrine. Her services would hardly be expensive for the benefits she brings:

[134] Alexandria, Greco-Roman Museum #P.445–46, in Adriani 1935/39:145–46, who infers from the monument's size that Isidorus may have donated the whole chapel (148). On plaquettes, see Reddé 1992:62. For an astute reconstruction of the religious context of votive offerings of an earlier period, see Pinch 1993:326–32.

[135] P.Oxy XIV.1627; cf. P.Sakaon 93, 6. The jury is presently out on the meaning of this liturgy, since two important documents for its currency don't imply the preservation of particularly religious functions: P.Oxy VIII.1116 (363 C.E.) assigns the guard to the Alexandrian temple of Augustus and P.Oxy XLV.3249 (326 C.E.) to the Oxyrhynchite Hadrianeum, at that time used as a prison. See Naphtali Lewis, The Compulsory Public Services of Roman Egypt, Papyrologica Florentina 11 (Florence: Gonnelli, 1982), 51–52.

[136] Isis shrines: Dunand 1981:144; Adriani 1935/39:148. Sobek shrines: Gallo 1992:121–23; BGU XIII.2215, iii, 1–4; see below, 3.2.

for the emperors, "for the rise of the Nile and increase of crops, and for favourable conditions of climate." And so it is likely that she was a part of the local civic budget for some time. But more important, if she visited only seasonally can we presume that the religion of the village depended entirely on her ministrations? Surely not, for the community itself would have long been able to sustain itself along traditional grounds, relying only on its own leadership and ritual knowledge.[137]

## 2.7 Religious Patronage and Its Challenges in Fifth-Century Atripe

That local commitment could maintain temples and their cults well past the third century is also evident in Shenoute's oblique approach to converting peasants in the region of Panopolis in the mid-fifth century. His sermons juxtapose a peasant audience to "pagan [hellēne]" landlords, whom Shenoute presents as oppressive and corrupt. In one sermon, "Not Because a Fox Barks," Shenoute berates his nemesis Gesios, a local noble; but he does so apostrophically before a largely Christian congregation:

> Your godlessness is matched by the way in which you afflict [thlibe] the poor with your oppressions [Copt. čons]. Is this not another kind of persecution [diōgmos], that you pursue the people, especially the elders of the Church, till you scare them out of their houses—and at such a time as this, too, when these great distresses [Copt. hise] are upon the earth! You go into their habitations; there are no children there, no parents, nobody at all in them, because they have fled; you carry off their beasts with their carts and their hay and take them to your plantations and make them drive them round and round beyond their powers. . . .
>
> . . . For any whose cattle or any other goods you covet, you people seize them from them, some for no payment at all, some for some trifling price; to say nothing of bread and wine, and fodder and hay and barley for your beasts, and all the rest. . . . And it is these same oppressions [thlipsis] with which you afflict [thlibe] them, with your forced labour and your putrid wine and all your hardships [hise] and oppressions [čons].[138]

It has often been assumed that this kind of scenario represents real socioeconomic tensions of the time, a historical situation of impoverished native Egyptians in incipient rebellion against ethnic "Greek" overlords

[137] *P.Oxy* XXXVI.2782, quoted above, 2.1. Compare the popular maintenance of religious tradition in rural Yucatan villages, discussed in Redfield 1941:101–3.

[138] Discourses 4: Not Because a Fox Barks, ed. Leipoldt 3:82, 83–84 (#24); tr. Barns 1964:157–58. See also Emmel 1993:892–93, 902–3, 1128.

who practiced and enforced paganism as an expression of their own hegemony. Into this scenario, the assumption goes, Shenoute contributed a nationalistic impulse, galvanizing "Egyptians" against "Greeks." What then brought the peasants to Christianity was Shenoute's implication that "Egyptian" and "Christian" might be equated and then juxtaposed to the equation, "pagan" equals "oppressor."[139]

As in many historical examples of charismatic demagoguery Shenoute's wielding of such all-encompassing binary categories may have functioned quite effectively for a portion of his audience: one angry sermon provokes ecstatic shouts of "Jesus! Jesus!"[140] But it is equally clear that traditional rites continued in the area, as Shenoute admonishes in his sermon "The Lord Thundered":

Accursed be he who worships or pours out (libations) or makes sacrifice to any creature [*ktisma*] whether in the sky or on the earth or under water! . . . Woe upon those who will worship the sun and the moon and the whole army [*stratia*] of heaven, putting their hearts in them as gods, when they are not gods . . . ! . . . Woe upon those who will worship wood and stone or anything made by man's handiwork (with) wood and stone, or (molded by putting) clay inside them, and the rest of the kind, and (making from these materials) birds and crocodiles and beasts and livestock and diverse beings! . . . Consider your foolishness, O pagans who serve and worship (things) that have no power to move whatsoever (and) especially (no power) to do something prodigious [Copt. *hōb nshpēre*]!

. . . Where are the crocodiles and all the things in the water, those things that you serve? Where is the sun and the moon and the stars—that God placed to illumine the earth? You are deceived, you who worship them as gods![141]

While this sermon was connected with his crusade against the nearby town of Plewit, which at that time was maintaining its full allegiance to native religious traditions and institutions, Shenoute must here have also been addressing practices among his audience. His descriptions of traditional piety, albeit polemical, conform generally to what we know about religious practices and attitudes from archaeology and ancient historians; and with Plewit so close by it would be inconceivable that a Christianized audience (in the loosest sense) could have been unfamiliar with the actual traditions to which he was referring.[142] Indeed, there is little evidence for

[139] Johannes Leipoldt, *Schenute von Atripe und die Enstehung des national ägyptischen Christentums*, TU 25 (Leipzig: Hinrichs, 1903), 175–82, followed by Barns 1964 and most recently by Trombley 1993/94, 2:210, 214–19.

[140] Ed. Leipoldt 3:87, 18 (#26) = "Only I Tell Everyone Who Dwells in This Village" (see Emmel 1993:994–95). Cf. Leipoldt 3:86, 1–3 (#25) = Discourses 4: The Lord Thundered, ms. 1–2 (see Emmel 1993:898).

[141] Discourses 4: The Lord Thundered, 46, 47, 49, 55, ed. Amélineau 1909:379–83.

[142] See Van der Vliet 1993:109–12.

Shenoute's success in the region beyond those who cheered him on in church and accompanied him on iconoclastic crusades against neighboring villages.[143] Even in the late fifth century Shenoute's successor Besa had to appeal to local villagers not to fight among themselves "for nothing [Copt. *jinjē*] over a piece of wood"—most likely a reference to an Egyptian religious image and the object (along with its devotees) of a local iconoclastic movement.[144] With the implication, then, of a broad-based local religion one cannot ascribe the adherence to traditional practices to a circumscribed "Greek" élite, nor for that matter can one conclude that Shenoute's audience collectively viewed Coptic Christianity as a rational extension of Egyptian identity.[145]

Some scholars have also come to question the reality or sense of categories like "Greek" and "Egyptian" in the world of Shenoute's audiences. *Hellēnē* did not carry the sense of ethnically "Greek" and therefore different from "Egyptian," but simply "pagan"—"not Christian," in Shenoute's view; Coptic monks were not by any means "purely" Egyptian, often coming from quite urbane and literate settings; and while gross socioeconomic disparities existed in Panopolis and elsewhere, there is no evidence that these disparities translated into ethnic, nationalistic, or religious opposition.[146] Shenoute's apostrophic condemnation of Gesios and his ilk bears a largely rhetorical plan, *creating* an image of an "oppressive pagan élite" through appeal to scriptural proof-texts (e.g., 1 Cor 6:9–10; 1 Tim 1:9–10) and the repetition of terms attractive to a peasant audience's self-definition: *čons, hise, diōgmos,* and *thlipsis.* When Shenoute proceeds to vandalize Gesios's home, an act for which he has to answer in both court and church, it is meant symbolically to force the social polarity he was trying to create.[147] Thus Shenoute's "socio-economic" juxtaposition seems to have functioned as a rhetorical means of convincing a peasant audience of the appropriateness, indeed the protective power, of Christianity through identifying traditional religion exclusively with the people who own the land and patronize the culture (and, to be sure, would occasionally oppress them). "Rich pagan" and

[143] Shenoute's claims of popular support in the lectionary tract "On Shenoute's harms" (= Leipoldt #28, 3:90–92) must be taken *cum grano salis.*

[144] Besa, "To the Dignitaries and People of the Villages" 2 = Paris copte 130⁵, 127v, ed. Kuhn 1956, 1:129. Kuhn himself suggests a dispute over a relic, which would be unlikely at this time or region as a point of popular dispute ("A Fifth-Century Egyptian Abbot, II," *JTS* ns. 5 [1954]:179). See further discussion below, 7.3.

[145] Wipszycka 1988:153, 159.

[146] Wipszycka 1992. On the realities of economic class in late antique Egypt, see Bagnall 1993:225–29, and as applied to Shenoute's discourses, Behlmer 1993.

[147] References to the incident in "Not Because a Fox Barks," subsequently narrated in Besa's *Life of Shenoute* 125–27. On the historical implications of the texts in general, see the careful survey by Emmel 1993:891–93. Trombley's reconstruction (1993/94, 2:212–18) should be used with great caution.

"poor oppressed" are polarized in order that the audience might identify with the latter and thus choose as protectors *not* the former but rather Shenoute and the Christians. It was a clever sort of "Christian populism," as Peter Brown has described:

> To have presented Christianity in this manner was a masterstroke of writers who were, themselves, highly educated men. Christian writers of the fourth and fifth centuries wielded with dazzling effect the rhetoric of paradox. It was a rhetoric that owed its effect to the close juxtaposition of the high with the low, of traditional marks of status, wealth, and culture with their charged absence.[148]

By these means Shenoute aimed to bring about a shift in regional patrons, and specifically a shift away from the traditional landlord, for patrons with their munificence and festival contributions stood very much in the role of local protectors and maintainers of tradition.[149] Gesios of Panopolis, who is probably the veiled opponent of a number of sermons, bears all the attributes of an important regional patron of the local temples and their festivals.[150] He maintains a household shrine with sacred images of sufficient local importance that Shenoute both knows of them and believes their destruction would have a decisive effect on traditional local piety.[151] He is a vocal and articulate defender of traditional piety and critic of Christianity (at one point comparing Jesus' miracles to those of Apollonios of Tyana).[152] He seems to be the regional supplier of ritual wine and festival meat. And he publicly performs various rituals, including "praying towards the West," the land of the dead, "pouring out (libations) to Kronos over the waters," and ultimately asperging the temple of Atripe with various scented plants after Shenoute had burned it through.[153] In a typical rural peasant world, where such ongoing devo-

[148] Brown 1992:74; cf. 77–78, 141.

[149] See Bagnall 1993:214–19 on festival patronage and on a larger, urban scale Brown 1992:82–84. Compare accounts of Syrian ascetics who likewise set themselves up as improved, Christian patrons in Theodoret of Cyrrhus, *Historia Religiosa* 14.4; 17.3, with Brown 1995:63–64.

[150] Behlmer (1993:14) discusses evidence that the various mentions of a single "pagan" opponent refer to Gesios.

[151] Shenoute, "Not Because a Fox Barks"; Besa, *Life of Shenoute* 88, 125–27.

[152] Turin codex IV, fol. XLIv–XLIIIr, ed. Behlmer 1996a:92–93, cf. lxxxviii–lxxxvii, 247–48. It is these characteristics that might identify him with a Gessius who studied under Libanius (*Ep.* 892, 948, 1042, 1524) and/or with another Gessius who was executed in late-fourth-century Egypt after tying his political career to oracle pronouncements (Palladas, *Anthologia Palatina* 7.681–88). See C. M. Bowra, "The Fate of Gessius," *Classical Review* n.s. 10 (1960):91–95; Alan Cameron, "Palladas and the Fate of Gessius," *Byzantinische Zeitschrift* 57 (1964):279–92; Thissen 1992/93.

[153] "Not Because a Fox Barks," ed. Leipoldt 3:82, 1–4; Turin cod. IV, "On the Last Judgment," fol. XLIr–v, ed. Behlmer 1996a:91–92, tr. 247. See Behlmer 1993:13 and Van der Vliet 1993:108–9. It should be noted with regard to Gesios's supplying of comestibles

tions structure collective life and symbolize a village's or region's relationship to its environment and economy, one cannot separate the piety of a Gesios from that of most of the peasants. Like Agrius of Panopolis, the second- or third-century patron who donated both a garden and biannual religious feasts for priests and townspeople, Gesios of Panopolis is a figure deeply committed to ensuring the very traditions that the majority of local peasants themselves followed.[154] Indeed, with his domestic shrine Gesios also resembles the "village notables [gnōrimō-terous]" at whose homes, according to Libanius,

> the country folk [used] to assemble in large numbers . . . at holiday time, to make a sacrifice and then hold a feast. So, summoned on the usual day they dutifully honored it and the shrine in a manner that involved no risk.[155]

I would argue that Shenoute's pointed polemic against such traditional patrons as Gesios should be taken as evidence for these patrons' continuing importance in maintaining local religion, not only through munificence but also, the materials suggest, holding a leadership role vis-à-vis the very performance of cult (along with providing its wine and animals).

One might also compare the social and economic function of Shenoute vis-à-vis the peasants (as he himself presents that function) to Libanius's own complaint about the occurrences of military "protectors [prostateis]" in the late-fourth-century East. Like Shenoute the "protector" offered a new and powerful kind of security to peasants that, at least in Libanius's view, directly threatened their legally and traditionally established relationship with the landlord-patron: the protectors are "people capable of offering a protecting hand to the distressed"; but when a landlord attempts to get his due from the peasants either directly or through legal proceedings,

> the protector is more influential than the laws, so that what is to be seen is a pitiful spectacle—protests from the peasantry, the bandying of high words, . . . and the winning of the case. And off goes the owner with head downcast, and [his peasants] follow, jeering at him.[156]

Indeed, if even the landlords should complain about the arrogance of the "protector," the latter

---

for celebrations that excoriations of Gesios's "foul [loms] wine" in "Not Because a Fox Barks" (ed. Leipoldt 3:84, 2) may link him with the owners of the vineyard on the island of Penehēou, whom Besa accuses of having "each year forced on the farmers the foul [loms] wine of the island" (Besa, Life of Shenoute 85).

[154] See Van der Vliet 1993:102–4, 109, and on Agrius of Panopolis, Welles 1946. On the close relationship between members of Shenoute's audience and Gesios himself, see Behlmer 1993:14–15.

[155] Libanius, Or. 30.19, ed. and tr. Norman, LCL, 2:116–17.

[156] Libanius, Or. 47.11, 12, ed. and tr. Norman, LCL, 2:502–3.

make merry and laugh at them, and so far from showing fear that anybody should get to know of it, they cap their misdeeds with threats and the promise not to refrain from anything else at all.[157]

Openly displaying his personal stake in this issue Libanius cannot but exaggerate the extent of this kind of new financial arrangement in the Roman East.[158] The landlord-patron was still the most important economic figure and a significant contributor to the maintenance of traditional religion. But to the extent that Libanius does reflect socioeconomic realities of the late fourth century, and in light of the Shenoute materials, we begin to get a picture of the late fourth and early fifth centuries as a time of new types of counter-leadership arising in Egypt. Indeed, the very issue of patronage of peasant communities, it has been observed,

> became a topic of debate only in the context of the late antique competition for power and economic resources. Traditional patrons found themselves supplanted as patrons, but also impeded as landlords—and as tax-collectors—by men with local authority, secular or religious.[159]

Shenoute too presents himself to the rural peasantry in the rather novel and attractive role of "protector" of their interests and economic pursuits—but in a way explicitly juxtaposed to the demonized land-holder(s).

But was Shenoute therefore successfully perceptive in focusing his rhetorical energies on the local patron Gesios, insofar as Gesios was a primary contributor to the maintenance of Panopolitan religion? The evidence from his sermons would suggest the contrary: not only did native religion in Atripe continue regardless (as Shenoute himself bears witness), but the people of the neighboring village of Plewit actively resisted his crusade and Besa never records their conversion. "Religion" in this particular region was not simply a function of patronage and existing cults. As Shenoute alludes to it in his sermons it consisted of the various life-crisis and festival rites that addressed health and safety and the agricultural cycle, all integrated according to Egyptian traditions of the gods and focused upon local shrines such as Gesios, the local patron, helped maintain.

---

[157] Libanius, *Or.* 47.4, ed. and tr. Norman, LCL, 2:502–3.

[158] Jean-Michel Carrié, "Patronage et propriété militaires au IVè S. Objet rhétorique et objet réel du discours *Sur les patronages* de Libanius," *BCH* 100 (1976):159–76, and Bagnall 1993:177–80, 222–23.

[159] Peter Garnsey and Greg Woolf, "Patronage of the Rural Poor in the Roman World," in *Patronage in Ancient Society*, Leicester-Nottingham Studies in Ancient Society 1, ed. by A. Wallace-Hadrill (London and New York: Routledge, 1989), 167.

Plate 1. Militant Bes with feather crown. Terra-cotta. Late Ptolemaic/Roman. H: 21.0 cm. W: 11.5 cm. Kelsey Museum of Archaeology, inv. 71.2.208. Courtesy of Kelsey Museum.

Plate 2. Roman shrine of Isis and Serapis, Luxor. View from east, showing inscribed portal and image of Isis. Photo by author.

Plate 3. Temple of Hathor, Dendara: rear wall with face of Hathor (fronting interior chamber of greatest sanctity), mutilated from pilgrims' gouges. Like many centralized rear wall images, this Hathor face provided an accessible shrine for those ineligible to enter the temple. Photo by author.

Plate 4. Horus-*cippus* of tamarisk wood. Ptolemaic. H: 18 cm. W: 10.3 cm. Ashmolean Museum, Oxford (Ex Christy Collection), inv. 1874.279a. Courtesy of Ashmolean Museum.

Plate 5. Horus-*cippus* with hieroglyphic spell on reverse, meant to be worn as amulet. Stone. Fayyum. Late dynastic/Ptolemaic. H: 6.5 cm. W: 5.1 cm. D: 2.0 cm. Kelsey Museum of Archaeology, inv. 3242b. Courtesy of Kelsey Museum

Plate 6. (*left*) Horus-*cippus*. Roman. H: 11.2 cm. W: 4 cm. Ashmolean Museum, Oxford, inv. 1886.809. Courtesy of Ashmolean Museum.

Plate 7. (*right*) Isis holding agricultural emblem, her elbow on a pot. Terra-cotta with traces of plaster and paint. From Roman Karanis (surface find), University of Michigan excavation, 1927. H: 27.9 cm. W: 10.1 cm. D: 7.2 cm. Kelsey Museum of Archaeology, inv. 6468. Courtesy of Kelsey Museum.

Plate 8. (*left*) Isis-*anasyrmenē*. Terra-cotta. From Roman Karanis (Structure B168, Locus K), University of Michigan excavation, 1928. H: 7.1 cm. W: 2.1 cm. D: 1.45 cm. Kelsey Museum of Archaeology, inv. 6488. Courtesy of Kelsey Museum.

Plate 9. (*right*) Standing Harpocrates with pot and pronounced phallus. Terra-cotta. From Roman Karanis (South Temple Complex, Structure E44, Room A), University of Michigan excavation, 1929. H: 21.25 cm. W: 7.15 cm. D: 4.1 cm. Kelsey Museum of Archaeology, inv. 6452. Courtesy of Kelsey Museum.

Plate 10. (*left*) Image of Bes, Dendara temple precinct. Late Ptolemaic/early Roman. Photo by author.

Plate 11. (*right*) Nude Bes on palm capital, holding club. Terra-cotta. From Roman Fayyum. H: 22.5 cm. W: 7.5 cm. Kelsey Museum of Archaeology, inv. 4960. Courtesy of Kelsey Museum.

Plate 12. (*top left*) *Cippus* with militant Bes holding sword and serpent and standing on crocodiles. Reverse has Greek prayer for Bes's maternal protection. Roman. Collection Michaeilidis (publ. *BIE* 42/43 [1960/62]:87, pl. Ia).

Plate 13. (*top right*) Bes in feather crown, flanked with bread loaves and jug. Terra-cotta. Roman. H: 12 cm. Budapest Museum of Fine Arts, inv. T.506 (Coll. P.Arndt). Courtesy of Budapest Museum of Fine Arts.

Plate 14. (*bottom left*) Lamp in shape of militant Bes. Terra-cotta. Roman. H: 19 cm. W: 9 cm. Musées Royaux d'Art et d'Histoire, Brussells, inv. E.3851. Courtesy of Musées Royaux.

Plate 15. (*bottom right*) Lamp (missing handle) with Bes and consort Beset. Terra-cotta. Roman, probably from Fayyum. H: 7.2 cm. W: 4.7 cm. Kelsey Museum of Archaeology, inv. 6573. Courtesy of Kelsey Museum.

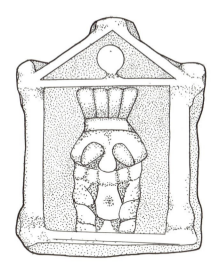

Plate 16. Amulet of Bes in shrine. Roman. Faience with heavy blue and yellow-green glaze. H: 4.0 cm. W: 3.2 cm. D: 0.7 cm. Museum of Fine Arts, Boston (Gift of Dr. and Mrs. Jerome Eisenberg), inv. 1995.710. Drawing by Y. Markowitz.

Plate 17. Domestic shrine niche from Roman Karanis (House C119), University of Michigan excavation, 1932. Courtesy of Kelsey Museum.

Plate 18. Female (maternity?) figurines with nimbi. Terra-cotta. Coptic period. From Abu Mina. Greco-Roman Museum, Alexandria, inv. 18968 (H: 18.2 cm), 18967 (H: 19 cm), 18965 (H: 16.5 cm). Courtesy of Greco-Roman Museum.

Plate 19. Mural of priests carrying bier with image of crocodile-god Sobek. The priests at right may be interpreting movements of the god through his image on the priests' shoulders. Copy from temple of Pnepheros at Theadelphia. From Breccia, *Monuments de l'Égypte gréco-romaine* (1926), pl. lxiv, 3.

Plate 20. Remains of secondary brick extension to temple of Isis and Serapis in Kysis (Douch), Kharga oasis, showing oracle chamber at center, with oracle hole just visible through original rear wall of temple. Cliché IFAO J.-F. Gout. Courtesy of Institut français d'archéologie orientale, Cairo.

Plate 21. Pilgrim gouges on northwest corner of temple of local god Arensnuphis, Philae. Photo by author.

Plate 22. Roman era sanatorium, Dendara temple precinct, with hydraulic system in foreground, Roman mammisi (birth-temple) with Bes capitals in background. Photo by author.

Plate 23. Image of saint painted on column as part of Christianization of sanctuary. Hall of Thutmose III, Karnak. Photo by author.

# 3

# THE LOCAL SCOPE OF RELIGIOUS BELIEF

## 3.1 Religious Localism and Transregionalism

BY LOCATING the support of temples and temple religion, broadly conceived, in specific communities and regions during the third and subsequent centuries we begin to conceptualize religion itself in Roman Egypt according to Robert Redfield's model of local or little traditions. But so as not to caricature little traditions as somehow hermetically isolated from one another or from a great tradition as this was maintained by priesthoods (or as Hellenism itself) we must assume certain modes of overlap. One such mode, described by McKim Marriott for village India as "Sanskritization," concerns that ongoing cultural process whereby aspects of little traditions become elevated and assimilated to broad systematizations maintained by literate priesthoods. At the same time, little traditions will domesticate, localize, and quite often change significantly elements of the great tradition. The result of these two dynamics is a perpetual tendency toward divergence, even discontinuity, between local and Sanskritized systems, as aspects of little traditions become unrecognizably abstract and ideas from great traditions become delimited and parochialized.[1]

Little traditions influence each other as well, particularly through regional networks whose villages are united in certain beliefs and practices through various kinds of central interaction: markets, festivals, or simply the economic ties between rural villages and the cities in Roman Egypt.[2] As we have assumed a close relationship between everyday and life-crisis needs and economic realities on the one hand and the morphology of practice and belief on the other, so we might also expect similar religious responses to the similar problems encountered across peasant cultures.[3] Transregional religious forms, then, must be defined in terms of transregional realities, including afflictions and misfortunes, beyond simply theological ideas or mentalities.

---

[1] Marriott 1955:207–18; Srinivas 1989:58–61.

[2] See Redfield 1956:50–57; J. Scott 1977:8. On economic ties between cities and villages, see Bagnall 1993:138–42, 148–60.

[3] J. Scott 1977:8–9.

Rather than centered in the large regional or "national" temples that received imperial munificence, popular Egyptian religion normally focused on the local temple or shrine. The minimal remains of local religion in Egypt obscure an astounding complexity of minor shrines and temples, which emerges only idiosyncratically from the texts and archaeological sites.

It is New Kingdom sites that best illustrate the traditional topography of the sacred in the small-scale Egyptian community. A workers' town like Deir el-Medina might disclose wayside shrines, household shrines, and an oracle of the local god Amenhotep I, whose image in procession would resolve mundane disputes. The homes of Amarna reveal an extensive domestic cult with elaborate house shrines. A record of judicial proceedings in the Thebaid during the New Kingdom discloses three different local "Amuns," each with regional authority to judge criminal cases. In Middle Egypt we find Horus-of-the-Camp addressing problems in a small community. Indeed, so much was the local shrine established in the "official" religious landscape of Egypt that the Egyptian priestly writing system contained a special word for "local god," using the hieroglyph for "town" to point specifically to its parochial identity.[4] Quite apart from the vicissitudes of gods like Amun and Horus in their "national" temples, classical Egyptian religion evidently comprised a host of little traditions, local gods, their respective temples, and the various shrines that sanctified home and land. And even in the cases of transregional gods like Amun, Horus, or Isis, we find not the integrated worship of a single deity but, as Redfield declared for India, "those many regional shrines which house the images of those deities that are intermediate between great and little traditions, being local forms of the one and universalized forms of the other."[5]

## 3.2 The Places of Isis and the Names of Sobek

One still finds evidence for local Horuses and Amuns in the Roman period: a "Horus of Shenwet" still worshiped on Philae in the fifth century; a Horus-like "Amun-Nakht" as the focus of the Augustan temple of 'Ain

---

[4] On the term "local god [*ntr niwti*]," see Erik Hornung, *Conceptions of God in Ancient Egypt,* tr. J. Baines (Ithaca, N.Y.: Cornell University Press, 1982), 69–74, and Gallo 1992:128–29 for Demotic examples from the second century C.E. Deir el-Medina: Sadek 1987:72–78. Amarna: Ikram 1989. Local Amuns in Thebaid: A. Blackman 1925:249–53. Horus-of-the-Camp: Ryholt 1993:195–98.

[5] Redfield 1956:99. In general on local temples in Egypt, see David P. Silverman, "Divinity and Deities in Ancient Egypt," in Shafer (ed.) 1991:38–41 (pharaonic); and Dunand 1979:85–86; 1991b:229–30; Alan K. Bowman, *Egypt after the Pharaohs* (Berkeley: University of California Press, 1986), 171–72; Lewis 1983:92–94 (Greco-Roman).

Birbiya in the Dakhla oasis, as well as local versions of Osiris, Seth, Mut, and Thoth throughout the same region.[6] Indeed, the numerous little shrines excavated in Deir el-Medina are themselves echoed in a list of buildings in early-fourth-century Panopolis: along one street are no less than nine shrines (*hiera*), including ones for national gods like Amun, Egyptian gods like Chnoubis, and Hellenistic syntheses like the *Agathos Daimon*, the beneficent spirit of Alexandria.[7] But the kind of network of local traditions reflected in the pharaonic sources is most evident in the cults of the crocodile-god Sobek in the Fayyum and of Isis in her varying manifestations throughout Egypt. As in the above cases of the Theban Amuns and Horus-of-the-Camp, *the local character* of Isis and Sobek in their particular shrines exceeded in immediate functional importance their official universalism. Indeed, it is those moments of universalism (literary or iconographic) that stand out as conscious endeavors by the peculiarly inspired.

The religion of the Fayyum is distinctive in Roman Egypt for its population's special veneration of such a uniquely Egyptian god as Sobek in a region deeply affected by Hellenism and in a period of active religious synthesis.[8] Numerous oracle "tickets" in Greek from various Fayyum towns and the extensive use of Greek for maintaining temple records and contracts there both argue that, far from an Egyptian assimilation of a "greater Hellenism," Greeks and Greek culture were undergoing a rapid indigenization. Even the Roman twin gods, the Dioscuri, seem to have been regionally popularized as a "twin" form of Sobek.[9] But the network of diverse Sobek cults and their indigenizing effect on aliens who came to settle in the traditional villages may rather be representative of the way most deities functioned locally in Greco-Roman Egypt. Sobek was manifestly individualized with different names—Soknebtunis, Petesouchos, Pnepheros, Soknopaios, Soknobraisis, Sokonnokonni, Souxei— according to individual cult; and each town in the Fayyum (or elsewhere on the Nile where Sobek was also popular) might have one or more cults with their respective priests and shrines of different sizes.[10]

[6] Horus of Shenwet: Žabkar 1975:150–51; Amun-Nakht: Kaper 1987; 1997:65–82; and below, 3.4.1.

[7] *P.Berlin* 16365, i.8; ii.21; vi.2–4; ix.3; xiv.27 (Ammon); xv.27 (Chnoubis); xvii.3; Aii.5 (*agathodaimon*); Aiv.12 (Persephone), ed. Borkowski 1975:24–26.

[8] Étienne Bernand, "Épigraphie grecque et histoire des cultes au fayoum," in *Hommages à la mémoire de Serge Sauneron*, vol. 2 (Cairo: IFAO, 1979), 68, 76.

[9] *P.Fayyum* 138; *BGU* XIII.2217, ii, 2; IGFayyum 1.74; 2.123, 143–44; 3.183. See Quaegebeur 1983a:313–16. Cf. Török 1995:43 and #33 on evidence for distinctively Greek Dioscuri cults.

[10] Toutain 1915; Gilliam 1947:183–86; Evans 1961:176–78. Souxei only mentioned in *P.Lond.* III.1267d. Sobek was also the regional god of Kom Ombo and parts of the Delta: see, in general, Brovarski 1984:1010–15.

The little traditions of the individual towns of Sobek in the Fayyum at the same time participated in a great tradition of sorts through the administration of priestly centers. Most evidence comes from the second century C.E. A scribal official in the town of Soknopaiou Nesos, a center of the Sobek priesthood, appends a note to a list of Sobek cults instructing that local priests should provide ritual services (*thrēskias*) for those nearby shrines lacking permanent priests.[11] The list of cults itself may refer to temples in the Fayyum served in some way by the priests of Soknopaiou Nesos, for a series of Demotic ostraca from second-century Narmouthis contains instructions and itineraries for priests making rounds of local shrines and performing various rites there.[12]

The cults of Isis in Egypt also show strongly local characteristics. Indeed, the practice of sending priests to officiate at (or simply to open) local shrines without priests appears also in the letter to the "[priestess-]basket-carrier" of the second or third century, instructing her to go to a local Isis shrine and perform the various rituals for empire and field. And excavated shrines like that of Luxor seem also to reflect this kind of priestly "circuit-riding" in their need for only occasional officiation.[13]

However, this traditional complex of local Isis cults must be understood in the context of a universalizing tendency that, over the course of the Greco-Roman period, endeavored to render Isis as a *pantokratrix*, a world-ruler, transcendent of any particular cult and merely manifest through the diverse local goddesses, who function as her avatars. While implicit in the typically Hellenistic popular iconography of Isis during the Roman period, which presented her in a fashion more broadly comprehensible in a multicultural society than did temple reliefs, this universalizing tendency is most evident in the Greek "Isis aretalogies," extensive hymns in which the goddess defines her purposes and identifies herself with a variety of local goddesses.

The most important of these aretalogies for interpreting the religion of Egypt is a series of hymns inscribed on a temple in the Fayyum during the late Ptolemaic period and attributed to one Isidorus, a priest, and a second-century C.E. papyrus from Oxyrhynchus.[14] In acclaiming Isis's singular power over agricultural fertility Isidorus associates her with two regional Sobek cults, Suchos of Arsinoë and Sokonopis of Anchoes, with the implication that Isis herself transcends these parochial gods (III.30,

---

[11] *BGU* XIII.2215, iii, 1–4. On the character of Soknopaiou Nesos, see Hobson 1984:106–8.

[12] Gallo 1992.

[13] Cf. *Gnomon of the Idios Logos* 85 (ed. Emil Seckel and Wilhelm Schubart, *Ägyptische Urkunden aus den Staatlichen Museen zu Berlin,* Gr. 5 [Berlin: Weidmann, 1919], 1:32); *P.Oxy* XXXVI.2782 ("[priestess-]basket-carrier"), on which see above, 2.1.

[14] Isis hymns of Isidorus, ed. Vanderlip 1972. *P.Oxy* XI.1380.

33). In another hymn she is associated with explicitly foreign goddesses like Astarte, Leto, Aphrodite, and Demeter (I.14–24). In the Oxyrhynchus aretalogy she is systematically identified with a vast catalogue of goddesses from around the known world, although a good half of the catalogue lists cult places in Egypt: Hermopolis, Sais, Sebennytus, Busiris, Heracleopolis, and others. More than simply synthesizing a conglomerate *Isis pantokratrix* transcendent of all places, however, the author apparently wishes to erase the typical local functions of the goddess; and he does so by relabeling the particular, indigenous manifestations of Isis in terms of Greco-Roman virtues and goddesses:

> . . . at Buto [she is viewed as] skilled in calculation . . . . ; at Thonis love . . . ; in the Saïte nome, victorious, Athena, nymph; . . . at Caene joy; . . . at Sebennytus inventiveness, mistress, Hera, holy; at Hermopolis Aphrodite, queen, holy; at Diospolis Parva ruler.[15]

It is, of course, conceivable that some overlap existed between the local characteristics that the aretalogy imputes to these different avatars and those characteristics functioning in the historical cults of the goddess. But to the degree that we can use local evidence for comparison on the one hand and identify the author's ideological program in labeling cults on the other, it is most likely that this text represents an attempt to promote a universal Isis while admitting her local cults as mere occurrences, manifestations, of her diverse virtues.[16]

This tendency to universalize Isis was no alien innovation but, as Isidorus and the Oxyrhynchus aretalogy illustrate, a development rooted in priestly interests. It derived, in fact, from the royal ideology of classical Egypt, in which Isis represented the throne and cosmic protection of the king.[17] Yet it is clear that the aretalogies—or at least the Oxyrhynchus aretalogy above—reflect the agenda of particular syncretistic constituencies more than religion "on the ground." (The hymns of Isidorus seem to represent a synthesis of the two.) What we find when we read beyond this agenda is a broad network of Isis cults throughout Egypt that had sufficiently distinct characteristics that the author felt constrained to reinterpret them as virtues, and yet sufficiently similar interests in agri-

---

[15] *P.Oxy* XI.1380, ii.27–37. The papyrus is quite fragmentary in this section.

[16] Compare an Egyptian "aretalogy" of Isis at her temple at Dendara, in which her universality is articulated expressly in terms of local goddess cults: "She is Nekbet at El-Kab, Tjenenet at Hermonthis, Iounyt at Dendara, Isis at Abydos, Sechat at Ounet, Heket at Hirour . . . , Neith at Saïs, . . . in each nome it is she who is in every town, in every nome with her son Horus" (tr. Daumas 1969:90).

[17] On Isis's royal associations as the root of the tradition of the Isis aretalogies, see Jan Bergman, *Ich bin Isis: Studien zum memphitischen Hintergrund der griechischen Isis-aretalogien,* Acta Universitatis Upsaliensis, Historia Religionum 3 (Uppsala: Universitets biblioteket, 1968), esp. 121–71.

cultural fertility that Isidorus saw fit to emphasize this particular range of powers.[18]

The universal Isis does not seem to have occupied the majority of devotees of Isis shrines except insofar as the ideology itself endowed her particular shrines and icons with a kind of authority unavailable to, say, traditional theriomorphic gods like Sobek, Taweret, or Tutu. Inscriptions from the Delta region and from Philae, for example, show that the forms "Isis of Philae," "Isis of Pharos," and "Isis of Menouthis" were considered quite distinctly, whether we choose to designate them as aspects, avatars, or independent goddesses. Serenus, "brought up near Isis of Pharos, came here" to worship "Isis at Philae" in 191 C.E.; a statue of "Isis of Menouthis" is sent "to Isis of Pharos" in honor of an emperor during the mid-second to early third century. Three inscriptions from the region of Theadelphia dedicate objects to an Isis-Sasypsis (spelled differently each time), and one inscription refers at the same time to Isis-Nepherses ("with beautiful throne") and Isis-Nephremmis ("of the beautiful arms"), both commonly affiliated with Sobek.[19] In Upper Egypt it is Isis of Philae herself to whom the Blemmyes make pilgrimage annually and maintain the cult in the fifth and sixth centuries, and it is her image that they borrowed for oracular proceedings.[20] One is reminded of localized devotion to the major saints in medieval rural Christianity: "Universal figures like Mary and Christ," William Christian describes for sixteenth-century Spain, "are particularized in specific shrine images and become Our Lady of Riansares or the Christ of Urda, and are valued above other Marys and Christs."[21]

Even in places for which no documents exist to indicate the terms of local veneration one can deduce the "parochialized" character of the Isis cult by the relationship between the particular Isis and the local economy and society. This is especially true of the agricultural Isises found at the

---

[18] Isidorus I.8–13, and on immediate agricultural associations of Isis cults: Dunand 1979:128–31. In general on the implications of syncretistic universalism on Isis religion, see Françoise Dunand, "Les syncrétismes dans la religion de l'Égypte romaine," *Les syncrétismes dans les religions de l'antiquité*, EPRO 46, ed. by F. Dunand and P. Lévêque (Leiden: Brill, 1975), 159–62.

[19] Serenus: IGPhilae 168; Isis of Menouthis: *CIG* III.4683b; Isis Sasypsis: IGFayyum 2.121, 123, 130; Isis Nepherses/Isis Nephremmis: IGFayyum 1.76. See Letronne, cited in A. Bernand 1970:298–99, on implications of local designators for Isis, and further on local Isises: Annie Forgeau, "Prêtres isiaques: Essai d'anthropologie religieuse," *BIFAO* 84 (1984):155–87.

[20] Priscus, fr. 27, ed. Blockley 1981/82, 2:322.

[21] Christian 1981:178. Cf. Marriott 1955:200 on "parochialization" of Hindu gods. On the relationship between the universal and the local Isis, see esp. Jean Leclant, "Isis, déesse universelle et divinité locale, dans le monde gréco-romaine," in *Iconographie classique et identités régionales*, BCH Supplément 14, ed. by L. Kahil, Ch. Augé, and P. Linant de Bellefonds (Athens: École française d'Athènes, 1986), 341–53.

temple of Kysis (where an inscription hails her powers in this domain), at the minor shrine by the Luxor temple (where her image carries a cornucopia), or in the domestic sphere (the terra-cotta figurines that emphasize agricultural and maternal fertility with a variety of symbols). A deity operating, providing power, in these domains would inevitably be conceived in local terms and often in direct connection with the main local divine image. The Isis of Ras el-Soda in the Delta is distinctive in expressing fertility (by a bared breast), apotropaic power (by a crocodile beneath her foot), or (if the crocodile refers to Sobek) a regional affiliation with the god of the region.[22] It is likely that people in the region of this small shrine also regarded this Isis as distinctive in these respects, just as Christian icons have historically tended to accumulate unique regional powers according to their distinctive traits.[23] Even in the Amesysia festival, celebrated quite fervently throughout Egypt during the third century C.E., it was the local Isis in "her" shrine whose image was carried around fields that had grounded the peasant communities for generations.[24]

In the Roman period it was, ironically, Hellenism itself that aided in the particularization of such an omnipresent figure as Isis. The statues of Isis found at the second-century shrines of Luxor and Ras el-Soda and the Roman terra-cotta figurines found throughout Egypt all show a pronounced Hellenistic style of dress (including nudity), hair, and accoutrements (see pls. 2 and 7–8). But far from reflecting a broad ideological tendency toward a transcendent and altogether Greek conceptualization of the goddess among Egyptians and Greco-Egyptians of the Roman period, so Françoise Dunand has argued, the Hellenized iconography of Isis figurines (as well as those of Horus) had become, like Greek itself, a medium for the articulation of indigenous ideas, an available, authoritative, and by now entirely popular form of representation. The Hellenizing style functioned as a mode of interpretation, rendering accessible and portable those images and concepts of divine power visible on the outside of temples. It allowed a range of accoutrements that focused Isis appealingly within local cultures, such as cornucopias, an emphasis upon specific parts of the body, or simply the "magical" power of the frontal posture.[25]

---

[22] Cf. László Kákosy, "Zeus in Egypt," *BSAA* 45 (1993):173–76, esp. 174 on similar iconography of a "Zeus" in the Cairo Museum.

[23] Alexandria, G.-R. Museum inv. P. 440, in Adriani 1935/39:139–40; Dunand 1979:65–66. On the local character of Christian icons, see Ernst Kitzinger, "The Cult of Images in the Age before Iconoclasm," *DOP* 8 (1954):84–150, esp. 100–115.

[24] See Bonneau 1974, 1984/85; Perpillou-Thomas 1993:66–71.

[25] Dunand 1979:13–16, 62–70, 150–58; 1981:136–39; Török 1995:20–22; and in general on this interpretive function of Hellenism, Bowersock 1990. Note that contemporaneous images of Isis in faience conform generally to Egyptian, not Hellenistic, iconographic tradition: Marie-Dominique Nenna and Mervat Seif el-Din, "La petite plastique en faïence du Musée Gréco-Romain d'Alexandrie," *BCH* 118 (1994):295–97, 315.

Thus the cobra-torsoed Isis-Thermouthis incorporates the ancient serpent-goddess Renenoutet, native to the Fayyum and long responsible for the grain harvest. The full-body modeling of Greco-Roman terra-cottas produced a more vivid synthesis of the two goddesses than the traditional temple relief, which located identity and synthesis almost exclusively in the crown design or head. Through iconographic aspects of Aphrodite (especially nudity) Isis could express the functions of assuring marital happiness and maternal fertility that were traditionally associated with Hathor.[26] The related image of Isis *anasyrmenē,* in which she raises her robes to expose her vulva (pl. 8), may derive artistically from Greco-Roman erotic art but reflects a quite ancient "folk" custom practiced by ordinary women before the Apis bull and by priestesses on sacred barges at the Bubastis festival toward people on the banks of the Nile, a form of acquiring or (in the latter case) radiating fertility.[27] Such cases do admit a syncretistic and universalizing tendency in their centralizing of Isis, but the tendency expressly brings out functions of indigenous popular relevance. It does not, for example, obliterate the traditional importance of Hathor or other goddesses whose fertility characteristics Isis might borrow in these postures or functions.

In such local forms the cults of Isis were able to maintain themselves and even prosper through late antiquity: the agricultural Amesysia through at least the end of the third century; the temple of Kysis through the beginning of the fourth century; and the incubation cult at Menouthis through the end of the fifth century, whose regional reputation and net-

---

[26] Isis-Aphrodite: Dunand 1979:67–70. Isis-Thermouthis: Gisèle Deschênes, "Isis Thermouthis: à propos d'une statuette dans la collection du professeur M. J. Vermaseren," in *Hommages à Maarten J. Vermaseren* vol. 1, EPRO 68 (Leiden: Brill, 1978), 305–15, pls. XLVII–LIII. Note that many terra-cottas preserve the crown from classical Egyptian tradition to clarify a particular synthesis: Isis with the crown of Hathor (Dunand 1984, #4a–c and p. 26), Harpocrates with the crown of Amun (Nachtergael 1988:11, #7; Dunand 1979, #284).

[27] Herodotus II.60.2; Diodorus I.85.3. *Figurines:* Cairo Museum inv. 26964 (= Dunand 1979, #60), 26965 + 27675 (= Dunand 1979, #61); Adriani 1933/35:156, #11 (Alexandria, G.-R. Museum); Breccia 1930/34, inv. 9223 (= Breccia 1930/34, #181), 9227 (= Breccia 1930/34, #182), 23936 (Ptol.-early Rom.); Louvre inv. E 20732 B (Dunand 1990, #4), E 20787 B–C (= Dunand 1990, #5; with scallop shell in place of vulva). *Interpretations:* Perdrizet 1921, 1:54–56; Lloyd 1976:275–76; Dunand 1979:33. In the story of Horus and Seth the goddess Hathor "uncovers her vagina [*kfi k3t.st*]" before Re, who laughs (IV.2, ed. Alan H. Gardiner, *Late Egyptian Stories* [Brussels: Fondation Reine Élisabeth, 1932), 41), much as Baubo "exposes of her body the whole improper part" to make the grieving Demeter laugh (*Fragmentum Orphicum* 52 = Clement of Alexandria, *Protrept.* 2.21). Both scenes apparently reflect the same kind of ancient Mediterranean lewd gesture. Performed another way the gesture had clearly erotic connotations: a Coptic love-spell (sixth to seventh century) imagines that the desired "will draw her robe to her neck, and she will call out to me, 'Come here!'" (Ms. London Hay 10414 = Meyer/Smith [eds.] 1994, #79).

work of priests and priestesses provide a detailed glimpse of a local Isis cult persevering quietly out of view of Christian forces.[28]

We would certainly expect the historical presence of numerous other such local Isis cults. The temple of Philae, which continued into the sixth century, may best represent the resilience of established Isis cults. Philae's importance and attraction to pilgrims throughout Egypt indeed over-shadowed the local Christian presence to such a degree that emperors did not attempt its closure until 540.[29] Its particular importance, we might imagine in light of the long-persisting Nile cults, derived from the first cataract's location in the cultural topography as a "source" of the river, the boundary land of rocks and whitewater where the Nile's surge was really sensible. Indeed, Philae's regional significance in late antiquity is evident in the fact that, like Menouthis (with its subsequent cult of John and Cyrus), its effective ideological "conversion" only occurred with the ignition of a full-scale Christian pilgrimage center in nearby Elephantine (with some Christian pilgrims declaring pious visits to Philae itself).[30]

Philae's ability to represent a more general survival of local Egyptian cults has been questioned on the basis of its patronage by Blemmyes in the latter centuries.[31] But a dichotomy between "Egyptian" and "Blem-myes" inaccurately characterizes the regional culture of the first cataract, which stood on a continuum of economy, religion, and language stretch-ing from Upper Egypt south through lower Nubia. Along this continuum one finds, for example, the same iconographic details (falcons, feathered crowns) and the same deities. This temple, after all, was dedicated to an Isis, and a scribe of Isis there proudly mentions his figurine of the Nubian god Mandulis in a fourth-century inscription.[32] While Hellenized Blem-myes, organized in cultic societies called *synodoi,* maintained the temple of Talmis (Kalabsha) after the third century, Philae's fourth- and fifth-century priesthood was the property of a family of mixed Egyptian and Blemmye heritage, literate in Greek, Demotic, hieroglyphic, and even the Meroitic writing system of the south. Some of the priests resided in Philae and some with the nomadic Blemmye tribes who annually came to bor-

[28] See Dunand 1981:139–41, 142–43, on evidence for Isis cults in third- and fourth-century Egypt. On Isis of Menouthis see 2.1 and 4.3.1.

[29] Trombley's discussion (1993/94, 2:225–35) of the fourth- and fifth-century Philae cult provides an effective digest of the inscriptional data. On Philae and Christianization, see Munier 1938:41–42. On the later use of Demotic at Philae, see Griffith 1937:10–11.

[30] Nautin 1967:29–33; Leslie S. B. MacCoull, "Christianity at Syene/Elephantine/Philae," *BASP* 27 (1990):151–62, with Ballet/Mahmoud 1987; and Trombley 1993/94, 2:235–39. On Menouthis, see Wipszycka 1988:138–42.

[31] See Wilcken 1901:405–7; Bagnall 1993:147; but even Griffith speaks of the "barbaric frequenters of the temple" in the fifth century (1937:11).

[32] IDemPhilae 436, ed. Griffith 1937:126–27. On religious continuities between Nubia (Blemmyes) and temples of the first cataract, see Castiglione 1970; Desroches Noblecourt 1985; Török 1989.

row an image of Isis.[33] As much as it attracted pilgrims from Lower Egypt, Talmis and the region of the first cataract represented "our land and our gods" to Blemmyes, as their king, Phonen, writes in the fifth century.[34] None of these details would support a notion of Philae "taken over" by alien tribes.

Thus it is hardly surprising that the Egyptian monk Paphnuti makes no ethnic or cultural distinction between Egyptian and non-Egyptian when he recounts the Christianization of Philae, even while the outsider Procopius, writing about Philae at the same time, is highly attuned to ethnic groups.[35] Indeed, the tremendous damage inflicted by monks and soldiers under the emperor Justinian in the sixth century implies that the temple could not simply have been "neutralized" through the expulsion of Blemmyes—it bore too much regional power.[36] The temple of Philae functioned as an axis for a number of traditional cults, all of which had come to express themselves—their social groups, their religious practices, their bureaucratic records—through the terminology of Hellenism even while maintaining rites of considerable antiquity.

### 3.3 The Persistence of Local Deities

The documentation for Sobek cults over much of Egypt through at least the end of the third century shows the importance of local religion, to be sure, but also the continuing value of indigenous gods during the Roman period. One must inevitably replace the older view of an Egypt increasingly identifying itself with Hellenistic hybrids like Serapis and the *Agathos Daimon* of Alexandria and leaving behind its theriomorphic "monsters" like so much parochial baggage. Indeed, indigenous gods are increasingly documented for the third century and later in papyri, inscriptions, and iconography, replete with references to Taweret, Montou, Triphis, Metasytmis, Mandulis, Tutu, Shai, and Bes.

It is telling, indeed, to find such local deities venerated and even promoted in their local forms by the Greco-Roman constituencies we might once have expected to look toward ecumenical powers. In one case, a set

[33] IGPhilae 197; on the borrowing of the Isis: Priscus fr. 21 (see below, 4.2.1). On the heritage, distribution, and functions of this family, see É. Bernand 1969b, 2:237–46; Burkhardt 1984; Trombley 1993/94, 2:229–30. In general on Blemmye culture at Philae, see Wilcken 1901:396–419; Žabkar 1975:145–47. IDemPhilae 371, 6–8, seems to reflect political tensions between "Nubians" and *Ble(?).w* (= *Blhm.w,* "Blemmyes"?) that led to the processional figure of Isis being retained for two years; cf. Griffith 1937:104–5.

[34] Letter of Phonen to Aburni, ll.21–22 etc., ed. John Rea, "The Letter of Phonen to Aburni," *ZPE* 34 (1979):147–62.

[35] Paphnuti 31–36, tr. Vivian 1993:87–89; cf. Procopius, *Hist.* I.19.34–37.

[36] See O'Leary 1938:55–57; Nautin 1967:25–27, and 6–8 on the political context of destruction.

of Roman era dedications to the goddess "Leto" from Medamud (north of Luxor), the Greek name plainly masks some local goddess: a Hathor, an Isis, a Sekhmet, in her specific form.[37] But in the deeply Hellenized area of Panopolis reverence for the local goddess Triphis was such even by the end of the third century that many children of the higher citizenry bore her name in either Greek ("Triphodoros") or Egyptian ("Pete-triphis"). These theophoric names invariably indicated ritual circumstances associated with conception or a local deity supplicated for a child's ongoing protection.[38]

Other local or regional cults continued with widely varying degrees of Hellenization. In early-fourth-century Panopolis one would still refer to the shrine of Chnoubis using the god's Egyptian name, while the goddess Nekhbet of El Kab (Fayyum) was registered as the Greek goddess Eileithyia in a tax receipt for her priest. A local god of popular appeal in the Fayyum, still invoked in the third century by the Egyptian Mestasytmis ("the ears [of the divinity] hear"), had a religious association organized in Greek fashion as a *synod*. Panopolis, which provides a microcosm of local religion in late antique Egypt, also records a resilient cult of the archaic god Min well into the fifth century. Though Min is celebrated in the city's name and at least one important inscription by the Greek name Pan, abbot Shenoute still refers to him as Min when he reveals to an audience that he has just stolen an image of the god from a private house.[39]

The god Montu, whose worship was essentially restricted to the region of Thebes, enjoyed a spate of munificence under Antoninus Pius, with a series of small temples continuing at least through the third century. The Bucheum at Armant, necropolis of the sacred bulls of Montu, continued to receive ritual burials as late as 340 C.E. The Bucheum's priesthood, still capable in hieroglyphs in the fourth century, had the rare perspicacity about an increasingly oppressive Christendom to revolt in the very wording of the last bull's funerary stela. By dating the bull by the "era" of Diocletian rather than the reigning emperor Constantius II, so the stela's most recent interpreter has suggested, the Buchis priests could deny (in the ritually powerful medium of the hieroglyphic stele) the advent and

---

[37] Pierre Jouguet, "Dédicace grecque de Médamoud," BIFAO 31 (1931):1–29, esp. 3–10; É. Bernand 1992:82–84 (#31).

[38] Borkowski 1990, with Yoyotte 1955:140 and Quaegebeur 1977 on the religious signifiance of onomastics. Mummy labels of the Ptolemaic period show the antiquity of invoking Triphis in names in this area: Henri Gauthier, "La déesse Triphis," BIFAO 3 (1903):170–72. On Triphis and her temple in general, see ibid., 165–81.

[39] Chnoubis: = *P.Berlin* inv. 16365, xv, 27 (ed. Borkowsi 1975). Nekhbet: *O. Fayyum* 23. Mestasytmis: Wagner/Quaegebeur 1973. Min of Panopolis: Welles 1946 (on Cairo JE 26903, the inscription of Ptolemagrius, most recently edited by É. Bernand 1969a, #114); Emmel 1994; Van der Vliet 1993:101–2, 107, regarding Leipoldt 3, #26.

authority of the Christian emperors. But the cult attracted more than local Egyptians: promoted as Apollo during the Ptolemaic period, Montu became the local object of dedications to "(our) native god Didymus Helios Apollo" from a company of Miletians living in the area around the end of the second century.[40]

The cult of the Nubian god Mandulis at Talmis (Kalabsha) attracted Greek and Roman pilgrims from well beyond its region south of the first cataract, demonstrating that the local distinctiveness of such cults made them no less accessible—and seems indeed to have rendered them increasingly attractive in their peripheral location. Built in association with Talmis's Roman garrison in the first century, the temple of Mandulis maintained an incubation oracle through the third century, at which point it seems to have continued without the influx of Roman pilgrims through the fifth century. But its roots go even farther back, originating as an attempt on the part of Ptolemy Philadelphus and then Augustus to establish common holy sites for the military and the nomadic tribes they were supposed to control, since Mandulis was himself a nomadic god and his establishment at Talmis an act of deliberate priestly syncretism. Thus he became the son of Horus and, for the soldiers and the Roman pilgrims who increasingly went to the ends of the Nile to seek advice, a form of the Alexandrian god Aion. It was in this essentially Greco-Roman guise that most pilgrims extolled Mandulis in their dedicatory inscriptions. As one reads in Nock's evocative translation:

> O rayshooting lord Mandulis, Titan, Makareus, having beheld some radiant signs of thy power I pondered on them and was busied therewith, wishing to know with confidence whether thou art the sungod. . . . I had a vision and found rest for my soul. For thou didst grant my prayer and show me thyself going though the heavenly vault; then washing thyself in the holy water of immortality thou appearedst again. . . . Then I knew thee, Mandulis, to be the Sun, the allseeing master, king of all, allpowerful Eternity [*Aiōn*]. O happy folk that dwell in the city beloved by the Sun Mandulis.[41]

The typical Hellenistic language of enlightenment and conversion suggests that Talmis may have represented to many of its pilgrims an outpost of Greco-Roman religious synthesis, a remote springboard for achieving those distinctive late Roman revelations. For one Ethiopian pilgrim its

[40] Grenier 1983; *P-M* 5:158–59. On the second-century Miletian inscription, on a column (Cairo SB 1530) found in Medinet Habu, see Guy Lecuyot, "Un sanctuaire romain transformé en monastère: le Deir el-Roumi," in *Sesto Congresso internazionale di Egittologia: Atti*, vol. 2 (Turin: Società Italiana per il Gas p.A., 1993), 383–85; Bataille 1952:92–94.

[41] Preisigke, *Sammelbuch* #4127, tr. Nock 1972a:366. On Mandulis-Aion synthesis, see Nock 1972a; Festugière 1950, 1:46–62. On establishment of cult at Talmis (Kalabsha): F. Ll. Griffith, "Meroitic Studies VI," *JEA* 15 (1929):72–74. See also Milne 1924:189–90.

peripheral location offered an entry to the Hellenistic *oikumenē:* preparing his votive inscription in metrical Greek with lofty references to Greek mythology, he explicitly desires to surpass "barbaric Ethiopian" and to "sing in sweet Greek verses," sentiments suggestive of a conscious antiparochialism—a view of Talmis as a step toward universalism.[42] Still, one must resist the urge to oppose such hybrid cultural sentiments to Egyptian culture. The identification of Mandulis with the sun, Re, the quintessential "Great God" in Egyptian priestly culture, bespeaks an Egyptian cosmos; and all these inscriptions must have required, as at all temples offering their walls for such votive insignia, a priesthood to compose, choose a place for, and inscribe the words.[43] Indeed, it would be this priesthood that reappears when Talmis is under Blemmye control, bearing theophoric names derived from Mandulis, associating in priestly *synodoi,* sponsoring festivals, and inscribing dedicatory stelae in Greek during the mid-fifth century.[44]

As at Philae, the cult of Mandulis at Talmis continued to function as an indigenous regional cult for Blemmyes and other local communities, while the Blemmye priesthoods that shared control by the fourth century had come, after centuries of pilgrimage to Greco-Roman sanctuaries, to define themselves through Hellenism. At the same time, the overall Egyptian imagery in the Mandulis inscriptions may reflect the same kind of Egyptianization of Greco-Roman supplicants' piety that provoked, for example, the numerous figurines of Egyptian gods in Roman military uniform. And epitomizing this remarkable synthesis of Hellenistic, Egyptian, and Roman military culture in Talmis, a graffito on the hypostyle wall portrays some nomadic ruler or god mounted and armored as a Roman emperor, spearing a barbarian enemy, and also being crowned with the feathers of Amun.[45]

Another long-lasting cult on Philae, devoted to a form of Horus, shows an additional dimension to the religious culture of the region—in this case an Egyptian-Blemmye syncretism that was Hellenized only minimally. Reports of the worship of a falcon-deity on Philae go back to

---

[42] Sayce 1894:284–91, #I, 24–25.

[43] On priestly inscribers, see *P.Oxy* VII.1029; Griffith 1937:8–9; Beard 1991:39–42, 45. Other Egyptian priests gifted in Greek poetic composition have been documented in Ptolemaic Edfu (Yoyotte 1969) and fourth-century Panopolis (Browne 1977); in general, see Cameron 1965. A first-/second-century epitaph for one Apollo of Lycopolis, dead at sixteen, full of Hellenistic mythological allusions, must reflect a poet-for-hire, although not necessarily a priest (É. Bernand 1992, #93). On Mandulis as Re, see Hans Lewy, "A Dream of Mandulis," *ASAE* 44 (1944):227–34 (*pace* Nock 1972a:374–77).

[44] *CIG* III.5071b and in general Wilcken 1901:411–19; Žabkar 1975:146. On Blemmye culture in Talmis, see also Desroches Noblecourt 1985.

[45] See Castiglione 1970:98 (abb. 7), 99–101. Trigger (1978:116–17) identifies this figure as the fifth-century C.E. Meroitic king Silko.

Strabo, who alludes to its mixed cultural background: "Here also, a bird is held in honour, which they call a hawk [*hieraka*]. . . . They said that it was an Ethiopian bird, and that another was brought from Ethiopia whenever the one at hand died, or before."[46] But we learn more about this cult from the beginning of the fifth century. Three Greek *proskunēmata* by Blemmye priests from this period accompany small images of falcon-headed crocodiles.[47] And a fifth-century Coptic account of Christians on Philae in the late fourth century records the following episode, beginning as the memoirs of one Abba Macedonius:

> "Now, I saw [the residents of Philae] going into their temples and worshiping a certain bird that they call 'the falcon' inside some kind of [secret contrivance].[48] Now it happened that after some days I came into [the courtyard of the temple]. The priest had left the city on business, [and] his two sons were performing his duties: they would take turns offering sacrifice to the idol. Now I, Macedonius, went up to them and using deceit spoke with them. I said, 'I would like to offer a sacrifice to God today.' And they said [to me], 'Come and offer it.' One of them went inside and ordered that wood be laid on the altar and a fire kindled beneath it, and the two sons of the priest watched over the wood until it burned down to the coals." . . . [Meanwhile] the bishop Abba Macedonius went to where the [secret contrivance] was. He removed the falcon, chopped off its head, and threw it upon the roaring fire. He left the temple and went away.[49]

The account is certainly heir to scriptural *topoi* of idol destruction. But in at least two points it links with other evidence: the mid- to late-fourth-century date of a Christian mission's establishment and, for our purposes, the falcon cult itself (to which Macedonius himself did only passing damage—and notably without even a mention of the cult of Isis).[50]

[46] Strabo, *Geog.* 17.1.49, tr. Jones, LCL, 8:131.

[47] IGPhilae 190–92, ed. É. Bernand 1969b, 2:221–25; cf. Žabkar 1975:145–47. IDemPhilae 77, 406 (ed. Griffiths 1937, 1:59, 406) refer to individuals whose names end in *Bk*, "falcon"; cf. Crum 1939:48b s.v. *Bĕč*.

[48] Copt. *henmangkanon*. Vivian translates "mechanical device," apparently taking it for Greek *mēchanē*. Spiegelberg (1924:188n.1) more convincingly derived the Coptic from *mangenon*, "means of charming," but interpreted it, probably in connection with Strabo's report, as a *living* falcon's cage. The context makes it quite clear that what is described is the icon's *naos,* which would be opened to display the god's image at certain times. The author's choice of the negative term *mangenon* simply points to the importance of the *naos* in secreting and then revealing the god himself; there is no reason to assume mechanical devices.

[49] Paphnutius, *Histories of the Monks of Upper Egypt* 31 (= B.M. Or. ms. 7029, fol. 13a–b, ed. Budge 1915:445), tr. Vivian 1993:87 (with modifications).

[50] See, in general, Spiegelberg 1924; Vivian 1993:54–69. Among scriptural *topoi* behind the narrative the most likely would be Daniel and Bel from the Daniel cycle (Bel and the Dragon 10–13).

Whereas the Coptic text describes a cult restricted to local priests and devotees, the bulk of evidence from the area shows the extensive role of Blemmyes as priests and pilgrims. So also the deity manifest in the falcon, occasionally depicted with a crocodile's body or other theriomorphic attributes, was an Egyptian form of Horus—"Horus who is in Shenwet." But this Horus had become particularly popular among the southern peoples congregating around the first cataract, perhaps due to his special protective powers (an increasingly important attribute of local gods, as we will see shortly).[51] This phenomenon of a local Egyptian god assimilated by Blemmyes and maintained alongside Isis into the fifth century in a Hellenized milieu shows the abiding appeal of local deities even in cultural crossroads like the region of the first cataract.

Many of these examples of local gods in the Roman period—Mandulis, Triphis, Horus of Shenwet—reflect the gods' success with often circumscribed clienteles but specifically within overtly "Hellenized" milieus. "Hellenism" in these cases can become the means for such indigenous cults to assert their continuing local or regional vitality, not to become subsumed within a Greco-Roman pantheism and not to be uprooted or replaced by Christian ideology.

## 3.4 Cults of Protection

Many cultures have a form or class of supernatural being so frightening in its iconography that the outsider is often at a loss to understand why anyone would portray it at all. Today one often associates such images with the outside of temples in India, Tibet, and Indonesia, but they are to be found on masks, doorposts, and gates throughout world cultures, occasionally describing a maleficent demonic world but more often representing the key figures in the mythology of repelling that same demonic world. These figures ward off evil from sanctuary, village, home, and person often by virtue of their mythologically marginal status: demonic appearance, demonic lethality against malevolent spirits, and even a genetic association with the demonic world that gives them some control over the activities of demons. Occasionally one must propitiate this kind of figure to avert its otherwise devastating wrath—to forge a protective alliance between this quasi-demon and the village.[52]

The presence of these figures has never implied any more than the artistic and mythopoeic creativity normal to any people preoccupied with illness and accident, drought and famine, infertility and dispute. One

---

[51] Žabkar 1975:150–53.

[52] See, for example, Christopher A. Faraone, *Talismans and Trojan Horses: Guardian Statues in Ancient Greek Myth and Ritual* (New York: Oxford University Press, 1992).

would, for example, be hard-pressed to relate the mere presence or extravagant imagery of these universal figures to cultural anxiety or decline. In Egypt, too, what appears to be a rise in evidence for this kind of protective figure just at the Roman period probably represents only the appearance of a quite ancient religious phenomenon now in the materials, iconography, or social circumstances of the Roman period. The protective deities represent a quite important phenomenon for the reconstruction of local religion, however, since their propitiation inevitably corresponds to the most basic concerns in the local peasant's (or traveling merchant's) world and often emerges in ritual spells preserved for their power to protect. Indeed, it is striking to discover in such spells a whole synthetic universe of apotropaic (and otherwise accessible) deities from all over the Mediterranean world, including Syria's Ereshkigal and Greece's Hekate and Persephone.

### 3.4.1 Seth

In the documents and remains of priestly ritual in classical Egypt the god Seth (Greek *Tuphōn*) seems most often to have functioned as the object of curses—by making and immolating his name or image, by portraying him bound or speared, by reciting his destruction to represent the decimation of chaotic "foreign" elements in the cosmos. Plutarch's thoroughly negative description of Seth in mythology and his reports of local festivals for Seth's destruction would seem to reflect the most common views in second-century Egypt. The vitality of this counter-Seth mythology in the early Roman period was such that Jews came to be regarded in some priestly quarters as "Typhonic," a perspective that culminated in the Egyptians' extirpation of Jews there in 117.[53]

Yet there was another tradition (often placed historically antecedent to the negative one) wherein Seth carried the vital role, according to a Late Egyptian text, of "slay[ing] the opponent of P-Re daily while I am at the prow of the Bark of Millions, whereas not any (other) god is able to do it"—that is, a god of singular apotropaic force.[54] There had long been a temple devoted to such a Seth in Ombos, and traces of ancient Seth cults have been found in the western oases as well as in the northeastern Delta.[55]

[53] Plutarch, *De Iside,* esp. 30–32, 49–50; P.Jumilhac (mid-Ptolemaic) xvii.10–11, ed. Vandier 1961:129 (cf. ibid., 108–9); Te Velde 1977:138–51; Ritner 1993, ch. 4. On evidence from the Roman period, see Frankfurter 1992:208–15.

[54] P.Chest.Beatty 1, iv, 4–5, tr. Wente, in William Kelly Simpson, ed., *The Literature of Ancient Egypt,* 2nd ed. (New Haven, Conn.: Yale University Press, 1973), 112–13. See also Te Velde 1977:99–108.

[55] Cf. Te Velde 1977:115–18; Kaper 1997, ch. 3.

It is in the temples of the Dakhla oasis that the cult of Seth as protector- and fertility-god is most abundantly documented into the Roman period. At Deir el-Hagar a relief from the reign of Vespasian celebrates him as "Lord of the oasis, who slays Apophis"; and at the temple of Tutu at Kellis Seth is the one who "has slain Apophis in the prow of the barque [of Re]." A graffito at Kellis portrays Seth's local cult image, a winged figure spearing a serpent. Reliefs and inscriptions throughout the oasis reflect a Seth festival, an oracular cult image, and the god's strongly local significance.[56]

In the Kharga oasis as well, in the court of the Amun temple of Hibis, "Seth, great of strength, the great god, residing in Hibis," is represented in a large relief, spearing the Apophis serpent.[57] But this link with the Theban deity Amun raises the question of how these cults could have cooperated, given the increasing hostility of many Theban priesthoods to Seth veneration over the Persian and Greco-Roman periods. Indeed, this hostility may explain the cultivation of an alternative protector-god in the oases, often with similar iconography: Amun-Nakht, who "runs fast over the desert, while he makes an end of the enemy," according to an inscription at 'Ain Birbiya in the Dakhla oasis.[58] Acclamations of Amun-Nakht describe the god in explicitly "anti-Seth" terms (e.g., as avenger of his father against Seth), suggesting his role in priestly attempts to suppress and replace Seth in the oases over the course of the Greco-Roman period.[59] At the same time, Amun-Nakht's character as warrior, protector, and repeller of chaotic forces, and his realization of the power of the Theban Amun in these functions, point to an abiding need in Egyptian religion of the time for such militant gods: a protector could only be supplanted by another protector.[60]

Indeed, enough tantalizing references to Seth-Typhon have come out of the Roman Fayyum and Nile Valley that it seems impossible that Egyptians of this period could have regarded this god merely as the object of execration. A Fayyum temple keeps among its collection of votive figurines a small image of Seth. The image may well have resembled a figure of Typhon that Plutarch recalled in Hermopolis, represented as a falcon

[56] Deir el-Hagar: P-M 7:298 (including a relief of Vespasian offering to Seth); Kaper 1997:58, 3.1.2.7–9. Kellis temple: Kaper 1997:60–62, 3.1.2.11, 16. In general on Seth veneration in the oases: Te Velde 1977:115–16, 133–34; Kaper 1997:63–64.

[57] P-M 7:280; Jean Capart, "Contribution à l'iconographie du dieu Seth," CdÉ 41 (1946):29–31; Kaper 1997:56–58, 3.1.2.5. On the date of the Hibis cult's demise, see Winlock et al. 1941, 1:48, cf. 45, and in general Wagner 1987:157, 360–61.

[58] 'Ain Birbiya temple: EB 1411, tr. Kaper 1987:151, with the temple's prominent iconography of Amun-Nakht discussed in Kaper 1997:69–74, 3.2.4.1–9.

[59] See Kaper 1997:81–85.

[60] The consequent prominence of the Amun cults of the oases during the Roman period seems to contrast with the decline of Amun cults in the Thebaid: cf. Kákosy 1995:2963–68.

fighting with a snake.[61] Both figures were probably designed to function as apotropaia, repelling evil forces. And so also the festival "regarding the Typhonians" in second-century Dendara would have provided participants with the ritual opportunity either to execrate Seth as harbinger of evils or to placate him as controller of them. At the same time Ombos and an obscure "village of Seth" in the Fayyum may actually have venerated Seth as the chief local deity.[62]

Given the demonic character of Seth in documents of Egyptian priestly tradition of the Greco-Roman period, it is particularly striking to find the god invoked in ritual spells of the third and fourth centuries:

> [*voces magicae*] . . . this is the chief name of Typhon, at whom the ground, the depths of the sea, Hades, heaven, the sun, the moon, the visible chorus of stars, the whole universe all tremble, the name which, when it is uttered, forcibly brings gods and spirits [*daimōnes*] to it. . . .
>
>   . . . [The invocation:]

> > I call you who did first control gods' wrath,
> > You who hold royal scepter o'er the heavens,
> > You who are midpoint of the stars above,
> > You, master Typhon, you I call, who are
> > The dreaded sovereign o'er the firmament.
> > You who are fearful, awesome, threatening,
> > You who're obscure and irresistible
> > And hater of the wicked, you I call,
> > Typhon . . .
> >
> >   .  .  .
> >
> > You who hold sovereignty over the Moirai,
> > I invoked you in pray'r, I call, almighty one.[63]

Seth's accessibility to the ritualist in this spell might almost imply a demonolatry or subversive mode of ritual. But the priestly provenance of these spells (to be discussed in ch. 5) militates against older scholarly—Roman, in fact—models of a subversive and demonolatrous "sorcery" lurking beneath a more exoteric and heaven-oriented "religion." One can

  61 *P.Oxy* XII.1449, 14 (cf. the bronze statuette of Greco-Roman date portraying Seth in military pose, published by J. Leibovitch, "Une statuette du dieu Seth," *ASAE* 44 [1944]:101–7, pl. 13); Plutarch, *De Iside* 50 (371C–D). Plutarch describes the falcon and snake as set upon a hippopotamus, a traditional image of the *execrated* Seth at Edfu, but he then clearly would be confusing two types of Seth image (cf. Griffiths 1970:490–91). That the falcon/snake figure existed as an image of Seth's own apotropaic powers is suggested by its parallel in the Hibis relief (see above, n. 57).

  62 Dendara festival: *P.Heid.* 1818, on which see above, 2.4. Ombos: see above, 2.6.1. "Village [*niw.t*] of Seth [determinative]": Gallo 1992:128–29.

  63 *PGM* IV.244–47, 251–68, 270–72, tr. O'Neil in Betz 1986:42–43.

easily understand the promotion of Seth here as an extension of his traditionally apotropaic function, persisting as it did in temples through the Roman period. His subordination of supernatural powers, including the wholly negative Moirai ("fate-demons"), resembles the chief attributes of other protective gods like Tutu and Petbe-Nemesis, to whom we now turn.

### 3.4.2 Tutu

Like Seth the god Tutu (Greek *Tithoēs*) had once been acclaimed as vanquisher of Apophis, the traditional enemy of the sun and cosmic order; but he came to achieve immense popularity throughout Roman Egypt by virtue of his mythical chiefdom over the "genii" of Sekhmet, an army of dangerous and capricious forces that could be harnessed only by particular gods. Tutu, like Horus, Bes, and certain forms of Amun, would thus be represented on apotropaic stelae, temple reliefs, and even amulets and coins as a sphinx that either stands upon, wears, or is accompanied by these same dangerous forces. His gaze, often turned toward the viewer (atypical in Egyptian relief art), would have borne particular power to repel maleficent forces.[64]

What is particularly striking in the case of Tutu is the extent to which the popular invocation of this apotropaic divinity extended to full-fledged cults throughout Roman Egypt. The existence of personal names incorporating "Tutu" or his "appearance" in a region of the Delta during the early Roman period indicates his normative presence as a local god with some power over maternal fertility.[65] Tutu was also the object of particular priestly elevation, appearing in such "official" temple media as *naoi* and temple reliefs—and in human form, not as a sphinx. In a large relief from Athribis, wherein he is represented with a local form of Horus, Tutu wears a crown with the theriomorphic heads of the genii.

[64] See esp. Picard 1958; Sauneron 1960b; Quaegebeur 1986; Kaper 1991 (pp. 60, 67n.5 on Tutu versus Apophis); Kákosy 1995:2982–84. On the "genii" of Sekhmet, see Meeks 1971:45–49. Important discussions of Roman era stelae include Guéraud 1935 and Kákosy 1964 (Sauneron 1960b reviews the corpus as a whole). On temple reliefs Tutu appears more often as a man than a sphinx. It should be noted that Sauneron's intepretation of the multiple heads or faces on gods like Tutu supersedes previous theories that this construction designated a *pantheos*, and Quaegebeur's interpretation of gods standing on beasts effectively challenges much of the consensus about Horus on the crocodiles and other gods in similar poses ("Divinités égyptiennes sur des animaux dangereux," *L'Animal, l'homme, le dieu dans le Proche-Orient ancien*, Cahiers du CEPOA 2 [Louvain: Peeters, 1984], 131–43; cf. Ritner 1993:119–36).

[65] Yoyotte 1955:135–38; Quaegebeur 1977. Subsequently Quaegebeur (1997) directed attention to the temple of Shenhur, from whose "voice" oracles, he proposed, Tutu granted these benefits.

But it is imagery such as one finds on a late-first-century *naos* that seems to suggest that militant powers once tied to the pharaoh were coalescing in gods like Tutu: he is "the most violent, the valiant lion who strikes whomever opposes (him) eternally and forever." And still in the third century he is invoked at Esna as "chief of the emissaries of Sekhmet."[66]

The progressive exaltation of Tutu from apotropaic "chief of demons" to central deity culminates in several temples of the Roman period in which he gains virtually focal status. At the temple of Shenhur (near Coptos), built and expanded during the first century C.E., Tutu is the companion of Isis of Shenhur and seems to have delivered voice oracles. On a part of the Roman temple in Coptos he is hailed as "Touou [*sic*], great of valour, the great god in the middle of Coptos, the chief of the entire land." Two dedication stelae of the early third century, found at Coptos, present apotropaic composites of the sphinx Tutu. One of these stelae serves our reconstruction of the life-context of such protective deities in documenting an actual "association [*sunodos*] of the great god Toutou." In the remains of the ancient town of Kellis in the Dakhla oasis stands a temple of the early Roman period that was active into the fourth century and devoted entirely to "the supreme god Tithoes and accompanying gods," including his consort, the local goddess Tapshay, both of whom are pictured in anthropomorphic guise enthroned over the doorway. Tutu himself is invoked as in the apotropaic stelae as "master of the demons."[67]

### 3.4.3 Petbe-Nemesis

By name the figure Petbe signified divine retribution as directed against wrongdoers, much in the way the pharaoh had once been imbued with vengeful power against enemies. Petbe and Tutu may thus have represented a trend in the "hypostasization" and independent representation of royal powers. Petbe served also as one element or aspect of the capricious and vindictive genii over which Tutu was often regarded as chief. Represented as a griffin on stelae, either alone or accompanying another

[66] Athribis relief: Alexandria, G.-R. Museum, inv. 3211 = Sauneron 1960b, #13 (1960b:271–72); see also Yoyotte 1955:136–37. Naos: Rondot 1990 (quotation tr. p. 306) = Sauneron 1960b, #14. Esna reliefs: Esna 486, 490, 626 = Sauneron 1960b, ##5–7.

[67] Tutu of Shenhur: Claude Traunecker, "Schanhur," *LexÄg* 5 (1984):528–31 and Quaegebeur 1997. Tutu of Coptos: *P-M* 5:128; see Sauneron 1960b:271, #12, fig. 1. Third-century Tutu stelae: Cairo JE #37538, in Guéraud 1935:5 = Sauneron 1960b, #29 (cf. p. 287); Cairo JE 64938, in Guéraud 1935:9–10 = Sauneron 1960b, #30. Tutu of Kellis: Wagner/Quaegebeur 1973:177–80; Hope et al. 1989:13–15; Kaper 1991:64–66; as "master of demons": Kaper 1991:64.

deity like Tutu, Petbe functioned as one more iconographic weapon in the total armory of village and temple apotropaia.[68]

Allegiance to Petbe appears most vividly in Egyptian names (onomastics), in festivals of the Roman period, and in a sermon by Shenoute. It is in the onomastics, in fact, that the explicit equation of Egyptian Petbe and Greek Nemesis appears. We may consequently take a *Nemesia* of 117 C.E. as a celebration of this god. And indeed, several references to festivals of Nemes*es* (in the plural) in the beginning of the Roman period quite likely reflect the complex army of vindictive and protective genii out of which such figures as Petbe and Tutu would occasionally be consolidated.[69]

Shenoute refers to Petbe as "Kronos," a god he portrays as still worshiped in his vicinity in the fifth century. But Kronos for Shenoute is really a form of Satan. "There is no liberty for those who put their trust in Kronos," Shenoute apostrophically addresses Gesios after ransacking his house; indeed Kronos "is you yourself and those like you in all belief and impurity. . . . you belong to Satan."[70] In his sermon "The Lord Thundered" he decorates "Kronos" with Greek mythological themes; and yet he also situates his subject in local terms: "Where is Kronos—who is himself Petbe—who trapped his parents while they were together and cut off his father's genitals with a sickle?"[71] The Kronos of Hesiodic tradition is thus identified with the Egyptian figure of Petbe. Such a brief clarification, not an obvious or even necessary translation of "Kronos," appears to have localized Shenoute's discussion of a quite nonindigenous Satan figure in the belief-system of the immediate community. In thus grounding his diatribe against a Satanic Kronos Shenoute suggests that it is this popular extratemple cult that best represents the opposing ideology.[72]

---

[68] Meeks 1971:43–44; Quaegebeur 1983b:50–54 (see also 41–50 on iconography); Kákosy 1995:2984–86. Claude Traunecker has more recently argued that Petbe represented the divine vengeance that a person could invoke against an aggressor before a temple or that would inflict someone who swore falsely before a temple: "L'Appel au Divin: La crainte des dieux et les serments de temple," in Heintz (ed.) 1997:35–54.

[69] Onomastics: Quaegebeur 1983b:52–53. See also Pettazzoni 1949:288–91: late antique astrologers commonly associated Nemesis with the planet Kronos-Saturn. Nemesia: *SB* XIV.11958, I, 39, on which see Perpillou-Thomas 1993:117–19. A celebration of the birth of Kronos (also identified with Petbe) recorded in late-third-century Oxyrhynchus may actually translate some form of Sobek: *P.Oxy* VII.1025 = W.Chr. 493, on which see Perpillou-Thomas 1993:107–9 (potential identification with Sobek based on *P. Tebtunis* II.294, 295, 298, 599; cf. Pettazzoni 1949:296–98 and IGFayyum III.217). On the festival of *Nemeses:* Perpillou-Thomas 1993:118, and compare plural *tuphōniois* in *P.Heid.* 1818 (above, 3.4.1).

[70] Shenoute, Discourses 4: Not Because a Fox Barks, ms. pp. 168–69, ed. Leipoldt 3:79.23–27 (#24), tr. Barns 1964:156.

[71] Shenoute, Discourses 4: The Lord Thundered, p. 55, ed. Amélineau 1909:383–84.

[72] See Van der Vliet 1993:112–14.

Two Coptic invocations from the fifth to seventh centuries illustrate the final stage in the understanding of Petbe.[73] Despite their late dates, these spells seem to preserve much older Egyptian traditions, one spell demonstrating a significant knowledge of traditional afterlife beliefs (addressing at one point "the sun of the underworld") and the construction of divine names from hybrids of "Horus": another name for Petbe here is "Hor-asias P-han-kapres."[74] But in both spells the figure of Petbe has been transformed into a chthonic power to be called *up* for personal purposes:

> Yea, shake yourself today with your power, Petbe, who is in the abyss; shake yourself today with your power, Thunder, the true name of Petbe, since I drag you up to ask you, Hor-asias P-han-kapres, you whose front part looks [like] a lion, whose rear part looks like a bear, whose head is fixed in heaven, whose feet are fixed on earth.[75]

To some extent the name has been simply inserted into a standard "chthonic invocation" formula that exalts, for the purpose of harnessing, powers believed to be located in the underworld, Amente.[76] However, "Petbe" is certainly the central power in the above spell; and the multiple animal attributes recall the iconographic construction of apotropaic and vindictive genii of the Roman period.[77] Despite Petbe's chthonic nature here, he is not polarized as a demon but (the spells elsewhere describe) has a harmonious relationship with a figure called "the father almighty," roughly identifiable in the ritual universe with the Christian god. Thus the cosmos projected in these texts consists of interacting and even harmonious heavenly and chthonic powers—again, roughly continuing the relationship of the local cosmos of capricious, vindictive, and apotropaic spirits and the regional or "national" cosmos of victorious, ordering, and beneficent deities.

Through such disparate documentation the popularity of the "cult" of Petbe in the Roman period serves to illustrate the more general phenomenon of apotropaic powers in Egyptian local religion. Figures with quite

---

73 Collection Lange, ed. Lange 1932:162–63 = Meyer/Smith (eds.) 1994, #118; P.Mil.Vogl. copt. 16, ed. Pernigotti 1979, ii.

74 See Irene Grumach, "On the History of a Coptic Figura Magica," in *Proceedings of the Twelfth International Congress of Papyrology*, ASP 7, ed. by D. Samuel (Toronto: Hakkert, 1970), 169–81.

75 Coll.Lange, ll. 11–20, ed. Lange 1932:162–63, tr. Meyer, in Meyer/Smith (eds.) 1994:238. Compare P.Mil.Vogl. copt. 16, invoking "Petbe in the form of a bull" to "subvert the foundation of the earth" to gain a loved one and "to shake the foundation of the earth and . . . the firmament [*nestereōma*] of heaven with the Thrones and those who sit upon them" (II.5–13, ed. Pernigotti 1979:33, 41–44).

76 The formula is used, for example, for "a demon whose name is Theumatha" in London Hay 10414 = Meyer/Smith (eds.) 1994, #79.

77 On Petbe and apotropaic composites, see Kákosy 1995:2985.

terrifying names, attributes, or iconographies functioned in extratemple religion as protective figures. Such apotropaic figures had considerable importance in priestly and temple milieus and their "official" iconography, as we see in an Isis figurine of the second century whose throne is flanked by the Nemesis griffin as well as other frightening theriomorphs.[78] But the appearance of these figures in people's names suggests a domestic or personal context for the ritual and beliefs surrounding such apotropaic spirits.

### 3.4.4 Protective Deities in Roman Egypt

As with so much data on particular Egyptian gods it is difficult to speak of a "rise" in the worship or popularity of Tutu and Petbe rather than a continuity that is supplemented by an increase in particular types of evidence. Yet virtually all the documentation of both figures comes from the Greco-Roman period. Moreover, the iconographic emphasis on Tutu's powers over capricious genii and demons, and Petbe-Nemesis's derivation from this very order of the supernatural, seem to indicate specific preoccupations or fears underlying these figures' popularity. Indeed, the spate of apotropaic images surrounding Harpocrates (the Horus-*cippi*), Bes, Amun, and even Isis and Taweret during the Greco-Roman period suggests at least a vital industry for producing personal, domestic, and communal apotropaia. It may well be in this context that we ought to situate the militant, armored Horus and Anubis figurines so typical of the Roman period.[79]

The particular concern in the case of Tutu for harnessing and directing an army of capricious or malicious powers points to elemental fears. James Scott has pointed to the basic capriciousness of the local "nature" spirits in peasant villages cross-culturally: they can act viciously, yet their propitiation can bring great benefits; and the everyday religion of little traditions consists to a large degree in the negotiation of such benefits and avoidance of the spirits' wrath. The capriciousness of genii or demons in this sense would translate a more profound organization of the environment and experience into both liminal (capricious) and fixed contexts, the former linked with some species of demon and some rite for propitiating or expelling it.[80]

Applying these observations to Roman Egypt we can discern two ma-

---

[78] Berlin 20004, in Quaegebeur 1983b:46–47. A small nemesis-griffin also appears in the throne of Amun in an offering scene with the emperor Trajan (?): Hildesheim, Pelizaeus Museum 1537 = *Cleopatra's Egypt: Age of the Ptolemies* (Brooklyn, N.Y.: Brooklyn Museum, 1988), #22.

[79] See Grenier 1978:408.

[80] J. Scott 1977:23–24. Cf. C. Stewart 1991:162–91, 211–21, on similar dynamics in contemporary Greek orthodox culture.

jor themes in the local religion. On the one hand, we see a new interest in identifying such an order of supernatural power and representing it on stelae and in temple reliefs as a means of turning their danger into a force against even greater dangers.[81] One can certainly see this trend in the theriomorphic figures that accompany Tutu, Bes, and sometimes Harpocrates. But one can equally see its basis in popular life. This was a time when "a certain evil demon" might cause a couple's divorce (so blamed in an early-fourth-century divorce contract), when more and more children were given the name *abaskantos,* "secure from supernatural harm," or names drawn not from the main local gods but from a host of apotropaic genii: Panorseus, Pechytes, Terouterou.[82]

On the other hand we can make out the work of local priesthoods, conjuring specific indigenous gods as chiefs or masters of these capricious genii, by the singular power of whom the local spirits and demons that occupied the peasant environment might be harnessed for beneficence and safety. Thus the function of providing apotropaic power, of protecting people from natural and supernatural malevolence, seems to rest increasingly on individual temples and regional traditions—and no longer, perhaps, on the "national" force of the pharaoh as mediated explicitly in local temple rituals.

The hypostasization of royal protective power is indeed one of the most striking aspects of the genesis of the protective gods. It is certainly the context in which Domitian and other early Roman emperors (or their Egyptian proponents) cultivated an association with Tutu. And it is not unlikely that Antoninus Pius and some of his Ptolemaic forebears became linked with the Theban cult of Montu, a warrior-god also expressing the pharaoh's vengeful capacities, for similar reasons: the foreign rulers' appropriation, for their own charisma or confidence, of the most powerful forces associated with the Egyptian throne.[83] But in the popular invocation of Tutu, Petbe, and Seth in domestic ritual and the naming of children, the "central" power of the pharaoh has shifted centrifugally out to the local stele or statue.

[81] Quaegebeur sees "un développement typique des croyances indigènes à l'époque tardive: . . . la prolifération de groupes de génies" (1983b:52). Compare the guardian deities on Edfu and Pharbaethos: Jean-Claude Goyon, *Les dieux-gardiens et la genèse des temples (d'après les textes égyptiens de l'époque gréco-romaine),* vols. 1–2, Bibliothèque d'Étude 93 (Cairo: IFAO, 1985).

[82] Divorce-demons: *P.Grenfell* II.76, 3–5; cf. *P.Lond.* V.1713, 18–21. *Abaskantos:* Danielle Bonneau, "L'apotropaïque 'Abaskantos' en Égypte," *RHR* 199 (1982):23–36. Names of apotropaic genii: Jan Quaegebeur, "A propos de Teilouteilou, nom magique, et de Tēroutērou, nom de femme," *Enchoria* 4 (1974):19–29.

[83] Tutu and emperors: Rondot 1990; Kaper 1991:60–61. Patronage of Montu cult: Bataille 1952:92 (argues that it checked the power of the Amun cult in Thebes) and above, 4.2. See, in general, Kákosy 1995:2916–17 (appropriation of Egyptian culture under Domitian), 2983 (royal hypostasization in Tutu), and Quaegebeur 1983b:50.

## 3.5 Gods of Safe Fertility

Among the diverse local communities of Egypt and their respective super-natural worlds a figure dedicated to fertility in one place might be under-stood as primarily apotropaic in another, often under different names. Thus there is some arbitrariness in distinguishing Taweret and Bes (or his image) from the figures above. "Bes"—a name that only in Greco-Roman times became the predominant term for an archaic dwarf figure with both leonine and ithyphallic traits—clearly functioned in a protec-tive role for multiple communities and homes in Roman Egypt, often in conjunction with Tutu. So also the goddess Taweret (also one of several ancient names for the female hippopotamus image) often assimilated the protective functions of a frightening analogue: knife-wielding hippo-potami inscribed on ancient ivory wands and on the walls of many tem-ples.[84] But well before the Greco-Roman period both figures seem to have assumed predominantly "fertility" traits: sexuality, conception, and maternal, obstetrical, and pediatric safety.[85] Indeed, Bes's increasingly important protective functions at this time are intrinsically linked to his powers for safety in childbirth.

### 3.5.1 Taweret

We might reconstruct a "popular" cult of Taweret (Greek *Thoēris*) as consisting of the following phenomena: priestly performances of rituals in her name before lay supplicants; temples' provision of stelae, incuba-tion areas, or other kinds of accessible "places" for drawing on the god-dess's powers; and the extension of her power from the temple into the domestic or village sphere with amulets, domestic shrines, and accom-panying rites. But the evidence for such a popular cult, vivid as it is, derives almost entirely from the Ptolemaic period. A jug in the shape of Taweret with a hole in one breast from which fluid—an expression of the goddess's power—would pour, found in the pilgrims' "arcade" at Saq-qara, suggests priestly ministrations to women seeking to protect a preg-nancy or lactation. A stela portraying "Isis of Sheta," a local goddess with the body of Taweret, presents her holding snakes and scorpions and mounted on a crocodile in a variation of the iconography of the Horus-*cippi*. The stela shows the extent of local variation in understand-ing Taweret and invoking her power.[86]

---

[84] See, for example, Cairo ## 9433–34, 9437, 9439, in Daressy 1903:43–48. On Deir el-Bahri, see Laskowska-Kusztal 1984:77–81.

[85] See Baines 1991:127–31.

[86] Taweret jug: Saqqara #1032, in G. Martin 1981:91, pl. 32; cf. Berlin inv. 19791, on which Morenz 1973:106–7. Isis of Sheta stela: Bernand Bruyère, "Un ex-voto d'Isis-Toëris au Musée d'Ismaïla," *ASAE* 50 (1950):515–22.

These materials might not necessarily pertain beyond the Ptolemaic period. But given the scope of Taweret's powers illustrated in these materials it is hardly surprising that papyri of the Roman period document the persistence of her temples in some form as late as the fifth century. This cult seems to have been valued highly enough at the local and domestic levels that popular support and reverence could make up for social and economic pressures for its demise.

The fullest documentation for the cult of Thoēris during the Roman period comes from Oxyrhynchus. By the size of her temple there it would seem that Oxyrhynchus was the regional center of the Thoēris cult. The structure and its processional avenue become a landmark from which an entire city quarter takes its name by the late first century C.E. Its civic importance and, presumably, continual visits by supplicants earned the Thoērion an unusually large guard staff for the end of the third century; and even in 342 the Oxyrhynchus town council was keeping the post of guard to the Thoērion as a required civic duty. An individual is still specified as "priest of Thoēris" in 339.[87]

The last mention of this temple comes as late as 462, when a symposium is to be held in it. The space evidently continued to maintain at least some holiness. The Thoērion had been the site of ritual dinners through the third century, so a symposium may not have constituted a break with the temple's ritual tradition.[88]

Beyond these sacral meals there is some evidence for a popular religion connected with the Oxyrhynchus Thoērion, perhaps similar to the kind of piety evident in the Ptolemaic materials. For example, Taweret of Oxyrhynchus maintains her Egyptian significance rather than being assimilated entirely to Athena, her Hellenistic alter ego—a compelling example of the cultural limits of Hellenism as a medium for local religion. And when a second-century man writes his wife that "every day and evening I perform the devotions on your behalf to Thoēris, who loves you," he reflects some dimension of private or domestic piety. "Devotions [*proskunēmata*]" here would certainly involve a domestic shrine of sorts, while the specific reference to Thoēris's love seems to reflect the special protection this goddess expressed toward women.[89]

The main Oxyrhynchus Thoērion also represented the axis for a net-

---

[87] PSI III.215, 6. Thoērion post as liturgy: *P.Oxy* I.43v = W.Chr. 474, iv, 14–23; *P.Oxy* XIV.1627. In general on Oxyrhynchus Thoērion: documentation in Quaegebeur et al. 1985:225n.46, extending to 331 C.E., with fullest discussion in Whitehorne 1995:3080–82.

[88] PSI III.175, on which text see Quaegebeur et al. 1985:225. On other Thoērion ritual meals, see Ludwig Koenen, "Eine Einladung zur Kline des Sarapis," *ZPE* 1 (1967):121–26; *P.Oxy* XLI.2976, 2 (second century C.E.).

[89] *P.Oxy* III.528, 4–6. On women's devotion to fecundity goddesses in the New Kingdom, see Pinch 1993:342–43.

work of other Taweret shrines, also still operating through the third century and extending well beyond the city: a "tetrastyle" (probably a small shrine like that of Isis at Luxor), a temple "of Thoēris of the Revealing Gods" and another shrine of "Thoēris Sintano," an Egyptian title ("seat of the fair of countenance") that might reflect this shrine's Egyptian character.[90]

What went on in these temples obviously amounted to more than a simple fertility cult and extends our understanding of how local gods could become quite successful in this period even while preserving their Egyptian character. The "revealing gods [*exagoreioi*]" seem to denote a type of oracular image borne in procession by cult servants, mentioned in a mid-third-century papyrus as *theagoi*.[91] That a traditional Egyptian processional oracle would be continuing out of these small native temples in this period, when a diversity of oracular forms were operating also, suggests the resilience of the cult's Egyptian character—a cleaving to Egyptian religious performance in a culture where gymnasium-based spectacles were already in the ascendance.

But the Oxyrhynchite had more than one option in seeking Taweret's mantic powers: another text, of the second century, seems to refer to incubation. In the form of a letter "to Thoēris, greatest goddess," the writer declares that "I was dining yesterday with my friends in your most blessed precinct. [I was?] overcome by sleep [ . . . ]"[92] The letter was probably meant as a request to the goddess that some fortune she had revealed in a dream would come to pass. The supplicant's reference to a collective meal eaten before incubation in the sacred precinct may reveal a connection between the ritual *symposia* mentioned in other papyri and the incubation cult itself.

The Oxyrhynchus evidence shows not so much an increase in the veneration of Taweret as the strong hold such traditional fertility deities exerted on the Egyptian and Greco-Egyptian population. By all accounts the cult continued throughout much of the fourth century, vital both to civic fortune and to the fertility, maternity, and broader religious needs of the regional populace, whose connection to the central temple would long have been secured through the multiple Taweret shrines in the area, of both Egyptian and Greek character. But the language of the papyri implies that Taweret's Egyptian meaning and the Egyptian character of her cult were maintained and communicated in Hellenistic terms, anchoring a city wed to gymnasium culture, Greek literature, and spectacles.

---

[90] *P.Oxy* I.43v iv.12–13; *P.Lond.* 2554, 9–11 (ed. Roberts 1934). On Sintano, see Quaegebeur et al. 1985:229 and Whitehorne 1995:3082.

[91] See Roberts 1934:23–25; *P.Heid.* IV.334, 5, with Bärbel Kramer in *P.Heid.* IV, pp. 240–42, and below, 4.2.1.

[92] *P.Oxy* XLI.2976.

Finally, the continuing *symposia* in the Thoērion might remind us of the fourth-century ironworkers of Hermonthis who made pilgrimage to the abandoned temple at Deir el-Bahri for a ritual symposium.[93] These ritual meals among religious societies remained a form of honoring traditional sacred places and preparing for some sort of oracular presence from the god.

### 3.5.2 Bes

The god Bes has been the subject of extensive Egyptological study, usually tracing the origin of an image that stands out from much other Egyptian iconography: the dwarflike, leonine, ithyphallic, frontally posed figure that served as a widely popular guardian of maternity and infants from the Middle Kingdom on.[94] And whereas the widespread appearance of this image in small domestic figurines, domestic murals, and infants' coffins testifies to its deep popular roots, other appearances in such "priestly" contexts as temple reliefs and ritual texts show that the Bes image also functioned in—or was perpetually appropriated by—official ritual and myth. The link was Bes's protection of the Horus-child in his mythical distresses, an archetype for all children in distress.[95]

It is only in the XXI Dynasty that this protective image begins to assume the name "Bes" (a word perhaps originally signifying "premature"), concurrently with the development of the Harpocrates (Horus-child) figure; and from that point Bes gathers increasing popularity as a multivalent "savior" figure in a diversity of media. On the Horus-*cippi,* where Bes's face surmounts the child Horus on the crocodiles like a fearsome mask (whence, it has been argued, the distinctive frontality of the Bes image arose), Bes is often invoked as the protector of the supplicant (pls. 4 and 6). On some *cippi* and stelae the mask, as it were, falls to the neck, and it is Bes himself who assumes the sole protective and apotropaic role: winged, clutching or trampling enemies, and occasionally surmounted by the vindictive genii under his control, like Tutu (pl. 12). In the Brooklyn Bes stela a winged Bes crowned with multiple heads stands over bound human enemies on a limestone relief that evidently framed the outlet of a water pipe by a temple, probably to deliver "apotropaic water" much like the older Horus-*cippi.*[96]

---

[93] Łajtar 1991:70.

[94] See esp. Michailidis 1960/62; James F. Romano, "The Origin of the Bes-Image," *BES* 2 (1980):39–56, and "The Bes-image in Pharaonic Egypt" (Ph.D. dissertation, New York University, 1989); Malaise 1990; Jeanne Bulté, *Talismans égyptiens d'heureuse maternité* (Paris: CNRS, 1991); Meeks 1992; Dasen 1993, ch. 6.

[95] Malaise 1990:701–11.

[96] Brooklyn 37.229 (unpubl.). On Bes's function on Horus-*cippi:* Malaise 1990:703–

As a protective force in general the Bes image was appropriated also into private or priestly media of the Late Period: he is "Sopd who smites Asiatics" on a royal *naos* and "Bes of the seven faces . . . [who] represents the invincible forces of Amun-Re" in the Brooklyn Magical Papyrus.[97] But the many terra-cotta images of Bes with sword and shield, or less frequently Roman armor, show an apotropaic Bes produced largely for domestic protection (pls. 1, 11, 14). It was by virtue of his popular apotropaic powers that Bes became a common symbol in the production of magical gems during the Greco-Roman period, becoming thus associated with ever more deities in the Greco-Roman world. One notes, however, that despite the international dissemination of his image (under a variety of names), Bes maintained a particular resistance to Hellenistic influence in posture and detail. Such iconographic resilience can only be ascribed to the profound connection Egyptians felt between Bes and the Bes image and the most basic ritual needs of domestic life: protection, maternity, and healing.[98]

There exists no clearer demonstration of this connection, and of the very breadth of power with which Bes was perceived as operating in domestic life, than a crude stela of the Roman period that presents Bes atop crocodiles, the traditional apotropaic posture of the Horus-*cippi,* holding a weapon, his phallus clearly visible (pl. 12). But Bes is not just a warrior here: a Greek inscription on the reverse invokes him in intimately maternal terms:

> Greatest god of the maternity of women, bounteous god of the maternity of women, planter of female maternity, benefactor of the maternity of women, sower of the maternity of women, protector of female maternity, guardian of the maternity of women, healer of the maternity of women, father of female

17; Borghouts 1978, #93. On the derivation of frontality from the mask, see Youri Volokhine, "Dieux, masques et hommes: à propos de la formation de l'iconographie de Bès," *BSE* 18 (1994):81–95. On consolidation of Bes as a protective image: Jean Leclant, "A propos d'une terre cuite de Bès à l'oryx," in *Hommages à Lucien Lerat* 1, ed. by H. Walter, Centres de recherches d'histoire ancienne 55 (Paris: Les Belles Lettres, 1984), 409–19; Michailidis 1960/62:61–62, pls. IX–XII. On Bes's amalgamation of protective powers, see, on the Brooklyn Magical Papyrus, Sauneron 1960b:277–87; 1970:11–17; Malaise 1990:719–22. In general on the development of dwarf figure as Bes: Meeks 1992.

[97] Naos of Nectanebos II from Saft el-Hinna: Roeder 1914:58–99, #70021 = Edouard Naville, *The Shrine of Saft el Henneh,* Egypt Exploration Fund, Memoirs 5 (London: Trübner, 1887), 10, pls. 2–3; Brooklyn Magical Papyrus iv, 1–2, tr. Sauneron 1970:23.

[98] Armored Bes figurines: Dunand 1990:39–41, 47, ##34–40, 58–59, plus British Museum GR 1888.6—1.110 and 1.96 = Terra-cottas C574, C608. Török 1995, #119, portrays a terra-cotta armored Bes on a horse rampant. Dissemination of Bes on amulets and gems: H.-C. Puech, "Le dieu Bésa et la magie hellénistique," *Documents* 2, 7 (1930):415–25; A. Delatte, "Études sur la magie grecque, IV. Amulettes inédites des Musées d'Athènes," *Le Musée belge* 18 (1914):33–37; Delatte/Derchain 1964:126–41.

maternity, redeemer of female maternity, master of the maternity of women, nourisher of the maternity of women, guardian of the maternity of women, rain of the maternity of women, awakener of the maternity of women, quickener of the maternity of women.[99]

In light of this invocation it is likely that the abundant terra-cotta Bes figurines, some coupled with a feminine consort "Beset" (pl. 15), may have been placed by beds to facilitate conception, to guard over pregnancies, or to protect infants. Ritual veneration of such images appears in a small faience amulet of the Roman period, in which Bes is framed in a shrine or wall niche (pl. 16; cf. pl. 17) and even more vividly in a stela posing a Bes figure next to bread loaves and wine or water jug, typical domestic offerings (pl. 13). Terra-cotta jugs in the shape of Bes or his head may have been part of such devotional rites, or for bringing back consecrated fluids from temples, or part of some kind of ritual to facilitate childbirth.[100] Two obstetrical spells of the XIX Dynasty suggest such a use of the Bes image in instructing that a "dwarf of clay" be placed on the belly of a woman in labor. In one spell the woman is supposed to appeal to the dwarf figurine to fetch an amulet from the goddess Hathor. Thus we see the dramatic modes in which Bes figurines might function in ritual: like images of saints in medieval Europe they could be expected to provide active mediation between supplicant and national god.[101] Egyptians of the Roman era evidently saw Bes's powers as extending from protection, as in the stelae and the warrior postures, to the most physical aspects of maternity.

Given the popular, even domestic sphere in which cults of Bes evidently took place, we may ask whether the veneration of Bes translated into a priesthood or institution of sorts. In earlier times (pharaonic and Ptolemaic) it seems that a ritual specialist would be associated with Bes through her or his capacity as healer and obstetrician. A house excavated in Kahun, east of the Fayyum, contained a large Bes mask of painted canvas, as well as other ritual accoutrements associated with the god; and one is tempted to ascribe these materials to someone with the status of

[99] Collection Michailidis, in Michailidis 1960/62:67–68.

[100] Bes shrine amulet: Boston, Museum of Fine Arts, amulet 1995.710. Stela of Bes and jugs: Budapest inv. T.506, in Castiglione 1957 and Török 1995, #11. Compare similar altar between Bes and Tutu in Brooklyn inv. 58.98 = Sauneron 1960b, #3, pl. XIV. Bes jugs: Alexandria, G.-R. Museum, inv. 16318 (= Breccia 1930/34, #274); 13706 (Rm 2), 1099 (Rm 10); Louvre inv. E 12470 (= Dunand 1990, #993), E 12472 (= Dunand 1990, #994), E 20707 (= Dunand 1990, #995), E 4667 (= Dunand 1990, #996). See Török 1995:58 on the use of Bes jugs (cf. 39, ##23–24). See also Bruyère 1939:102–3 on domestic Bes cult in Deir el-Medina (New Kingdom).

[101] P.Leiden I.348, spells 30–31, tr. Borghouts 1971:29 (= Borghouts 1978, ##60–61). See discussions in Borghouts 1971:154n.370 and Dasen 1993:52–53, 70–71.

midwife or obstetrical healer, perhaps associated with a local temple.[102] A vivid example of a full-fledged "Bes shrine" was uncovered at the pilgrims' arcade at Ptolemaic Saqqara: a series of rooms decorated with enormous paintings and terra-cotta reliefs of Bes (accompanied by nude females); and from these rooms (or in connection with them) an extensive array of phallic and Bes figurines were apparently purveyed. Both the erotic figures and the shrine itself served popular desires for maternity, as focused upon conception and the erotic component of fecundity. The shrine certainly would have required some kind of attendants with quasi-priestly authority to receive and store offerings.[103] Infants' coffins of terra-cotta decorated with Bes heads (Late or Hellenistic Period) may provide another glimpse of Bes "priests'" ritual services: mortuary rites for those whom Bes could not protect in this life.[104]

Ritual accoutrements of the Roman period that are associated with Bes—torches, jugs—make it likely that this type of Bes "priest" could have persisted, a local specialist in obstetrical ritual with some links to the temple institution, whose procedures involved appealing to (or through) Bes and the god's images. And even in the Roman period the cult of Bes was in no way exclusive to the domestic sphere. Even though most terra-cotta images suggest domestic contexts, local temples might own finer images, like the bronze and silver Beses listed in a late-second-century inventory of the temple of Soknopaiou Nesos, or larger ones—many terra-cottas measure over a meter high.[105] The Hathor temple at Dendara itself seems to have been some sort of regional center of Bes veneration, probably due to the traditional affiliation of Bes with the goddess Hathor, whose major temple stood there. Its second birth-temple, begun under Trajan with continued construction and decoration under Antoninus Pius, places special emphasis on the figure of Bes—both

---

[102] W. M. Flinders Petrie, *Kahun, Gurob, and Hawara* (London: Kegan Paul, Trench, Trübner, 1890), 30 (#58); pl. VIII, ##13–14, 27, with interpretations in Dasen 1993:70, 80.

[103] On Saqqara Bes rooms, see J. E. Quibell, *Excavations at Saqqara (1905–1906)* (Cairo: IFAO, 1907), 12–14, pls. XXVI–XXXIII; H. S. Smith, "Saqqara. Late Period," *LexÄg* 5 (1984):424. On the interpretation of Saqqara "erotica," see Philippe Derchain, "Observations sur les erotica," in G. Martin 1981:166–70, and Pinch's astute remarks on the erotic component of Middle and New Kingdom fertility figurines (1993:219–25). On the concept of a Bes "cult," see Dasen 1993:80–82.

[104] Meeks 1992:428–29; Dasen 1993:77; and on Bes coffins (found at Abydos): E. R. Ayrton, C. T. Currelly, and A. E. P. Weigall, *Abydos* 3 (London: Egypt Exploration Fund, 1904), 52, pls. XXXVIII, 6; XXIII, 5.

[105] *BGU* II.387, ii, 9–11. On terra-cottas, see Nachtergael 1985. Bes figurines rank as the third most common in collections of terra-cottas (following Harpocrates and Isis): Dunand 1984:21 (Cairo Museum); 1990:29 (Louvre). Among larger terra-cottas are Alexandria, G.-R. Museum, Rm 1 #23379 and Rm 20 #21123; Louvre inv. E 20698 (= Dunand 1990, #56).

the apotropaic power of his militant pose on column capitals (pls. 10 and 22) and scenes of his dance before Ihy-Harsomtus (a type of Harpocrates) above the outer corridor. During the same period, according to a papyrus, Dendara celebrated an annual festival of Bes—perhaps the most opportune time for appealing to the god for favors in childbirth and children's health.[106]

If we can suppose the existence in the Roman period of ritual specialists operating under the authority of, or as mediators of, Bes in their obstetrical capacity, then such specialists may have been officiants at festivals like Dendara's Bēsia; and perhaps there is some relationship between the local authority of such specialists and the prominent Bes images in birth-temples like that at Dendara. But even these hypotheses of Bes priesthoods stem from data—masks, shrines, crude coffins—that reveal the same sphere of domestic and protective piety as the Roman terracotta images. They point not to an exclusive priesthood but to specialists in the ritual service of domestic life and its misfortunes. The images on the birth-temple of Dendara and the Bes festival there seem to have sprung not so much from priestly texts as from the world of domestic ritual and its inevitable need for binding centers or axes. In this respect, Bes seems to have remained essentially a "folk" deity, a part of the cycle of life for Roman Egyptians. And in this intimate role the god seems to have resisted decline as much as his iconography did through Hellenization.

At Dendara itself, Bes's abiding "presence" and popularity through at least the fourth century are evident paradoxically in the meticulous Christian mutilation of the Bes images on the birth-temple. Whereas the extensive lower reliefs of Hathor and the child-god Ihy-Harsomtus remain largely intact, most of the Bes heads have been systematically mutilated, suggesting that Christians recognized the abiding power these images held for people in the vicinity (see pl. 22).

But popular allegiance to Bes was even more widespread through the cultural stresses of the third and fourth centuries, as we find in two historical incidents reported in literary texts for their political or ideological significance. "In the furthest part of the Thebaid," begins Ammianus Marcellinus, "there is a town called Abydos, where a god locally called Besa used to reveal the future through an oracle and was worshipped with traditional rites by the inhabitants of the surrounding regions."

---

[106] *P.Heid.* inv. 1818, 8, in Youtie 1973; cf. 188–89 on *Bēsia*. On Bes at Dendara, see Bruyère 1939:103–5; Daumas 1958:135–44; Malaise 1990:690. Cf. Metropolitan Museum of Art inv. 23.2.35 and 1971.226 as samples of Dendara iconography. On the construction of the Roman birth-temple, see François Daumas, *Les mammisis de Denderah* (Cairo: IFAO, 1959), xix–xxv.

We will discuss the singular development of this Bes oracle in the following chapter as a phenomenon of both priestly innovation and, more broadly, the widespread oracular activities of the Roman period (see below, 4.3.2). But Ammianus here provides evidence of the same popular Bes veneration represented in the terra-cottas, inasmuch as the oracle is an extension of what is "worshipped with traditional rites [*priscis . . . caerimoniis*] by the inhabitants of the surrounding regions."[108] Moreover, one Demetrius of Alexandria, brought to trial for allegedly subversive inquiries of this oracle, was apparently accustomed to performing some ritual veneration to Bes: "he maintained that he had observed this practice [of propitiating Bes] from early youth."[109] Such piety on the part of Demetrius, who was surely not a native of Abydos, indicates that the everyday cult of Bes extended well beyond regional "centers" like Dendara and, at this point, Abydos.

Bes's strong hold in Abydos by the fourth century is evident not only in Ammianus's distanced account but also in a more proximate (if less sympathetic) source, the Coptic *Life of Apa Moses,* who sought to eradicate traditional religion in the region of Abydos in the late fifth century.[110] His encounter with a "demon" Bes, complete with features recognizable from Bes iconography, in a temple that is identifiably the very Memnonion of Abydos where the oracles were delivered, shows that the god in his popular apotropaic function continued to be viewed as a force in the temple until late in the fifth century.[111] The lacunose manuscript begins here with the appeal of some Christian villagers:

[ . . . ]They prostrated themselves at the feet of our father Apa Moses, they implored him because there was an evil demon that had entered the temple that was called Bes, which was situated to the north of the monastery, and it was going out and attacking passersby, and some of those attacked had become blind in one eye, the hands of others had dried up, the feet of others had become lame, the faces of others had grown distorted, and others had been rendered deaf and dumb. For there was a multitude that had seen him leaping on the ground in the temple and changing into a host of forms. And this, then, was the demon that was doing so much harm, God maintaining him until he should manifest his miracles.

But the holy Apa Moses took with him seven brothers courageous in the faith: Apa Paul, Apa Andrew, Apa Elijah, Apa Joseph, Apa Psate, and Apa Phoibamon; I also went with them, me a sinner. He led us forth and entered

---

[107] Ammianus 19.12.3, tr. Hamilton 1986:181.
[108] Ammianus 19.12.3.
[109] *propitiandi . . . a prima aduliscentia* (Ammianus 19.12.12).
[110] Texts and translations: Amélineau 1888/95:680–706; Till 1936:46–81. Discussions: Coquin 1986; Wipszycka 1988:155–56.
[111] Kákosy 1966a:189–95.

in the evening. The saint said to us, "Pray with perseverance as we implore the Lord." As soon as we had begun to pray the sanctuary [Copt. *p-ma*] shook around us and there were great noises before us like lightning-bolts and thunder-claps. Our father said, "Fear not! It is (only) deceptions of demons!" And seeing his great courage we recovered ourselves and persevered in prayer.

In the middle of the night the demon cried out, "How long will you make us suffer, O Moses? But know that I am not afraid of you and your prayers can do nothing to me, O you who wait in vain all this night. Flee! Don't get yourself killed and don't kill those with you, for I have caused the death of a host of arrogant ones like you![ . . .

. . . ] again we heard the noise of the multitudes who ran after us and did not approach us at all. Once again he shook the sanctuary in which we stood, such that it was on the point of tumbling down on us and one of us fell on his face—so much did the ground tremble under us. But my father grabbed us and raised us up, saying "Fear not, but be confident, as you will see the glory of god!"[ . . . ][112]

The details of the dramatic combat of forces have little historical value, but the legend does attest to an identifiable god with an indigenous name, Bes, believed to be residing in a temple with which he had been associated a hundred or so years earlier.[113]

The abiding presence of the "cult" of Bes in the homes and villages of Roman Egypt must be attributed to the intrinsic relationship of Bes and the Bes image with the most intimate and critical points of life in ancient and traditional cultures. Whereas many deities like Isis and Taweret might guarantee maternal fertility, Bes functioned primarily to protect it—hence his later iconography shows as close a relationship to apotropaic figures like Tutu as to "fertility" figures like Hathor and Taweret.

Furthermore, whatever we might propose about the structure of a Bes priesthood, the degree of centralization of Bes cults, or the dependency of domestic Bes cults on particular temples, the various intimations of a great tradition of Bes do not seem to have been so extensive that they were subject to the vicissitudes of imperial patronage, munificence, and legislation. The exception, of course, is the Abydos oracle, for that local sphere of ritual authority associated with Bes would not in itself explain the rise of a Greek-literate scribal institution for the Bes oracle there. Does it show, in fact, the consolidation and Hellenization of such Bes

---

[112] Ed. Amélineau 1888/95:689–90; tr. based on Amélineau's.

[113] It is likewise tempting to see in Jerome's description of a demonic "dwarf [*homunculus*] . . . its forehead bristling with horns" in his Life of Paul of Thebes (8, *PL* 23:23) a distant perversion (and relegation to the desert) of an image that was widely popular in Egyptian homes.

priests, the diversification of priestly functions serving an oracle that had begun on a simpler scale under Bes priests, or the clever appropriation by Mediterranean-savvy priests of a popular god's authority? However one accounts for this important religious development and its relationship to the popular domain, allegiance to Bes on the part of the common people did not decline significantly in the third and fourth centuries. Indeed, here we see precisely the kind of pervasive cult that would be overlooked by monasteries and Christian governors, limited as it was to the local and domestic spheres of life. It may indeed have been Bes's deep significance to traditional civic and home life that led to the synthesis and expansion of the Abydos oracle cult over the first four centuries of the Roman era, as I argue in 4.3.

## 3.6 Domestic Religion

With Bes and to a lesser extent Taweret the evidence for the continuity of traditional deities comes increasingly to point to local and domestic contexts: small images that might be set in wall niches, appeals for divine favor and power in intimate aspects of life, rites performed in private, often family settings. Both Bes and Taweret continued as identifiable forces in local communities because of this domestic context, this interweaving of their images with the cycle of life in traditional peasant and urban settings. And yet one cannot thereby polarize domestic against temple religion as if the former were fundamentally autonomous from the latter. The importance of the Thoērion in Oxyrhynchus demonstrates that individual domestic cults of a traditional fertility deity might be understood in connection with that god's local (or regional) cultic "center."

A local "center" of domestic cults would exert continuing influence on those cults through its festivals, processions, and external services like stelae and oracles. Conversely, local and domestic devotions to these "popular" gods of protection and fertility would lend social support and popular credence to their central temples (e.g., the Bes oracle at Abydos in its connection with popular Bes worship). It is likely that the relationship between these two points in the axis, the local or regional temple on the one hand (as center) and the domestic shrines on the other (as peripheral anchors), provided the context for both continuity and the appearance of decline, as religious activity shifted centripetally toward flourishing temple or centrifugally to the home altar depending on political and cultural circumstances.

This axis appears vividly in the Coptic narrative of the fall of the temple of "Kothos," discussed earlier (2.6.1), in which the local populace takes up arms to defend the temple against Makarios of Tkôw and his monks:

> There was a village on the west side of the river in which they worship an idol called Kothos which is mounted in the niches of their houses. And when they go inside their doors, they are accustomed to bow down their head and worship him. . . . And when we had come northward in the region for about five or six miles, I saw one of their temples by some vineyards beside the road. And my father [Apa Macarius] went toward the temple. . . . But he had not yet reached the door of the temple when the demon who dwells in Kothos, the idol, cried out: Make haste and cast Macarius of Tkôw out of this place, for a tremor has come over me when I saw him. And if he spends one more hour in this place, I shall go away from this very place, and you will never find me.[114]

This passage offers an important glimpse of traditional domestic piety as it continued in the fifth century.[115] Houses contain wall niches (Copt. *shousht*) in which small figurines of the local god are set. Devotion to the local god through the medium of his figurine takes the form of formal gestures performed at transition points like entry—a typical occasion for minor "rites of passage" as Arnold Van Gennep once described.[116] And the piety expressed by means of the figurine is continuous with the piety and social solidarity generated by local temples with priesthoods. Indeed, the figurine in its niche or altar would serve to some degree as an extension, even a microcosm, of the temple and its cult.

### 3.6.1 Domestic Images and Figurines

To what degree does material and documentary evidence bear out this Coptic author's vignette? The sizable corpora of terra-cotta figurines and stelae that were manufactured continuously through the fourth century certainly corroborate one essential element of the picture.[117] Even in the fifth century Shenoute seems quite aware of the manufacture of such domestic icons when he pronounces, "Woe upon those who will worship wood and stone or anything made by man's handiwork (with) wood and stone, or (modeled by putting) clay inside them."[118] And after vandalizing the domestic shrine of the local patron Gesios, Shenoute tells a con-

---

[114] *Panegyric* ms. M609 V.1, 3–4, ed. and tr. D. W. Johnson 1980, 1:29–31, 2:21–24.

[115] See above, 1.3.3, on the historical interpretation of such hagiographical witnesses to late Egyptian religion.

[116] See Arnold Van Gennep, *The Rites of Passage* (Chicago: University of Chicago Press, 1960), 24–25.

[117] On dates of manufacture, see Dunand 1979:29–31; 1990:9–13. On archaeological levels of finds, see Nachtergael 1985.

[118] Discourses 4: The Lord Thundered, ed. Amélineau 1909:381. See Van der Vliet 1993:111–12.

gregation that he removed an "idol" of Pan-Min, the traditional local god of Panopolis.[119] The name "Kothos" in the Coptic text above has not yet been recognized and may be imaginary—decorating a typical portrait of traditional local piety of the Coptic period. But the range of deities represented in figurines extends from the local or regional, like Tutu or Sobek, to the transregional, like Isis or Harpocrates or Amun; and one can presume that any local cult such as "Kothos" represents would have had its corresponding domestic icons.[120]

The domestic image of greatest popularity according to the proportion of his terra-cotta figurines among various excavations was Harpocrates, a youthful form of Horus (and related gods) fairly distinct from the royal or warrior Horus of major temples like Edfu (pl. 9). The iconography suggests the abiding strength of popular or domestic cult in determining the objects and form of everyday piety; and we might thus use the Harpocrates image as an example of the importance of domestic figurines in general in connecting people to temples.[121]

While the Harpocrates figure certainly arose as a priestly synthesis, the terra-cottas of the Roman period reflect the figure's thorough domestication. Through the same "Hellenistic" techniques of representation that developed the Isis figurines Harpocrates becomes a medium of fertility in field (with a pot), flock (on a goose), and family (with enlarged phallus), as well as an apotropaion (with military accoutrements, accompanied by the sphinx Tutu, or most commonly on the Horus-*cippi*).[122]

Piety around the Harpocrates image often extended to a social dimension—*Harpocrateia* festivals are documented from early-second-century Fayyum—but the actual priestly rites of this form of Horus would be peripheral to local temples' cults. On the basis of the popular Harpocrates figurines, many of which show the child-god stirring or eating from a pot, one may infer a domestic cult tradition of preparing festival food in the god's honor, presumably for children. "Official" Harpocrates worship may simply have taken the form of an image's procession along with others or its mere display and adornment (perhaps ritually clothed on certain days) in an interior or exterior niche, as in the small Isis shrines of Luxor and Ras el-Soda.[123] The temple's figure of Harpoc-

---

[119] Shenoute, "Only I Tell Everyone Who Dwells in This Village," = Leipoldt #26 (3:89), on which see Emmel 1994. Cf. Bataille 1952:103–4 on Pan-Min in Ptolemaic Thebes.

[120] See Perdrizet 1921. Sobek figurines are rare: Dunand 1990:294, ##887–88 (Louvre), and collection James H. Schwartz (New York).

[121] Nachtergael 1985; Dunand 1990:28–29.

[122] Dunand 1979:73–87.

[123] On *Harpocrateia,* see Perpillou-Thomas 1993:88–89 re: P.Fayyum 117, 11; *SPP* XXII.183, 113. Perpillou-Thomas connects this festival with that "of the child" in the calendar of the Roman Esna temple (Sauneron 1962a:17); but this latter calendar renders this Harpocrates cult quite peripheral to those of Neith and Heka. On Harpocrates figu-

rates may well have constituted a "center" for the domestic cult by the mere fact that its grandeur and size exceeded that of the domestic terra-cotta figures. If it emerged only occasionally, as at most traditional temples, the image's appearance may have been all the more striking, perhaps inspiring the purchase of identical miniatures or a longing for some contact with the image to bring home. A fourth-century rite for making an amulet reflects the kind of intrinsic power borne by the temple's Harpocrates figure as well as the private world of devotion to it: "On [a strip] from a linen cloth taken from a marble statue of Harpokrates in any temple [whatever] write with myrrh these things: . . . "[124] In the Harpocrates images one sees the overall religious importance of the terra-cotta figurine in Roman Egypt: the endorsement, yet also appropriation, of temple tradition by domestic religion and its axis, the home shrine.[125]

### 3.6.2 Domestic Shrines

It is quite certain that these figurines stood in homes. Many of the extant figurines were actually found in houses (and some graves); and other house sites have provided evidence of just the kind of wall niches described in the above "Kothos" episode. The Fayyum town of Karanis in particular has yielded a wealth of such niches, all from the Roman period, some decorated with Hellenistic molding and motifs or even with paintings. Many terra-cotta images, like the enshrined Bes amulet in plate 16, portray gods within shrine porticoes much like those that framed wall niches in the Roman period (pl. 17).[126]

But beyond such figurines the domestic cults of Roman Egypt (as cross-culturally) involved all manner of paraphernalia, often miniature or cheaper (wood, terra-cotta) versions of temple paraphernalia. Lamps and

---

rines in temples, see Adriani 1935/39:140–42, pl. LVI; and Leclant 1951:456. On festival food at *Harpocrateia*, see Török 1995:119 (#159), with additional images in Dunand 1979, ##134–87 (cf. ibid., 74–75).

124 *PGM* IV.1073–75, tr. Grese, in Betz (ed.) 1986:59. The linen cloth would presumably refer to the image's sacred garments, wrapped on special festival days.

125 Cf. Dunand 1979:134–36 and Török 1995:20–21.

126 Nachtergael 1985:225; Rassart-Debergh 1990:48–49 on niches. See also Dunand 1979:8–9, 103–6. Enshrined Bes amulet: Boston, Museum of Fine Arts, Amulet 1995.710. On Karanis: Gazda 1983:31, fig. 54, with numerous archives on the Karanis site in the Kelsey Museum, University of Michigan. Compare the extensive data on domestic wall shrines and their contents in Ostia of the imperial and late antique periods in Jan Theo Bakker, *Living and Working with the Gods: Studies of Evidence for Private Religion and Its Material Environment in the City of Ostia (100–500 AD)*, Dutch Monographs on Ancient History and Archaeology 12 (Amsterdam: Gieben, 1994), 8–17, 32–42, 186–91; and more broadly David G. Orr, "Roman Domestic Religion: The Evidence of the Household Shrines," *ANRW* II.16.2 (1978):1557–91, noting the fundamental *independence* of the Roman domestic cult from any priestly "center."

incense-burners in the shape of temples, miniature altars, and even the miniature *cippi* of Horus represent a process of domestication-through-miniaturization of temple cult and, perhaps, an increasing importance of domestic cults in the Roman period.[127] And in the Fayyum the novel display of painted portraits of gods within domestic shrines was growing in popularity from the second century C.E., an iconography that would be wholly appropriated by fourth-century Christian craftspeople to portray its martyrs and saints.[128]

The small niche altars recalled in the "Kothos" episode and suggested in the archaeological remains would have contrasted with the larger domestic shrines maintained by priests and some village landowners. Private cultic structures appended to homes are certainly known from New Kingdom Egypt; and Libanius assumes their existence in the fourth-century Near East when he describes the festival gatherings of villagers at the homes of "village notables": "So, summoned on the usual day, they dutifully honored it and the shrine [*hedos*] in a manner that involved no risk."[129] But our best witness for such private shrines is Besa's Life of Shenoute, in an incident corroborated in the abbot's own sermons:

> One day, our father went to the city of Shmin to carry off in secrecy by night the idols in Gesios' house. . . . When they came to the pagans' door, the doors of the house opened immediately one after another until they entered the place where the idols were. So with the brothers who were with him, he picked them up, took them down to the river, smashed them in pieces and threw them in the river.[130]

Among these images, Shenoute later describes in a sermon, he found the figure of Pan-Min (mentioned above, 3.3), religious books of some sort, a lampstand, and offerings of bread and some liquid in a vessel.[131] Besa implies that the shrine was reached only from deep inside the house, more likely a traditional domestic arrangement that associated the shrine with the fortune of the home than secrecy. Yet, as we have discussed (2.7), Gesios's house may have been a mainstay of local religion in its traditional rites and festivities; and we may see this occasionally public

[127] Altars: Étienne Drioton, "Objets de culte domestique provenant de Médinet-Qoûta," *ASAE* 40 (1941):923–35, with Dunand 1990:310–13. Lamps as temples: Dunand 1976:75–76; 1990:317–18. Domestic Horus-*cippi*: László Kákosy, "Les stèles d'‘Horus sur les crocodiles' du Musée des beaux-arts," *Bulletin du Musée hongrois des beaux-arts* 34/35 (1970):22; Sternberg-El Hotabi 1994:242–43.

[128] Rassart-Debergh 1990:48–55.

[129] Libanius, *Or.* 30.19, ed. and tr. Norman, LCL, 2:116–17. On domestic sanctuaries in New Kingdom Egypt, see Ikram 1989 (Amarna).

[130] Besa, *Life of Shenoute* 125–26, ed. Leipoldt 1:57, tr. D. Bell 1983:77–78. Shenoute makes repeated reference to the episode in Discourses 4: Not Because a Fox Barks (Leipoldt 3, #24 = Barns 1964). See also Van der Vliet 1993:102–3.

[131] Shenoute, "Only I Tell Everyone Who Dwells in This Village" = Leipoldt 3:89, #26.

function in Besa's use of the plural—"pagans' [*ntenihellēnos*] door"—as much as to say it was a congregating place for all local "pagans."[132]

Such private shrines may have resembled in arrangement the layout of figurines and statues in the Luxor and Ras el-Soda temples: a central table on which a selection of popular divinities are arranged, with additional images in wall niches and set on bases. By comparison with domestic altars of other cultures we would expect that the layout of images and offerings expressed links between the home and the various dimensions of religious authority: the broader "national" deities, the local temple, minor protective or beneficent deities (e.g., Bes or Tutu), and rough, even aniconic "images" of domestic spirits.

### 3.6.3 Domestic Ritual

It is hard to estimate, merely on the basis of extant materials, the complexity and abundance of local and domestic rituals in a typical peasant village, even those in close communication with urban centers. But we can reconstruct some ritual elements of domestic religion in light of the domestic rites of other cultures. The "Kothos" episode, for example, envisions ritual in a domestic cult as involving private gesture. One would expect a similar use of gesture in the devotions of one Aelius Theon, who writes his girlfriend's father in the second century that "every day I make her [the girl's] devotions [*proskunēma*] before the god, the [ . . . ] Lord Serapis—and yours and her mother's" (*P.Oxy* LIX.3992, 13–17). It is more likely that such daily devotions would take place in a home or a small street shrine than in a major temple. The word *proskunēma* here clearly involves a combination of formal utterance, gesture, and perhaps an offering of some simplicity (since it would be produced daily).

The domestic cult offering seems to escape the papyri, which instead document sacrificial requirements for temple and festival. But a terracotta image of Bes in the Budapest Museum poses him between a jug and two loaves of bread, represented like the collections of offerings on classical Egyptian offering tables and offering scenes on temples (pl. 13). Likewise a protective stela of the same era in the Brooklyn Museum shows an offering table piled high and two jugs between Tutu and a warrior Bes.[133] Both stelae show that domestic cults of Bes (and presumably Tutu) involved the setting out of offerings—bread and some liquid, much

---

[132] A Coptic legend envisions a similar arrangement in the home of an Alexandrian devotee of Egyptian gods: inside the house is a "room [*koitōn*] . . . —the (sacred) place [*ma*] where his gods (stood)" (Ps-Cyril, "Miracles of the Three Children," 6 = Ms. Vat. copte 62, f. 180v–181r, ed. De Vis 1990, 2:187). The "Kothos" priest Homer in the Panegyric on Makarios is burned "along with the idols that had been found in his house" (5.11).

[133] Budapest inv. T.506, in Castiglione 1957 and now Török 1995, #11; Brooklyn Museum 58.98, in Sauneron 1960b, #3. See also Pinch 1993:335–36 on "folk" food offerings during the New Kingdom.

as Shenoute at one point describes as standing on Gesios's private altar, or even sweet-smelling plants, as he finds Gesios scattering in the demolished temple of Atripe.[134] The use of such offerings would in turn imply that sacred figurines were not always relegated to niches in homes but were often set up in the context of a domestic altar, with room for offerings and their vessels, lamps and incense, and additional decoration during festival time. The terra-cotta Bes "jugs," whose crudeness of manufacture points toward a context more at the "domestic pole" than the "temple pole," may have held sacred liquids brought home from temples during festivals.

The fourth-century *Life of Pachomius* provides another angle on the offerings of the domestic cult: "As a child [Pachomius's] parents took him with them somewhere on the river to sacrifice to those [creatures] that are in the waters."[135] Here the devotions made toward local supernatural powers are truly a family activity. They articulate a bond between the family unit in its susceptibility to misfortune and need for agricultural fortune, and an exclusively local type of supernatural being that was propitiated apart from the temples' major deities and traditionally held the ability both to protect and to motivate river and field.

As in many cultures, the domestic cult (like private piety within temples) often involves the lighting of lamps to symbolize a continuous devotion at certain times of the week, month, or year; and Roman Egypt provides an abundance of such lamps.[136] In an earlier time Herodotus had described a "festival of lamps" in Saïs that revolved around the home, the domestic space; and this festival may have been the context of an early Ptolemaic letter's admonition to two sisters to "light a lamp for the shrines [*hierois*] and spread the cushions."[137] Centuries later, Shenoute alerts his devotees to Gesios's ritual lampstand and, at a different point, castigates those "who give thanks to demons, . . . while burning lamps and offering incense in the name of phantoms"—testimony to the continuity of traditional domestic piety through the fifth century (see above, 2.5.3). Shenoute ignores, of course, the swelling industry of Christian devotional lamps during this same period.[138]

But the continuity of such practices would have been due precisely to their familial dimension, their interconnection with the concept of the home and its protection and favor.[139] Indeed, those who light lamps in

---

[134] Shenoute, "On the Last Judgment," Turin codex IV, fol. XLIr–v, ed. Behlmer 1996a:91–92.

[135] *V. Pachomii* SBo 4, tr. Veilleux 1980:25. See above, 2.2.

[136] Dunand 1976.

[137] *P.Athens* 60, 5–8. Cf. Herodotus 2.26.1–2.

[138] See Ballet/Mahmoud 1987.

[139] See Tran Tam Tinh 1986:360–61 on the importance of lamp function in the design of terra-cottas.

Panopolis, according to Shenoute, do so out of devotion to Shai, a folk-spirit of protective favor as it pertained to the various spheres of social identity, interaction, and vulnerability in the peasant world—it was to "*šai* of the village or *šai* of the home" that people lit lamps.[140] This protective function of domestic lamplighting is particularly evident in the lamps and "torches"—elongated cylindrical lamps with vertical decoration—with the image of Bes: one such lamp in the Brussels museum of a warrior Bes (with armor, shield, and upraised sword) makes the apotropaic character of the flame particularly vivid (pl. 14).[141]

### 3.6.4 Significance of Domestic Cult

With the domestic shrine and its family cult we have moved to the very taproot of religion in Roman Egypt, that life-context for which so many of the gods popular in the Roman period offered benefits of fertility (maternal, agricultural), healing, and protection. It is particularly useful to emphasize the evidence for home altars (which appear in some form wherever Egyptian houses of the New Kingdom or later have been excavated) because, cross-culturally, they have allowed a maintenance of traditional ritual and belief even in circumstances of a weak or weakening "center"—temple, church, or whatever it is that represents the great tradition in a village.

It should be stated at this point that any endeavor to flesh out domestic religion in Roman Egypt cannot but work through comparison to domestic religion cross-culturally. The Egyptian evidence, as we have seen, is quite fragmentary and scattered. Yet the piety that takes form out of Christian texts and papyri, terra-cottas and archaeology, echoes many of the same forms and orientations of domestic religion current in other cultures; and it is these parallels that provide an idea of the functions, contexts, and attitudes that prompted the manufacture of the Egyptian materials (or lay behind their literary witnesses).[142] In modern rural Mayan culture, for example, the domestic altar supports the often elaborate rituals that concern the safety and well-being of the family; and while they invoke divine figures associated with a great tradition, these

---

140 Shenoute, Discourses 4: The Lord Thundered, 45, ed. Amélineau 1909:379. Inscribed lamps from late antique Corinth invoke angels and other powers for favors or mercy or protection: David Jordan, "Inscribed Lamps from a Cult at Corinth in Late Antiquity," *HTR* 87 (1994):223–29. These lamps, found in a single enormous cache, may have been dedicated to a particular sanctuary.

141 Bes "torches": Louvre inv. E 21518 (= Dunand 1990, #970), E 21535 (= Dunand 1990, #972), E 30318 (= Dunand 1990, #973). Warrior-Bes lamp: Nachtergael 1988:16, #17 (= Brussels M.R.A.H. inv. E3851).

142 Besides the works of Redfield, J. Scott, and Marriott, useful points of comparison on domestic religion in peasant societies can be found in Vogt 1976 and esp. Feuchtwang 1974.

rituals are constructed most immediately out of the local tradition and tend in fact to preserve quite archaic religious elements.[143]

The religious dimension of the home functions variously as satellite, extension, and miniaturization of the local temple. Rural Taiwan provides an example of the complementary symbolism and ritual between domestic altar and temple that goes far in explaining the Egyptian evidence. The domestic altar and the temple (as in Egypt, a building restricted to priests) are indeed complementary ritual axes, expressed most vividly in the popular view of domestic incense-burners "as a division of the local temple's main incense-burner." Temple festivals become the occasion for affirming this connection: people exchange their altars' incense sticks for those carried in the temple's procession. Festivals involve a complex of ritual activities at both the village and domestic dimensions, devoted to local gods and capricious local ghosts; and thus both dimensions gain protection and beneficent supernatural relationships through the concentric powers of home altar and temple altar.[144]

In such cases domestic altars locate and articulate the holy within the family setting, forming a kind of microcosm of religious life and calendar as well as a vivid line of defense against misfortune. But in more complex or transitional cultures they constitute an iconographic *bricolage* of the familiar and familial with an "other"—the official, the hierocratic, or some other cultural idiom of authority. In domestic altars of Mexican and African American traditions the "official" idiom might consist of mass-produced images of Catholic saints, which are combined on the altar with vessels of holy sand or water, ad hoc images prepared by local healers, colorful stones or other objects, and common tools or implements that might represent the types of powers invoked on the altar, all "renewed" at festal times by the addition of food and flowers. Often what is most meaningful in the cultic setting of the domestic altar is not the "official" images but these cruder materials, which are often accumulated in pilgrimages or crisis-motivated requests of healers. These cruder materials both articulate holiness itself in the life of the family and interpret the meaning of the official images.[145]

---

[143] Redfield 1941:248–49. It should be noted that, in contrast to (for example) the Taiwanese emphasis on temple–home reciprocity discussed in Feuchtwang (1974), Vogt detects an orientation in domestic ritual among the Zinacanteco of Southeastern Mexico toward the *separation* of the domestic space from the main deity, the "Earth Lord," symbolically demarcating the limits of his territory (Vogt 1976:59). Domestic rituals instead articulate the reciprocity between domestic religious space and centralized religious space (1976:123).

[144] Feuchtwang 1974:105–11 (quotation from p. 108).

[145] I base these and following observations especially on two exhibition catalogues, Elizabeth Carmichael and Chloë Sayer, *The Skeleton at the Feast: The Day of the Dead in Mexico* (London: British Museum, 1991), and Robert Farris Thompson, *Face of the Gods: Art and Altars of Africa and the African-Americas* (New York: Museum for African Art,

It is likely (if hardly provable) that the terra-cotta images in Roman Egypt functioned analogously to the official images of contemporary popular Christianities. Their Hellenistic style both represented the dominant idiom of Hellenistic culture and articulated the great tradition, the mythological idiom of the Egyptian temples, in a more popular or available format. Set up in their wall niches they formed a focus of sorts for the addition of offerings, sanctified materials from temple precincts (water poured over healing stelae, sand rubbed from temple walls, etc.), amulets from local healers. During festival times, when the temples themselves would adorn their processional images with clothing, households may have added more images or even, as in the contemporary Mexican Day of the Dead, an additional altar space.

How did Egyptians choose and install their central domestic figurines? The sheer variety of Bes, Harpocrates, and Isis figurines implies some choice in purchasing from local craftspeople.[146] Drawing on a study of the private acquisition of sacred images in rural India (among the Mina of Rajasthan) we might expect some of the following procedures to have taken place. A local priest often advises a family on the type of image most suitable, especially when the purchase is meant to offset some past or possible calamity; and the priest will recommend a particular form of a deity to express the power needed. Consequently the family will often purchase the image at an auspicious time, especially at a festival associated with the divinity represented and from craftspeople in the vicinity of the festival temple. Egyptian terra-cotta figures were painted; and so also in Rajasthan sacred images may well be painted to order and occasionally made to order if the craftsperson has insufficient stock. The image would then be consecrated at the temple itself, a service that would earn local priests some extra income, and then installed in a niche, a shrine structure, or some sanctified place near the home with an additional ceremony.[147]

Another important aspect of domestic cult is signaled in the very form in which some lamps and figures were manufactured (or framed): the miniature temple. This kind of iconography, which was certainly not unique to the Roman period, would have maintained an explicit link between the domestic altar and the edifices of the great tradition, those

---

1993), plus discussions of contemporary Greek domestic altars in C. Stewart 1991:51–53 and Hart 1992:147–50. Mexico has provided particularly rich examples of the complexity of domestic altar construction: see Hugo G. Nutini, *Todos Santos in Rural Tlaxcala* (Princeton, N.J.: Princeton University Press, 1988), chs. 6–7, and William H. Beezley, "Home Altars: Private Reflections of Public Life,' in Dana Salvo, *Home Altars of Mexico* (Albuquerque: University of New Mexico Press, 1997), 91–107.

[146] See Pinch 1993:326–32.

[147] Kumar 1984, esp. 17–29.

temples and shrines recognizable throughout the landscape. But there is something singularly powerful about the miniature in itself, as Susan Stewart has observed. It has a revelatory aspect: "That the world of things can open itself to reveal a secret life—indeed, to reveal a set of actions and hence a narrativity and history outside the given field of perception—is a constant daydream that the miniature presents."[148] Thus the common image of a god emerging from his or her temple or posed in its doorway (pl. 16) would recall and even invoke the festival appearance of the temple image, whether in the traditional procession or at the opening of a shrine's doors (the evident mode of "appearance" in the Luxor Isis shrine [pl. 2]). The miniature temple breaches the exclusivity of the temple sanctuary.

The miniature also takes a repeated episode of the real world and renders it in a state of perfection—perfect ritual, perfect continuity, and a merging of mythic past and performative present, transcending the real temple cult as much as the idealized processions on temple reliefs.[149] The correlation in real life between the stone of the temple and the stone of the image is lost in the terra-cotta, where the temple seems to frame a "living" image. Here not only the terra-cotta temples would have relevance but also the images of festival characters (priests, shrine-bearers) as they might have been displayed on domestic altars, since they preserve a concept of perfect festival even through times when festivals or their patronage might be in decline. Like Christian crèche displays they bring into the home a state of ritual festivity that is iconographically associated with the outside.

The domestic altar's function as the demarcation and articulation of the sacred would extend, of course, to those more-than-domestic altars maintained by local patrons like Gesios on the one hand and, on the other, actual priests. Gesios's shrine, accessible only through "doors . . . one after another," the many images kept by the priest of Kothos, and the collection of images kept in a back room of the temple of Isis of Menouthis bring to mind the elaborate domestic altars constructed by priests and priestesses of syncretistic African religions.[150] Kept in homes and easily closed off (in closets or back rooms) from outside eyes, these domestic priests' altars project a secrecy and concentric ritual holiness traditionally associated with established temples; but in their availability to the eyes of devotees and service for special rites the altars carry not only an exoteric familiarity but even a mark of status and authority for the hierophant who assembled the altar. The parallel with African syn-

[148] S. Stewart 1993:54. See also Smith 1995:24–27, analyzing cultic miniaturization in the *PGM*.

[149] S. Stewart 1993:122–23.

[150] Gesios: Besa, *Life of Shenoute* 126. Priest of Kothos: *Panegyric on Makarios* 5.11. Menouthis: Zachariah of Mytilene, *V. Sev.* = A. Bernand 1970:211.

cretistic religions may convey to us in addition the resilience—through cultural stresses—that such an ambivalently esoteric-exoteric altar, constructed and maintained by a priest in his or her own domestic space, might have in the local religious context.

Thus domestic altars function as demarcations of sacred space, according to the various ways this idea of "sacred" might be construed in a society in transition. But another function, evidently quite real to the homes of Roman Egypt, would have been the altar's ability to protect the home and to assure safety. A third-century letter reflects these sentiments in a general sense when it asserts that "our ancestral gods continually assist us, granting us health and safety [sōtēria]"—the sense of "ancestral gods" almost certainly implying some representation thereof in the home.[151] But we have also seen the use of apotropaic names, often quite local like Tutu, Teilouteilou, and Bes; and these names may have corresponded to domestic images. The threshold rites of the "Kothos" story offer the most vivid example of a domestic deity's apotropaic function.

And yet by the fifth century, with native religious traditions increasingly spun out into village and domestic contexts, traditional ritual practice itself came to assume a form increasingly easy to recast in the Christian idiom. The Coptic Mary homily discussed above (1.4.2) provides a good example of a late stage of Egyptian local religion that consisted primarily of family-centered rites of protection, rites so pragmatic in scope and so removed from a developing great tradition of Christianity that they might only be noticed as antithetical by this perspicacious Coptic author: "They pour all over themselves water with incantations (spoken over it), and they break their clay pots claiming it repels the evil eye. Some tie amulets on their children."[152] The rites described in this text would have been continuous with those preserving the Shai of home or village that Shenoute knows in Panopolis, only differing in the latter's festal context.

It is notable that by the fifth century a Coptic "folk" religious art had developed, often with minimal adjustment from traditional iconography, to accommodate this shift in religious idiom: crude terra-cotta and bone maternity figurines (pl. 18), oil lamps, small censers and braziers like those required in Coptic ritual spells, and even portable altars: Besa mentions a silver one that belonged to Shenoute.[153]

---

[151] *P.Oxy* VI.935, 8–12.

[152] Ps-Athanasius, Homily on the Virgin (ed. Lefort 1958:35–36), quoted above, 1.4.2.

[153] Figurines: Charles Palanque, "Notes sur quelques jouets coptes en terre cuite," *BIFAO* 3 (1903):97–103; Malgorzata Martens, "Figurines en terre-cuite coptes découvertes à Kôm el-Dikka (Alexandrie)," *BSAA* 43 (1975):53–77; Nachtergael 1988:27; Piotr Parandowski, "Coptic Terra-cotta Figurines from Kôm el-Dikka," in *Coptic Studies: Acts of the Third International Congress of Coptic Studies,* ed. by W. Godlewski (Warsaw: PWN, 1990), 303–7; Török 1993:30–48, 59–64 (it is unlikely that these figurines were

## 3.7 Localization and Continuity in Egyptian Religion

It has been common to gauge the evolution of Egyptian religion in terms of the rise and fall of various deities. One imagines a graph on which could be plotted the fortunes of Amun, Isis, Montu, Horus, Re, Sobek, and others. For much of Egyptian history this gauge might have had some usefulness in signifying the relative power of certain priesthoods under changing dominions of pharaohs, Persians, and Ptolemies. Through the second century of the Common Era we can still trace the affection of one emperor (or his proponents) for Montu, another for Tutu, another for the Nile cult, another for Serapis.

But by this time the power of imperial affection or disaffection regarding Egyptian institutions carried such dire (or exaggeratedly beneficial) implications that our graph of gods comes to resemble a kaleidoscope of the emperors' own curious religious sentiments and suspicions of an exoticized Egypt, rather than the significance of certain gods in the land. By this time we need a different interpretation of Egyptian religion from that which emphasizes priesthoods, the historic centers of certain gods, and the magnificence of their infrastructures. Did "the" cult of Isis or of the Nile at this time rise or fall according to a single Egyptian priestly institution or, as we have seen, according to regional, even local, organizations and even the private and festival devotions of a village?

This "relocation" of basic religious dynamics becomes essential as we move, over the third century, through the near-elimination of all official temple support and then, progressively over the fourth and fifth centuries, through the proscription and persecution of the temples' cultic activities. We are faced then with either a facile assumption of Egyptian religion's "end" or, as the scattered witnesses to continuing religion impel us to follow, a more subtle concept of what religion might be that could sustain these traumas.

That concept of religion must begin with the local context, assess its mainstays in everyday life, and move concentrically wider to understand the religions of regions and across regions. Whereas in chapter 2 we saw the social forces and attitudes that would maintain religion at both local and regional levels, in this chapter we have seen the way the gods themselves during the Roman period reflected these local and regional scopes of piety. Even more, our attention to the deities most popular in the domestic sphere allows us to recognize a process increasingly evident in the Coptic sources: the centrifugal shift of traditional religion from the

---

*poupées* or *jouets* as implied by Palanque and Martens). Oil lamps: Ballet/Mahmoud 1987. Censers and braziers: London Hay 10391 = Meyer/Smith #127, l.37, London Or. 6795 = Meyer/Smith #130, l.55, London Or. 6796 [4]v = Meyer/Smith #132, l.47, inter alia. Portable altar (= Coptic *trapeza nčismou*): Besa, *Life of Shenoute* 48–51.

transregional pilgrimage cult (or priestly center) to the regional cult, then to the local cult, and finally to the domestic sphere, that island of survival in changing or disintegrating cultures.

It is a shift, as noted, historically paralleled in Central and South American cultures. It was also by no means uniform even in any one region: some traditional practices might be maintained exclusively in the household while others were alive and well in a regional temple like those of Menouthis or Abydos that might be long overlooked by Christian authorities. But it is a shift that allowed people to maintain traditions critical to life, to social identity and solidarity, and even to spatial orientation.

# 4

## MUTATIONS OF THE EGYPTIAN ORACLE

### 4.1. Foundations and Traditions of the Temple Oracle

IN YEAR 14 of Psamtik I, on the fifth day of the first month of Shomu (October 4, 651 BC), the occasion being the festival of the new lunar month, there was a procession of the august god, lord of all the gods, Amon-Reʻ, King of Gods. His shrine was borne by twenty priests out onto the Floor of Silver in order to go around the temple. Before the shrine were several more important priests, including the First Prophet or High Priest, the Third Prophet and the Chief Lector-priest with the venerable Montemhet, Fourth Prophet of Amon and Overseer of Upper Egypt, heading them and offering incense. In its course the procession arrived at the . . . Hall of Review, where the ordinary people awaited it. It was here that Pemou, son of Harsiese, son of Peftjau, stood and announced to the great god his presence and besought of him an oracle in favor of his father, Harsiese, who wished to leave the service of Amon for that of Montu-Reʻ-Harakhti. This petition the great god was pleased to grant and he signified his approval by responding to the voice of Pemou and advancing.[1]

The record of this auspicious event now hangs on a wall in the Brooklyn Museum: a colored vignette on papyrus showing the priests bearing the lavish shrine of Amon-Re on poles toward Pemou and the high priests.[2]

Another papyrus, in the British Museum, offers a vivid scenario of local oracles in practice: a man responsible for sacred garments finds they have been stolen and appeals to the god Amun of Pe-Khenty during the god's festival to find the clothes. The names of possible suspects are read before the god—that is, a portable shrine akin to that in the Brooklyn Papyrus—and a local farmer is accused. But the farmer claims innocence and demands another "trial" before the god Amun of Te-Shenyt. When this Amun, too, finds him guilty and he again claims innocence, he is sent before the god Amun of Bukenen, where he finally confesses and is punished.[3]

[1] Parker 1962:1.
[2] Parker 1962:3–6.
[3] A. Blackman 1925:249–55.

These typical instances of the oracle in classical Egypt (respectively of the Late Period and New Kingdom) provide the indigenous background against which the evolution of oracles in the Roman period must be understood. The Egyptian oracle served to integrate and maintain social order through adjudicating disputes and guiding people through crises. Oracles bridged the world of the priesthood with the world of the laity, the unity of the "great" Amun with the particularity of the local, speaking Amun, and the esoteric world enclosed in temples with the exoteric space of the public procession. This "bridging" role of oracles is expressed most importantly in their principal social context: the god's festival. In a mood of popular enthusiasm, accompanied by musicians and dancers, the god and its priests would process out of a local temple that was entirely proscribed to villagers.

Several alternatives existed for consulting the god. One might, as in the British Museum Papyrus, appeal personally to the god, often at a designated point in the procession. One supplicant of the late Ramesside period hoped for such a personal audience "to tell you some affairs of mine, (but) you happened to be concealed in your holy of holies, and there was nobody having access to it to send in to you. . . . See, you must discard seclusion today and come out in procession in order that you may decide upon the issues." Perhaps more often, as in the Brooklyn Papyrus, it would be a priest who would address a client's question to the god; and when the situations requiring the god's adjudication demanded a public reading of a list of people, it was inevitably priests who would compile and read these lists before the god.[4]

The sizable collection of oracular ostraca from Deir El-Medina in western Thebes shows that by the New Kingdom local oracle rites might commonly work through the medium of writing, addressing not (or not only) spoken questions but questions and names that had been written on ostraca and placed before the "god," the shrine box borne by the priests or villagers: for example, "Shall one appoint Sety as priest?"; "Is it he who has stolen this mat?"; "Is this calf good so that I may accept it?"; and "My good Lord! This axe belongs to Pakhy"—which was probably set out with the ostracon of another who claimed the axe.[5] Thutmose the scribe closes his letter to another priest with the promise that "I am submitting your (case) [lit. placing you in front of] (the oracle of) Amenophis [= Amenhotep I] whenever he appears in procession," and he

---

[4] Priests' surrogate appeals to oracles: Černý 1941:138f.; McDowell 1990:109–10; cf. Barns 1949:69, on awareness of priestly control. Besides the Brooklyn Oracle Papyrus, cf. O. B.M. 2625, in A. Blackman 1926:182. On clients' own appeals: Černý 1962:43; cf. 1935:41; McDowell 1990:107–9. Late Ramesside letter to god: P. Nevill, tr. Wente 1990:219, #355; cf. Barns 1949:59.

[5] From Černý 1962:46.

claims that the god blesses his colleague each time.[6] Such documents, as well as the preserved ostraca themselves, show that a common method of asking a question to the god would be to commission the affirmative and negative answers to be written on ostraca and then placed before the shrine in procession; and in one striking judicial case the names of at least twelve suspects were written on reeds, evidently to be spread out before or sequentially presented to the god.[7] The written questions, especially those in dual affirmative and negative presentations, tend to conform to formulas, a fact that both indicates the importance of priestly scribes in mediating supplicants' problems for the oracular rites and also provides an important prototype for the equally formulaic oracle questions of the Greco-Roman period.[8]

And how, in fact, did the god answer? The priestly documents that describe the oracular rites, such as the Brooklyn and British Museum papyri, describe the god as "nodding" or "saying no"; yet given the public nature of the oracular procession it is doubtful that an actual "voice" could have been feigned. At the same time the dual and multiple oracular ostraca meant to be placed on the ground before the procession suggest that some movement on the part of the shrine in procession would have been required to "choose" the appropriate ostracon. Thus Egyptologists have concluded that the priests bearing the shrine would move forward or backward according to whether the god's answer was, respectively, affirmative or negative, or it would move toward the "correct" of multiple options.[9] To audiences such movements would certainly appear as the will of the god: in the Brooklyn Papyrus the shrine "draws toward [Eg. *st3*]" the supplicant "by (the power of) the great god."[10] Diodorus, reflecting late Hellenistic witnesses, thus described the procession of the Amun oracle on the Siwa oasis: "The image of the god . . . is carried about upon a golden boat by eighty priests, and these, with the god on their shoulders, go without their own volition wherever the god directs their path."[11]

---

[6] P. B.M. 10417, tr. Wente 1990:179, #296; cf. A. Blackman 1926:184–85. Whether or not "place you in front of [*w3h*]" had become a perfunctory formula by the time this letter was written, it certainly derived from the physical act of placing an ostracon or papyrus before the god's shrine.

[7] Černý 1941; cf. idem 1935, plus "Nouvelle série de questions adressées aux oracles," *BIFAO* 41 (1942):13–24, and "Troisième série de questions adressées aux oracles," *BIFAO* 72 (1972):49–69. In general on the Deir el-Medina oracle procedure, see McDowell 1990:107–14.

[8] Černý 1935:55–56; Schubart 1931. See also Browne 1987.

[9] Černý 1935:56–57; 1962:44–45; McDowell 1990:108–11.

[10] Parker 1962:11.

[11] Diodorus Siculus, Hist. 17.50.6, tr. Welles, LCL, 8:265. Compare Lucian's satirical description of a similar oracle in Syrian Heliopolis: "This god takes the initiative himself

No doubt the movements of such portable shrines were often much more subtle than simply backward and forward—Strabo speaks of their "nods and signs [neumasi kai sumbolois]"—and often required interpretation by a priest, as in the Brooklyn Papyrus and other ancient illustrations of oracle procedure, or else (in smaller-scale village oracles) public discussion.[12] Such nuances became particularly important (and their priestly interpreters particularly powerful) when the god's message came through the movement of an animal like the Apis bull of Memphis or even, as Plutarch and other authors detail, through the sounds of children playing by the temple.[13]

The intrinsic function of the written word in many oracle rites, including the written documentation of the results of the god's movements, might also allow the god to "speak" apart from the public procession—that is, in the temple itself. In such a case priests would then transmit the divine words to the client. The divinized Amenhotep I (as oracle-god) assigns a specific tomb to one Amenemope "by a writing."[14] Already in the Third Intermediate Period the priests of the local god Horus-of-the-Camp (in the area of modern El-Hiba, south of the Fayyum) were employing a system, probably widespread at the time, whereby an oracle request was submitted in two versions, phrasing the alternative answers, and the petitioner would receive back the "correct" answer as proof of the god's decision.[15] This system would have released the divination rite from the context of public performance yet still have offered a guarantee that the god had in fact rendered an oracle. By this period some temples were also extending the ritual guarantee of an individual's safety, traditionally performed with an inscribed ostracon placed before the proces-

---

and completes the oracle of his own accord. This is his method. Whenever he wishes to deliver an oracle, he first moves on his throne, and the priests immediately lift him up. If they do not lift him, he begins to sweat and moves still more. When they put him on their shoulders and carry him, he leads them in every direction as he spins around and leaps from one place to another. Finally the chief priest meets him face to face and asks him about all sorts of things. If the god does not want something done, he moves backwards. If he approves of something, like a charioteer he leads forward those who are carrying him. In this manner they collect divine utterances, and without this ritual they conduct no religious or personal business" (De Dea Syria 36, tr. Harold W. Attridge and Robert A. Oden, The Syrian Goddess [De Dea Syria], SBL Texts and Translations 9 [Missoula, Mont.: Scholars, 1976], 47–49).

12 Strabo 17.1.43. Compare public discussion of local oracles in Surinam (Price 1975:41–42) and in divining the cause of an Ethiopian woman's illness (Mercier 1979:14).

13 Plutarch De Iside 356e; Dio Chrysostom, Or. ad Alexandrinos 32.13; Aelian, De nat. animal. 11.10; texts and discussion in Pierre Courcelle, "L'oracle d'Apis et l'oracle du jardin de Milan," RHR 139 (1951):218–22. On Apis bull: Sadek 1987:271–72; Thompson 1988:190–95. On the special authority of priests in these matters, see Dunand 1979:123.

14 BM Ostracon 5624.5, in A. Blackman 1926:177, 180.

15 Ryholt 1993.

sional shrine, to inscribed "amuletic decrees"—promises of the god's protection against long lists of maleficent powers, which would have been prepared in the temples themselves. Presented to clients as the local god's own "oral" decree, the inscribed papyri would subsequently be worn in a tube around the neck as both an apotropaion and a bond of security between the client and the god.[16] And indeed, in a culture where writing itself was a prerogative of the priestly and administrative élite and viewed as sacred in its very letters, such written records of the god's words inevitably carried a talismanic numinosity: even in the third century C.E. a papyrus recording oracular predictions of a political and agricultural nature calls itself an "amulet [*alexētērion*]" for the year, with instructions for its further ritual empowerment.[17]

The issuing of oracles within the temples allowed the oracles themselves to assume a more extensive, even discursive quality than could be achieved in spontaneous public performance. The evidence for this extension of the oracle "genre" comes mainly from the Hellenistic period, although this does not imply a change from the priestly oracle compositions of the Late Period. Herodotus, for example, understands oracles' judicial functions not in the context of festival processions but of the shrine itself and its ongoing service (2.174). Herodotus also describes how the oracle shrine of "Leto" (Wadjet) in the Delta city of Buto transmitted a warning of imminent death to one pharaoh and to another the prophecy that vengeance and "bronze men" would come from the sea. Thus in Herodotus's time an oracle was such a thing as could be sent.[18] Papyrus Dodgson, from the Ptolemaic period, records a series of messages that had apparently been delivered in the first-person singular as the voice of the local oracular gods of Elephantine transmitted through some kind of personal (ecstatic?) intermediary. In vehemently chastising a local citizen for neglecting the cult of Osiris the oracles reflect an origin in a temple (or its grounds), not a procession.[19] And by the Roman period the formula for oracle requests comes to consist of the instruction, "If [this is the answer], deliver this [ticket] to me," written on two tickets for both alternatives.[20] Thus the oracle rite becomes an ongoing ticket exchange with the priests as mediators.

It is in the context of such written oracles that the extensive oracular

[16] Edwards 1960; A. Klasens, "An Amuletic Papyrus of the 25th Dynasty," *OMRO 56* (1975):20–28.

[17] *P.Oxy* XXXI.2554. See, in general, Ritner 1993:36, 214–17.

[18] Herodotus 2.133.1; 152.3. Cf. Černý 1962:46–47.

[19] Ed. De Cenival 1987; cf. Griffith 1909 and now C. Martin 1994, who views the oracle as emitting from a *naos*.

[20] See esp. Schubart 1931 and Browne 1987, with further discussion and bibliography below, 4.2.

texts of the Greco-Roman period should also be understood, for they are framed explicitly as the recorded utterances of oracular-gods. The Oracles of the Lamb and the Potter, ostensibly the direct transmissions from the ram-god Khnum in one of his temples at Herakleopolis and Elephantine, both deliver extensive tableaux of social chaos that would occur with the lapse of kingship and be reversed with a new king.[21] These Khnum oracles seem to have been issued in connection with various anti-Greek movements around these temples, and together constitute a series of successive "clarifications" of Khnum's words as they were taken to refer to political events of the mid-second century B.C.E. Both the Khnum oracles and the Demotic Chronicle, a political commentary on oracles of the god Harsaphes in Herakleopolis from the early Hellenistic period, show the very concept of the oracle evolving into a priestly literary tradition with little evident attachment to ritual.[22]

More extensive divine pronouncements than could be interpreted from a shrine's (or, later, an Apis bull's) movements might also be produced before an audience with a "talking statue" or some like contrivance for issuing mysterious sounds. While a mechanism widespread in the ancient and medieval worlds, one of the only Egyptian examples of a hollow statue with a mouth-hole, through which a hidden priest could speak, in fact derives from the Roman period, a bust of the god Re-Harmachis in Roman armor.[23] The statue would have stood on a substantial base and against the wall of a temple chamber prepared to receive audiences of a modest size (given the height of the bust [51 cm]). A priest must have hid on the other side of the wall to deliver the oracles through a hole or tube that led to the image's mouth.

The existence of such rooms and the extent of such talking statues are confirmed again by data of the Roman period—in this case an oracular statue's apparatus found at Kom el-Wist, outside Alexandria, and the two oracle temples of Sobek in the Fayyum town of Karanis. The Kom el-Wist find consisted of a bronze tube leading to a bronze base that held the image of a bull, out of whose mouth presumably would have passed words uttered secretly by a priest at the other end of the tube.[24] The

---

[21] Oracle of the Lamb: Zauzich 1983. Oracle of the Potter: Koenen 1968, 1970, 1974, 1984; Dunand 1977.

[22] On the evolution of the oracle as text, see John D. Ray, "Ancient Egypt" in *Oracles and Divination*, ed. by M. Loewe and C. Blacker (Boulder, Colo.: Shambhala, 1981), 182–83.

[23] Cairo 66143, in Loukianoff 1936. In general, see Poulsen 1945 and László Kákosy, "Orakel," *LexÄg* 4 (1982):600–601.

[24] Labib Habachi, "Finds at Kôm el-Wist," *ASAE* 47 (1947):285–87; Guy Brunton, "The Oracle of Kôm el-Wist," *ASAE* 47 (1947):293–95.

mechanics here resemble a Christian description of oracular statues operating in fourth-century Alexandria:

> [The priests] had constructed statues of bronze and wood hollow within, and fastened the backs of them to the temple walls, leaving in these walls certain invisible openings. Then coming up from their secret chambers they got inside the statues, and through them gave any order they liked and the hearers, tricked and cheated, obeyed.[25]

In the Karanis temples, at the back of the shrines, stand huge plinths that apparently supported mummified crocodiles as images of Petesouchos, the local form of Sobek (an image of Petesouchos on a base was actually found in one of the temples).[26] Beneath these plinths are tiny rooms that could only have been entered from the far side of the base, just large enough to conceal a priest.[27] Thus an audience (or those privileged enough to be invited near the sanctuary) might hear Petesouchos actually speaking in his shrine. Finally, four *naoi* (stone box chambers for cultic images) in the Cairo Museum, each large enough to accommodate a person, have large holes drilled in their sides: an oracular function seems quite likely.[28]

It is tempting to imagine the eruption of such oracular contrivances as a phenomenon of the Greco-Roman period, perhaps as a means of appealing to new types of audiences and their expectations. But as with the literary oracles we cannot assume that such phenomena did not exist earlier among the diverse oracle cults of Egypt. The fact that the very earliest New Kingdom documents describe gods as "speaking" to people (usually pharaohs) suggests that something was actually heard.[29] In essence, the talking statues were only a synthesis of a type of ecstatic oracle from ancient times with the silent drama of the processional oracle. Indeed, the "voice" oracles' lineage with the processional oracle is vividly confirmed in an early Roman (47–44 B.C.E.) shrine at Coptos: although it is proportioned and decorated as an enclosure for the local gods' sacred

[25] Theodoret, *H.E.* 5.22, tr. Jackson in *NPNF* 3:147–48. Cf. Rufinus, *H.E.* 11.23.

[26] Boak (ed.) 1933, fig. 10; Gazda 1978, #31.

[27] Hogarth in P.Fayyum, p. 30; Boak (ed.) 1933:9; Enoch E. Peterson, "The Temple of Pnepheros and Petesuchos," in Boak (ed.) 1933:53–54; Poulsen 1945:184.

[28] Roeder 1914:25 (#70007), 37 (#70010), 46 (#70014), 55 (#70019). Roeder interprets the holes as *Abflusslochen* although they are all above floor level. The card by #70014 in the Cairo Museum associates the hole with "speaking" oracles. See C. Martin 1994 for one possible historical scenario of oracular *naoi*.

[29] Černý 1962:35–36; Kuhlmann 1988:22–23, 133–34, on "royal" speaking oracles at Siwa; and cf. Baines 1987:89–90. On evidence for pre-Hellenistic contrivances for spoken oracles, see Gaston Maspero, *Égypte* (Paris: Hachette et Cie, 1912), 242 (Khonsou at Karnak) and Fakhry 1944:43, 87–88 (Siwa).

processional barque, it is far too small for this purpose. A small, richly decorated wall blocks off the barque's would-be sanctuary. This wall also frames a hole from which voice oracles were apparently issued.[30] The god's messages were invariably understood in oral terms, as "speaking."[31]

Two main conclusions follow from these general observations of the oracle in traditional Egyptian culture: the localized nature of the oracle, and the evolution of a priestly scribal apparatus to develop local oracles from a ritual form into a literary tradition.

Location is intrinsic to the Egyptian oracle. From the three local Amuns of the British Museum Papyrus, to the local oracular service of the cult of Amenhotep I in the workmen's town of Deir el-Medina, to the recorded travels of one Hor, a priest of the Thoth cult, to various sanctuaries of the Ptolemaic period that received dream oracles, the god was understood as communicating in particular places. Whereas the documents of the Amenhotep oracle demonstrate how a god of almost exclusively local relevance would function among the populace through oracle processions,[32] the local Amuns (of the same region) show a god of transregional appeal localized and so individualized among different Theban villages that they would be viewed as independent recourses for judicial proceedings.[33] The phenomenon continues into the Roman period, especially in the oases with the cult of Amun and in the Fayyum with the cult of Sobek, where (we have seen) local forms of the crocodile-god assume slightly different names. And in the cases of both Amun and Sobek, at least some of the shrines were renowned for oracles.[34]

The existence or spread of multiple shrines was not merely a priestly contrivance. It is quite evident that local forms bespeak strong local context, even enmeshment, in the little tradition. Moreover, from the oracle requests of Deir el-Medina to those of the late Roman period one can see clearly that most local oracles did not merely serve the pilgrimage needs of well-heeled Roman youth but answered the perennial social and agricultural needs of their respective regions.

On the other side, one perceives a priesthood with literary inclinations

---

[30] Traunecker 1992:49–53, 379–87.

[31] Even as literary a document as the Oracle of the Lamb was based on the widespread tradition that in the time of one King Bocchoris "a lamb spoke" (Manetho, frags. 64–65, on which passage see Kákosy 1966b:345).

[32] Sadek 1987:131–38.

[33] See A. Blackman 1925:253; Černý 1962:40–41. See also J. F. Borghouts, "The Ram as a Protector and Prophesier," *RdÉ* 32 (1980):33–46, on powers ascribed to a "ram" without actual theology; Kákosy 1966b:342–43 on transregional authority of Amun, 343–44 on affiliation of Harsaphes of Herakleopolis with Khnum, and 346–47 on growth of local (Herakleopolis/Elephantine/Esna) Khnums through affiliation with Amun.

[34] Amun: Wagner 1987:329–35. Sobek: Toutain 1915; Brovarski 1984:998–99, 1013–15; Quaegebeur 1984. See above, 3.2.

that go beyond the mere preparation of supplicants' ostraca and the simple documenting of important oracular pronouncements. From the Late Period (e.g., the Brooklyn Oracle Papyrus) through the Roman period (as witnessed by the manuscripts of the Potter's Oracle) the recording, interpretation, literary preservation, and even invention of oracles becomes a major pursuit of the temple scriptorium and possibly one of the earliest priestly literary endeavors for which Greek is brought into service. Whether this evolution of oracular literature testifies to internal literary inclinations or a need for propaganda in the religious competition of the Greco-Roman world, the Egyptian oracle comes to cover a wide range of phenomena, from ritual to text, linked by the integral function of the priesthood.

## 4.2 The Persistence of the Temple Oracle in the Roman Period

### 4.2.1 Processional Oracles

The development and proliferation of the "ticket" oracle does not imply the simultaneous demise of the oracle procession. A Roman edict from the end of the second century C.E. attempts to proscribe oracles whether "in writings as it were divinely delivered or through the procession of images." Shortly thereafter we find a shrine of Taweret in Oxyrhynchus sponsoring processions of "the revealing gods," borne in the traditional manner by shrine-bearing priests, where "revealing [*exagoreuoi*]" indicates the oracular function of the borne images.[35]

Much more widespread evidence for processions that carried "oracular" powers appears in Egyptian theophoric names constructed with the prefix "appearance of [god's name]" or the suffix "[god's name] (is) the speaking appearance."[36] In these cases, which come for the most part from the late-second-century Delta (with much more ancient roots), it is often popular gods that appear, like Tutu, reflecting a phenomenon of popular birth oracles as locally based as it was widespread in Egypt.[37] This popular dimension might imply that the god's "appearance" as it

[35] Second-century edict: P.Coll.Youtie I.30 = P.Yale 299, 12–15, ed. Parássoglou 1976 and Rea 1977. On its doubtful effectiveness, see Lane Fox 1986:213, *pace* Ritner 1995:3355–56. Revealing gods of Oxyrhynchus: *P.Lond.* 2554, ed. Roberts 1934. On the sense of *exagoreuoi,* see Roberts 1934:25; Kramer in *P.Heid.* IV.334, pp. 240–42. See also Perpillou-Thomas 1993:216–17 on oracular functions of *kōmasia,* described by Clement in the third century (*Strom.* V.671).

[36] Greek NN + *teōs* = Eg. *djed-her* + NN, proposed by Vergote 1954; see also Yoyotte 1955:135–40; Quaegebeur 1977.

[37] Kákosy 1964; Sauneron 1960b:286–87; Quaegebeur 1986.

was honored in names more likely consisted of the procession of an image at a festival than of incubation in a temple.[38]

Perhaps the most vivid document of the processional oracle in Roman Egypt (at least through the third century) is a wall painting in the temple of Pnepheros, an avatar of Sobek, in the Fayyum town of Theadelphia (pl. 19). Much like the regal ceremony of the Amun oracle described in the Brooklyn Papyrus (above), this painting shows shrine-bearers holding an image of the god—in this case, what appears to be a mummified crocodile on a long bier, wearing the *atef* crown associated with Amun.[39] They carry the bier before several priests who face it, presumably to interpret the god's movements. As we will see, numerous Sobek oracles were operating simultaneously in the Fayyum: not only the "voice" oracles of Karanis but also several "ticket" oracles. The Theadelphia painting makes clear that at least one processional oracle continued as well. Indeed, it is likely that the painting was commissioned, just like the Brooklyn Papyrus, to commemorate an auspicious oracle in the time-honored form of memorial.

The lack of documentation for processional oracles after the middle of the third century does not reflect the dwindling of this highly traditional religious form but rather the local and performative nature of the rite. Solving common problems on the spot, it does not seem to have lent itself to much written documentation after the priestly records of the Ptolemaic period—even the early Roman materials are idiosyncratic.[40] But iconographic sources provide some illustration of the continuing tradition. Roman era terra-cottas represent various forms of shrine procession; and such wooden icons as were traditionally carried in procession are listed in temple inventories of the second and third centuries.[41] These

[38] Vergote 1954:23; Yoyotte 1955:139–40. See also Jan Quaegebeur on the name *Teephibis,* "the appearance of the Ibis has spoken," arguing that the reference to Ibis as opposed to Thoth seems to imply a popular oracular form of Thoth attached to his official cult ("Teëphibis, dieu oraculaire?" *Enchoria* 5 [1975]:19–24, esp. 21 on Roman era papyri). On popular Thoth veneration in the later Roman period, see László Kákosy, "Problems of the Thoth-Cult in Roman Egypt," *Acta archaeologica Hungaricae* 15 (1963):123–28. On the priestly Thoth oracle at Saqqâra during the Ptolemaic period, see T. C. Skeat and E. G. Turner, "An Oracle of Hermes Trismegistos at Saqqâra," *JEA* 54 (1968):199–208, and Ray 1976:1–6, 130–36, 158–61.

[39] The Greco-Roman Museum of Alexandria contains a wooden bier for carrying such a crocodile mummy (inv. 19680), a wooden shrine for the bier (inv. 19679), and a wooden model of a crocodile's head, hollowed out as if for placing over a crocodile mummy's head and bearing a wooden socket on top as if to receive a crown (inv. 19691). All objects were apparently found in Theadelphia. One is, of course, tempted to regard these materials as the oracle's processional equipment.

[40] See McDowell 1990:107–8.

[41] Terra-cotta models: Dunand 1979:93–94, ##329–30, 332–39. Temple inventories: P.Yale 363, ll. 9–10, on which see Gilliam 1947:211n. ad loc.; *BGU* XIII.2217; and

kinds of public rites are also recalled in Christian texts—for example, the procession that Apa Apollo encounters, carrying the divine image out of the local temple and through the villages.[42] So also the historian Priscus describes an "ancient custom [*palios nomos*]" at the Isis temple on Philae that was still maintained under Maximinus (305–13), whereby the Blemmyes

> were to have the right to cross unhindered to the temple of Isis, while the Egyptians had the care of the river boat in which the statue of the goddess was placed and ferried across the river. At a fixed time the barbarians take the statue across to their own land and, when they have taken oracles [*khrēstēriasamenoi*] from it, return it safely to the island.[43]

Priscus's testimony does not imply that the priests of Isis held such rituals at Philae itself, although the fact that the Isis cult there continued for another two hundred years makes it quite likely. Indeed, a fourth-century Demotic Egyptian inscription at Philae lamenting the absence of "the barque [Eg. *wtn*] of Isis" for two years during a period of political tension suggests that the oracular Isis to which Priscus refers took the form of a traditional Egyptian processional barque shrine.[44]

One additional reason to doubt the total evaporation of the processional oracle is its resilience in other cultures. What seems to have been an autochthonous African form of divination has reappeared throughout the African diaspora since the eighteenth century. The following example of a twentieth-century oracle rite among Africans in Surinam, in its close formal parallel to the Egyptian rite, suggests not so much a common ritual pool as the inevitable reappearance of the rite in cultures in which it was traditional:

> [The god] Gaan Tata replied to questions through the movements of the bearers of his oracle. This was a small bundle tied to a plank which two Gaan Tata priests carried. . . . It was hidden from view by long draperies which touched the ground when the ends of the plank rested on the heads of two bearers. Other priests standing in front of the bearers put questions to the oracle. Gaan Tata replied through the movements of the bearers in this way, a forward move signified an affirmative, a backward or sideways one a negative answer. Wild chaotic movements indicated the High God's vivid displeasure. . . . A high priest was in charge of the oracle: after receiving a whispered report from his subordinate priests, he issued a final communiqué to the meeting of elders. As a rule, the oracle sessions were held in public in

---

contents of Menouthis Isis temple mentioned by Zachariah of Mytilene, ed. Kugener 1907:29 = A. Bernand 1970:211.

[42] *Hist. Mon.* 8.25–26. See above, 2.2.

[43] Priscus, fr. 27, ed. and tr. Blockley 1981/82, 2:322–23.

[44] IDemPhilae 371, 7, on which see Griffith 1937:104–5, 144 (#84 on *wtn*).

front of the temple, an ordinary but bigger hut where sacred objects were stored.[45]

It would appear that the processional oracle might continue in communities as a ritual form in spite of decline in religious infrastructure (and far worse than decline in the case of Surinam!), requiring only a temporal context—a calendar or schedule—for its appearance, a community in perpetual need of divination, an image and its bearers, and probably an authoritative interpreter such as a priest or elder. As temples like Esna maintained complex processional calendars at least through the third century C.E., one would tend to expect many more processions on a smaller, more localized scale continuing throughout the fourth century.

### 4.2.2 Alternative Media

Might there have been a tendency within Egyptian religion itself away from such processions and toward other types of divination? The early Roman shrine at Coptos was constructed to resemble the sanctuary of a processional barque and yet to deliver "voice" oracles to supplicants who entered. Should this chapel be taken to indicate a broader Egyptian tendency of replacing processional oracles with other types during the late Greco-Roman period? In this case the iconography of the barque sanctuary was only an architectural conceit for a shrine planned from the beginning to issue "voice" oracles.[46] The choice of a "voice" oracle signified a local need for the god's continual availability to render decisions, in contrast to the pomp and drama of the procession, which itself was probably irreplaceable as a calendrical event and ritual process.[47]

The social changes and increasing stress of the Roman period may well have led to a diversification of the means of divination, which as a ritual process typically functions to resolve social tensions and private anxieties, to direct action in unstable circumstances, and to integrate the individual with a coherent religious cosmology. We find a mother in the second century C.E. who, concerned about her distant son's affairs and

[45] Bonno Thoden van Velzen, "Bush Negro Regional Cults: A Materialist Explanation," in Werbner (ed.) 1977:108, with photo of contemporary version of oracle in Richard and Sally Price, *Afro-American Arts of the Suriname Rain Forest* (Berkeley: University of California Press, 1980), 65, pl. VI, and general analysis in Price 1975:38–43. Compare parallels attested in eighteenth- and nineteenth-century Jamaica collected in Roger D. Abrahams and John F. Szwed, *After Africa* (New Haven, Conn., and London: Yale University Press, 1983), 163–64, 165–66, 171–73; W. Blackman 1927:113 and Sauneron 1960a:95–96 for modern Egypt; and Sidney W. Mintz and Richard Price, *The Birth of African American Culture* (Boston: Beacon, 1976), 55–56, on the nature of the rite's continuity in cultures of the African diaspora.

[46] Traunecker 1992:51, 383.

[47] Traunecker 1992:379–80.

potential journey to Rome, does not await a scheduled procession of the god but "consults the oracle [*manteuomai*] every ten days" and thereby (*oun*) finds "that good opportunities were not available [to him] this present quarter."[48] A society of greater mobility and economic opportunity might well require oracles in more continuous accessibility than could have been offered by traditional processional oracles. Thus even as they may have changed their mode of oracle rite from public procession to private audience, several important Egyptian oracles continue from pharaonic times until well into the Roman period. The oracle of Amun at the Siwa oasis, the oracles of Sobek throughout the Fayyum, and the cult of Amenhotep I at Deir el-Bahri (the same divinity once questioned in New Kingdom Deir el-Medina, about a kilometer away) represent the best examples of this continuity of ancient shrines.

The oracle of Amun at Siwa, first attested in the XVIII Dynasty and achieving renown throughout the eastern Mediterranean world in the fifth and fourth centuries B.C.E., seemed to Strabo "nearly abandoned" by the turn of the eras.[49] Yet Strabo here may be guided by his agenda of contrasting the Egyptian cult to a superior Roman divination. For, in the first or second century C.E., one Nearchos writes of his trip to Siwa, "where Amun utters oracles for all mankind; and I sought auspicious words, and I inscribed the names of my loved ones on the temples as an eternal devotion [*proskunēsis*]."[50]

Apparently two oracle rites were functioning when Nearchos made his trip: the traditional processional oracle (as Diodorus records) and a "voice" oracle by the inner sanctuary of the temple, such as Alexander the Great was reputed to have encountered. The latter had become an incubation oracle by the Roman period, through which Amun might "utter oracles for all mankind." Whether or not both were still operating in the sixth century C.E., when Procopius describes Siwa as an outpost of native piety, it is quite evident that the temple maintained its local tradition of Amun's accessibility for centuries.[51] One might explain the persistence of the Siwa Amun cult simply by its position on the periphery of Roman administration and Christianization, available only to devoted pilgrims and nomadic tribes (indeed, the builder of the oracle temple called himself "Chief of the desert-dwellers").[52]

---

[48] *P.Merton* II.81, 3–7.

[49] Strabo 17.1.43. On the history of the Siwa oracle, see Fakhry 1944:28–46 and Kuhlmann 1988.

[50] *P.Lond.* III.854 = W.Chr. 117. Cf. also Lucan, *Pharsalia* 9.511–86.

[51] Procopius, *Aedif.* 6.2.16–17. See further discussion of the oracle's continuity in Wagner 1987:329–30, and on the two distinct oracle cults there, Kuhlmann 1988, ch. 8 and p. 158. Diodorus's discussion of the processional oracle: 17.50.6 (quoted above, 4.1).

[52] Fakhry 1944:91–95.

Although shorter-lived than the cults of Amun, the temple of Amenhotep I or Amenothis at Deir el-Bahri had indigenous, popular roots in
the New Kingdom cult of a historical figure, a divinized scribe. At Deir el-
Bahri the cult continued its broad appeal until at least the end of the
second century C.E., the sanctuary already known as a place of healing
through incubation by the beginning of the Hellenistic period (the testimony of devotional inscriptions, ostraca, and papyri).[53]

The cult seems to have been a crucible of popular Egyptian Hellenization, since its largely Egyptian clientele commissioned votive inscriptions
in Greek, and the roster of a religious society (or *sunodos*) probably connected with this cult consists entirely of Egyptian names.[54] Here also one
finds a striking document: a priestly "romance" in Greek, created in the
second century C.E. and preserved on Oxyrhynchus Papyrus 1381. In its
enthusiastic account of how the writer, a scribe, gained health for himself
and his mother by the power of the temple's gods, the text shows the
development of a priestly propaganda for the cult.[55] The text is in Greek,
but its central narrative, the drama of a legendary pharaoh encountering
an ancient book, is written according to the typical archaizing features of
the Egyptian *Königsnovelle*, a literary genre traditional to priestly circles
in pharaonic Egypt that is similarly used in the Oracles of the Lamb and
the Potter. Such propaganda would have maintained the Egyptian
priestly authority of the healing cult while being available in the dominant language of written dissemination.[56]

Incubation as a form of gaining the voice of the temple's god (if not,
originally, his healing power) had a long tradition in Egypt. Although the
most explicit evidence for this type of oracle in pre-Roman Egypt (such as
the dream records of the priest Hor) suggest that incubation may have been
more systematically pursued by members of the priesthood before the later
Hellenistic period, there is some evidence for "popular" incubation as well.[57]
From the votive inscriptions left on the temple walls of Deir el-Bahri we
learn that incubation had become the central "oracular" ritual in a healing
cult of Amenhotep I and his associate gods Imouthes-Asclepius and Hygeia.
But these gods may not have restricted themselves to dreams: a special

---

[53] Octave Guéraud, "Quelques textes du Musée du Caire: II. Inscription en l'honneur
d'Aménôthès," *BIFAO* 27 (1927):121–25; Bataille 1951, esp. xix–xx; Dietrich Wildung,
*Egyptian Saints: Deification in Pharaonic Egypt* (New York: New York University Press,
1977), 94–100; Laskowska-Kusztal 1984:106–27. On the evolution of the cult of Amenhotep I, see Wildung, op. cit., ch. 3.

[54] *O.Theb.* 142 (second century C.E.). On the character of worshipers from inscriptions,
see Bataille 1951:xv–xvii.

[55] See discussion in *P.Oxy* XI, pp. 222–25; and Kákosy 1995:2977–78; and below, 6.1.

[56] See below, 6.2.

[57] See Sauneron 1959:40–45; Ray 1976:130–36. On popular incubation in New Kingdom Egypt, see Assmann 1978.

opening above the door to the temple's inner sanctuary probably allowed the gods' "voices" to speak to clients out of their own holiest abode.[58]

Whereas the dated votive inscriptions at Deir el-Bahri seem to cease in the late second century, the decline of the cult of Amenhotep I should not be fixed too strictly to the same period.[59] With texts like the Oxyrhynchus "romance" still circulating in the second century, it may be more sensible to ascribe the cult's decline to the third century, whose economic crises claimed many such temples. When a guild of ironworkers made annual pilgrimage there during the mid-fourth century, however, their "devotions [proskunēmata]" make no mention of oracles.[60]

The Fayyum cults of Sobek provide unique papyrological evidence for at least three oracle temples functioning from the late pharaonic period through the third century C.E., when the Fayyum's irrigation systems fell into disrepair and at least its outlying areas were abandoned. The evidence consists of numerous written appeals for answers and blessings, first (historically) in Demotic and then in Greek, expressing both a phraseology and a range of concerns much like those on the New Kingdom ostraca of Deir el-Medina. The cult of Sobek at Tebtunis, under the name of Soknebtunis, provides indisputable evidence that the Sobek oracle was indigenous to the Fayyum and an entirely Egyptian phenomenon in all its constitutive forms, for Demotic Egyptian papyri associated with Soknebtunis go back to the early Hellenistic period.[61] While oracle requests from the Roman period do not survive, other evidence for the continuity of the temple's priesthood into the fourth century suggests the continuity also of its oracle "service."

The Demotic oracle requests already show a development of the oracle "ticket" from their ancient prototypes as visible in the oracle requests to Horus-of-the-Camp. In Tebtunis the divination procedure is made explicit in the text of the oracle request, instructing: "If [this alternative is the god's answer] bring this [ticket] out [of the temple]." The same formula would ultimately continue into Greek and then Coptic.[62]

The cult of Pnepheros and Petesuchos, twin aspects of Sobek at Ka-

[58] Bataille 1951:xxiii–xxiv; Laskowska-Kusztal 1984:118–27 (esp. 123–24 on the portal). As with the temples of Karanis and Siwa, one must assume that some clients were admitted to an area quite close to the sanctuary and the "voice" hole emitting from it.

[59] See Bataille 1951:xxiv–xxv.

[60] Łajtar 1992. See above, 3.3, on parallels with ritual in the Oxyrhynchus Thoērion.

[61] Demotic oracles: W. Erichsen, *Demotische Orakelfragen*, Kgl. Danske Videnskabernes Selskab. Historisk-filologiske Meddelelser 28, 3 (Copenhagen: Munksgaard, 1942); Giuseppe Botti, "Biglietti per l'oracolo di Soknebtynis in caratteri demotici," *Studi in memoria di Ippolito Rosellini* 2 (Pisa: Lischi & Figli, 1955), 10–26; Edda Bresciani and P. Pestman, "Tre Domandi oracolari," *P. Mil. Vogliano* 3 (1965):195–99; Bresciani 1975. Greek oracles: P.Mil.Vogl. III.127; *P.Tebtunis* II.284 = Schubart 1931, #1.

[62] See Schubart 1931:114; Henrichs 1973:116–17; Clarysse 1984:1348–49.

ranis, may not have provided a "ticket" oracle cult like that of Soknebtunis since there are no extant oracle papyri addressed to these gods. Yet
the "voice" oracle in the Karanis temple, described above, would have
continued from at least the time of the temple's beginnings at the turn of
the eras through its demise in the late third century C.E.[63] In this case the
oracle may have had an essentially local clientele: dedicatory inscriptions
from the temple's substantial rebuilding in the late second century C.E.
suggest that it was a communal rather than individual or imperial effort.[64] This popular support of the Karanis temple again shows the degree to which the Sobek cult was indigenized in the Fayyum; thus, the
"voice" oracle was an extension of normal ritual around the chief local
and regional god.[65]

The priestly town of Soknopaiou Nesos developed an oracular cult of
Sobek with a much broader appeal, using inscribed questions and responses instead of the "voice" oracles. A considerable number of papyri
from this town dating from the second century B.C.E. through the third
century C.E. show the continuity of the oracle cult over several centuries,
in both Demotic Egyptian and Greek.[66] An interesting addition to the
cult of Soknopaios, undoubtedly developed to bring maximum authority
to its oracle, was the great god Amun (long associated with authoritative
oracles) to the divine voices accessible there: multiple requests appeal to
"my lord Soknopaios and Amun, the great gods."[67] One request, apparently from the same temple archive of the god, is addressed exclusively
"to the lord Amun."[68] The resulting importance of the Soknopaiou
Nesos oracle may partially explain how the priest-dominated town could
thrive into the third century with little dependence on agriculture.[69]

The existence of single oracle requests addressed to other local forms
of Sobek—Sokonnokonni in his temple at Bacchias, Souxei at some unknown location in the Fayyum—shows that the much larger archives
that remain from Tebtunis and Soknopaiou Nesos do not represent the
full extent of Sobek oracle cults in the Fayyum during the early Roman
period.[70] Even by the middle of the third century, a variety of local ora-

[63] See Gazda 1978:9–10, 13.

[64] IGFayyum I.88–89, on which see É. Bernand 1984:80 (##27–28), 83–84.

[65] See also Toutain 1915:180–87.

[66] Ptolemaic period: *P.Ox.Griffith* 1–12, ed. Bresciani 1975:2–11. Roman period:
Schubart 1931, ##2, 4, 7–10 = Preisendanz 1973/74, 2, P XXXb–f; *P.Lond.* 2935–36,
ed. Coles 1967; *P.Wien* G297, ed. Henrichs 1973; *P.Berlin* 21713, 21716, 21875, 25044,
ed. Aly 1987; *P.Köln* IV.201. On the history of cult, see Rübsam 1974:162–66.

[67] *P.Berlin* 21875 = Aly 1987, #6; cf. Aly 1987, ##2, 4–5; Henrichs 1973, #2; Coles
1967, ##1–2; Schubart 1931, ##7–8; *P.Köln* IV.201; *P.Heid.* IV.335.

[68] *P.Berlin* 25044 = Aly 1987, #8. See Aly 1987:99 on site.

[69] See Hobson 1984:106–8.

[70] *P.Fayyum* 137 = Schubart 1931, #3; *P.Lond.* III.1267d = Schubart 1931, #11.

cles were being maintained in temples up and down the Nile, using traditional rites as well as developing those rites that were, perhaps, more attractive to outsiders and the munificence they could bring: "ticket" exchanges with their amuletic potential, incubation, and healing as a component of the oracle.

## 4.3 New Egyptian Oracles of the Roman Period

Alongside the extant oracle "tickets" used for cults of Sobek are many for cults about which we know nothing else. The Fayyum towns of Soknopaiou Nesos and Bacchias, while centered around their respective cults of Sobek, also held shrines to the Greco-Roman Dioscuri—at least the Bacchian version, which provided oracles.[71] An oracle of Serapis in Oxyrhynchus continued to provide answers for the problems of city-dwellers into the third century.[72] And hitherto unknown oracles of Isis, Harpsenisis, and Thonis appear in single requests from the same period.[73] That the latter are indigenous gods with known temples shows that the addition of oracles could not have been simply an innovation for Greco-Roman clients but actually served a predominantly Egyptian or Egyptianized population.

The great number of such "ticket" oracles in the Roman period may in some way reflect a general popularization of the written medium within the sphere of religion during this time—that people desired the actual words of gods in concrete form.[74] To the extent that oracles often were produced as amulets in pharaonic Egypt they would also have served this function in the Roman period. But we have seen that the "ticket" oracle itself derives from a ritual tradition at least as old as the Third Intermediate Period; and in both ancient and Greco-Roman forms the essential preparatory stage of the rite, the presentation of the written alternatives

[71] P.Fayyum 138 = Schubart 1931, #6; cf. PSI Congr. XX, 3, ed. Paola Prunetti, Dai Papiri della Società Italiana (Florence: Papyrological Institute, 1992), 13–15. Other shrines of Dioscuri are mentioned in P.Oxy II.254, BGU XIII.2217, II, 2 (post-161 C.E., Soknopaiou Nesos) and P.Giss. 20 = W.Chr. 94 (beginning of second century, Apollinopolis Heptakomia), in which Alinē, the author, claims to have built a topos for the Dioscuri after receiving an oracle to this effect. Quaegebeur has argued compellingly that over the course of the Greco-Roman period the Dioscuri came to function as a Hellenized version of an indigenous "twin" form of Sobek (1983a:313–16). See above, 3.2, on Sobek cults.

[72] Schubart 1931, ##5, 12–14; P.Oxy XXXI.2613.

[73] Isis: P.Mich. 1258, ed. Henrichs 1973. Harpsenisis: P.Carlsberg 24, ed. Adam Bülow-Jacobsen, "P. Carlsberg 24: Question to an Oracle," ZPE 57 (1984):91–92. Thonis: P.Köln IV.202. This god is rather ill-attested: a temple is known through P.Oslo III.143, 8 (first century C.E.) and it may be related to some aspect of Horus (Jean Yoyotte, "Notes de toponomie égyptienne," MDAIK 16 [1958]:78).

[74] Beard 1991:49–53.

to the god, suggests that the tickets themselves would not necessarily be viewed as empowered, but rather as "tools" of divination. It is more likely due to the ease of the "ticket" oracle, its capability to provide the traditional service of an oracle cult without the need for processions and apparatus, that numerous such oracles appear in Egypt during the early Roman period, in cults often with little previous association with oracles.

### 4.3.1 Incubation and New Temple Facilities

The Roman period did see several incubation cults grow to regional prominence while maintaining roots in traditional sacred space and cultic practice through association with temples, local deities, and their rites and priesthoods. The structure of an early Roman "sanatorium" at Dendara—private chambers surrounding a central room, each with wall niches to hold divine images—suggests that along with the water and various healing rituals conducted by priests one was supposed to gain a healing vision of a divinity (probably Hathor herself) through incubation (pl. 22). The central stela's hieroglyphic characters are themselves typical of the early second century, and the cult could not have died very soon thereafter.[75]

It is the incubation cults of Isis in Canopus and Menouthis that may best exemplify an oracle's continuity into the late Roman period. Inscriptions show that temples of Serapis and Isis were attracting prominent pilgrims to the town of Canopus (east of Alexandria) increasingly over the course of the Ptolemaic period.[76] Already at this time the various cults of Isis in the Alexandrian orbit had acquired, or had begun to maintain assertively, the strongly local characters and functions one finds in Roman inscriptions. Indeed, it is likely that the notion of a "marine" Isis, Isis *pharia*, developed in the context of the Canopus cult.[77] Yet it is only in the late first century B.C.E. that one finds the first notice of an oracle cult. Strabo describes

> the temple of Sarapis, which is honoured with great reverence and effects such cures that even the most reputable men believe in it and sleep in it—themselves on their own behalf or others for them. Some writers go on to record the cures, and others the virtues, of the oracles there.[78]

In the same period Diodorus describes generally the powers of Isis in incubation. His remarks most probably reflect the Canopus cult, since he would be dependent on traditions and reputations in circulation around

[75] Daumas 1957:50–57, and above, 2.3.

[76] A. Bernand 1970:232–36, 308–9, 317–18.

[77] Ladislas Castiglione, "Isis Pharia: Remarque sur la statue de Budapest," *Bulletin du Musée hongrois des beaux-arts* 34/35 (1970):37–55.

[78] Strabo 17.1.17, tr. Jones, LCL, 8:62–65.

Alexandria (and Isis's powers in incubation are not known for certain elsewhere during Diodorus's time):[79]

> Isis . . . finds her greatest delight in the healing of mankind and gives aid in their sleep to those who call upon her, plainly manifesting both her very presence and her beneficence towards men who ask her help. . . . For standing above the sick in their sleep she gives them aid for their diseases and works remarkable cures upon such as submit themselves to her.[80]

A distinct cult of Isis in the neighboring town of Menouthis first comes to light during the late second or early third century through both an inscription describing an image of "Isis of Menouthis" sent to "Isis of Pharos" and the Oxyrhynchus Isis aretalogy, Oxyrhynchus Papyrus 1380.[81] While one should beware of the terms by which such aretalogies describe local cults (the genre, as we have noted, tended to organize Isis cults according to Greco-Roman virtues rather than indigenous functions), the attribution of "truth" to Isis in Menouthis quite likely refers to her "true" oracular words. At the very least these sources show an arrangement of independent and localized institutions.[82]

We glean more about the Egyptian nature of this cult from a set of votive stelae from about the second century, dedicated to Isis of Menouthis as "she who hears (prayers, requests)." The stelae include symbols highly traditional to such votive signs, the feathered *atef* crown associated with Osiris and a pair of "hearing ears" long associated with local shrines of popular access.[83] This kind of iconography would have expressed the cultural distance of at least some adherents of the Menouthis cult from the Hellenistic world of Alexandria. And yet these or a similar shrine's votive stelae were well known to the Christian Clement, also in the second century, who refers to "those who fashion ears and eyes of costly material and consecrated them, dedicated them in the temples to the gods."[84]

Apparently the Isis cults of Menouthis and Canopus did not decline significantly during the third century, for dedicatory inscriptions con-

---

[79] Cf. *P.Oxy* 1380, 42–43 and *P.Mich.* 1258, ed. Henrichs 1973, on later witnesses to Isis oracles.

[80] Diodorus Siculus, *Hist.* 1.25.3, 5, tr. Oldfather, LCL, 1:81.

[81] Inscription: *CIG* III.4683b, on which see A. Bernand 1970:296–99.

[82] *P.Oxy* XI.1380, 62–63. The oracular Bes of Abydos is also called *alēthēs* and *pan-alēthēs* (Perdrizet/Lefebvre 1919, ##489, 492–93). In IGPhilae 168 Serenus, "brought up near Isis of Pharos," is sent by an oracle of "Apollo [= Horus?]" to make *proskunēsis* to Isis of Philae. The inscription reflects a world of deities conceptualized in respect to their locales. See É. Bernand 1969, 2:170n. *ad* 6, and above, 3.2.

[83] François Kayser, "Oreilles et couronnes: à propos des cultes de Canope," *BIFAO* 91 (1991):207–17, with Sadek 1987, ch. 9 and pls.

[84] Clement, *Strom.* 5.7., tr. Wilson, *ANCL*, 2:246.

tinue at least through the third century and references to vibrant religious activity there in both Epiphanius and Rufinus imply persistence through the fourth century.[85] One reason for this continuity may be the cults' special attraction to the Alexandrian élite and regional priests. The picture of these towns in Rufinus, Eunapius, and the sixth-century Zachariah of Mytilene gives one the impression that they were becoming a social focus and rallying point for an intellectual "paganism" evolving during the fourth century.[86] Nonetheless, the cult of Canopus fell in about 389 during the same iconoclastic campaign that destroyed the Alexandrian Serapeum.[87]

A vague reconstruction of the events in the region by the seventh-century ecclesiarch Sophronius of Jerusalem once led scholars to believe that the Isis temple of Menouthis fell around 414. Yet Zachariah of Mytilene, who himself accompanied a destructive mob into Menouthis around 484, plainly refers to a structure covered in hieroglyphs and arranged with secret rooms—that is, a temple or temple chamber—as the locus of an Isis cult that was still providing the power of the goddess Isis through incubation for a regional population.[88] It was here that an Alexandrian philosopher, Asclepiodotes, received

> an oracle (or, rather, he was deceived by the demon appearing as Isis) according to which the goddess promised him children if he went with his wife into the temple that the goddess had in Menouthis, a village forty miles away from Alexandria.
>
> He stayed some time in Menouthis and offered a considerable number of sacrifices to the demons. But it was to no avail. The sterility of his wife persisted nonetheless. Having believed that he saw in a dream Isis lying beside him he heard it declared by those who interpreted dreams there and who served the demon expressed in Isis, that he ought to join himself to the idol of that goddess, then to have sex with his wife—that thus a child would be born to him.[89]

[85] Inscriptions: A. Bernand 1970:241–45, 250–52, ##13–15, 24–26—all to Serapis and Isis. Literary sources: Epiphanius, *De fide* 12.1–4 (quoted above, 2.5.1), and Rufinus, *H.E.* 26–27, both in A. Bernand 1970:199–201. On Rufinus's picture of Canopic piety, see Thelamon 1981:207–43. A large black basalt statue of Isis holding a cornucopia, found in Abukir and now in the Greco-Roman Museum of Alexandria, probably belonged to one of these temples (inv. 31424).

[86] See Eunapius, *V.P.* 6.9.17 [470–71], Zachariah, *V.Sev.*, in A. Bernand 1970:202–5, 207–13; and discussion above, 2.6.2.

[87] Rufinus in A. Bernand 1970:201. See also p. 321 and Thelamon 1981:258.

[88] Zachariah, *V.Sev.*, in A. Bernand 1970:211; Duchesne 1910:10–12; Wipszycka 1988:138–42, rejecting Hippolyte Delehaye, "Les saints d'Aboukir," *AnBoll* 30 (1911):448–50. On proposals regarding this hieroglyph-covered building, see A. Bernand 1970:322–23 and Kákosy 1984:68–69.

[89] Zachariah, *V.Sev.*, tr. Kugener 1907:18, in A. Bernand 1970:208.

When she did not conceive by these means, the priest sent him to the nearby town of "Astu," where a local priestess would give him a baby.

That this cult maintained itself regardless of a local Christian community and that, when destroyed in 484, it was replaced by a church with relics claimed explicitly to have healing powers (Saints Cyrus and John), both suggest the vital importance of the Isis oracle in serving regional needs. Indeed, when analyzed over a broader period of time, the oracle cults of Isis east of Alexandria seem to have gone through several stages: (a) competition in Canopus with a neighboring incubation oracle of Serapis through the beginning of the Roman period; (b) still in Canopus, an eclipsing of the Serapis oracle in the early Roman period as the cult of Isis itself grows in popularity and, in Egypt, indigenous character and function; (c) the steady growth of the Menouthis cult of Isis, such that (d) with the demise of her Canopus temple in 389 the major regional incubation cult (and no doubt its displaced priesthood) could shift to Menouthis, which may have already laid claim to Isis's words of "truth." It would be reasonable to take as a final stage (e) the translation of the cult of Cyrus and John to Menouthis (initiated on the basis of an oracular dream!), since this cult too involved incubation for healing.[90] Indeed, the bishop under whose aegis the translation took place made clear in a homily at the time that the conversion of the site was merely a replacement of healing cults:

> Approach, all those who have long wandered, come to the true and non-profit [akapēleuton] cure! For none of us (on our side) invents dreams! Nobody says to visitors, "Cyrus says, 'Do this or that.'" The power is altogether Cyrus and God. . . . Come to the true and celestial doctors to whom God of all powers bestowed the authority to be able to cure, saying "Cure the sick—receive a gift, give a gift!"[91]

The vicissitudes of the Menouthis site show a persistent regional need for an oracle cult as well as the continuing ability to maintain it in the Canopus–Menouthis area. In addition, the attractiveness of the cult to intellectual "pagans" in the fourth and fifth centuries shows how the local oracle was viewed as a symbol of native religion in the late Roman period.

At the other end of Roman Egypt, in the region of the first cataract, the

---

[90] On the translation, see Sophronius, in A. Bernand 1970:214–17; on incubation in the cult of John and Cyrus, see Duchesne 1910:9–10. In general on continuities between the cults, see Gérard Viaud, *Les pèlerinages coptes en Égypte,* Bibliothèque d'études coptes 15 (Cairo: IFAO, 1979), 6–7, and Sarolta Takács, "The Magic of Isis Replaced, or Cyril of Alexandria's Attempt at Redirecting Religious Devotion," *Poikila Byzantina* 13 (1994):489–507.

[91] *PG* 77:1105.

garrison of Talmis developed and maintained an incubation oracle of the god Mandulis from the beginning of the Roman period through the third century, at which point it seems to have continued without the influx of Roman pilgrims through the fifth century. The incubation oracle itself probably only played a temporary part in the overall history of the cult of Mandulis at Talmis. Attested only by inscriptions of the first three centuries C.E., it may have been developed as precisely an apparatus of Hellenization (incubation's antiquity in Egypt notwithstanding), eventually to be abandoned or modified to serve the less individualized piety of the Blemmyes and, eventually, the installation of a Christian sanctuary.[92]

The graffiti themselves preserve a curiously ethereal tendency among pilgrims (or those of the type to leave graffiti), in contrast to the mundane and somewhat desperate appeals at places like Abydos and (it would seem) Menouthis. The anonymous inscription that identifies Mandulis with Aion presents the acquisition of this knowledge as spiritual conversion, not a night in a temple: "I had a vision and found rest for my soul. For thou didst grant my prayer and show me thyself going through the heavenly vault. . . . Then I knew thee, Mandulis, to be the Sun, allpowerful Eternity [*Aiōn*]."[93] The oracle was evidently appropriated by a culture of young men in search of heavenly knowledge, *gnōsis*, as a means of revealing gods' true essences.

But then it is striking that the god with whom the elsewhere transcendent Aion is identified in this passage is the distant, barbarian, and quite parochialized Mandulis.[94] This irony points to a subtle dynamic in the interaction of Greco-Roman and native Egyptian cultures in the Roman period: that exoticist lure toward a late antique "heart of darkness"— the distant, alien, and therefore "most" thoroughly indigenous cultic wisdom—as the locus of revelation and *gnōsis*. Here in practice is the theme of the Egyptomanic spiritual quest described in numerous late antique literary sources: the youthful Clement of the Pseudo-Clementine *Recognitions*, Eucrates in Lucian's *Philopseudes*, Thessalos of Tralles in his herbal tract.[95] In the same way, the Talmis pilgrim came from afar to find the true Aion in the local, even barbarian, god Mandulis. So one Serenus, "brought up near Isis of Pharos" (Alexandria), receives an oracle from "Apollo" to make a pilgrimage to Isis of Philae, off at the distant periphery of Roman civilization, in 191 C.E.[96] Nearchos sought an oracle

---

[92] Sayce 1894, ##IV–VI. See above, 3.3.

[93] Preisigke, *Sammelbuch* #4127, tr. Nock 1972a:366.

[94] On the god Aion in the Roman world, see esp. Nock 1972a:388–96; Bowersock 1990:22–28.

[95] Ps-Clement, *Recognitions* 1.5; Lucian, *Philopseudes* 34–36; Thessalos, *De virtutibus herbarum* 12–13, ed. Friedrich 1968:48–49. See below, 5.3.1.

[96] IGPhilae 168, ed. É. Bernand 1969, 2:166–74.

at Siwa after visiting "the region of the cataract." The late antique historian Olympiodorus procures an invitation from "the phylarchs and prophets" of the Blemmyes to visit them at Talmis and then beyond, "so that I could investigate those lands five days distant from Philae" where he learned there were emerald mines.[97] These texts all express a Greco-Roman pilgrimage ideology of forging as far as one could get from the center (Greco-Roman culture and its cities) to the periphery of the empire, deep into alien land, and thereby to a new "center," as it were, of alien wisdom.[98]

The cult of Isis and Serapis at Kysis in the Kharga oasis reflects a similar phenomenon of appealing to different constituencies from the periphery of the empire. Epigraphy and archaeology at Kysis reflect first an agricultural and then a military society. It was a region in which the Hellenized deities Serapis and Isis might be promoted despite the traditional association of oasis cultures with the god Amun.[99]

The history of the cult and the appearance of its oracle offer an important gauge of religious developments in the Roman period since the town itself does not seem to have existed beforehand. Its temple to Isis and Osiris-Serapis was begun under Domitian and finished under Trajan, and the town's "boom" period began in the fourth century with the installation of an army garrison.[100] The dedicatory inscriptions, which date from the time of Domitian, disclose a devotion to Isis and Serapis as "supreme gods of Kysis" and to Isis in her specific powers over agricultural fertility, as well as a priesthood bearing theophoric (Isiac) names and skilled in both Demotic and hieratic Egyptian. All this is evidence for the cult's traditional character and the basis of its powers and functions in the agricultural life of the oasis's southern region.[101] At the same time, an inscription "to Aminibis, supreme god" shows the incursion of, or extension of, the temple's authority to the traditional oasis-god Amun.[102] Traditional piety seems to have continued well into the fourth century (during which time Christian inscriptions and ostraca also begin to appear), and the town's prosperity is indicated by a set of gold priestly jewelry still in use during the fourth century.[103] In the fifth century the town was completely abandoned.

---

[97] Olympiodorus, frag. 35.2 (= Photius, *Bibl. Cod.* 80, p. 182), ed. Blockley 1981/82, 2:198–200.

[98] See also Festugière 1950, 1:59–66.

[99] Wagner 1987:329–34.

[100] See summary in Wagner 1987:176–78 and Reddé 1990.

[101] Wagner 1987:48–53, 336, 345; Vernus 1979:12.

[102] *SB* 8440; Wagner 1987:333.

[103] Reddé 1990:290; 1992.

The significant development in Kysis is the addition of an oracle "chapel" to the south end of its temple at some point following the decline of its temple cult proper in the mid- to late fourth century. Those parts of temples' outer walls closest to their inner sanctuaries were commonly the location of public or popular cults, and temples like Dendara, Karnak, and Kom Ombo even carried special iconographic reliefs at this spot to focus such piety (pl. 3). In this case, the area just outside the south wall was surrounded with brick walls, which were plastered over and decorated, and the south wall and its reliefs were covered in gilt.[104] Then a hole was broken through the temple's wall between the brick chapel and the inner sanctum of the temple itself, providing the means for a "voice" oracle to enter the new chapel outside the wall (pl. 20). The new structure preserved the sacred exclusiveness of the temple's own rooms while making the god immediately accessible to pilgrims, who could hear the god's voice coming from the sanctuary itself, as at Deir el-Bahri.[105]

These materials give a striking picture of religious innovation in the face of economic decline. The oracle cult clearly succeeded the fuller temple cult, for the oracle was based in sacred areas that, in the temple's greater days, had been either taboo (the sanctuary out of which came the "voice") or objects of popular veneration (the exterior south wall, just outside the sanctuary). This development was no unique phenomenon. The Menouthis temple of Isis may itself have been such an extension or portion of a larger temple. And the story of Thessalos of Tralles also may reflect the use of nether portions of temples for incubation ritual.

Thessalos, apparently writing in the first century C.E., travels south to Diospolis in order to learn the mysteries of the priests there. After he gains their trust, he claims, one priest "promised to reveal to me the craft of divination in secret." They fast for three days and then, in a prepared chamber [*oikos*], he is offered a choice of encountering a dead soul or a god of his choosing. Thessalos decides upon the god Asclepius, is shut in the chamber and told to face the "throne," receives an auspicious theophany, and goes his way. While the text bears all the trappings of a Greco-Roman novel in its view of Egypt, it seems also to carry some verisimilitude. In this case the "chamber"—complete with a physical locus for the theophany reminiscent of the ancient Egyptian "false por-

---

[104] Compare the gilding associated with the building of the contra-temple at Kellis (Dakhla oasis): Hope et al. 1989:15.

[105] Serge Sauneron, "Douch—Rapport préliminaire de la compagne de fouilles 1976," *BIFAO* 78 (1978):7, pl. II; Vernus 1979:9; Dunand 1991a:246. Cf. Reddé 1990:290, who dates the oracle earlier, and Grimal in *BIFAO* 90 (1990):394. Quaegebeur 1997 proposes a similar "voice" oracle of the god Tutu at the Roman Isis temple of Shenhur. On Deir el-Bahri, see above, 4.2.2.

tal" (through which the god's *ba* manifests itself)—suggests a temple alcove or additional room, redesigned for oracles.[106]

As in Thessalos's Thebes, the historical and religious contexts in which the phenomenon was understood would have been manifold. The direct "visionary" experience proffered by the incubation cult in Kysis may have answered the cultural needs of a new clientele unaccustomed to or unfulfilled by the traditional ritual dramas of Egyptian temples (as these were visible to townspeople); and the fourth-century militarization of Kysis may well have been the occasion to offer a new, individualized or psychologically dramatic kind of rite like that at Talmis. There were certainly other religious reasons as well for the Kysis oracle: if the voice from the temple were Isis it would represent the extension of the Greco-Roman Isis oracle as we find it in Canopus, Menouthis, and elsewhere. If Serapis or Amun, of course, the cult's development of an oracle would be in line with their temple cults elsewhere in Egypt at this time.[107]

### 4.3.2 The Voice of Bes in Abydos

A shift from Isis to Amun would not be impossible in the genesis of an oracle cult, for changes of gods did occur at oracle sites. It is this important phenomenon that the Memnonion of Sethos I at Abydos represents so vividly. Erected in the XIX Dynasty as a monument to seven gods, most particularly Osiris, on a site long associated with mortuary divinities, a goal for pilgrims and a sacred burial ground for Egyptians of all ranks since the Middle Kingdom and for Greeks from before Alexander, the Memnonion also provided a renowned incubation oracle of Osiris-Serapis throughout the Ptolemaic period.[108] Historically, the Serapis oracle must have been a shift in ritual program from previous rites for the god Osiris. These Osiris rites themselves declined in the Late Period, opening up hitherto sacrosanct sections of the temple to graffiti in honor of Serapis.[109] The indigenous "Osirian" roots of the Abydos oracle cult seem to have been popularly understood, however: some votive inscrip-

[106] See also Festugière 1939 (esp. 61n.21 on the *oikos*); Smith 1978a; Fowden 1986:162–65; and Ritner 1995:3356–58. On the novelistic perspective on Egyptian religion, see below, 5.3.1, 5.3.3.

[107] A profusion of gold *ex voto* medallions bearing the image of Serapis and the Apis bull imply a continuing veneration of this god through at least the beginning of the fourth century (see Reddé 1992:62). But this does not mean that the development of the oracle chamber involved the same divinity.

[108] On Greek views of the Memnonion, see Strabo 17.1.42, 44; Plutarch, *De Iside* 20, 359A–B.

[109] A. H. Sayce, "Some Greek Graffiti from Abydos," *PSBA* 10 (1888):380–81; Perdrizet/Lefebvre 1919:xiv–xix.

tions appeal to Osiris, and even in the fourth century C.E. two ritual spells for gaining oracles invoke Osiris as "he who gives a message [Copt. *ji ouō*] in Abydos."[110]

In the Roman period a curious transformation occurs in the Memnonion: the "voice" becomes that of the god Bes, hitherto known best as an apotropaic figure of terra-cottas, stelae, amulets, and temple birth-chambers, and quite popular in these media throughout the Roman period. At least twenty-eight individual graffiti in the Memnonium of Abydos, carved through the fourth century, directly invoke Bes, often repeating the name several times for efficacious contact.[111] And in the fourth century there is also an external witness to the cult, Ammianus Marcellinus, who describes the circumstances of its forced closure in 359:

> In the furthest part of the Thebaid there is a town called Abydos, where a god locally called Besa used to reveal the future through an oracle and was worshipped with traditional rites by the inhabitants of the surrounding regions. Some of those who consulted the oracle did so in person, others sent a letter by an intermediary containing an explicit statement of their requests. In consequence, records of their petitions on paper or parchment sometimes remained in the temple even after the replies had been given. Some of these documents were sent to the emperor [Constantius II] out of malice. His small mind made him deaf to other matters, however serious, but on this point he was more sensitive than the proverbial ear-lobe, suspicious and petty.[112]

The emperor immediately dispatched the infamous notary Paul to the region, and a full-scale inquisition was held to root out the subversiveness to which the oracle had given voice and to close the Abydos shrine itself (an echo of the Roman proscription of Egyptian oracles in 199, for similar fears of subversion). Among those whom Paul brought to trial was the Alexandrian philosopher Demetrius, who

> was shown to have offered sacrifice to Besa on several occasions. He could not deny it, but maintained that, though he had observed this practice from early youth, his purpose was simply to propitiate the deity, not to inquire into his own prospects of advancement; nor did he know of anybody who made this his aim.[113]

Thus the popular Bes image widely employed to protect children, homes, and life in general had somehow evolved in the Roman period

---

[110] *PGM* IV.12; *PDM* xiv.628. See Griffith 1900:87 and Crum 1939:475A.

[111] Abydos, Memnon graffiti ##1[x4], 22, 386, 458[x4], 480–81, 488–89, 493–95, 497, 499–500, 507, 509–10, 518, 520, 523–24, 528, 552, 560, 580 in Perdrizet/Lefebvre 1919. See analysis of Bes oracle pilgrims in Dunand 1997.

[112] Ammianus 19.12.3–6, tr. Hamilton 1986:181–82.

[113] Ammianus 19.12.12, tr. Hamilton 1986:182.

into a large-scale pilgrimage cult that even operated by correspondence. Where there is hitherto little evidence for a "cult" of Bes, the Abydos materials reflect a considerable priesthood. Not only would the international correspondence and the archives have required several trained scribes, but the arrangement of the graffiti implies that some staff was able to maintain sacred limits around the inner portions of the temple, whether by placing the inscriptions themselves or restricting the places where they might be put: twenty-five out of twenty-nine votive inscriptions explicitly to Bes are outside the temple walls. One verse inscription records the visit of a member of a family of priests.[114] And the Coptic *Life of Moses* (late fifth century) assumes the activity of some priesthood—the author uses the traditional terminology for priestly ranks—but with what local temple they were associated is now unclear.[115]

Ammianus himself indicates the oracle cult's association with the local veneration of Bes—that is, with his connotations as protector of maternity and home, as discussed above. But this change of Bes to "oracle-giving [*khrēsmodotas*]," as one pilgrim clearly reveres him, seems to transcend the locale of Abydos.[116] Fourth-century spells for gaining one's own incubation oracle refer to Bes's oracular capacity: one is entitled "Request for a dream-oracle [*oneiraitēton*] of Bes"; another invokes him as "the oracle-giving god [*khrēsmōdos theos*]."[117]

Do these Bes oracle spells suggest that the Abydos oracle was part of a broader transformation of Bes into an oracle-god? Or do they assume the prior popularity of the Abydos cult of Bes? Since the oracle spells bear sufficiently close parallels in imagery and wording to suppose a common "master" (and thus not independent, isolated production), and since they appear in manuscripts of the fourth century, their general reflection of the authority of the Abydos oracle seems the most likely relationship. But then the oracle of Bes itself must be attributed to local ingenuity. What circumstances would impel priests—the likely innovators—to promote the god Bes as oracular and as speaking from Abydos in particular?

Like the god Tutu, who was invoked as a protector of sleep and dreams in a third-century (B.C.E.) stela, Bes was invoked in classical and Ptolemaic Egypt to "repel the demon-prowlers by night as well as by

---

[114] Abydos, Memnon graffito #528, ed. Perdrizet/Lefebvre 1919:94.

[115] Moses is said to kill twenty-three *ouēēb*-priests and seven *hont*-priests associated with a nearby temple of "Apollo." *Life of Moses,* ed. and tr. Till 1936:2, 49, 68; Amélineau 1888/95:687. Cf. Wipszycka 1988:156; Coquin 1986:8. In general on Bes devotion in Roman Egypt, see above, 3.5.2.

[116] Abydos, Memnon graffito #488.

[117] *PGM* VII.222; VIII.101–2. Cf. *PGM* CII.1–17 and A. Delatte, "Études sur la magie grecque, V. AKEPHALOS THEOS," *BCH* 38 (1914):201–13.

day," as an inscription on one small Bes figurine puts it.[118] The Bes image often appears in bedrooms or on beds, suggesting its protection of sleep or of sexuality and fertility—or most likely both, in the sense of granting dreams suggestive of fertility and safe maternity.[119] This interpretation has been proposed for the Bes chambers at the pilgrims' arcade at Ptolemaic Saqqara, for example: the enormous reliefs of Bes with nude females would provoke dreams of happy and safe maternity—oracles, in fact. Unfortunately, there is no evidence from the early Roman period that Bes was commonly construed as granting oracles.

One must hence look elsewhere for the roots of this singular innovation of a Bes oracle in the Memnonium of Roman Abydos. And given the implicit activity of a priesthood in negotiating the oracles for both pilgrims and correspondents, one ought to look to the priestly world for the sources of this innovation. Whereas the discussion of Bes in chapter 3 concentrated on the evidence of figurines and other materials to illustrate the consistent religious themes of maternal fertility and protection (especially of children), the ritual texts invoking Bes seem to present a more diverse figure, an extension of major deities for multiple purposes. Thus in the Brooklyn Magical Papyrus, in which spells originally composed to protect the pharaoh as child and adult are reassigned to a nonroyal client, Bes is invoked—and drawn—as an amalgamation of divine powers to repel and attack demonic "enemies."[120] Through such multivalent representations the texts reflect the typical archaizing tendency of temple scribes, looking back to the constructions of the Bes image in ancient traditions in order to synthesize a "Bes" god in the Late and Greco-Roman periods. For this reason we may point to descriptions such as the following from the Harris Magical Papyrus (XIX–XX Dynasties) as bound to have a continuing effect on the priestly development of Bes:

> Oh dwarf here of heaven, the great dwarf whose head is large, whose back is long, whose thighs are short, the great support that extends from heaven unto the Underworld, the lord of the great corpse, which rests in Heliopolis, the great living god who rests in Busiris! Pay attention [to] NN born of NN! Guard him by day, watch him by night, protect him [as] you protected Osiris.[121]

[118] Michailidis 1963/64:70, fig. 23. On Tutu as protector of sleep, see Picard 1958: 59–64.

[119] See Bruyère 1939:99, 103, on bed chambers at Deir el-Medina; Michailidis 1963/64:70–73; and in general, Dasen 1993:71–73, 75–76.

[120] See esp. Sauneron 1970:11–17, with review by László Kákosy, *Bibliotheca Orientalis* 29, 1–2 (1972):28–29; and Malaise 1990:719–22.

[121] P.Harris Magic viii.9–11, ed. Lange 1927:72–73, tr. Borghouts 1978:90, #134. See discussion in Dasen 1993:51–53.

It is precisely the "dwarf's" function here as protector of Osiris's corpse, probably an extension of the Bes image's connection with still-born and deceased infants, which reappears in the Roman period in the three spells for private oracles.[122] Found in separate ritual grimoires dated to the fourth century, these spells were apparently based on a master-spell quite close to that in the Harris Papyrus, since they invoke Bes as "the god placed over Necessity . . . the one lying on a coffin of myrrh, having resin and asphalt as an elbow cushion. . . . You are not a daimon but the blood of the two falcons who chatter and watch before the head of Osiris."[123] The mortuary details in these spells are largely vestigial, much like the royal terminology in the Brooklyn Papyrus: in both cases a new application was drawn from older rituals of a narrower and traditionally pharaonic scope.

The existence of this "literary" ritual tradition of Bes must reflect a continuing priestly interest in developing and rearticulating an image of overwhelming popularity.[124] And it is perhaps this priestly interest in Bes's mortuary powers that best explains the shift in oracular gods in the Memnonium of Abydos from Osiris to Bes in the first or second centuries C.E.[125]

The Memnonion itself functioned as a center of the Osiris cult in Egypt, arranged as it was with a particularly extensive set of rooms devoted to Osiris, penetrating deep into the temple, with two halls spacious enough (even if not originally designed) to host a number of pilgrims. This would have been the location of the Osiris and subsequent Serapis oracles through the Ptolemaic period. These same Osiris rooms, alone among the Memnonion's seven shrines, also show a peculiar concentration of Christian mutilation—activity that generally indicates a place's abiding power at the point when a local Christian group was able to gain control. But the "speaking" god at Abydos at this time was Bes, not Osiris. Indeed, devotions (*proskunēmata*) to Bes are inscribed on the (south)west exterior wall of the Memnonion, just outside the Osiris chambers.[126] Thus at one level of religious development, that of priestly

---

[122] See Meeks 1992:427–34 on Bes's mortuary character, and on this spell, Dasen 1993:51–53.

[123] *PGM* VIII.95–101, tr. Grese in Betz 1986:147; cf. VII.236–40; CII = *Suppl. Mag.* 90.7–16 = *P.Oxy* XXXVI.2753.

[124] See Sauneron 1970:viii, 17.

[125] See Kákosy 1966a:193–94; 1995:2981–82. On the proposition of a "Bes clergy," see Meeks 1992:428–29; Dunand 1997:70; and above, 3.5.2. One is tempted to attribute some original creative spark in this change to one Saprion, an *engkatokhos* (hermit of sorts who resides in temple) who claims a devotion to "the Lord Bes" already in the early first century B.C.E. (Perdrizet/Lefebvre 1919:xvii–xix, #506).

[126] *P-M* 6:4, with Murnane 1983:210 on layout; Perdrizet/Lefebvre 1919:86–96 on

innovation, there must have been some continuity between Osiris and Bes such as that expressed in the Harris Magical Papyrus and its late antique parallels.

Since the Memnonion lacks any suggestion of a birth-chapel in which Bes might have had some traditional presence in the temple, we cannot otherwise explain the particular choice of Bes as ascendant god of Abydos in the Roman period. What is clear is that a god of broad popularity both within and beyond Greco-Roman Egypt for the negotiation of life-crises was promoted to the object of a full-scale cult with priesthood and pilgrims, and that a century following that cult's imperial closure the temple itself was still popularly identified as the habitat of Bes, according to the Coptic *Life of Moses of Abydos*. Thus beyond the context of priestly scribal synthesis one must also regard the phenomenon of the Bes oracle at Abydos as an example of a domestic cult with transregional *recognition* that was subsequently elevated to the status of transregional *cult*. This process of "elevation" is really identical to the long-standing Egyptian practice of extending the regional scope and authority of cults through syncretism, an endeavor directly attributable to priesthoods and therefore comparable to the process of universalizing elements of little traditions in other cultures. In India, for example,

> Identification [of local with great gods] not only enables wide cultural gulfs to be spanned, but also provides a means for the eventual transformation of the name and character of the deity, and the mode of worshipping him. Many Sanskritic deities worshipped in India today began their existence in the dim past as the deities of low castes or tribes.[127]

Furthermore, as McKim Marriott has pointed out, the great tradition itself gains and galvanizes authority "in so far as it constitutes a more articulate and refined restatement or systematization of what is already there."[128] The process of universalizing deities of the little tradition into elements of great tradition mythology inevitably draws upon "folk" gods like Bes.[129]

### 4.3.3 Oracles in Ascendance or Transformation

Overall we have seen documentary evidence for at least fifteen traditional Egyptian oracles operating successfully through the third century and

---

distribution of graffiti. It is conceivable that the secret crypt in the northwest corner of the building (behind the shrines to Isis, Horus, and Sethos I) served as the source of a speaking oracle (similarly proposed by Dunand 1997:70).

[127] Srinivas 1989:61.
[128] Marriott 1955:197.
[129] See Srinivas 1989:60.

four—Kysis, Abydos, Canopus-Menouthis, and Siwa—extending well beyond that. And these are only minimum numbers: their existence is only documented through the most haphazard of literary remains.

Those oracles whose origins or period of most dynamic growth lie in the Roman period continue to reflect those two important elements of the Egyptian oracle: its essentially localized nature and the integral participation of priesthoods. Priesthoods are implicit in every oracular function, from the maintenance of archives and dissemination of answers at Abydos to the "voices" of Sobek and Re-Harmakhis, from the promotion of Amun oracles to the invention of a Bes oracle, and in the cooperation of local shrines and priests among the towns east of Alexandria. A late-third-century letter from Oxyrhynchus refers to a "one-eyed astrologer" affiliated with an incubation cult much in the way the *muqaddam*, or guardian, of a Moroccan saint shrine provides dream interpretation to pilgrims today.[130]

What I have designated "new" oracles were also highly traditional, located as they were in temples of great antiquity, which often (Kysis, Abydos) had been receiving pilgrims for centuries. Given this affiliation between oracles and the prevailing local tradition, my division between "continuing oracles" like those of Sobek in the Fayyum or Amenhotep I at Deir el-Bahri and "new oracles" like Bes of Abydos or Mandulis of Talmis has no more than convenient, heuristic value. Even the Isis oracles of Canopus and Menouthis, which extend to the end of the fifth century, are developments of cults that go back at least to the early Ptolemaic period.

The division between continuing and new Roman oracles does, however, allow us to address the question, Was there a rise of oracles in the Roman period? Traditionally, affirmative answers to this question tended to be based on pan-Mediterranean appraisals of a Greco-Roman or late antique spiritual need. Bell saw the popularity of oracles in Roman Egypt as evidence of "a more personal trend of religious feeling," even "a craving for a redemptive religion and a closer union with God." Another papyrologist likewise attributed the draw of oracles to people's need for something more emotionally fulfilling at a time when "the major religions tended . . . toward ever-increasing formalism."[131] And yet, as a more circumspect historian of the period has remarked,

Theories of a psychological change, or a "new mood," are no longer helpful. There had been no sharp rise in credulity, no pressure from new, unsatisfied

130 *P.Oxy* LXI.4126. On the *muqaddam*, see Elizabeth Fernea, *Saints and Spirits: Religious Expression in Morocco* (Austin, Tex.: Center for Middle Eastern Studies, 1979), 6, 12, and the accompanying documentary film.
131 Bell 1953:68, 70; Lewis 1983:98.

anxieties. Almost all of this range of persons, places and techniques had been credited for centuries, flourishing because they met enduring needs. In the second century, inspired oracular shrines were merely establishing themselves once more in the market: the market itself was not new.[132]

To a large extent the concept of a "rise" of oracles is a function of the evidence itself, especially when one looks only at the Greco-Roman period and neglects the broader context. A profusion of remains of incubation and "voice" oracles, as well as the many "ticket" oracles from the Fayyum, give the impression of a new kind of piety or, in the case of the "ticket" oracles, a new anxiety in the Roman period preserved in its *ipsissima verba*. But when one follows the cults, the techniques, and the very questions asked, back into Ptolemaic and pharaonic times, the picture offered is very much one of continuity. Even distinctive Greco-Roman traits like the names of gods and the apparent expansion of the "ticket" oracle can be attributed to cultural circumstances apart from pan-Mediterranean anxiety. The use of Greek even at local oracles like those of Sobek in the Fayyum, as also for quasi-nationalist tracts like the Oracle of the Potter, testifies not so much to cultural syncretism or Mediterranean clienteles as to a growing preference for Greek among temple scribes, a "linguistic" Hellenization that often communicated a highly traditional Egyptian outlook.[133] Thus from a broader Egyptological perspective the Roman period is but a chapter in the perpetual rise and decline of regional oracle cults spanning well over a millennium.

And yet certain distinctively Roman needs seem to lurk behind portions of the evidence. The particularly poetic *ex voto* graffiti on the walls of the temple of Mandulis, whether inscribed by priests or the pilgrims themselves; the peripatetic piety of Nearchos, who visited Siwa after one of the Nile cataracts, or Serenus, who traveled up to Philae at the urging of an oracle of "Apollo"; the vision quest that inspired pilgrimages to Talmis and apparently also Abydos, Kysis, and Deir el-Bahri—all these historical vignettes we have surveyed seem to reflect a distinctive religious attitude among a particular constituency in Roman Egypt. The problem is, How important or representative was this constituency to Egyptian religious developments, and how can one characterize its attitude?

For example, the putative "individualism" of oracular questions and rites in the Roman period merely reflects the basic function of any divina-

---

[132] Lane Fox 1986:213. Cf. Dodds 1965:55 and Brown 1975:11–13, for whom traditional temple oracles retained their integral social status only to *decline* in about the third and fourth centuries due to competition with seers and prophets. Polymnia Athanassiadi, "The Fate of Oracles in Late Antiquity: Didyma and Delphi," *Deltion tēs Khristianikēs Archaiologikēs Hetaireias* 15 (1989/90):271–78, tracks the abiding authority of the Didyma and Delphic oracles until their forced closure in the later fourth century.

[133] See Clarysse 1984:1348–49; 1993, esp. 188 on oracles; and below, ch. 6.

tion system, which articulates and reconciles individuals' concerns within a traditional cosmology and ritual system (e.g., the woman who consults an oracle every ten days out of anxiety for her distant son, in Papyrus Merton 81).[134] The oracle "tickets" of the third-century Fayyum are no more individualistic than those from Deir el-Medina (or those delivered to Horus-of-the-Camp) in classical Egypt. And the perception of different shrines as offering distinctive "revelations" seems to have had some antiquity at least within the temple priesthood. The priest Hor of Sebennytos travels to and around Memphite shrines receiving incubation oracles of Thoth and Isis; and although he lives in the mid-second century B.C.E., his practices have no distinctively Hellenistic traits.[135]

Certainly the extension of the temple incubation rite to a clientele beyond that of the priesthood and the subsequent development of incubation oracles in temples to accommodate lay pilgrims would appear to be a new development, a "democratization" of priestly tradition. In this sense the written word, through the medium of votive graffiti, does provide a crucial link between the lay supplicant and the god he or she came to visit, for Greek and the ability to write allow, at least in some cases, the supplicant to participate directly in a version of temple "cult."[136] But this does not change structurally the system that was already in place for individuals like Hor. Priests were on hand to interpret the dreams received; and their instruction would have earned them particular authority with those clients who sought "revelations" from the divine world.

In interpreting the new oracles one should not be misled by the spirituality of a Thessalos or a pilgrim to Mandulis Aion. Temple oracles traditionally functioned to provide advice on life-crises and protection. In many temples they served as regional cults, supplementing rather than supplanting local and domestic cults, as we should infer from the agricultural promises of Isis at Kysis, which served the southern portion of the Kharga oasis; the reputation of Isis at Menouthis for impregnating the barren in the region of Alexandria and the western Delta; and the sanatorium at Dendara, whose sacred waterworks simply extended the ancient practice of collecting the water passed over magical stelae. The appeal of Bes at Abydos undoubtedly lay more in this area of "affliction"—with Abydos as the regional locus of the domestic god of protection—than in the political oracles for which it was closed, since the popular cult of Bes remained deeply rooted in Egypt through the Roman period. And throughout the third century in the Fayyum it is clear that several local avatars of the regional (even pan-Egyptian) god Sobek offered oracular advice through both "tickets" and "voices." In all such cases one should view the oracle as

---

[134] *P.Merton* II.81; see above, 4.2.2.
[135] Ray 1976:117–21, 130–36; cf. Sauneron 1959:38–43.
[136] Beard 1991:45–46.

designed and maintained not for the Roman youth in search of mystical revelation or the governor inquiring about his political future but for popular physical and everyday concerns.

Yet it is precisely this patronage of the Roman youth and the politician that explains the economic resilience of the temple oracle. It is almost certain that a request for an oracle by "ticket," enchambered "voice," incubation, or letter would have been accompanied by a gift of some sort. Normally in the Roman period both local shrines and regional temples were to varying degrees dependent on gifts to supplement a declining imperial patronage.[137] Donation would function as an acknowledgment of the symbolic and authoritative role the temple and its cult would play in the area. A donation might well be in exchange for an act or token of sacred beneficence such as an inscribed amulet or an empowered substance or some kind of divine "guarantee" of safety, all of which were prepared or available through the shrine's priesthood.[138] But an oracle cult provided a particular service, and one of extraordinary utility in a society undergoing rapid economic change: divination. Through oracles a shrine could become a thoroughly active participant in the life of a local community, multiplying considerably the ritual "exchanges" customarily performed from inscribing the occasional amulet or promoting divine guarantees to, with oracles, answering the regular questioner. Thus an oracle cult could be virtually self-supporting; and with the decline of such imperial patronage in the Roman period and complete withdrawal following Constantine the oracles could, and in fact did, persist. Evidence for the economic potential of oracles appears, for example, in an early-second-century letter from Middle Egypt in which a woman claims to have built a shrine (*topos*) for the Dioscuri at the prompting of an oracle, and in the homily at the installation of a Christian healing cult at Menouthis, criticizing its native predecessor for demanding donations.[139]

While the evidence for local processional oracles continuing beyond the third century should militate against the assumption of this public oracle's utter demise, one would expect that many temples could not afford the large-scale dramas recorded in the Brooklyn and British Museum papyri. A "ticket," "voice," or incubation oracle, on the other hand, required minimal staff and minimal portions of temples to main-

---

[137] See Nock 1972b:571, and above, 2.6.4.

[138] Edwards 1960, 1:xvii–xviii; Ritner 1993:216; 1989:105–7; and, particularly for the Roman period, Evans 1961:233–36.

[139] Letter: *P.Giss.* 20 = W.Chr. 94. Homily: Ps-Cyril of Alexandria in *PG* 77:1105 (tr. above, 4.3.1). Lucian mentions "the price set for each oracle" given at the cult of Glycon through Alexander of Abonuteichos (*Alexander,* 23), many of which were apparently delivered already inscribed on papyrus (19).

tain. Thus it was clearly in the economic interest of a temple to develop and promote an oracle, particularly one that could speak also trans-regionally to the concerns and needs of politicians and Roman pilgrims. Ingenious "voice" oracles like those at Coptos, Karanis, Kom el-Wist, and the unknown shrine that held the speaking image of Re-Har-makhis would only have contributed to the unique and broad appeal of a regional oracle.

That these endeavors worked in some places and not others is due to local variations in temple economy, administrative enforcement of edicts, and Christian influence on administrators and mobs. The oracles of Sobek in the Fayyum, as dependent as they were on local clients, could not sustain the depopulation of the Fayyum due to the decline of irrigation during the third century. But the oracle of Isis at Menouthis, which not only held regional renown as a healing shrine but became a rallying place for intellectual "pagans" of the fourth century, was able to maintain itself until the forced replacement of its divinity in the late fifth century. It may perhaps be suggested that smaller, more localized shrines with traditional support from the community through religious societies and local patronage outlasted larger temples that had arisen under royal munificence and become dependent on it (thus also forsaking popular religious needs as the major context for cult activity). Indeed, it is largely such local cults that seem to persevere into the fifth century according to hagiographical sources.

## 4.4 Mutations of the Oracle in the Late Roman Period

### 4.4.1 The Oracular Text

As innovative as the temples were in promoting oracles in the Roman period with incubation, talking statues, long-distance oracular correspondence, and the opening of sacred galleries to the votive graffiti of Roman élite, the locating of oracles within the temples gave them a traditional, archaic authority that could not be acquired by other modes of encountering divinities. Yet it is precisely in this period, beginning with evidence of the third century, that the traditional Egyptian oracle comes also to be marketed in literary form, as a ritual that could be performed virtually anywhere, given the right preparations and materials. Iamblichus himself provides an extreme example of this trend as he tries to develop a philosophical theurgy on the basis of traditional Egyptian incubation oracles.[140] But there is a more immediate corpus of evidence: oracular "spells" in the Greek and Demotic magical papyri,

[140] See Athanassiadi 1993b.

and the *Sortes Astrampsychi,* a complex divination text that could produce answers to the typical questions asked of temple oracles.

Both types of literature continued to lay claim to a kind of temple authority—the oracular spells through their details and invocations; the *Sortes* through the pretended lineage of the text (they were supposedly revelations by the priestly sage Astrampsychos) and the presumed importance of the individual trained to use the text with appropriate authority. The Bes oracle spells discussed above constitute only the briefest sample of a great number of oracle and dream rites (*manteion* or *oneiraitēton*) in the Greek magical texts and of spells for a "god's arrival [*pḥ-nṯr*]" or for "divination [*šn*]" in the Demotic magical texts.[141]

The Demotic spells clearly reflect temple oracle traditions, although in their assumption of privacy probably the traditions of priests rather than those available to supplicants.[142] The Greek spells often employ Hellenistic terminology and divine names that would have been broadly accessible in a Greco-Egyptian culture. But more telling among the Greek texts are those preparatory and invocational details drawn clearly from priestly liturgy and the world of the temple. By their mutual similarity to a spell in the Egyptian magical papyrus Harris the three Bes oracles, I have suggested, probably depended on some kind of Egyptian master-spell. An appeal for a *mantia* of Kronos expects one to "be clothed with clean linen in the garb of a priest of Isis."[143] A dream oracle depends on Egyptian solar mythology to invoke "the one who shakes, who thunders, who has swallowed the serpent, surrounds the moon, and hour by hour raises the disk of the sun."[144] A ritual designed "to see a true dream" invokes the Egyptian goddess Neith in Greek and Egyptian with the adjuration, "if I shall succeed in a certain activity, show me water, if not, fire."[145] And the following spell ascribes (no doubt pretentiously) a solitary divinatory procedure to a temple's archives:

> "Great is the Lady Isis!" Copy of a holy book [*antigraphon*] found in the archives of Hermes: The method is that concerning the 29 letters through which letters Hermes and Isis, who was seeking Osiris, her brother and husband, [found him].
>
> Call upon Helios and all the gods in the deep concerning those things for which you want to receive an omen [*klēdonisthēnai*]. Take 29 leaves of a male date palm and write on each of the leaves the names of the gods. Pray and then pick them up two by two. Read the last remaining leaf and you will

[141] J. Johnson 1977:90–91, and see further below, 5.2.3.
[142] J. Johnson 1986:lvii; Ritner 1993:215, 231–32.
[143] *PGM* IV.3095–96, tr. Grese in Betz 1986:98.
[144] *PGM* VII.366–68, tr. Grese in Betz 1986:127.
[145] *Suppl. Mag.* II.79 = *P.Oxy* LVI.3834, ll. 12–18. On invocations of Neith, cf. *PGM* VII.341; XIXa.1.

find your omen, how things are, and you will be answered [*khrēmatisthēsē*] clearly.[146]

Thus the practitioner might have confidence in and promote the traditional efficacy of this form of divination as an alternative to temple oracles. The very notion of oracle rite has therefore clearly shifted into a self-conscious textuality; and it would seem that one of the major functions of this textuality is its independence from the temple structure, its mobility, efficiency, and general practicality (even if restricted to a limited and literate number of specialists).

Who were the practitioners? As we will see further, in the context of the priestly culture itself, the promulgation of these divination spells in ritual corpora typical of priests suggests that they represent a distinctive development within the priesthood: an interest (or a diversification of much older priestly interests) in personally "beholding" deities that had traditionally served as ritual analogies for healing and cult performance.[147] One can then suppose, in the light of the story of Thessalos of Tralles, that some priests came to offer the same divination "experiences" to private clients at a price. For the client the divination spells would represent a "freelance" version of temple oracles, indeed as an actual alternative to them, not ideologically exclusive of temple oracles but promoting the same access to the voices of, quite often, the same divinities.[148]

Viewed in the same context as, for example, the guides for using Homeric texts as devices for divination, the profusion of divination spells in the ritual corpora must also reflect a new assumption on the part of both priests (in their capacity as local ritual specialists) and their clients that the text might provide (or ground) similar access to divine messages as temple structures, "a tendency," in the words of Mary Beard, "to define communication between humans and gods in written terms."[149] It is a tendency clearly rooted in Egyptian temple tradition itself, wherein one can observe the evolution of oracle texts in the service of temples, and not in the spread of Greek or Hellenistic concepts of democratic literacy. But it is a phenomenon that paralleled and drew upon similar developments in Greco-Roman culture.

It is this self-conscious textuality that emerges most clearly in the phenomenon of the *Sortes Astrampsychi*; and in this case the "oracle" consists not in an esoteric dream vision achieved through following the

---

[146] *PGM* XXIVa.1–25, tr. Grese in Betz 1986:264. See ibid., 264n.3.

[147] Podemann Sørensen 1992:170–72, 177–79.

[148] See Smith 1978a, 1995; and below, 5.3.

[149] Beard 1991:52. *Sortes Homericae: PGM* VII.167–86; IV.467–68; *Suppl. Mag.* II.77; *P.Oxy* LVI.3831. See Franco Maltomini, "P.Lond. 121 (= *PGM* VII), 1–221: Homeromanteion," *ZPE* 106 (1995):107–22.

text's instructions but in the extraction of a simple answer to the practical question, an exact mirror of the temple oracles of the Roman period as we know them from extant oracle request "tickets." As it has been reconstructed from various manuscripts of the third through fifth centuries, the *Sortes Astrampsychi* assembled 90 to 110 different questions typical of Greco-Egyptian concerns of the third century C.E., with a corresponding number of "decades" of answers to those questions (ten possible answers for each question).[150] The answers are carefully dispersed among different columns so that the "true" answer would depend upon: (a) a random number to be chosen by the client (between 1 and 10), which is (b) added to the number accorded the question asked, and (c) the sum matched to a second number through a table in the book. This second number guides the diviner, the owner of the *Sortes,* to the appropriate column, and the client's number indicates the appropriate answer within the column. Following these procedures one could gain ten different possible answers to whether one should become a fugitive (question 86) or be sold (question 74), all scattered among the columns, to be mysteriously produced by the diviner and his book.[151]

Thus it is the text itself, which circulated in at least some manuscripts under the attribution of the legendary Egyptian seer Astrampsychos, that produces the oracle; and one might well imagine the respect a nonliterate client would accord the *Sortes* as itself the negotiator of often quite vital crises. Indeed, this text would have required little training on the part of the owner beyond literacy itself, and it would not have conveyed charisma or authority to the one who was able to use it beyond the authority incumbent upon any owner of sacred texts in antiquity.[152]

There is a clear formal relationship between the *Sortes Astrampsychi* and Egyptian "ticket" oracles: each question begins "If [*ei*] I should find what is lost," "If I should give birth," "If I have been poisoned," just like

---

[150] In two editions: *P.Oxy* XXXVIII.2832, ed. Browne 1974 + XLVII.3330; *P.Oxy* 2833, ed. Browne 1974; *P.Oxy* XII.1477, ed. Browne 1974; P.L. Batavia 573v, ed. Hoogendijk/Van Minnen 1991; *P.Oxy* ined., ed. Gerald M. Browne, "A New Papyrus Codex of the *Sortes Astrampsychi,*" in *Arktouros: Hellenic Studies Presented to Bernard M. W. Knox,* ed. by G. Bowersock, W. Burkert, and M. Putnam (Berlin: de Gruyter, 1979), 434–39. Other mss.: P.Gent inv. 85, ed. W. Clarysse and R. Stewart, "P. Gent inv. 85: A New Fragment of the Sortes Astrampsychi," *CdÉ* 63 (1988):309–14; P.Rainer I.33, ed. Lenaerts 1983; R. Stewart 1987; P.Iand. 5.71, ed. Lenaerts 1983; R. Stewart 1987; P.Berol. 21341, ed. Brashear [forthcoming]. See now Gerald Browne's critical edition: *Sortes Astrampsychi* 1 (Leipzig: Teubner, 1983).

[151] Gerald M. Browne, "The Composition of the *Sortes Astrampsychi,*" *BICS* 17 (1970):95–100, and Browne 1974a:8–14. On historical realities reflected in the questions, see Strobel 1992.

[152] See Beard 1991:52–53; Potter 1994:25–26. Astrampsychos also appears as the authority behind spells in *PGM* VIII.1.

the oracle request "tickets" preserved in Demotic, Greek, and Coptic.[153] The grammatical sense of the "if [*ei*]" in the *Sortes* has changed from creating a condition for the issuing of one of the answer tickets to posing a hypothesis of sorts: "Am I to give birth?", as it were, instead of "If I am to give birth return this half of the ticket to me." But this change would reflect the nature of recasting such questions for the text rather than the influence of another oracle tradition altogether.[154] So also with other differences: the absence of a direct address to the deity or of the dual (affirmative and negative) question forms both accord with the technique of the book. (Of course, some oracle-mongers may well have included a variation on the divine address orally as a preparatory rite to the questioning of the text.) One can clearly see the text as arising out of the same needs as maintained temple oracles, and no doubt out of the same (priestly) milieu that promulgated the "ticket" exchange and maintained the oracles' archives.

It is the success of the *Sortes Astrampsychi,* undergoing two editions in antiquity and extant in at least nine manuscripts of the third through fifth centuries, that suggests its reflection of a distinctive trend of the Roman period. It may well have supplemented or extended the temple oracles for regions beyond their reach, as one historian has proposed:

> Oracular books in the hands of private diviners could circulate widely, reaching where the spoken word of god was rarely or never heard. Any town could have its own alphabetic oracle, ready for the casual use of its citizens on whatever trivial, or not so trivial, matters were troubling them.[155]

The "ritual" of consulting such a text through the mediation of a lone professional would have been quite distinct from the pilgrimage—personal or epistolary—to an oracle shrine. The essential change that the *Sortes* signal is the mobility of hitherto locative points of sacred communication, their accessibility through the mediation and ritual expertise of solitary *literati* (of real or pretended priestly background), and thus, it seems, an increased sense of competition among the various human and architectural points in a sacred topography—what Peter Brown has described as a shift and ensuing crisis in the locus of the holy in late antiquity.[156]

Perhaps nowhere is this dislocation more evident than in a concordance that apparently prefaced a third-century manuscript of the *Sortes.*

---

[153] Gerald M. Browne, "The Origin and Date of the *Sortes Astrampsychi,*" *ICS* 1 (1974):56–58; Browne 1987.

[154] See Randall Stewart, "The Oracular *ei,*" *GRBS* 26 (1985):67–73.

[155] Beard 1991:53.

[156] Brown 1975:11–12; cf. Strobel 1992:138–41.

The concordance assigned a deity to each of the hundred or so "decades" of answers, all with the heading, "gods giving oracles and signs [*khrēmatistai kai sēmantores*]."[157] The gods range from Egyptian (Amun, Osiris, Anubis) to Alexandrian (Serapis, *Agathos Daimon*) to Greco-Roman (Athena, Apollo) and personifications ("lightning," "power"), but the list seems to have been randomly compiled and it is "useless to look for a relationship between the question to be answered and the god who is supposed to lead to the answer."[158] Nevertheless the text's conceit of a hundred-some gods "speaking" answers through the book, rather than through their oracular *loci* around the Mediterranean, certainly extends the *Sortes* beyond simply an ingenious divinatory device: it now contains the gods themselves, brought together in one place, the book.

Given the concurrence of the dates of the *Sortes Astrampsychi,* the Greek and Demotic oracle spells, and the demise of the temple oracles of Sobek for social and economic reasons all in the third century, it seems wiser to attribute such a transformation of basic aspects of Egyptian religious culture to the dire economic circumstances as they affected the religious infrastructure, than to some general late antique *mentalité*. In this way one observes innovation as a function of real needs—not only for oracles per se as the reconciliation of life-crisis and social tension but for new media of oracles that could withstand economic and political stresses and could achieve authority in a world of diverse religious authorities and spiritual yearnings. The special charisma of the oracular text then, while deriving ultimately from traditions of the sacred book in the temple's scriptorium, comes to participate in a broader Greco-Roman veneration of the sacred revelatory book.

### 4.4.2 The Seer

Among the rivals to the temple oracle following the third century stood the regional seer, who performed many of the same functions as the temple oracle: resolution of disputes and other juridical acts, moral and ritual exhortation, agricultural predictions, speculation and guarantees of healing and safety, and more general, often political, prophecy. In literally "embodying" such a traditionally earth- and architecturally bound ritual, the seer reflects that tendency toward the dislocation of temple functions as much as the oracle book. In "the rise of the holy man as the bearer of objectivity in society," observes Peter Brown, who has demonstrated this functional inheritance in most detail (and over a much

[157] *P.Lugd.-Bat.* inv. 573v, ed. Hoogendijk/Van Minnen 1991:15–22.
[158] Hoogendijk/Van Minnen 1991:18.

broader area), one finds "a final playing out of the long history of oracles and divination in the ancient world."[159]

The seer was a relatively new social role in late antique Egypt, and one in which Christian types seem to have gained a competitive edge. Yet seers were not unprecedented in Egyptian history, and the Roman period itself offers considerable evidence for such dramatic personifications of the oracle. Those sparse examples of seers in earlier (New Kingdom) times suggest their complementary relationship with temple cults. One individual in Deir el-Medina addressed the oracle of Amenhotep I, "Does Horus come through him? Send the truth!", as if the god's guarantee was required to authenticate some local seer's charisma. A Demotic Egyptian oracle from the mid-Ptolemaic period seems to "speak" with the combined authority of the oracle-god and a seer based in the temple, known as "the Child born in Elephantine."[160] But in the mid-third century C.E. there is already evidence of a more independent breed of seer: a "*mantis and instigator of evils*" who appeared in Alexandria in 248 C.E. and incited a pogrom against Christians. The church historian Eusebius, who would certainly have blamed the temples if they were responsible, gives no information as to the seer's affiliation, although in describing the man's appeal to "popular superstition [*tēn epikhōrion . . . deisidaimonian*]" he implies a rhetoric probably consistent with religious discourse.[161]

Eunapius's portrayal of fourth-century philosopher-saints in Alexandria gives an impression of charismatic seers again with loose affiliations to local temples; and it is Eunapius's clear intention to present them as new "oracles." The pronouncements (*ta lekhthenta*) of the scholar Sosipatra "had the same force as an immutable oracle [*akinētōn manteiōn*], so absolutely did it come to pass and transpire as had been foretold by her."[162] She had access to omens (*sēmeia*) and to ecstatic states in which she received prescient visions.[163] Her son Antoninus, who established himself in Canopus at the temple of Isis discussed above, held similar oracular powers according to both Eunapius and, apparently, local legend. Among his pedagogical discourses Antoninus

> foretold to all his followers that after his death the temple would cease to be, and even the great and holy temples of Serapis would pass into formless

---

[159] Brown 1982:134. Cf. Potter 1994:29–37.

[160] Horus-seer of Deir el-Medina: Cairo ost. J.59465, ed. Černý 1935:48. "Child of Elephantine": De Cenival 1987; C. Martin 1994 (viewing the "Child" as a deceased saint); Griffith 1909:102–3. In general on seers in ancient Egypt: Baines 1987:93.

[161] Eusebius, *H.E.* 6.41.1.

[162] Eunapius, *V.P.* 6.8.6 [469], tr. Wright, LCL, 411.

[163] Eunapius, *V.P.* 6.9.7, 12–13 (470).

darkness and be transformed, and that a fabulous [*muthōdes*] and unseemly gloom would hold sway over the fairest things on earth.[164]

No doubt at this point in the late fourth century it was not a stretch of the imagination to expect the imminent destruction of the religious infrastructure or to foresee the resulting despondency of a populace without holy centers. Yet the source of Antoninus's language here, the symbolism that would have had popular resonance as issued from a temple, is clearly the tradition of *Chaosbeschreibung*, the literary tableaux of social, political, and environmental reversal that drove ancient kingship propaganda, Hellenistic political oracles like those of the Potter and the Lamb, and even prophecies of doom during the Roman era like the Christian *Apocalypse of Elijah* and the Hermetic *Perfect Discourse*.[165] As part of his rather extravagant affiliation with the Canopic temples, it seems, Antoninus learned to communicate in the symbolic language of such literary oracles, which (by the manuscript evidence) had gained considerable popularity since the second and third centuries C.E.[166] The fact that the Serapeum did, in fact, succumb to mobs soon after his death earned Antoninus particular fame. Indeed, to Eunapius his prophecy of the collapse of things "gained the force of an oracle [*khrēsmou*]"—using the traditional word for a temple-pronouncement.

It is impossible to judge from such panegyrical discourse as Eunapius's the size or geographical breadth of the constituency that would have revered either Sosipatra or Antoninus or any of the other "pagan holy men" recorded in Egypt. The imputation of oracular function may be Eunapius's own device or the view of a very small band of disciples and enthusiasts. But it is significant that these philosophers earn clairvoyant status in some relationship to their degree of piety and allegiance to the temples themselves.[167] Thus there is not so much a "shift" in the locus of oracles from temple to seer as an extension of the temple through the seer.

The Christian ascetic seers stand in considerable contrast to these spiritual gurus, for they represented—at least on the outside—a shift of the oracle function through juxtaposition, not extension. Their oracular abilities are invariably cast under the term *prophēteia*, implying a basis in legends of biblical prophets, their visions and otherworldly journeys. Yet in cases like the virgin Piamoun, a desert seer, the "gift of prophecy"

[164] Eunapius, *V.P.* 6.9.17 [471], tr. Wright, LCL, 417. See above, 2.6.2.
[165] Mahé 1982:68–97; Fowden 1986:38–44; Frankfurter 1993:159–211; and below, 6.2.
[166] See Thelamon 1981:260–61; Mahé 1982:59; *pace* Athanassiadi 1993a:13–16.
[167] Fowden 1982:52–54. On the broader issue of the constituencies of "pagan holy men," see Fowden 1982:45–48; Athanassiadi 1993a:19.

pertains to her supernatural ability to resolve a violent dispute between two villages over water rights.[168]

One John of Lycopolis, according to the fifth-century travelogue *Historia monachorum in aegypto,* is also distinguished as possessing "the gift of prophecy" (1.1) but is perhaps the most vivid example of the desert hermits' appropriation of the social function of the oracle. The author provides a catalogue of John's pronouncements on issues identical to those on which temple oracles were traditionally consulted: the fate of the empire, to the monarch (Theodosius; 1.1); the outcome of a prospective battle, to a local army officer (1.2); the safety of a tribune's wife en route to Alexandria (1.4–9); the safe birth of a son, to a man evidently come to ensure the same (1.10); and the eventually natural death of the emperor to the author himself, who evidently asked precisely the kind of question that had, a half century earlier, resulted in the closure of the Abydos Bes oracle (1.2, 64).[169] Thus the author concludes the catalogue of pronouncements:

> These are the wonders which he performed before strangers who came to see him [*tous exōthen erkhomenous*]. As regards his own fellow-citizens [*tois autou politais sunekhōs*], who frequently came to him for their needs, he foreknew and revealed things hidden in the future; he told each man what he had done in secret; and he predicted the rise and fall of the Nile and the annual yield of the crops. In the same way he used to foretell when some divine threat was going to come upon them and exposed those who were to blame for it.[170]

Drawing an important distinction between John's transregional ("strangers") and regional/local ("fellow-citizens") services, the author ascribes to John the traditional oracles' roles of giving authoritative agricultural advice, judicial resolution, advice in mundane concerns, moral warnings of a more general nature, and even (the author discusses in much detail) healing oil much like the healing water of the Dendara shrine and the Horus-*cippi*. John thus becomes a central integrating authority in the region, the vestibule of his hermitage enlarged by necessity to hold about a hundred people.[171]

Some texts make the juxtaposition of holy man to oracle quite explicit. Bishop Athanasius, according to one legend, was able to interpret the squawks of crows in the court of the temple of Serapis in Memphis as

---

[168] Palladius, *Historia Lausiaca* 31.

[169] Compare Isaac the Monk, who predicts and thus effects the death of the emperor Valens in late-fourth-century Constantinople (Sozomen, *H.E.* 6.40).

[170] *Hist. Mon.* 1.11, tr. Russell 1980:53. John's renown is also reported in Sozomen, *H.E.* 7.22.

[171] Palladius, *Historia Lausiaca* 35.4.

predicting the death of Julian (a possible satire on Memphite priests' alleged divination by children's games).[172] And Athanasius's own *Life of Antony* wages such a sustained polemic *against* the oracle that one infers the continuing importance of oracles as the hermits' major rivals in fourth-century Egypt. Among the acts of demons of which one should beware is their "divining [*manteuesthai*] and foretelling things to come" (23). Yet, Athanasius continues in an extended discussion of oracles,

> if they pretend also to foretell the future, let no one give heed. Often, for instance, they tell us days beforehand of brothers coming to visit us; and they do come. But it is not because they care for their hearers that they do this, but in order to induce them to place their confidence in them, and then, when they have them well in hand, to destroy them. Hence, we must not listen to them, but send them off, for we have no need of them. What is wonderful about that, if they who have lighter bodies than men, seeing that men have set out on a journey, outdistance them and announce their arrival?
>
> .  .  .
>
> So, too, they sometimes talk nonsense in regard to the water of the River [i.e., the impending level of the Nile's annual surge]. For example, seeing heavy rains falling in the regions of Ethiopia and knowing that the flooding of the River originates there, they run ahead and tell it before the water reaches Egypt. Men could tell it too, if they could run as fast as these.[173]

Athanasius demonstrates considerable familiarity with the popular function of oracles in the life of Egyptians: the Nile surge, concerns around traveling, and even their medical and meteorological scopes (33).[174] Sometimes the demons behind oracles "come to you at night and want to tell of future things" (35), an apparent reference to the incubation oracle as might be practiced in solitude since the dissemination of oracle spells. But Athanasius never actually rejects oracles' supernatural credibility: "They do, sometimes, speak the truth"; just "let nobody be amazed at them for this" (33).

Often a person will indeed desire to know the future (*proginōskein*), Athanasius admits, and in that case one should approach the task in spiritual purity (34)—much as contemporaneous oracle spells required. But it is evidently the hermit Antony himself who represents the *legitimate* center for oracular functions. He controls the destiny of travelers: "As for those who came to him, he frequently foretold their coming, days and sometimes a month in advance and for what reason they were coming" (62). He is able to resolve judicial disputes (87). And he has the gift

---

[172] *Apophth. Pat.* Epiphanius 1 (*PG* 65:161–63); Sozomen, *H.E.* 4.10.

[173] Athanasius, *V.Ant.* 31–32, tr. Meyer 1950:96–97. All subsequent translations from *V.Ant.* are from Meyer 1950.

[174] On travel oracles, see Schubart 1931, ##6, 14; *P.Köln* IV.202; *Sortes Astrampsychi,* qq. 73, 80, 89.

of "discerning spirits"; he could perceive "their movements and was well aware in what direction each of them directed his effort and attack," a cosmological expertise hitherto reserved for temple priests (88). Thus it was against the loom of Antony's *charismata* that Athanasius could address Egyptians apostrophically, "where now are your oracles [*manteia*]?" (79).[175]

Seers and hermits, particularly the Christian ones, therefore appear during the course of the third and fourth centuries as a new form of oracle. In their native contexts they seem to supplement temple oracles and their functions in integrating local and regional life; but with Christianity they become exclusivist, ultimately to function (at least in the promotional literature of the time) as a simple replacement for the temple oracle.

Two additional observations arise from these data. First, Athanasius's explicit anti-oracle agenda in the *Life of Antony* and the close replication of oracular functions by other Christian hermits in the Greek sources present a picture, not of indigenous oracles in decline, but rather of oracles as the hermits' principal opponents, sturdy in their deep local roots and service to everyday anxieties. Second, given the popularity of the hermits' typically oral and gestural mode of communication, one must be wary of pushing too far that image of a general "bibliocentrism" that seems to arise from the multiplication of written religious materials like the *Sortes*.[176] A popular Greco-Egyptian fascination with the written word, fueled by priestly translations and innovations of the Roman period, certainly contributes to the historical context in which the proliferation of *Sortes* books arose, but would not have characterized all of Egypt.

The rise of hermits as a replacement for oracles is not in itself explained with such formulas as the "dislocation of the Holy," or with assumptions about cultural conversion at the ideological level. Egyptian individuals still had their fields to sow, their produce to sell, and their offspring to generate in the fourth century, each a sphere of religious need that could not have been addressed through the piety of an otherworldly sect—hence the scramble for relics and corpses already by the middle of the fourth century.[177] What, then, was the appeal of a Christian hermit within the Egyptian context?

Studies of traditional African religions, especially those undergoing

---

[175] Athanasius generally linked the ascetic virtue of the desert hermit with the power of prognostication: see David Brakke, *Athanasius and the Politics of Asceticism* (Oxford: Clarendon, 1995), 250–52.

[176] Rubenson (1995) makes the important point that hermits such as Antony could be both literate and rather learned in Greek philosophy, suggesting that their hagiographers' depiction of ignorant and populist rustics may have exaggerated their opposition to urban intellectual currents and pushed their "natural piety" toward an ahistorical ideal. Nevertheless, the (apparent) literacy of some like Antony would certainly not have constrained the hermits to serving literate conventicles.

[177] Lefort 1954; Frankfurter 1994a.

some measure of political and economic transformation, have emphasized the complementarity of the local priest-staffed cults that resolve the ongoing concerns of one to several villages and the regional prophet cults that arise occasionally to address broader needs of an entire region.[178] Often these regional cults will address disputes unresolvable at the local level, theological questions about changes in the local cult, or supernatural problems too imposing for a local shrine to negotiate. Consultation of the regional cult invariably requires pilgrimage from one's home, a social process that in itself renders the object of pilgrimage a "greater center" of mythic quality, as we have seen in the case of Greco-Roman pilgrimage to Siwa and to temples of the first cataract.[179]

To the extent that one can derive some comparative insights from these modern African examples, the triumph of the Christian hermits seems to constitute a triumph of the regional or transregional cult in a period when local cults were not viewed as sufficiently strong or authoritative.

In classical Egypt, of course, the regional cults would consist of established temples, like those of Memphis, Abydos, or Karnak, which would articulate the royal mythologies, rather than of seers, the sparse evidence for whom seems to suggest a fairly local scope of activity in some complementary relationship with local temples.[180] The evidence for oracles in the New Kingdom, in particular, the Deir el-Medina ostraca and the British Museum papyri, demonstrates the strength of the local cults: of Amenhotep I at Deir el-Medina and of the local Amun cults in the Thebaid, the latter perhaps through their association with the universalistic god of the great tradition, Amun.[181] If the proliferation of Greek-"speaking" oracles of Sobek in the Fayyum is any indication, it seems that the dawn of the Hellenistic period saw a new rivalry for regional and transregional authority among cults of hitherto local significance. Virtually all the Roman-era oracles addressed in this chapter had no less than regional authority and, more often, claims to universalism: Kysis for much of the southern portion of the Kharga oasis; Amun of Siwa and Bes of Abydos each with pan-Mediterranean authority; and cults of Canopus

[178] Werbner (ed.) 1977; Werbner 1989; E. E. Evans-Pritchard, *Nuer Religion* (New York and Oxford: Oxford University Press, 1956), 304–10 (with D. H. Johnson 1992, 1994); Redmayne 1970.

[179] Turner 1974:189–90, 195–98. Goody 1975:96–99. Compare the discussion of the oracle of Delphi as a "pan-Hellenic" cult in Catherine Morgan, "The Origins of Pan-Hellenism," in *Greek Sanctuaries: New Approaches*, ed. by N. Marinatos and R. Hägg (London and New York: Routledge, 1993), 27–32.

[180] Examples cited—person channeling Horus at Deir el-Medina (Černý 1935:48), "the Child [Eg. *p3 ḥrd.t*]" at Elephantine (De Cenival 1987:4–5 and Martin 1994:206, 209)—suggest fairly restricted authority.

[181] Cf. Richard P. Werbner, "Continuity and Policy in Southern Africa's High God Cult," in Werbner (ed.) 1977:179–218, and Werbner 1989 on local cults of high gods.

and Menouthis drawing Alexandrines. In some cases we have proposed an actual state of competition between cults. Egyptian local cultures may then have become accustomed to local cults that were vastly overshadowed by Greco-Egyptian regional cults in terms of authority and power—hence the growth of a culture of popular pilgrimage in the Hellenistic period.[182]

We would not expect this trend to lead to a concomitant demise of local cults, since local cults define communities geographically, socially, and morally; and of course we know such cults did continue throughout the Roman period.[183] But it might accustom people to construing and appealing problems in a regional or transregional scope: journeying to the oracle of Kysis, for example, to ensure one's wife's maternity rather than working ritually with the staff of the local shrine. And it is this context in which a rise of prophet cults makes sense as a hybrid of oracle cults: that quality of power uniquely vested in a particular human being offers an attractive ultimate authority for those already seeking resolutions through pilgrimage. In the African cases, for example,

> a medium who establishes a reputation for wisdom in settling disputes, for exorcising malevolent spirits, for effective cures and for bringing rain may draw supplicants to him from a wider vicinity that extends far beyond the boundaries of his spirit province or even his region.[184]

Differing in self-presentation not substantially from indigenous African prophets, the Christian hermits represent a type of regional prophet cult. As the description of John of Lycopolis makes vividly clear, the hermit constitutes a forum of appeal for both local folk and distant pilgrims. Piamoun has regional authority to resolve disputes among villages. At least in the hagiographers' presentations, most of the hermits attract pilgrims from far and wide. And their often quite remote locations, symbolically transcending the bounded community and projecting equal access from all domains, reflects the "peripheralizing" tendency of regional and transregional cults.[185]

The essential difference reflected in these Christian prophets, however, is their resolute rejection of the piety of the local cults rather than comple-

---

[182] Jean Yoyotte, "Les pèlerinages dans l'Égypte ancienne," *Les pèlerinages,* Sources orientales 3 (Paris: Éditions du Seuil, 1960), 54–57.

[183] On the functions of local cults, see Malaise 1987:68–69, and more generally, Garbett 1977 and Colson 1977. On their persisting significance in the Roman period, see Brown 1975:36–38.

[184] Garbett 1977:71.

[185] See Turner 1974:179, 184–87, 191–95; Werbner (ed.) 1977:xxiii–xxiv; although cf. James E. Goehring, "The Encroaching Desert: Literary Production and Ascetic Space in Early Christian Egypt," *JECS* 1 (1993):281–96, on substantial evidence for urban hermits as well.

mentary critique or endorsement of them (a role the hermits would later acquire toward churches and bishops). The ideology within which this rejection is framed, demonology and exorcism, is in itself typical of regional prophet cults and so not specifically "anti-pagan." Indeed, what can be appealing about a new pilgrimage shrine or prophet cult is the new moral system it often presents to or requires of devotees. Nuer prophets of the twentieth century actually established themselves as instruments of the High God against sorcery and the use of magical substances: "In this way the prophets appeared to regulate spiritual activity, both that which was harmful and that which was beneficial, for the general good and well being of the moral community in which they operated."[186]

As we saw in the sermons of Shenoute of Atripe, local suppliants did not necessarily follow the hermits' rejection of local religion.[187] Nevertheless, this ideology would ultimately create a tension at the local level between an attitude that viewed local and regional cults as complementary (i.e., appealing to the prophet when local means fail) and one that accepted them as exclusive (i.e., appealing to the prophet or his surrogate at every point of crisis, however minor). And this tension would presumably grow if, as sometimes occurs, a widening "catchment area" (the geographical breadth from which pilgrims travel) required the seer to bring his or her particular idiom of supernatural forces and ritual performance into line with those institutions claiming authority over religious ideology in the area. The means of power would then become great saints or angels or the cross, for example, rather than local spirits or deceased sheikhs.[188]

Indeed, to embrace an exclusive allegiance to the regional prophet cult as it was promoted by the hermits would have also required some sort of localized "cult." Redmayne notes "the sheer quantity of misfortune, particularly sickness, infertility, and death, and the mental uneasiness caused by smouldering quarrels" that an African diviner of the late 1950s had perennially to address.[189] The localized form of the Christian hermit comes about through the efforts of pilgrims in importing *eulogia*, "blessings": amulets, holy water and oil, holy dust, relics, and other objects with sympathetic and contagious association with the prophet—in one fifth-century case, snake heads, crocodile teeth, and fox claws.[190] Such

[186] D. H. Johnson 1992:4. Compare also Redmayne 1970; Goody 1975:99–100.

[187] See esp. Shenoute's *Sermon* 11, ed. Amélineau 1909:379–81.

[188] Cf. Carl-Martin Edsman's discussion of an eighteenth-century Swedish mantic in her relationship with ecclesiastical authority: "A Swedish Female Folk Healer from the Beginning of the Eighteenth Century," in *Studies in Shamanism*, ed. by C.-M. Edsman (Stockholm: Almqvist & Wiksell, 1962), 120–65, esp. 124.

[189] Redmayne 1970:117. See Baines 1991:132–34 on religious responses to everyday affliction in ancient Egypt.

[190] Shenoute, "Catechesis against Apocrypha" = Paris copte 129² 66 + DS 59, tr. Orlandi 1982:90.

materials were certainly believed to work, and were promoted as working, as the hermits' surrogates in any of the aspects of life that the hermit would personally address, including those that could be placed under the rubric "oracular"—advice and resolution, protection, healing.[191] Thus a local cult, the surrogate, could exist in a complementary relationship with the prophet cult, the holy man.

### 4.4.3 The Christian Shrine and the Restoration of the Local Oracle

This local scope was evidently also fulfilled by churches and monasteries, and most interestingly in the form of oracles. As the cult of Saints Cyrus and John explicitly took over the function of "healing center" in the region east of Alexandria from the previous cult of Isis and came similarly to integrate the ritual of incubation, so also the cult of Saint Menas, which ministered to both nomads and Mediterranean pilgrims, employed incubation as a primary form of healing for pilgrims who had made their way out to its enclave in the desert west of Alexandria.[192] That oracular incubation continued in at least this healing context, and no doubt for broader functions, may be confirmed by a Coptic text that criticizes the use of dreams and advocates strict discernment to avoid "false" messages.[193] Shenoute criticizes "those who sleep in tombs to behold dreams and who question the dead about the living," a popular practice that had already received Athanasius's explicit disapproval in 370.[194] In this respect the growth of the major Coptic sanctuaries and their reputations for healing powers can be largely attributed to their appropriation of traditional incubation ritual from native oracle shrines—often, as in the case of Menouthis, shrines recently supplanted or displaced.[195]

There exists a substantial corpus of Greek and Coptic papyri with typical oracular questions addressed to or through Christian saints. The corpus vividly illustrates how ecclesiastical and monastic institutions in some cases inherited the local role of temple oracles, from the scope of

---

[191] On continuation of the healing function in Coptic saint cults, cf. Drescher 1946:xi, xx–xxi, 119, 123; and on continuity of a saint through *eulogia*, Vikan 1982.

[192] References to successful incubation practices in *Miracles of Apa Mena* (text, pp. 30–32) and *Encomium on Apa Mena* (text, pp. 64–65), in Drescher 1946. On "sanatorium" facilities at the site of Abu Mena, see Grossmann/Jaritz 1980:214–16.

[193] MacCoull 1991. Cf. propaganda for a Christian incubation cult at the Alexandrian shrine of "The Three Children," in a miracle cycle attributed to Cyril of Alexandria: Ps-Cyril, "Miracles," 7 = Ms. Vat. copte 62, fols. 182v–184r, ed. De Vis 1990, 2:190–93.

[194] Shenoute, "Those Who Work Evil," ed. Amélineau 1909:219–20, tr. Lefort 1954:230, and Vienna K 9040, ed. Dwight Young, *Coptic Manuscripts from the White Monastery: Works of Shenute* (Vienna: Verlag Brüder Hollinek, 1993), 23–24; Athanasius, *Ep.* 42 (370 C.E.), ed. Lefort 1955:65 (fr. 15), on which see Baumeister 1972:70–71; Brakke 1994:414–16.

[195] Cf. Gregory 1986:237–39 for Roman examples of this replacement of local shrines.

issues addressed to the very formulation of questions.[196] Rylands 100 requests assurance of maternity from the "God of St. Leontius." Berlin 21269 asks for advice on a betrothal. Oxyrhynchus Papyrus 925 desires travel advice and a guarantee of safety from God and Christ: "Do you wish me to go to Chiout, and shall I find that you are of help to me and gracious?" Another expresses concern about a proposed move to Antinoë: "O God Pantokrator, if you command me, your servant Paul, to go to Antinoë and stay, order me in this ticket"—using Coptic *pittagn* (= Greek *pittakion*) for "ticket," just like the earlier temple oracles. The latter text was probably part of a dual-ticket request, originally accompanied by another ticket asking "if you command me *not* to go . . . order me in *this* ticket."[197] Indeed, a remarkable pair of just such dual tickets survives for someone's inquiry about financial affairs, apparently prepared by the same hand on a piece of papyrus that was then cut in half:

> My lord God almighty and St. Philoxenus my patron, I beseech you through the great name of the lord God, if it is your will and you help me to get the banking business, I invoke you to direct me to find out and to speak.

> My lord God almighty and St. Philoxenus my patron, I beseech you through the great name of the lord God, if it is not your will for me to speak about the bank or about the weighing office, direct me to find out that I may not speak.[198]

The extent of this corpus of Christian oracle tickets, and especially such formal oracle requests as the above, suggests that oracles were no "behind-the-scenes" favor but rather a common service to the community that was offered by certain churches or monasteries. The archives of an oracle of Saint Colluthos in Antinoë, consisting of seventy-one oracle tickets from about the fifth century, demonstrates the prominence of this form of divination as a normative extension of a martyrial cult.[199] Most important, all such cases—and even written oracular responses like Papyrus Berlin

---

[196] De Nie 1942; Sergio Donadoni, "Una domanda oracolare cristiana da Antinoe," *RSO* 29 (1954):183–86; Youtie 1975; *PGM* P1, P8a–b, P24; Papini 1985; Meyer/Smith (eds.) 1994:##30–35, 65; and esp. Papaconstantinou 1994.

[197] Coll.von Scherling, ed. de Nie 616, pl. XXXII; cf. P.Berlin 21269 = Meyer/Smith (eds.) 1994, #34, which includes one of the possible answers, "yes," on the slip, and Treu 1986:29. P.Rylands 100, ed. W. E. Crum, *Catalogue of the Coptic Manuscripts in the Collection of the John Rylands Library* (Manchester: Manchester University Press, 1909), 52 = Meyer/Smith (eds.) 1994, #65. P.Berlin 21269, ed. Treu 1986:29–30 = Meyer/Smith (eds.) 1994, #34. P.Oxy VI.925 (= *PGM* P1), tr. Meyer, in Meyer/Smith (eds.)1994:52, #30.

[198] P.Harris 54, tr. Meyer, in Meyer/Smith (eds.) 1994:53–54, #33; P.Oxy XVI.1926 (= *PGM* P8a/b), tr. Meyer, in Meyer/Smith (eds.) 1994:53, #32. See also Youtie 1975:256–57.

[199] Papini 1985.

13232 ("Do not harm your soul, for what has come to pass is from God")— would have required scribes accustomed to translating clients' concerns into a form that could be ritually resolved by an oracular procedure.[200]

No doubt the same Christian scribal organization was responsible for the Christianization of the *Sortes Astrampsychi* and similar divination texts. A partial collection of answers for the *Sortes* in a seventh- or eighth-century Coptic manuscript shows that the medieval *Sortes Sanctorum,* in which each "decade" of answers was headed by a saint, were already taking root in Byzantine Coptic Christianity before the spread of such manuscripts in medieval Europe.[201] Was the *Sortes Sanctorum* the editorial work of a Coptic monk? As the original *Sortes* came under the aegis of the legendary seer Astrampsychos, then came to represent the literary voices of Greco-Roman gods, all within Egypt, it would be reasonable to expect the tradition to continue into Christian idiom within Egypt as well.[202] By the fourth century in Egypt there were already guides to using the gospels (especially John) for divination, which provided oracular "interpretations" for the various verses one might arrive upon in the process of divination.[203]

Like the Christian "ticket" oracles, the Christian oracular books suggest a life-world of monks or other types of literate ecclesiastical personnel offering the kind of religious service that historically had located a cult within the matrix of social relations, aspirations, and crises that defined a community's religious needs. Where the "ticket" oracles might have been exchanged on a particular feast day, as in the festal processions of the god in the indigenous oracle rites, the oracular books seem to point to private consultations with a "master" of divination and other ritual texts who himself held some authority in the Christian hierarchy. The "message" of such texts, that the "saints" or the gospels were the ultimate appeal in matters of divination, was fully consonant with the domestic orthodoxy of popular Coptic Christianity.

[200] P.Berlin 13232, ed. Kurt Treu, "Varia Christiana," *Archiv* 24/25 (1976):120, tr. Meyer, in Meyer/Smith (eds.) 1994:54–55, #35.

[201] Vatican copt. pap. 1, ed. A. Van Lantschoot, "Une collection sahidique de 'Sortes Sanctorum' (Papyrus Vatican copte 1)," *Le muséon* 69 (1956):35–52, tr. in Meyer/Smith (eds.) 1994, #126; on *Sortes sanctorum,* see T. C. Skeat, "An Early Mediaeval 'Book of Fate': The Sortes XII Patriarcharum," *Mediaeval and Renaissance Studies* 3 (1954):41–54.

[202] Strobel notes that a Gallic manuscript testifies to Christian redaction of the *Sortes* already in fourth-century Gaul (1992:135–38), although this does not establish a non-Egyptian provenance for its origin.

[203] Otto Stegmüller, "Zu den Bibelorakeln im Codex Bezae," *Biblica* 34 (1953):13–22; Paul Canart and Rosario Pintaudi, "PSI XVII Congr.5: Un système d'oracles chrétiens ('Sortes Sanctorum')," *ZPE* 57 (1984):85–90; and Joseph van Haelst, *Catalogue des papyrus littéraires juifs et chrétiens* (Paris: Sorbonne, 1976), ##429, 433, 438, 441–43, 445–46, 1124, 1172, 1177. Haelst #441 is from the late third to fourth centuries, others from the fifth to eighth centuries.

## 4.5 Egyptian Oracles in the Roman Period

The common inference that there was a rise of oracles in the Roman period, in itself a gauge of pervasive anxiety or more pressing spiritual needs, has repeatedly run up against evidence both extensive and subtle for the continuity of Egyptian oracle traditions over considerable time. To be sure, we have seen many ways in which the elaboration of oracular media, often within a particular temple or region, took on a certain energy in the Roman period. And yet much of this energy can be attributed to the cults' endeavors to persevere in a period when traditional media (like processional oracles) could not sustain the cultic infrastructure—attract extravagant patronage—as in earlier times. It was also a time when new types of pilgrims were defining themselves: youthful Roman "seekers," intellectual "pagans," and the passionately superstitious and paranoid Roman authorities, who might shut down oracles as easily as beg their advice. Oracles provided a means of support, and oracular innovation carried important financial implications.

Oracle cults in their late antique guise have opened windows on other religious dynamics as well. In their diverse Greek expressions—ticket oracles, inscribed *proskunēmata*, oracular texts, and cult propaganda—the Egyptian oracles show themselves to have been an actively synthetic ritual medium as well as one steeped in the traditions and authority of particular temples. Behind our excitingly diverse documents from the period we can see, in fact, priesthoods—perhaps diminished to small coteries of literate experts—maintaining the basic elements of oracular divination while experimenting with numerous idioms current in the Mediterranean world: new revealing gods (in the case of Bes, a god of wide indigenous appeal), a prevailing passion for revelatory books and for individual instruction, the "democratic" appeal of priestly rites and secrets, the numinous aura of a devotional testimony composed in florid metrical Greek. Priests also seem to have been the ones to recognize a temple's potential to be reconfigured so as to focus its exotic power (to outsiders) on an incubation cult. And we can see in texts like Papyrus Oxyrhynchus 1380 that inevitable priestly program to keep "cult propaganda" (as we might describe the heroic charter legends that grounded temples' divine authority) as a living, now Hellenistic literature. In the most general sense priests maintained their most dynamic scribal roles through oracles—writing, updating, translating, collecting, and systematizing, a subject to be broached in more detail in chapter 6.

Besides these literary endeavors, the oracle cults point toward ritual experts committed to the very drama of the oracle: the preparations for incubation and the procedure for interpreting the god's messages, the details of the ticket oracle exchange, and indeed, the choreography of the processional oracles, which still emerged from some local temples during the fourth century.

The phenomenon of the oracle as a regional or transregional cult, complementing local cults, has allowed us to take a new look at the rise of the Christian desert hermit in his or her structural relationship to local piety. These historical figures fulfilled many of the same roles as oracles, although with far more explicit (or at least more often recorded) tension with local piety. Their religious significance in third- and fourth-century Egypt may then stem not from new, Christian theologies of asceticism, but rather from autochthonous needs for transregional cults that stand on the periphery of society.

That is, religious needs in their most basic forms determine religious developments in late antique Egypt. It is a principle most vividly apparent in the Christian ticket oracles, although we have seen it before: the Nile cult, domestic figurines, even Shenoute's competitive fury toward the patron Gesios. The Christian oracle shrines and the mundane "oracular" services of a number of holy men and women demonstrate a pronounced tendency in Egyptian religion of this time toward the localized, the every-day needs and religious world of the small community as these might be centered in a particular place or person, and away from (if never entirely departing) the ideology of the great tradition.

# 5

## PRIEST TO MAGICIAN: EVOLVING MODES
## OF RELIGIOUS AUTHORITY

### 5.1 Decline and Persistence

FROM the Augustan reforms of the late first century B.C.E., through those of Septimius Severus around 200 C.E., to the Christian edicts of the fourth and later centuries, the Roman period can seem like one protracted attempt at controlling local cults. And whereas local communities and innovative cults could forestall the various pressures of decline, the elaborate priestly hierarchy that was indulged and swollen under the Ptolemies dwindled progressively with the systematic checks on their power.

The kingship no less than the great tradition of Egyptian religious systematization was a function of the priesthoods, who wielded tremendous control over royal authority and, by extension, over political discourse. By the end of the Ptolemaic period Egyptian priests had become quite powerful in the mixed Greco-Egyptian culture, for Augustus's own reforms seem to have been motivated by fear of native, priest-led revolts. The reforms, in effect by the end of the first century B.C.E., involved the reorganization of the entire hierarchy of the Egyptian priesthood, such that a Roman official became the "High Priest of Alexandria and All Egypt" or *Idios Logos,* temples and priesthoods were to rely entirely on imperial munificence (the *suntaxeis*) rather than their own lands (with few exceptions), and every aspect of priestly life was accounted for through a complex bureaucratic system laid out in the "*Gnomon* of the Idios Logos."[1] Thus, as Milne observed, "the power and influence of the Egyptian priesthood were diminished by their conversion (put in extreme terms) from territorial magnates into State pensioners."[2]

The vast paperwork that supported the *Gnomon*'s system actually provides abundant documentation for the success of local cults and mainte-

---

[1] See, in general, Seckel/Schubart 1919; Milne 1924:180–82, 286–89, 308 (3); and Allen Chester Johnson, *Roman Egypt to the Reign of Diocletian,* An Economic Survey of Ancient Rome 2 (Baltimore: Johns Hopkins Press, 1936), 711–17. On anti-insurrectionist motivations, see also Harold Idris Bell, "Egypt under the Early Principate," *CAH* 10 (1934):290–91; Lewis 1983:91–92.

[2] Milne 1924:289. See also Glare 1993.

nance of traditions during the second and early third centuries, despite evidence that priestly privileges (especially priests' economic distinction from layfolk) were being progressively undermined from above.[3] The *Gnomon,* for example, functioned partly to define and restrict the priesthood in a culture wherein a diversity of people had traditionally been involved in some way with the functioning of temples. By all accounts, candidates for priestly duties continued to be inspected for purity of lineage and body, and priests had to declare their pure behavior in an oath: "I will not eat and I will not drink the things that are not lawful nor all those things which have been written in the books nor will I attach my fingers to them."[4] In their official inventories to the government, temples report rich and varied cultic objects, complex ritual schedules, and often quite large staffs: the population of the priestly center of Soknopaiou Nesos still consists of around 60% priests in 178–79 c.e.[5] The hierarchy of priestly ranks continues and even expands with such quasi-priestly administrative categories as *arkhiprophētēs.*[6] Only in mortuary ranks do we find evidence of a diminishment of priestly activity, whether because these ranks became legally distinct from priests or their functions shifted to nonpriestly guilds.[7]

A broad look at the Egyptian cultic and priestly network during the first two and a half centuries shows little or no decline. Besides the evidence of the papyri, we see temples like Dendara, Philae, and Kom Ombo, whose inscriptions commemorate various building and refurbishing projects under numerous emperors into the third century. And both Plutarch and Clement of Alexandria portray Egyptian priesthoods and religion as practically thriving in the late second century.[8]

The economic reform of Septimius Severus at the beginning of the third century aimed at localizing government in multiple town councils

[3] See Lewis 1983:90–94, with Gilliam 1947:206–7 on the loss of privileges.

[4] Circumcision affidavits: P.Washington University inv. 138, ed. Verne B. Schuman, "A Second-Century Treatise on Egyptian Priests and Temples," *HTR* 53 (1960):159–70, and Reinhold Merkelbach, "Ein ägyptischer Priestereid," *ZPE* 2 (1968):7–30.

[5] P.Vindob.G. 24951, 24556, in Hobson 1984:106n.37. In general on required temple records, see *BGU* XIII.2215–19; Gilliam 1947; Evans 1961. Whether the great fluctuations in temple staffing at the temples of Soknokonnis (a decline from approximately twenty-three to twelve priests between 116 and 171 c.e.) and Soknobraisis (an increase from fourteen to sixteen between 171 and 188) are due to strict government control or typical demographic shifts is difficult to determine. Gilliam (1947:187) infers the former.

[6] Adam Bülow-Jacobsen, "The Archiprophetes," in *Actes du XV<sup>e</sup> congrès international de papyrologie* 4, ed. by J. Bingen and G. Nachtergael (Brussels: Fondation Reine Élisabeth, 1979), 124–31.

[7] See Rémondon 1951.

[8] Plutarch, *De Iside.* Clement of Alexandria, *Strom.* 6.4.35, 37; *Paed.* 3.2.4; *Protrept.* 2.39; and in general on Clement's interpretation of Egyptian religion, Deiber 1904. On early Roman munificence of Egyptian temples, see Kákosy 1995:2900–2927.

(*bouleutai*), themselves responsible for arranging civil services and the payment of taxes. The temples, too, were brought under the local administration of the *bouleutai,* but hardly to their benefit, as they had traditionally represented an organ of the kingship itself. Except for the sporadic and indirect munificence of emperors like Decius, the temple had now to persevere within the constraints of the local economy and under the supervision of the town council.[9] And, thus rendered so dependent upon the vicissitudes of local economies that were themselves falling rapidly into decline over the course of the third century, many temples were dragged down into disrepair, decay, and abandonment.[10]

Many temples, but certainly not all. For this scenario is largely inferred from the sudden drop in inscriptional and papyrological documentation after about 250 C.E. and not out of direct testimony. Indeed, despite this overall drop in data, priestly activities and even sacred landholdings are easily documented into the fourth century.[11] In a street census of early-fourth-century Panopolis priests still comprise a healthy 5% of the population.[12] Aurelios Sarapammon asserts his status as priest for the Oxyrhynchus Thoērion in 339.[13] Even at an Upper Egyptian temple like that of Akoris, which was clearly diminished by the late fourth century, priests still came annually to register the Nile surge on the Nilometer.[14] Zachariah of Mytilene's account of the fall of the Menouthis Isis temple assumes not only a functioning priesthood in this healing center still in the late fifth century but a priestess—a woman who retained her office for the sake of its public utility and implicitly its earnings—in at least one other town.[15]

And the priesthood still had social significance, providing a sense of identity, purpose, and importance among families through the fourth century. Aurelius Thonius swears in an affidavit of 336 C.E. that he received his priestly rank "in succession to my aforesaid father Demetrius, who was himself one of the said priests and celebrants [*kōmastoi*] of the

---

[9] Lewis 1983:48–49; Bagnall 1993:55–57; and on the administration of temples, *BGU* 362 = W.Chr. 96 and Corpus Papyrorum Hermopolitanarum 7 2, on which see Alan K. Bowman, *The Town Councils of Roman Egypt,* ASP 11 (Toronto: Hakkert, 1971), 97, 164; cf. Evans 1961:172; Dunand 1991b:291.

[10] Otto 1905/8, 1:403–5; Bagnall 1988:286–88.

[11] Zucker 1956; Dunand 1978:355–60; Glare 1993; and Whitehorne 1995:3081–82 on the Oxyrhynchus data alone, with the overall conclusion that "the extravagant religious sensibilities which had always characterised the inhabitants of Egypt at every level of society were by no means destroyed by the 'economic rationalism' of the Romans" (3058). Kákosy 1995 makes clear the imperial motivations for selected patronage in the later third century (2927–31).

[12] Borkowski 1975:43.

[13] PSI III.215.

[14] *IGAkoris* 40–41, with É. Bernand 1988:xxii.

[15] Zachariah of Mytilene, *V. Sev.,* in A. Bernand 1970:208.

divine images."[16] Priests in early-fifth-century Panopolis had enough political acumen and self-confidence to haul Abbot Shenoute before a magistrate in Antinoopolis (two hundred kilometers down the Nile).[17] The culture of the priestly family is still in the memory of a Theban monk of the late fourth or early fifth century: "I was the son of a priest of the pagans. When I was a child I would sit and watch my father proceeding many times to offer sacrifice to the image."[18] A contemporaneous legend recalls the purity of the priestly family: when a monk asked a village priest for his daughter's hand in marriage, the priest replied, "I cannot give her to you unless I learn [its appropriateness] from my god."[19]

The position of "priest" in Egyptian society still fell into particular ranks and functions through the fourth and fifth centuries. We find the "Sealer of the Sacred Calves," a traditionally vital role that ensured the purity of a temple's animals, seeking another priest's arrest in late-third- or early-fourth-century Oxyrhynchus.[20] The fifth-century hagiographer of Moses of Abydos counts the saint's murderous accomplishments in terms of *ouēēb*-priests (twenty-three dead) and *hont*-priests (the higher-ranking *ḥm nṯr* priests, commonly translated "prophets," seven dead).[21] In 373 C.E. the priesthood of Isis on Philae still includes functions of "first and second *ḥm-nṯr*" and a "high priest [Eg. *wʿb ʿ3*]"; "chief baker [Eg. *ʿmr3 ʿ3*]"; "scribe of the sacred book [Eg. *sḫ mtḏ-nṯr*]," who is responsible for gilding an image of Cleopatra; and other obscure titles. In 407 C.E. we find a "master of secrets [Eg. *(ḥry) sšt*]," and in 452 a "chief adorner of images [*prōtostolistēs*]."[22]

The priest in ritual procession seems still to have been a typical sight in the Egyptian landscape, whether in the massive processions of the boat of Khnum through the region of third-century Esna or the smaller group observed by Apa Apollo in fourth-century Hermopolis (Ashmunein),

---

[16] *P.Oxy* X.1265, 17–22.

[17] Shenoute, "The Lord Thundered" (= Leipoldt 3:85.1, #25); "Only I Tell Everyone Who Dwells in This Village" (= Leipoldt 3:88.11–16, #26).

[18] *Apophth. pat.* (anon.) 191, ed. Nau 1908:275.

[19] *Apophth. pat.* (anon.) 190, ed. Nau 1908:274–75. Note that in IDemPhilae 365 (452 C.E.) the first prophet of Isis is the grandson of a chief priest through his daughter.

[20] *P.Oxy* LXI.4116. On the office of *moskhosphragistēs*, see P. W. Pestman, *Recueil de textes démotiques et bilingues* 2 (Leiden: Brill, 1977), 117–21.

[21] *Life of Moses of Abydos*, ed. Amélineau 1888/95:687 = Till 1936:49. See also Wipszycka 1988:156. On *hont*, see Jaroslav Černý, *Coptic Etymological Dictionary* (Cambridge: Cambridge University Press, 1976), 288 s.v., and Anthony Alcock, "Coptic Words for 'Priest'," *ZÄS* 114 (1987):179.

[22] *ḥm-nṯr*: IDemPhilae 375. High priest: IDemPhilae 365. Chief baker: IDemPhilae 372; cf. 368. Scribe of sacred book: IDemPhilae 371 (gilding image: IDemPhilae 370); see Griffith 1937:304. Master of secrets: IDemPhilae 364. Chief adorner of images: IGPhilae 193, 196; cf. É. Bernand 1969, 2:235–36. Griffith takes *ʿnt3 ʿ3 n p-wʿb* (IDemPhilae 371) to be a priestly role meaning "chief pharmacist of the workshop" (1937:104; 289, #821).

whose "priests in Bacchic frenzy together with the people would carry [a divine image] in procession through the villages."[23] The sacrality of priests in processions was additionally conveyed in their occasional dramatic realization of gods: a masked Anubis in a late-third-century *Serapia* in Oxyrhynchus, and the "basket-carrying priestess [*kalatēphoros*]" officiating at a small village temple of (Isis-)Demeter in the second or third century, who almost certainly represented the goddess Isis in her agrarian form.[24]

Such priestly "power" could be preserved in the terra-cotta figurines of priests and priestesses that people brought home with them. Terra-cotta figurines of the Roman period in general tended to idealize and render accessible the image of priests in procession: for example, the nudity of terra-cotta priestesses does not record actual cultic attire but rather, in a concise form, the fertilizing power with which certain priestesses may have actually been imbued in ritual context.[25] Produced continually through the fourth century C.E., such figurines document the continuing reverence for the priestly role in Egyptian culture.

Did the priesthood continue? That is, did the priests continue to carry authority as priests when the infrastructure that defined their roles was disintegrating? A legacy from eighteenth-century scholarship that construed the priests of old religions as types of Catholic priests—whom Protestant caricature tended to retroject upon whatever in history could more vividly evoke a stilted and mercenary ritualism—still presses us to see ancient priesthoods as somehow in tension with society, only propped up by their ancient temples and their spiritless obsession with systematizing belief. When the temples collapse, the people are free and the priestly status becomes merely an anachronistic pretension on the part of certain élites.[26]

---

23 *Hist. Mon.* 8.25, ed. Festugière 1971:56. See above, 2.2.

24 *SB* V.7336, 24, ed. Wormald 1929; *P.Oxy* XXXVI.2782, on which see above, 2.1. The priest in the Anubis mask might belong to the order of *tarikheutai*, the quasi-priestly rank of embalmers who are represented iconographically in the image of Anubis (although scarcely appearing in papyri of the Roman period): see Bataille 1952:206–7; Diodorus I.91.5–6. Jean-Claude Grenier argues that Anubis-maskers (*anuboforoi* in a Latin inscription) were local volunteers, not priests (*Anubis alexandrin et romain*, EPRO 57 [Leiden: Brill, 1977], 177–81); but *hiereis* of Anubis are attested in *P.Mich.* IX.572 (131 C.E.) and *P.Oxy* X.1256 (282 C.E.). In general on ritual drama and masking in Egyptian religion, see Dunand 1991b:286 (on the Esna festival cycle); Wormald 1929:242; Griffiths 1975:217–18; and Arelene Wolinski, "Egyptian Masks: The Priest and His Role," *Archaeology* 40, 1 (1987):20, 22–29.

25 Dunand 1979:34–38, 100–102. See above, 3.2.

26 One notes, for example, Bagnall's reference to "the near-ghetto of the temples" and "a rickety formalism" in the priestly cult (1993:268, 324). On the roots of this perspective in anti-Catholic polemic, see Jonathan Z. Smith, *Drudgery Divine: On the Comparison of Early Christianities and the Religions of Late Antiquity* (Chicago: University of Chicago Press, 1990), esp. 33–35.

We would do well to look at native priesthoods in cultures overlooked by this Protestant polemic: in Africa, for example, where "priest" becomes more of a heuristic than an imported category for a type of ritual specialist with a fairly defined social status, with regulations for purity, and with an authority more extravagant than ordinary people but less marginal than that of prophets.[27] The priest is fundamentally a member of the society, who works for its good. And with this description in mind we can find at least three ways in which priestly status can continue to carry social value, meaning, and charisma.

One way for such continuity to occur, of course, is the necessity of a chief ritual expert for rendering the festivals, the agricultural passages, and other socially cohesive events complete and efficacious. The priest knows the rites. To be sure, a community can maintain religion in its broad sense of life-maintaining rituals without the constant presence of a priest. But the priest's expertise in staging rituals tends not to be borne by the community as a whole; and cross-culturally, villages with diminished access to such ritual experts tend to maintain only a fraction of the community rituals a priesthood might once have staged in full variety.[28] A community, guild, or family might hold onto some traditional rites, but it is the priests who made the holy stand out. In this sense a cultic procession such as the monk Apollo is supposed to have beheld functioned not simply as opportunities for temple–village interaction. They also framed the singular role of the priest or priesthood in adorning the images, opening the temple, carrying the images, and chanting the prayers—essentially in staging the procession for the benefit of fields and society. And doubtless the priesthoods were viewed in this vital role by the town councils that paid them.

But there are also two ways in which priests can maintain authority and status by changing it. A priest can become a prophetic figure, a mobilizer of a community or a region for defense or revolt.[29] And in what is perhaps the most resilient role for any ritual expert, the priest can diminish the scope of rituals performed, from a repertoire focused upon the temple-based festival rite to a repertoire encompassing more the crises and concerns of ordinary life: blessings and curses, childbirth and protection, love-spells and healing-spells, amulets and domestic altars.

[27] See, for example, Victor Turner, "Religious Specialists," *IESS* 13:437–44; Beidelmann 1971; Benjamin C. Ray, *African Religions: Symbol, Ritual, and Community* (Englewood Cliffs, N.J.: Prentice-Hall, 1976), 116–19; Lawson 1985:86–90.

[28] See Redfield 1941:96–98.

[29] Note that in this study "prophet" designates not the Egyptian priestly rank of *ḥm-nṯr* according to its Greek translation (*prophētēs*), but a charismatic leader who synthesizes received tradition and innovative ideology according to current circumstances and thus mobilizes a social group to some distinctive action.

## 5.2 Resilient Social Roles

### 5.2.1 Popular Charisma

Priestly charisma is typically a charisma of "office," meaning that leadership authority extends from the social position or rank one occupies rather than from one's unique presence or ideology. Priests' abilities to influence people, to convey ideology, thus tend to be constrained by their dramatic cultic roles. In the Roman period the erosion of priestly economic status may also have contributed to a diminution of social influence.

In many cultures undergoing the kinds of social and political stresses that might diminish priestly status, native priests have retained or successfully claimed a charismatic authority beyond that of village ritualist. Leaders of popular revolts in African and African American cultures invariably had prior authority as religious leaders—diviners, prophets, healers, priestly initiates, or other recognizable types of supernatural mediation—and galvanized their followers with traditional amulets and rites to resist opponents as well as with rhetoric based in native religious idiom.[30] Even without revolts societies undergoing any sort of political and cultural crisis will continue, at the village level, to exalt individuals holding any sort of traditional status or numinosity, such that the latter come to combine diverse types of leadership: prophetism, that is, can grow out of priesthood. This is what we may call the *charismatic potential* of local priests: an occasional social role that expands the authority, the significance, of a person already personally vested with some local authority but often unable to articulate a religious message through traditional cultic media.

A number of episodes during the course of Roman rule suggest that Egyptian priests in many regions and situations could likewise carry (or claim) charismatic influence in social affairs. What distinguishes the priests in these episodes from the far more marginalized prophet figures one finds, for example, in early Roman Palestine or fourth-century Egyptian asceticism is the means of influence: the principal means of communicating ideology for Egyptian priests (at least of the higher ranks) derived from ritual contexts, especially the oracle and the festival execration rite.

Plutarch describes one such execration rite during which priests sacrificed red cattle as images of the demonic Seth-Typhon. After preparing the animals with markings symbolic of Seth's destruction, the priests "in-

---

[30] Beidelman 1971, esp. 388; Michael Adas, *Prophets of Rebellion: Millenarian Protest Movements against the European Colonial Order* (Chapel Hill, N.C.: University of North Carolina Press, 1979), 102–5, 112–13, 120, 138–56. Cf. Margaret Creel's remarks on the 1820s slave revolt leaders Gullah Jack of Charleston and Boukman of San Domingo as particularly charismatic through their roles as African-born diviners (Creel 1988:153–55).

voke curses on the head of the sacrifice and cut it off."[31] These public curses, chanted in the midst (perhaps the high point) of the festival, recall the numerous Egyptian librettos for Seth execration rites preserved from the Ptolemaic and classical periods.[32] Plutarch is quite explicit about the enthusiastic public participation in these execration rites, which were still taking place throughout Egypt when he visited. Through their public curses, that is, priests galvanized and articulated a hostility, or at least a gleeful aggression, in the community much like that of modern Guy Fawkes' Day or Purim. And priests could easily mingle the mythology of the "ritual hostility" with perceived threats in the real world, thus launching an attack on anything they might cast as "Sethian."

Oracles, as we have seen, provided multiple media for priests' involvement in local, regional, and even more distant affairs. Some types of oracles seem to have established a quite intimate, if secretive, relationship of priest and supplicant. Almost like a Catholic communion booth, the oracular *naoi,* the small oracular consulting chamber at Coptos, and even the small anteroom of the sanctuary of Hatshepsut at Deir el-Bahri would have given response to only one or two supplicants at a time. Presumably the supplicant would approach the god in his shrine and present the problem as an appeal. The hidden priest would then deliver the answer as from the god, and the answer to such a question as above might well involve directing the supplicant to a priest for a blessing or an amulet: at the fifth-century Isis oracle of Menouthis, for example, the priest who interprets dreams directs the philosopher Asklepiodotos to the priestess of the village of Astu.[33] Then the next person would enter or approach the god. Even the larger sanctuaries, like those of Soknopaiou Nesos, Kysis, and Menouthis, seem to have served the quite intimate concerns of health, fertility, or even existential advice, like the "Apollo" oracle's admonition to Serenus of Pharos to make pilgrimage to Isis of Philae.[34] Such cases reveal priests and priesthoods forging interconnections among cults and thus, through the oracles, maintaining authority and sacrality in a changing religious landscape.

[31] Plutarch, *De Iside* 31.

[32] For example, P.Jumilhac (ed. Vandier 1961), P.Salt 825 (ed. Derchain 1965). See, in general, Ritner 1993:136–44, 168–71. The reliability of Plutarch's detail in describing these rites is quite apparent in ch. 30, where he mentions cakes stamped "with an image of a tied ass" (362F). These cakes correspond to vignettes in P.Salt 825 and a roughly contemporaneous stela in Hanover's Kestner Museum: see Philippe Derchain, "A propos d'une stèle magique du Musée Kestner, à Hanovre," *RdÉ* 16 (1964):19–23 (stela); Derchain 1965, fasc. 1b, 22a–23a (P.Salt 825), with Griffiths 1970:416–17; Jean Yoyotte, "Religion de l'Égypte ancienne," *Annuaire de l'École pratique des Hautes Études, V<sup>e</sup> section: Sciences religieuses* 77 (1969):185–91; and Ritner 1993:113–19, 175–77.

[33] Zachariah of Mytilene, *V.Sev.,* in A. Bernand 1970:208.

[34] IGPhilae 168. See above, 3.2.

From ancient times priests and priesthoods had used these same oracular media for much more inflammatory or ideological purposes, occasionally mobilizing or galvanizing large groups of people to act on the word of the god.[35] Such demagogic activism among Egyptian priests has a background in the regional mobilizations of the Theban priesthood during the Ptolemaic period. Indeed, the abiding importance of these earlier religious uprisings seems evident in the preservation of their prophetic oracles in the Oracle of the Lamb and the Potter's Oracle as late as the third century C.E.[36] Papyrus Dodgson, an oracular transcript from an early Ptolemaic oracle of Khnum at Elephantine, suggests that ecstatic prophecy may at some points have been the medium for oracles' delivery.[37] The early Roman officials seem to have designed the Augustan reforms of the Egyptian religious hierarchy to tighten control over the immense potential for popular leadership held by regional priesthoods as well as further efforts (the edict of Septimius Severus preserved in P.Yale 299 and the closing of the Abydos Bes oracle in 359 attempted to restrict traditional temple oracles as potentially subversive).[38]

But the best evidence that priests were, in fact, mobilizing circumscribed "holy wars" in the Roman period comes from the second century: in the Egyptian response to the Jewish revolt (116–17) and in a regional uprising in the Delta (172–73).

The Jewish revolt was itself religious in nature (there are hints of messianic rumors), sweeping from Cyrene in North Africa eastward to stimulate multiple Jewish communities and even terrorize their neighbors into committing preemptive massacres. With the Roman army on the Persian front it was left to Egyptian forces to put down the revolt in Egypt, and in the process they seem to have annihilated most of Egyptian Jewry.[39] The

[35] Dunand 1979:123.

[36] Préaux 1936; Eddy 1961:297–302, 314–18 (who vastly overstates ethnic factors); and K. Vandorpe, "City of Many a Gate, Harbour for Many a Rebel," in Vleeming (ed.) 1995:232–36. The use of symbolically loaded terms against indigenous pharaohs in the early second century B.C.E. would suggest hierocratic participation on both sides. See materials from counter-pharaoh revolts discussed in P. W. Pestman, "Haronnophris and Chaonnophris: Two Indigenous Pharaohs in Ptolemaic Egypt (205–186 B.C.)," in Vleeming (ed.) 1995:101–37. On Oracles of the Lamb and the Potter, see above, 4.1, 4.2.2, and below, 6.2. It should be noted that there is at least as much evidence for priestly promotion of Ptolemaic kingship as there is for priestly opposition to it: Koenen 1983 and Janet H. Johnson, "Is the Demotic Chronicle an Anti-Greek Tract?" *Grammata Demotika,* ed. by Heinz-J. Thissen and Karl-Th. Zauzich (Würzburg: Gisela Zauzich, 1984), 107–24.

[37] Griffith 1909; De Cenival 1987; C. Martin 1994. See above, 4.4.2.

[38] See Parássoglou 1976:262–66; Bowersock 1986; Milne 1924:180–81.

[39] On the annihilation of Egyptian Jewry through the response to the revolt, see Tcherikover/Fuks 1957/64, 1:92–93; Smallwood 1976:405–9; and Aryeh Kasher, *The Jews in Hellenistic and Roman Egypt* (Tübingen: Mohr [Siebeck], 1985), 28. In general, see Frankfurter 1992.

enthusiasm required to effect this degree of devastation (hardly unknown for the time, it should be said) can be convincingly linked to an oracle preserved from the period in two papyri, which urges its audiences to "attack the Jews," who are "opponents of order [*paranomoi*] once expelled from Egypt by the wrath of Isis," lest these "impious people despoil your temples" and "your largest temple become sand for horses." The oracle links the enthusiasm of the anti-Jewish response to a priestly tradition reaching back to the early Ptolemaic period that identified Jews as people of Seth-Typhon, dangerous foreigners.[40] Along with other details of the character of the Egyptian response to the Jewish revolt, the oracle indicates that priests were wielding a broader version of that same Seth execration ideology that Plutarch beheld in local festivals and that usually carried a more neutral significance, celebrating as it did the power of the kingship. Indeed, by the end of the second century the *victory* over the Jews had actually become a festival, the overt language of which would have focused on the repelling of Seth-Typhon.[41] During the revolt, however, the priests seem to have communicated the execration ideology through the medium of written (perhaps also recited) oracle texts and in the language of political execration that the Potter's Oracle had aimed against Greeks in general during the Ptolemaic period.[42]

By the end of the second century C.E. the Delta was awash with stories about either a gang of brigands or rampaging warriors of some district. Having been known as Neikochites in 166/67 C.E. according to a papyrus that details their depredations, they quickly came to be known as "*boukoloi*."[43] Their memory was preserved in the actual name of the

---

[40] *CPJ* 520 = PSI 982, plus an unpublished Oxyrhynchus fragment graciously shown me by Ludwig Koenen. See Georg V. Manteuffel, "Zur Prophetie in *P.S.I.*, VIII.982," *Mélanges Maspero* 2 (Cairo: IFAO, 1934), 119–24; Menachem Stern in Tcherikover/Fuks 1957/64, 3:119–21; Ludwig Koenen, review of *CPJ* 2–3, *Gnomon* 40 (1968):257–58. On the background of Egyptian anti-Jewish ideology, see Manetho fr. 54; Chaeremon fr. 1; Plutarch, *De Iside* 31; and in general Griffiths 1970:418–19; Van Der Horst 1984:49–50nn.1–8; John Gager, *Moses in Greco-Roman Paganism* (Nashville: Abingdon, 1972 ), 26–29, 113–22; and Yoyotte 1963. Memphis seems to have been a particular center of anti-Jewish sentiment before 116 (*CPJ* 141; *Sibylline Oracle* 5.60–62, 68–70; with Roger Rémondon, "Les antisémites de Memphis," *CdÉ* 35 [1960]:244–61, and Thompson 1988:99) and of anti-Jewish mobilization during the revolt (*CPJ* 439; Smallwood 1976:402).

[41] On *CPJ* 450, see Alexander Fuks, "The Jewish Revolt in Egypt (A.D. 115–117) in the Light of the Papyri," *Aegyptus* 33 (1953):153–54, and Tcherikover/Fuks 1957/64, 2:260n. ad loc. On the interpretation of the festival's probable structure, see Frankfurter 1992: 213–15.

[42] See Frankfurter 1992:209–11.

[43] Cassius Dio 72.4, with Winkler 1980:175–81 and Bertrand 1988. *Neikōkeitai:* P.Thmouis I, cols. 104, 116, cf. 114, ed. Sophie Kambitsis, *Le Papyrus Thmouis 1* (Paris: Sorbonne, 1985). See ibid., 28–29, and Bowersock 1994:52–53.

district (the boukolia) during the third and fourth centuries, and legends of their exploits flourished in the Greek novels of Achilles Tatius, Heliodorus, and others.[44] But in Cassius Dio's brief account of their threat to the Roman military, he mentions their leadership under a priest, Isidorus, and Heliodorus seems to echo this detail in placing a disenfranchised Memphite priest, Thyamis, over his fictional *Boukoloi*.[45]

Without pushing Isidorus's significance so far as to imply outright nationalistic rebellion, we can still make some tentative observations that would corroborate a priest's leadership. Isidorus's presence, for example, would explain the increasing threat of the *boukoloi* such that they came to be named no longer by a local designation, "Neichochites," but rather a term for 'herdsmen' of apparently more marginal and dangerous significance that may have carried negative Egyptian overtones. It might also explain the necessity of some temple, presumably of the Delta, to issue an oracle in the second century prophesying their defeat (and to send it up the Nile, where the oracle papyrus was found): it speaks of "a disturbance in Egypt" and a "death of *Boukoloi*."[46]

Isodorus's leadership of the Delta *boukoloi* simply contributes to a general picture of priests' charismatic leadership in the Roman period despite the progressive erosion of their *economic* status. The example of the *boukoloi* also alerts us to the local or regional boundaries of such charisma. Priestly authority, especially in its capacity to mobilize people beyond the context of festivals, was growing increasingly circumscribed, localized, as with the rest of Egyptian religion. The priest Sarapion might still presume the authority in 217 to predict Caracalla's imminent death

---

[44] *Boukolia:* W.Chr. I.21 = *BGU* II.625 (early third century C.E.); Athanasius, *V.Ant.* 49 (ca. 358 C.E.); Jerome, *V.Hil.* 31.2 (late fourth century C.E.). *Novels:* Xenophon of Ephesus, *Ephesiaca* 3.12.2 (second century C.E.; robber group in Delta called *poimēnes*); Achilles Tatius, *Leucippe and Clitophon* 3.9; 4.17–18 (ca. 175 C.E.); Heliodorus, *Aethiopica* 1.5–6; 2.24.1 (third/fourth century C.E.); cf. Lollianus, *Phoinikika* frs. A2r–B1r (late second century C.E.), in which atrocities are attributed to a bandit group much like the *boukoloi* of Achilles Tatius, Cassius Dio, and Heliodorus.

[45] Heliodorus, *Aethiopica* 1.19, 22.

[46] P.Stanford inv. G93bv, ed. John C. Shelton, "An Astrological Prediction of Disturbances in Egypt," *Ancient Society* 7 (1976):209–13. The marginal and dangerous significance of *boukoloi* is quite apparent in the word's use among the novelists (Winkler 1980:175–81; Bertrand 1988); but the term may be related to an ancient Egyptian word for "Asiatic" that had come by the Late Period to signify "herder," *'3m.w* ("Amu"). In both ancient and Ptolemaic times *'3m.w* carried the sense of marginal and warlike people: see Georges Posener, "Les asiatiques en Égypte sous les XIIè et XIIIè dynasties," *Syria* 34 (1957):145–63, on ancient views of *'3m.w*; Joseph G. Manning, "Land and Status in Ptolemaic Egypt," in *Grund und Boden im Altägypten,* ed. by S. Allam (Tübingen: Allam, 1994), 50–51, on the evolution of the term to mean "herder"; and Spiegelberg 1910:8–9 and glossary 10–11, showing that the negative sense of "Asiatic" was still preserved in a Demotic text of the early Roman period.

in the emperor's very court. But the uprisings for which we have evidence in the late third century are indeed quite circumscribed: Ptolemais and Coptos in 278 and another based in Thebes during the reign of Diocletian. When, in the late fourth century, the philosopher Antoninus offers an oracle on Egypt's doom in the spirit of the Potter's Oracle, he does so on the porch of a rural temple in the Delta.[47]

By the fifth century the charismatic authority of priests, when it could arise, was almost exclusively local. And yet such authority is quite vivid as it is presented in the Coptic sources. In the story of the defense of the cult of "Kothos," the god himself mobilizes the villagers against Dioscorus and his monks. To the extent that the story holds some verisimilitude, and I have argued so above, it suggests the issuing of a "voice" oracle: a priest of "Kothos" stood behind a temple wall and delivered the voice of the god to encourage people to defend the sanctuary.[48] The story of Shenoute's crusade against the village of Plewit, which holds more historical credibility, describes a united action among villagers to repel the abbot using the materials of traditional execration rites "according to their books." Inasmuch as Shenoute himself speaks of "books full of magic" that he plundered from the Plewit temple and even finds himself on trial in Antinoopolis at the instigation of Plewit's priests, it is likely that the villagers' ritual actions followed the directives of a priest (who could read such books).[49]

In the midst of the social and economic disintegrations that characterized the third century, and faced with the growing repression of a Christianized imperium, one would hardly expect local priests of the native religion not to respond occasionally as charismatic leaders—not nationalist revolutionaries, to be sure, but mobilizers of local or regional uprisings.[50] The Christianity that developed in the third-century countryside was itself a prophetic movement responding to cultural stresses of the period. The so-called Melitians whom Athanasius excoriated in the fourth century expressed the same millennialist fervor, no doubt continuing still. If this kind of Christianity continued to gain adherents in rural

---

[47] Sarapion before Caracalla: Cassius Dio 79.4.4–5. Third-century Theban uprisings: W. Seston, "Achilleus et la révolte de l'Égypte sous Dioclétien," *Mélanges d'archéologie et d'histoire* 55 (1938):184–200; Allan Chester Johnson, "Lucius Domitius Domitianus Augustus," *CP* 45 (1950):14–16; Alan K. Bowman, "The Military Occupation of Upper Egypt in the Reign of Diocletian," *BASP* 15 (1978):26–33, and idem, "The Revolt of Busiris and Coptos," *BASP* 21 (1984):33–36. Antoninus's oracle: Eunapius, *V.P.* 6.9.17 (471); see above, 4.4.2.

[48] See above, 1.3.3 and 2.6.1.

[49] Besa, *Life of Shenoute* 83–84, with Shenoute, "Only I Tell Everyone Who Dwells in This Village" (= Leipoldt 3:89.15–16 [cf. 88.11–16], #26) and "The Lord Thundered" (= Leipoldt 3:85.1, #25).

[50] See Wipszycka 1992:93.

communities through the force of charismatic leaders, we should expect that the broader phenomenon of prophecy extended to local priests as well (as it does in contemporary prophetic movements).[51] Here, at least, we have seen evidence that priests could assume such a charismatic role and did so under Roman rule.

### 5.2.2 Local Ritual Expertise

With the constraints of Christianization following upon the economic crisis of the third century, the authority of the priest increasingly devolved upon his generalized, extracultic, local ritual expertise and upon his unique aura of ancient tradition: he becomes the local healer, diviner, manufacturer of amulets, and dispenser of spells.

Every society has its ritual experts as well as its exotic images of magicians and sorcerers. Indeed, one might say that much of ancient peasant life involved negotiating problems and tensions through a network of charismatic individuals that spread over village and region. At the simplest dimension, the furthest removed from any kind of great tradition or institutional or guild affiliation, one would find midwives and wise women, while at the other extreme one would find the traditionally designated ritual authorities, representatives of a great tradition (if such a thing were to exist in the broader religious culture): priests. Where the charisma and ritual performance of wise women would arise essentially within the culture and sacred world of the local community and would remain oral, the priests' ritual expertise would, even if improvised, be perceived as conveying the traditional lore and authority of an archaic temple institution, particularly as that lore might be preserved and transmitted in sacred letters.

Ritual expertise in most rural communities in the late antique Mediterranean world seems to have clustered at the "wise women" part of the spectrum, the priesthoods that might once have influenced local culture having been gutted early in the Roman period. Thus Gaul had its local healers at the time of the shrine of Saint Martin of Tours; and the region of Sykeon in sixth-century Galatia had a "sorcerer" with particularly widespread religious authority.[52]

---

[51] See Frankfurter 1993:241–78. The *Apocalypse of Elijah,* an Egyptian Christian prophecy of the third century, seems to be the work of such a charismatic leader with some kind of training in Egyptian priestly literary composition: see, in general, Frankfurter 1993:101–2, 195–238.

[52] *Gaul* (sixth century): Gregory of Tours, *Miracles of St. Martin* 27, on which see Flint 1991:59–84. *Galatia: Life of St. Theodore of Sykeon* 35–38, 143, tr. Dawes/Baynes 1977:112–15, 181. Compare also evidence for local ritual experts in fourth- to fifth-century Asia Minor and Greece: Basil, *Ep.,* 211, 217.72, 83; *Greek Anthology* 365 (Agathias Scholasticus).

But Egypt's records project a different picture of local ritual expertise from the beginning. There were almost certainly wise women: several documents from the New Kingdom refer to such a figure, and the historian generally takes the role as a given even despite silence.[53] But even that sphere of ritual expertise most typically ascribed to wise women, obstetrical and gynecological healing and protection, is most richly documented not, as one might expect, in scattered precipitates from an oral, women's world but rather in ritual texts, documents of the House of Life, the temple scriptorium.[54]

The role associated with healing-spells, curse-spells, safety-spells, and the whole range of rites concerned with that obscure (sometimes personified) cosmic force known in Egyptian as *heka* was no freelance "magician" but the *ḥry ḥb*, or lector-priest, who fulfilled this role publicly by virtue of his (or her) professional association with the sacred books of the temple.[55] Indeed, not only are the legendary wizards of Egyptian literature all priests and masters of the book, but virtually all documentation for local ritual expertise in Egypt through the first two centuries of the Roman period shows some association between the alleged "magician" and the temple institution.[56] The most vivid link between popular or local ritual expertise and its charisma and the institution of the temple, however, is the corpus of ritual manuals. From pharaonic times through the fourth century C.E., these collections of spells for snakebite, safety, love, healing, success, and the rest could belong to no other constituency than one versed in Egyptian writing. And if Egyptian writing had once occupied scribes and clerks outside the temples proper, by the Greco-

[53] A local "wise woman [Eg. *t3 rḫ.t*]" in Deir el-Medina, on which see J. F. Borghouts, "Divine Intervention in Ancient Egypt and Its Manifestation (*b3w*)," in *Gleanings from Deir El-Medina*, ed. by R. Demarée and J. Janssen (Leiden: Nederlands Instituut voor het Nabije Oosten, 1982), 25–27; Baines 1987:93; Koenig 1994:34–35. Soranus mentions OB/GYN remedies purveyed by women, perhaps referring to Alexandria: *Gynecology* 1.2.4.

[54] J. F. Borghouts, "Magical Texts," *Textes et langages de l'Égypte pharaonique: Hommage à Jean-François Champollion* 3 (Cairo: IFAO, 1974), 7–19; Borghouts 1978:x–xi; Ritner 1995. On OB/GYN spells, see also Ritner 1984 and the profusion of (Greco-) Egyptian sources cited in Aubert 1989. This link between OB/GYN and the priesthood should not be taken as excluding women from sacred midwife roles, as such roles seem to have been long incorporated within the Egyptian priesthood, perhaps in connection with Bes: see above, 3.5.2.

[55] Among important demonstrations of this indigenous Egyptian link between "magic" and the institutional priesthood, see Derchain 1963:221; Sauneron 1960a:63–65; 1966; Baines 1991:166–72; Ritner 1993:204–5, 220–33; Pinch 1994:47–60; Koenig 1994:19–38.

[56] Subspecialties of ritual expertise in the pharaonic period (e.g., *ḥrp-srkt*, "scorpion-charmer") are not significantly distinct from priestly experts (see Alan H. Gardiner, "Professional Magicians in Ancient Egypt," *PSBA* 39 [1917]:31–43; Ritner 1993:222; Koenig 1994:32–34). *P.Oxy* VII.1050 (second century C.E.) mentions a nonpriestly *manganos*, a designation cognate with *mageia*, but he is a performer hired for public games (l.19).

Roman period literacy in Egyptian was the exclusive provenance—and requirement, no less—of the priesthood.[57]

In the culture of the scriptorium this link between writing and priestly service allowed a certain consistency to Egyptian religion as a whole, a kind of great tradition in perpetual dialectic with the strongly local characteristics of cults and popular practice. Writing allowed priests to maintain a mythology, an authoritative language, to which rituals of the most mundane sort might make appeal. Thus from the popular, illiterate viewpoint the lector-priest held the skills to resolve any crisis, passage, or need by rendering it in mythological terms, invoking the authority of temple discourse, transmitting the power of the written word into forms of everyday accessibility: blessed water, an amulet, the burning of a written name.[58] In this public role lector-priests operated as mediators between that great tradition of the temple scriptorium and the little tradition of the village or simply its regular activities and crises.

The Egyptian priesthood was a sprawling and often regionally idiosyncratic institution, and locating the bulk of popular ritual expertise within that institution reflects little more than how deeply the great tradition—the archaic temple culture (with its definition of priest and sacred power)—had thrust its roots into (or grown out of) the local religious cultures of Egypt. Different ranks of priests probably all had their "magic," their repertoires of talismans, spells, and rites that extended their "official" ritual activities into the everyday sphere: one thinks especially of the various mortuary priests in this respect. Incubation oracle cults certainly had their attendants, dream interpreters, and other specialists, like the one-eyed astrologer mentioned in a late-third-century letter from Oxyrhynchus and the priestess in fifth-century Menouthis who procures a baby to guarantee an oracle. Just as the Ptolemaic period offers an example of a "lector-priest among the people," there must have been a range of ways in which people associated with the priesthood could serve the popular ritual needs of ordinary villagers.[59]

The status of lector-priest itself probably indicated a range of institutional roles, from official festival reader to a lower "training" rank with only peripheral connection to established temple cults. Lector-priests may well have resembled, in their intermediary status between temple

---

[57] Sauneron 1962b, with *P.Tebtunis* II.291, 40–43.

[58] See Baines 1983; and on the construction of spells, Jørgen Podemann Sørensen, "The Argument in Ancient Egyptian Magical Formulae," *Acta Orientalia* 45 (1984):5–19, and Ritner 1992.

[59] "One-eyed astrologer" affiliated with incubation cult: *P.Oxy* LXI.4126. Alexander Jones (1994) has shown a consistent relationship between astrological texts of the Roman period and the temples. Menouthis priestess: see above, 2.1 and 4.3.1. The "ḥr-tb among the people" visited by the Ibis priest Hor (second century B.C.E.) is almost certainly the public role of a particular temple priest (Hor #12, ed. Ray 1976:51–53, esp. 53n.f).

and local religion and their relative marginality to village culture, the minor clerics of contemporary religious establishments in Sudan and Ethiopia: the Berti (Sudan) *faki* and the Ethiopian *debtera*. Like Egyptian priests, both figures gain local charisma and develop their "magical" repertoires by virtue of their literacy and their control of the religious idiom and texts of the greater tradition (Islam in the case of the *faki*, Christianity in the case of the *debtera*); their dress tends also to be distinctive of the religious institution. Both figures have formal religious duties during official worship, festivals, and rites of passage. But both also serve as exorcists, healers, and amulet manufacturers, primarily in their capacity of mediating the concrete efficacy of written texts to nonliterate clients through a diversity of rites, such as inscribing "magic" scrolls for the afflicted or erasing inscribed Qur'anic verses into liquid. As ritual expertise is a major source of revenue among the *debteras* there is a lively exchange of techniques and designs among them over the course of their formal training. Although neither figure constitutes the sole ritual expert in his respective culture, their common ability to mediate powers popularly associated with the greater tradition by virtue of its *texts* puts them in a unique charismatic position in local communities.[60]

It is likely that this same charismatic position—between local and great tradition, skilled at the "magical" application of the written word—provided a context for priests' continued authority at the local level through the late Roman period. As temple revenues shrunk, that is, many priests were increasingly thrown back on their roles as ritual specialists. From the villagers' perspective, the priests' usefulness, if not outright charisma, as ritual experts might continue on an individual basis long past the crumbling of the regional temples. And in times of crisis they might still be called to protect an entire village, as was the priest who was able to render curse materials according to books when Shenoute approached Plewit.[61]

Indeed, it has happened in the history of religions that, under certain types of cultural disintegration, a professional priestly class will scatter into so many local ritual specialists, each flung back upon his or her lineage, overt priestly traits, knowledge of traditional ritual language and gesture, as the only available means of professional income and social

---

[60] On *fakis*, see El-Tom 1985; on *debteras*, A. Young 1975, Mercier 1979, and Kay Kaufman Shelemay, "The Musician and Transmission of Religious Tradition: The Multiple Roles of the Ethiopian Däbtära," *JRAf* 22 (1992):242–60. Ernest Gellner records a similar role for the *foquaha* in Morocco (*Saints of the Atlas* [Chicago: University of Chicago Press, 1969], 286–87, 298). Herman Te Velde suggests that similar social dynamics influenced the role of the Egyptian lector-priest ("Theology, Priests, and Worship in Ancient Egypt," in *Civilizations of the Ancient Near East* 3, ed. by J. Sasson et al. [New York: Scribner's, 1995], 1747).

[61] Besa, *Life of Shenoute* 83–84, and above, 5.2.1.

esteem.[62] For example, out of the many African captives brought to the Americas in the eighteenth and nineteenth centuries who arrived with some training or specialty in ritual practices (healing, cursing, amulet manufacture, divination), some individuals seem to have preserved a certain prestige and mystique in the eyes of others, becoming "conjurers" in the slave communities. This diversified role of diviner, healer, sorcerer, and social mediator was sufficiently localized in clientele that conjurers came to have strong associations to specific places.[63] Becoming one of the chief religious leadership roles in rural African American culture, the conjurer seems to have grown out of the consolidation of traditional ritual expertise in certain individuals.

The status of "conjurer" came ultimately to settle on anyone convinced of his or her own abilities (and able to articulate that conviction in traditional terms), but it originally designated those of African birth who already had the status of ritual specialist or diviner. And thus in comparative terms a traditional social status of religious specialist can be maintained despite cultural trauma, changing from the role of cultic service or community leadership to the role of ritual expert.

The comparison serves a model of Egyptian priest that is not mindless performer and temple functionary but rather involves a popularly designated ritual expertise, a figure whose interest in maintaining archaic temple tradition serves as much popular religious need as any personal need for authority, a figure who can mediate among community need, broad traditions, and historical situation despite the trauma of the religious infrastructure to which he belongs.

### 5.2.3 The Multiplication of Ritual Experts

How central the social role of ritual expert remains in local religion emerges most clearly with the multiplication and competitive diversification of such figures after the third century. For here we can see people's

---

[62] See Arthur Darby Nock, "Paul and the Magus," in Nock 1972, 1:321.

[63] See Albert J. Raboteau, *Slave Religion: The "Invisible Institution" in the Antebellum South* (New York: Oxford University Press, 1978), 275–88. Evidence for Ibo, Gola, and Bakongo ritual experts on the Georgia/South Carolina coast includes Gullah Jack (Creel 1988:153–59); and from the Georgia Writers' Project ethnographic collection, *Drums and Shadows: Survival Studies among the Georgia Coastal Negroes* (Athens: University of Georgia Press, 1940; repr. Westport, Conn.: Greenwood, 1973), the following individuals: Dick Hamilton (67); grandfather of Jack Waldburg (68); grandfather of Rosanna Williams (70–71); Alexander the Conjurer (177, 179). On religious offices in regions of origin, see Creel 1988:56–58; and on the knowledge specific to secret societies, ibid., 47–52. On evidence for a "popular" ritual knowledge carried from Africa, see *Drums and Shadows*, 167. Lawson describes such African religious roles in their structural context, maintained and filled in each generation despite traumas and cultural shifts (1985:86–90).

everyday needs for supernatural power and conciliatory rites engendering all sorts of rural leaders, whose charisma very much depended on addressing these needs.

During the fourth century prophetic figures arose throughout rural Egypt, appropriating in charismatic form such traditional priestly services as divination, social mediation, healing, and supernatural protection: that is, the ascetic holy men, whom we have previously regarded in their competition with oracles (4.4.2). Figures like Paul of Thebes, Antony, Apollo, and John of Lycopolis are also recorded as ministering to people's needs in domains of health and safety and gaining great renown specifically through these services. Their cults differed from the local charisma of the remaining priestly ritual specialists in exerting attraction and influence over broad areas, requiring pilgrimage rather than the negotiation of normal intravillage consultation.

Thus we can imagine a multiplicity of ritual experts by the mid- to late fourth century, as the remaining priests were met with increasing competition from Christian holy people. The collection and consultation of ritual grimoires, for example, became also the province of a Christian and Manichaean book culture.[64] As is so often the case in the local reception of great traditions, especially those advancing new sacred books, Christianity was often viewed as a superior ritual technology for handling quotidian problems and its bishops and functionaries as particular experts in this technology.[65] The fourth century, that is, provides a diversity of new figures renowned for their devotion to sacred or revelatory texts, who by virtue of these literary associations would have become regional resources for private rites and charms.

The traditional crafts of Egyptian practical ritual, like amulets and minor sacred images, may also have devolved upon various nonliterate local figures with no priestly background: the fifth-century Homily on the Virgin discussed above (1.4.2) decries local manufacturers of traditional ("demonic") amulets, while the fourth-century (336–40 C.E.) Egyptian *Canon of Pseudo-Hippolytus* refers to Christian craftspersons of what are evidently traditional Egyptian images, amulets, and divination techniques; and the somewhat later *Canon of Pseudo-Athanasius* attacks

[64] Manichaean ritual texts from Kellis (Dakhla oasis) are still in the process of publication (Colin A. Hope, Olaf E. Kaper, and Gillian E. Bowen, "Excavations at Ismant El-Kharab 1992," *BACE* 3 [1992]:42). Among those found, Kellis ms. P88 (fourth century C.E.) is a Manichaean letter quoting a Coptic separation spell that the writer says he found on a loose papyrus.

[65] Cf. J. Scott 1977:28 on the reception of Buddhism in Burmese local culture; Schoffeleers 1994, on the common understanding of Jesus in modern sub-Saharan Africa according to the model of the local healer; and below, 7.1.

those who consult "astrologers, sorcerers [Copt. *refmoute*], diviners [Copt. *refsine*], magicians [*magos*]," and other local ritual specialists.[66] Shenoute offers a concise illustration of this multiplicity of specialists, local sources of amulets, advice, and power, as they operated in the fifth-century countryside of Panopolis:

> In the moments of the suffering, . . . [there are some who] when they fall into poverty or become ill—or indeed other temptations—abandon God and have recourse to enchanters or oracles or . . . other deceptive things: just as I myself have seen—the snake's head bound to the hand of some, and another with the crocodile tooth bound to an arm, another with fox claws bound to his legs: especially as there was a magistrate who told the latter that he was wise to do so. Indeed, when I reproachfully asked him whether it was the fox claws that would heal him, he said: "It was a great monk who gave me them saying, Bind them to you, and you will recover."[67]

That a monk is now offering fox claws is instructive. By the fifth century it is apparently those figures affiliated with the Christian hierarchy who are occupying the central roles of ritual expertise in villages, like the Ethiopian *debtera* conveying authority and power through their affiliation with the great tradition and proficiency in its ritual idioms. In an Arabic encomium on the sixth-century Coptic saint John of Paralos there is an account of a village priest (Christian) "who practiced astrology and magic. This occupation returned to him a great quantity of money. It was revealed to the bishop not to let him offer the holy sacrifice [Eucharist] any more."[68] One cannot assume that this priest saw in his "magical" practice anything heterodox or not incumbent upon his role as village priest.

By the seventh century and the advent of Islam, Egypt had gained the reputation as a veritable culture of magicians, far beyond the biblical portrait of Pharaoh's indomitable court wizards. Ritual expertise at the local level now consisted of a wide assortment of Coptic, Islamic, and more synthetic purveyors of spells and amulets, much as Winifred Blackman portrayed Egyptian villages in the 1920s. The vast corpora of medieval Jewish grimoires and amulets found in Cairo suggest that Jews also provided such services; and exchange among Jewish, Coptic, and Islamic ritual specialists is evident both in the abundant commonalities among their respective texts and in a trilingual (Coptic, Greek, and Aramaic)

---

[66] Ps-Ath. Homily on the Virgin, ed. Lefort 1958:36 (ms. p. 95); *Canon of Ps-Hipp.* 11, 15 (ed. René-Georges Coquin, "Les Canons d'Hippolyte," *PO* 31, 2 [1966]:96–97, 100–101); *Canon of Ps-Ath.* 41 (ed. Riedel/Crum 1904:88, 118).

[67] Paris copte 1292 66 + DS, p. 59, tr. Orlandi 1982:90.

[68] Synaxarium Jacobite, 19 Kihak: John of Paralos, ed. and tr. René Basset, "Le synaxaire arabe jacobite," *PO* 3 (1909):487.

grimoire of the fifth century.[69] Thus a late-tenth-century writer could pronounce:

> The Babylon of the magicians is in the land of Egypt. A person who has seen this [state of affairs] has told me that there still remain men and women magicians and that all of the exorcists and magicians assert that they have seals, charms of paper, sandal, *jazab,* smoke, and other things used for their arts.[70]

## 5.3 Roman Hellenism and the Revaluation of Priestly Service

### 5.3.1 The Egyptomanic Lens of Hellenism

The outsider's perception of Egypt as the land of "magic," of course, goes back to the literature of the Greco-Roman period, and more broadly to that combination of awe and disgust that characterizes the exoticism of any age but the Roman Empire above all. The "gazing" culture projects upon and then discovers in the exotic culture its own latent ideals and embarrassments. Thus the exotic culture serves to define the boundaries of the gazing culture through a series of polarities: the exotic culture is older, wiser; its commoners are cruder, more superstitious and morally primitive; its past comprises an ancient line of awesome rulers that puts the gazing culture at the level of childhood; and yet that past is indeed bygone, crumbled, a mere backdrop to the present primacy of the gazing culture. It is in this ideological context that "Greeks," so Heliodorus observed, would "find all Egyptian lore and legend irresistibly attractive."[71]

The travelogues and fiction of the Roman period have a fascination with the Egyptian priest, romanticizing him—invariably "him"—as the ultimate Oriental wise man.[72] This "Egyptomania" succeeded in recasting Egypt for most Mediterranean readers (and listeners) as a landscape

---

[69] P.Mil.Vogl. 16, ed. Sergio Pernigotti, Franco Maltomini, and Paolo Marrassini, *SCO* 29 (1979):15–130. Egyptian-Jewish exchange in the domain of ritual spells must have started well before the Byzantine period, as the *PGM* corpus contains numerous frame legends and divine names from Jewish lore (e.g., *PGM* XIII, the "Eighth Book of Moses"): see, in general, Campbell Bonner, *Studies in Magical Amulets, Chiefly Graeco-Egyptian* (Ann Arbor: University of Michigan Press, 1950), 26–32. The reconstruction of the Jewish ritual specialist (or spell compiler) in Schiffman/Swartz 1992:45–52 resembles that of the Egyptian priestly ritual specialist in late antiquity sufficiently to imagine some degree of social interaction.

[70] Ibn al-Nadim, *Kitab al-fihrist,* tr. Bayard Dodge, *The Fihrist of al-Nadim: A Tenth-Century Survey of Muslim Culture* (New York: Columbia University Press, 1970), 726.

[71] Heliodorus, *Aethiopica* 2.27, tr. Morgan 1989:401. My discussion of the exotic in its application to Roman views of Egyptian culture owes much to Edward W. Said, *Orientalism* (New York: Random House, 1978).

[72] Dunand 1978 collects materials on priestesses in Roman Egypt.

of gurus ready to teach and initiate Roman youths in all the esoteric mysteries and "philosophies" they might yearn for or imagine. "What, then, shall I do?" asks the fictional Clement in a novel of the third century:

> This shall I do. I shall proceed to Egypt, and there I shall cultivate the friendship of the hierophants or prophets, who preside at the shrines. Then I shall win over a magician by money, and entreat him, by what they call the necromantic art, to bring me a soul from the infernal regions, as if I were desirous of consulting it about some business. But this shall be my consultation, whether the soul be immortal.[73]

Priests who can be bought, masters of such perverse rites as necromancy, mystagogues for the inquiring élite, here is Egyptian religious leadership in the late antique imagination. Clement's "testimony" marks only a later, Christian stage of an Egyptomania and its concomitant rendering of priests as gurus that together permeate Greco-Roman literature: Lucian, Apuleius, Heliodorus.[74] To be sure, the Greco-Roman period saw a general exoticism toward Near Eastern cultures, appropriating the wisdom, the priests, and the texts of India, Persia, Palestine, and Mesopotamia as loci of spiritual authority, sources for Greeks of intellect to plumb, collect, extract, and imitate.[75] Hellenism's particular deference to Egypt, however, had begun before Plato and suffused the philosophy, geography, religious texts, and novels of the Greco-Roman period.[76] It found ritual expression in tourism, the circuit of its ancient sites and temples. One might say that early tourism almost always had a religious component, the acquisition of a series of encounters with holy places; but in the Roman period tourism to Egypt tended increasingly to function as pilgrimage. The statue of Memnon at Thebes received a vast increase in foreign visitors in the Roman period who regarded it as oracular.[77]

[73] Pseudo-Clement, *Recognitions* 1.5, tr. Smith, *ANF* 8:78.

[74] On the relationship of the Pseudo-Clementine *Recognitions* to the Greek novel, see Bowersock 1994:139–41.

[75] Useful studies of this exoticist yearning for Oriental wisdom include Arthur Darby Nock, *Conversion* (Oxford: Clarendon, 1933), 107–10; Festugière 1950, 1:17–44; Hengel 1974:210–18; and Arnaldo Momigliano, *Alien Wisdom: The Limits of Hellenization* (Cambridge: Cambridge University Press, 1975), which unfortunately does not touch on Egypt.

[76] *Phaedrus* 274C–75B; *Laws* 2.656D–57A; Joly 1982; and more generally on Greek idealizations of Egypt, Iversen 1961; Froidefond 1971; and Smelik/Hemelrijk 1984, esp. 1869–79, 1920–55.

[77] In general, J. Grafton Milne, "Greek and Roman Tourists in Egypt," *JEA* 3 (1916):76–80; N. Hohlwein, "Déplacements et tourisme dans l'Égypte romaine," *CdÉ* 30 (1940):253–78, esp. 261–62. On Thebes and the Memnon site: André Bataille, "Thèbes

Still, one must remember a typical facet of exoticism, that tourists are selective in what they value about the alien land, and pilgrims even more so. The pilgrims' Egypt was one of decrepit monuments of a bygone, a *superseded,* empire out of which lone voices spoke, and then only for those who had ears to hear. The oracular sounds of the Colossus of Memnon blew out of its fallen stones: when the statue was repaired in the 270s the sounds stopped.[78] As Clement makes a straight course to the wise "hierophants and prophets," so Thessalos of Tralles describes his own spiritual search and encounter with "high priests, devotees of letters, and old men full of diverse learning," who alone seem to represent the past glory of Thebes.[79] Strabo marvels, much like the Traveller in Shelley's "Ozymandias," at the ironic state of the great temple city of Heliopolis in the late first century B.C.E.:

> The city is now entirely deserted. . . . It is said that this place in particular was in ancient times a settlement of priests who studied philosophy and astronomy; but both this organization and its pursuits have now disappeared.[80]

The monuments are glorious in their decay only: they are not functioning temples that produce festival processions but authenticating backdrops to the gurus with their ancient mysteries.

Greco-Roman Egyptomania as a type of exoticism thus carried both romanticizing and negatively distorting sides. And the literary construction of the Egyptian priest was prone to both. He was, above all, a skilled *magos:* a master of supernatural forces for the most mundane as well as the most weighty purposes. *Magos* (akin to English "magician") and its corollary *mageia* (akin to "magic") had by the Roman period assumed the sense of ritual power such as an "Oriental" priest might control and dispense for any reason, but especially for subversive purposes in matters of competition: love, justice, politics, commerce, hatred. It was clearly an

gréco-romaine," *CdÉ* 26 (1952):345–52; Smelik/Hemelrijk 1984:1938–45; Bowersock 1984; and Aristide Théodoridès, "Pèlerinage au Colosse de Memnon," *CdÉ* 64 (1989):267–82.

[78] Bowersock 1984:30–32.

[79] Thessalos, *De virtutibus herbarum* 12–13, ed. Friederich 1968:49, with Smith 1978a:178. See discussions by Festugière 1939; Smith 1978a:172–89; and Fowden 1986:162–76.

[80] Strabo 17.1.27, 29, tr. Jones, LCL, 8:79, 83. Although Strabo elsewhere renders a cult dead that was actually quite alive (17.1.43 on Siwa Amun-oracle; cf. above, 4.2.2), inscriptional evidence confirms Strabo's general impression of Heliopolis, where Herodotus had placed "the most learned of the Egyptians" (2.3) and whose symbolic value was maintained in later texts like the Potter's Oracle. But both Strabo (17.1.29) and Plutarch (*De Iside* 6) refer to a priestly cult of some sort continuing in Heliopolis.

outsider's term, casting an aura of otherness to practical or quotidian ritual.[81]

*Mageia* and *magoi* seem to have fascinated Greco-Roman authors as a kind of mysterious Oriental "service" at the same time as the Roman Empire as a whole was growing ever more frightened of the subversive power of alien religious practices. Thus as Clement feigns an interest in the priests' necromancy, Thessalos of Tralles desires the old men of Thebes to divulge to him "the efficacious force of magic."[82] Lucian's satirical dialogue *Philopseudes* describes an otherwise historical figure, Panchrates, "a man of Memphis, one of the scribes of the temple, wonderfully learned, familiar with all the culture of the Egyptians," as having "lived underground for twenty-three years in . . . [Egyptian] sanctuaries, learning magic [*mageuein*] from Isis" and thus being blessed with such ludicrous powers as "riding on crocodiles and swimming in company with beasts while they fawned and wagged their tails."[83] The figure Kalasiris in Heliodorus's *Aethiopica* travels around the Mediterranean with a magnetic reputation for broad ritual expertise, including love-, healing-, protective-, and even necromantic spells, an expertise whose authority and effectiveness stem explicitly from his Memphite priestly background.[84] Jerome tells the story of a Gazan youth who travels to Memphis in search of an Egyptian love-spell to win over a girl. "And so after a year's instruction under the seers [*vatibus*] of Asclepius" he returned with "certain portentous formulae and monstrous figures engraved on a leaf of Cyprian brass," which he buried under the girl's door.[85] To the Greco-Roman novelists, and doubtless to much of their culture, the Egyptian priest had a wisdom in *mageia* that could be taught or bought—or imitated with dire consequences, as Panchrates's apprentice in the *Philopseudes* discovers when he tries to use the master's spells, or (in another culture) Lucius in Apuleius's *Metamorphoses* when he tries to use the mistress's flying cream.[86]

Besides a purveyor of magic the Egyptian priest was constructed (like all Near Eastern priests) as a philosopher, astrologer, and diviner: one who lived a life of perfect moderation, studied actual ancient texts, knew volumes about the heavens and their interpretation, and had numerous

---

[81] Among the better studies of the identification of *mageia* and *magoi* in the Roman world are Phillips 1986:2711–32; Alan F. Segal, "Hellenistic Magic: Some Questions of Definition," *The Other Judaisms of Late Antiquity*, BJS 127 (Atlanta: Scholars, 1987), 79–108; and Fritz Graf, *La magie dans l'antiquité gréco-romaine* (Paris: Les Belles Lettres, 1994), 31–105.

[82] Thessalos, *De virtutibus herbarum* 12–13, ed. Friederich 1968:49.

[83] Lucian, *Philopseudes* 34–35, tr. Harmon, LCL, 3:371–73.

[84] Heliodorus, *Aethiopica* 3.13, 16–19; 4.7; 6.14; etc.

[85] Jerome, *V.Hil.* 21, PL 23:39.

[86] Lucian, *Philops.* 35–36; Apuleius, *Met.* 3.23–24.

authentic techniques through which to tell the future. While dissembling before the native masses the Egyptian priest knew well the ecumenical significance or philosophical abstractions to which his gods' overt animal or human forms truly pointed.

But the priest's alluring control of the supernatural for divination or binding could ignite the fears of mantic subversion that were endemic to Roman culture.[87] The wishful image of priests philosophically transcending the animal forms of the Egyptian gods was merely the flip side of an attitude of scorn for "animal worship" in all its facets in Egyptian iconography and ritual: as Juvenal begins his vicious satire of an altercation during an Egyptian festival, "Who knows not what monsters demented Egypt worships?"[88] And most important, the emphasis on the priests' role as gurus, spiritual masters to Roman seekers, diminished respect for their primary, cultic duties and for their religious leadership among Egyptians.

### 5.3.2 Diverging Priestly Worlds

These stereotypes affected Egyptian priests according to the degree they had themselves assimilated Hellenistic culture. And the degree of Hellenistic culture seems most of all to have been dependent upon the relative scope or tendency of priestly identity: localization or ecumenization.

Local priests will typically operate in a liminal role socially, economically, politically, and in their positions as ritual experts. They represent a flexible combination of the great tradition and its political and ideological tendencies, and the little tradition, of which they are fundamentally members and participants and to which they have an implicit cultural allegiance.[89] In some cultures the local priest has an incidental role in the total religious life of the community, only contributing the authority of the great tradition at limited points of ritual. In other cultures the local priest acquires ritual functions and charismatic reputations that extend beyond those traditional to the role in its more conventional sense (ad hoc fertility magic or curses, for example).

[87] Ritner 1993:217–20.

[88] Juvenal, *Satire* 1. See Reinhold 1980; Smelik/Hemelrijk 1984; and Bertrand 1988.

[89] Frankfurter 1992:215–17. See also Marriott 1955:209–11 on the local religious character of Brahmins in village India. This primary identification with local or regional ideology on the part of some priests has been used to explain the (assumed) priestly leadership of the Theban revolts during the later Ptolemaic period: Eddy 1961:314–20; Dunand 1979:125–28 and "Grecs et égyptiens en Égypte lagide: Le problème de l'acculturation," in *Modes de contacts et processus de transformation dans les sociétés anciennes*, Collection de l'École française de Rome 67 (Pisa and Rome: École française de Rome, 1983), 59–62.

What we know of such local priests in the late third century and there-after is almost entirely due to the whims of papyri, but it follows the general picture of Egyptian local religion laid out in chapters 2 and 3. Among those who showed up to demonstrate their ritual devotions to "all the gods" in accordance with the edict of the emperor Decius was a priestess of Petesuchos in the Moeris region of the Fayyum. The temples of Anubis, Leto, and "associated gods" in a small Cynopolite village of the late third century seem to have a priest and a priestess, both with Egyptian names and neither able to write Greek. The "priest of the vil-lage of Chenetoris" in 312, whose father is known only by the single theophoric name Tithoës, also is illiterate in Greek. A Fayyum ostracon from 298 refers to a priest of "Eileithyia," the local goddess Nekhbet. Beyond the culture of the priest-philosophers and even that of the large Sobek priesthoods in the Fayyum this stratum of local priests was a con-tinuing factor of the religious landscape, part of local communities and their ritual lives.[90]

But a priestly "upper class" is also quite evident in the Roman period, one that actively sought to promote itself in the world and values of a "higher" or ecumenical Hellenism. Their traces appear most vividly be-hind such literary endeavors as the Hermetica, which continue the an-cient tradition of the "writings of Thoth" in Greek guise, and Iamb-lichus's *On the Mysteries*, which discusses the nature and forms of divination as conceived in the third and fourth centuries. These materials disclose a subculture both insular, in the sense of conviction in its own religious authority and fascination with various types of private visionary experience, and ecumenical, in the sense of promoting itself in a period of great religious competition as a network of philosopher-gurus, masters of ancient mysteries, accessible in Greek at a price to the Greco-Roman enthusiast.[91] The significant departure in this subculture is its apparent (or professed) independence from particular temples and cultic service, becoming a kind of extended fraternity of sacred masters under the aegis of Thoth.

In Panopolis such a cultivated Hellenism did come in tandem with a devotion to temple service and the august identity incumbent upon the priesthood. The archives of a priestly family affiliated with the temple of Pan-Min in the first half of the fourth century reveal its lively participa-tion in the intellectual and aesthetic life of the empire. The father, Au-relius Petearbeschinis, is patriarch of a family with considerable land-holdings in the Panopolite nome. His first wife, Aurelia Senpasis, was a

---

90 Priestess of Petesuchos: W.Chr. 125 = P.Alexandria, in Knipfing 1923:364–65. Cy-nopolite temples: *P.Oxy* X.1256. Priest of Chenetoris: *P.Oxy* LIX.3981. Priest of Eileithyia: *O.Fayyum* 23.
91 See Fowden 1986:155–95; Derchain 1963; Athanassiadi 1993b.

priestess. His eldest son, Horion, is not only priest but (in a papyrus of 299) nome-*arkhiprophētēs* (a new rank under Roman rule); and in 348, after Horion's death, his brother Ammon goes to Alexandria to secure some temple's rank of "prophet" for Horion's son, an endeavor that would have required great political skill with the Roman bureaucracy.[92]

Ammon himself is a scholar of considerable Greek facility and intellectual depth: to his hand are attributed a fragment of the *Odyssey* and a list of Greek philosophers with their pupils.[93] Aurelius's third son, Harpocration, is a professional panegyrist with the imperial court and travels around the Mediterranean world to acclaim "the triumphs of our victorious masters." We know from other testimony that Harpocration would be only one of a number of wandering poets who achieved great notoriety in late antique Egypt, several of whom were priests. Indeed, there is some evidence that such priestly poets were applying their versatility in Hellenistic literature to refining Egyptian literature itself: some Demotic literature shows the influence of Greek literary style.[94]

One can detect the same remarkable synthesis of high Hellenistic culture and deep traditionalism in another family of Panopolitan priests, that of Horapollo, author of the first ostensible explanation of hieroglyphs for outsiders. Details of this family appear in Horapollo's own letter of the fourth century and in the early-sixth-century writings of Damascius. Whereas Horapollo himself emphasizes the Hellenistic culture of his upbringing, Damascius describes his father Asklepiades and uncle Heraiskos earnestly pursuing the priestly traditions of their heritage with religious passion, if greatly diminished knowledge. In one climactic scene wherein Asklepiades entombs the body of Heraiskos according to "those customs appropriate for priests," the former beholds luminescent hieroglyphs on the shroud. This reverence for hieroglyphs continued into Horapollo's treatise, the *Hieroglyphica,* whose erroneous explanations of Egyptian determinative symbols reflected the demise of that form of Egyptian writing. Revered though they were as monuments of Egyptian tradition, it was Greek language and mythology that now provided the central vehicle for preserving priestly lore.[95]

This culture of priests and priestly families actively engaged in the broader Hellenistic culture and its philosophical idiom, of course, had

---

[92] Willis 1979.

[93] Willis 1978.

[94] Thissen 1992:80–83. Harpocration: *P.Köln* inv. 4533v, 23–27. Cf. Browne 1977:189–93 and Cameron 1965, esp. 474–75 on other priestly poets. É. Bernand publishes the Roman era mortuary stele of a twenty-one-year-old Egyptian poet buried at Abydos with a metrical Greek epitaph (1992:146, #94).

[95] Damascius, fr. 174; and in general Maspero 1914; Fowden 1982:46–47; 1986:184–86; Athanassiadi 1993a:20; and Bowersock 1990, ch. 5, esp. 60–61. On the *Hieroglyphica,* see below, 6.3.

roots in the much earlier endeavors of priests like Chaeremon (first century C.E.). It probably also reflected the different value of priestly rank in a period when such a thing could be bought and sold as status rather than service. One Apollonius, a resident of first- or second-century Lycopolis, describes himself in his epitaph as "gymnasiarch and *agoranomos* and high priest and performer of sacred rites [*hieropoios*]," which is inscribed right beneath an Egyptian vignette of himself offering to Osiris.[96] But what gods had he served?

This Hellenization of priestly tradition seems to have forced a kind of democratization (among the literate) of knowledge and authority once truly the privilege of priests. When the task and the pride of cultural conservator fell to poets like Nonnos or Cyrus of Panopolis the traditions became increasingly unrecognizable as Egyptian, increasingly in a line with the peripatetic intellectual "pagans" of fourth-century Alexandria. And yet the evolution of this priestly class and its interests in the late Roman period was authentically Egyptian. Emphasizing their own supralocal activity, private illumination rituals, their status as priests, and their concerted endeavor to translate Egyptian temple traditions into Hellenistic idiom, they sought to distinguish themselves from the ranks of those local priests whose scopes of authority and action were merely the shrine, the community, and its perennial ritual needs.[97]

### 5.3.3 The Mobilization of Temple Priests and the Assimilation of the Magos-Image

> Up to this point I have relied on the accounts given me by the Egyptians and their priests.[98]

Herodotus's Egyptian diary may have dubious ethnographic or historical value, but in its simultaneous reverence and gullibility for the words of priests around the Mediterranean it offers a good sense of what an Egyptian priest might tell an inquisitive foreigner in the fifth century B.C.E.: the Greek equivalents of Egyptian gods, the heroic legends of ancient kings as preserved in official texts, and the absolute priority of

---

[96] É. Bernand 1992:141, #91.

[97] On the character of this late antique priestly society, see Fowden 1986, ch. 7; Bowersock 1990:55–69. Ernest Gellner makes the important point that priesthoods (i.e., of higher ranks) in preindustrial societies tend to have just this kind of antilocal tendency and commitment to institutional status, thus (his argument goes) preventing anything like nationalist sentiments (*Nations and Nationalism* [Ithaca, N.Y.: Cornell University Press, 1983], 10–11, 16–18).

[98] Herodotus 2.142.1, tr. Aubrey de Sélincourt, *Herodotus: The Histories*, rev. A. R. Burn (Harmondsworth: Penguin, 1972), 186.

Egyptian culture in most achievements of civilization.[99] One might imagine similar priestly tradents bringing Plato to his strange Egyptocentrisms; and so also in the Hellenistic period, it is difficult to imagine that Egyptian priests, the widely perceived as well as self-defined bearers of the cultural traditions, did not actively participate in their own self-promotion.[100] The first-century C.E. Memphite priest Chaeremon described "the Egyptian priests . . . as philosophers among the Egyptians, that they chose the temples as the place to philosophize," and whose cultic functions were "no empty gesture, but an indication of some allegorical truth."[101] It is interesting, then, to find priests also actively embracing the exotic image of the Oriental "magician."

At this point it is useful to introduce a term, *stereotype appropriation,* to refer to the manifold ways indigenous cultures embrace and act out the stereotypes woven by a colonizing or otherwise dominant alien culture. While the latter creates its images of the exotic out of its own needs, aspirations, and insufficiencies (and only to some degree the realia of the indigenous culture), the indigenous cultures appropriate those same images as a means of gaining political and economic status in a broader culture now dominated by, in this case, Rome. One can think of myriad examples of stereotype appropriation in the contemporary world as well: Indian spiritual leaders in America, Native American powwows, Egyptian belly-dancing and other cultural performances for the sake of tourists, and the various assertions of parochialism or ethnicity (according to dominant stereotypes) in contemporary ecumenical societies. But gaining political and economic status by this means has historically meant the reification of stereotypes, even the redefinition of the indigenous culture itself, which becomes to a large degree a stage for the dramatization of others' truths. Thus we can observe Egyptian priests in the Roman period gaining power and prestige through assimilating the broader Mediterranean (and narrowly Roman) image of the *magos.*

Much like Heliodorus's character Kalasiris, the Memphite priest who travels around the Mediterranean resolving social crises with his wide knowledge of spells, the historical priest Harnouphis achieved great renown in the second century through his travels, chief among which in-

[99] For example, Herodotus 2.2.5–3.1; 13.1; 19.1; 54.1–2; 99.2; 100.1; and 42.2, in which "they say" Osiris is Dionysus. In general, see Lloyd 1976:89–100.

[100] Plato, *Phlb.* 18B–C, on which see Joly 1982; Frankfurter 1994b:203–5. Compare also Strabo 17.1.29; Diodorus 1.96.1–3; 97.5–98.9; Plutarch, *De Iside* 10; Heliodorus, *Aethiopica* 3.13–14. Cf. Solmsen 1979:31–41.

[101] Chaeremon, frag. 10 = Porphyry, *De abstinentia* IV.6, in Van der Horst 1984:16–23, 56–61. See also Pieter Willem Van der Horst, "The Way of Life of the Egyptian Priests According to Chaeremon," in *Studies in Egyptian Religion,* ed. by M. Heerma van Voss et al. (Leiden: Brill, 1982), 61–71; Fowden 1986:56; and in general on priestly "philosophizing" Derchain 1963:224–25.

volved casting curse-spells for Marcus Aurelius's German campaign, at
one point producing a miraculous rain when the troops were parched.
Cassius Dio thus designates him a *magos*. Sarapion, "a certain Egyptian"
whom the emperor Caracalla executed for predicting his imminent death
"to his face," would have held such intimacy with the emperor on the
basis of some traditional authority. His reputation for great supernatural
powers suggests this authority came from a priestly rank. Materials on
the spread of Egyptian cults in the Hellenistic and Roman periods also
document the many Egyptian priests who were devoting their efforts and
promoting their authority outside Egypt—and not by any means exclusively to expatriate Egyptians: Roman and Greek devotees were particularly welcoming.[102]

Yet this self-promotion as international *magos* above and beyond
other priestly roles (like festival leadership or care of images) was not
simply an invention of or capitulation to the wider Roman world's exoticism. It also reflected the idealization of priests in native Egyptian literature, as this literature was still being composed in both Egyptian and
Greek during the early Roman period.[103] A second-century fragment of a
lost Greco-Egyptian novel about a priest (*prophētēs*) Tinouphis calls
him also a *magos*.[104] The pharaoh Nectanebos in Pseudo-Callisthenes's
*Alexander-Romance* is portrayed with distinctly priestly functions: he
learns of the Persian invasion during a traditional divination rite (1.1–3);
he gains authority in the Macedonian court according to his ritual expertise (1.4); and he seduces Alexander's mother by managing to appear
to her as the god Amun (1.4–7). This story, originating in Egypt as
propaganda for Ptolemaic authority, carried an Egyptian image of
priestly thaumaturge wherever it circulated throughout the Mediterranean world.[105]

---

[102] Harnouphis: Cassius Dio, *Hist.* 72.8.4, tr. Cary, LCL, 9:28–29, with J. Guey, "En-
core la 'Pluie miraculeuse'," *RevPhil* 22 (1948):16–62; Kákosy 1995:2923–24. Sarapion:
Cassius Dio 79.4.4–5. On itinerant Egyptian priests, see also Philippe Bruneau, *Le sanctuaire et le culte des divinités égyptiennes à Érétrie*, EPRO 45 (Leiden: Brill, 1975), 104–5,
and Françoise Dunand, *Le culte d'Isis dans le bassin oriental de la méditerranée* 3, EPRO
26 (Leiden: Brill, 1973), 138–42. Michel Malaise argues that it was non-Egyptians who
imported the earliest Egyptian cults to Italy and that pronounced Egyptian influence on
these cults (including the importing of Egyptian priests) occurred with the Egyptomania of
the imperial period (*Les conditions de pénétration et de diffusion des cultes égyptiens en
Italie*, EPRO 22 [Leiden: Brill, 1972], 257–59, 321–30).

[103] Spiegelberg 1933:55–61; Barns 1956; Sauneron 1966:51–56; De Salvia 1987;
Heinz-Josef Thissen, "Ägyptologische Beiträge zu den griechischen magischen Papyri,"
*Religion und Philosophie im alten Ägypten: Festgabe für Philipppe Derchain*, Orientalia
Lovaniensia Analecta 39, ed. by U. Verhoeven and E. Graefe (Leuven: Peeters, 1991), 295–
97; Koenig 1994:38–47.

[104] P.Turner 8, 22, on which see Haslam in P.Turner, p. 38.

[105] On Nektanebos's ritual manipulation of miniature figures for divination (1.1–3),

Other royal figures appear in Egyptian literature as most powerful priest-magicians. The "Bentresh Stela," a work of the Late or Ptolemaic period, reports with an air of nostalgia how Ramses II could command healing gods to serve a foreign ruler. The legends of Setne Khamwas, still read in Egyptian in the Roman period (if unattested in Greek), portray this figure's search for a mysterious spell-book of Thoth, his visit to the underworld, and encounters with even more powerful priest-magicians.[106] The legendary king Psammetichus (seventh/sixth century B.C.E.) appears as the supreme hierophantic authority of a fourth-century ritual spell:

> Nephotes to Psammeticulos, immortal king of Egypt. Greetings. Since the great god has appointed you immortal king and nature has made you the best wise man, I too, with a desire to show you the industry in me, have sent you this ritual procedure [*praxis*] which, with complete ease, produces a holy power. And after you have tested it, you too will be amazed at the miraculous nature of this operation.
>
> . . . But you are not unaware, mighty king and leader of *magoi*, that this is the chief name of Typhon.[107]

This image of a great lector-priest sought by or gaining the patronage of a mighty ruler goes back to ancient Egyptian prototypes. In a cycle of stories from the Middle Kingdom, the legendary Djedy must be brought from a distant village, whence he astounds the court with his supernatural powers and prescience of coming pharaohs. The legend of Meryre, another ritual expert brought to the court because of his renown in order to cure a pharaoh, offers an ironic picture of a good pharaoh surrounded by malevolent "court-magicians." They urge Meryre's death as the only cure for the pharaoh and then obliterate Meryre's memory on earth; but Meryre exacts revenge from the underworld by sending a clay man to Pharaoh to urge their execution.[108]

The literary motif of the lector-priest in court was still popular in the Roman period, here assimilated distinctively to the realities of Roman rule:

---

compare II Setne 4.15–19; 5.19–23 (tr. Lichtheim 1973/80, 3:145, 147); and Pinch 1994:91–92.

[106] Bentresh Stela (Louvre C 284), tr. Lichtheim 1973/80, 3:90–94. On the Setne cycle, see now Tait 1991, esp. 33–34. A decree of the XXII Dynasty relates how Pharaoh Tutmosis found "a book of protection from the [time] of the ancestors" and thus alleviated his people's suffering (ed. Pascal Vernus, "Un décret de Thoutmosis III relatif à la santé publique," *Orientalia* 48 [1979]:176–84).

[107] *PGM* IV.154–60, 244, translation adjusted from that of O'Neil in Betz 1986:40.

[108] Djedy: P.Westcar = P.Berlin 3033, tr. Lichtheim 1973/80, 1:215–22. Meryre: P.Vandier, ed. Georges Posener, *Le papyrus Vandier*, Bibliothèque générale 7 (Cairo: IFAO, 1985).

Pachrates, the *prophētēs* of Heliopolis, revealed [this spell] to the emperor Hadrian, revealing the power of his own divine *mageia*. For it attracted in one hour; it made someone sick in 2 hours; it destroyed in 7 hours, sent the emperor himself dreams as he thoroughly tested the whole truth of the *mageia* within his power. And marveling at the prophet, he ordered double fees to be given to him.[109]

All these types of native materials about ideal priest-magicians and their international appeal provide suggestive links with, first, Egyptian priests' own historical self-promotion outside Egypt, and second, the character of the Egyptian priest as *magos* in Greek literature: Diogenes's Paapis, Lucian's Panchrates, Apuleius's Zatchlas, Aelian's Iachim, and Heliodorus's Kalasiris.[110] We might then suppose that Egyptian priests during the Roman period, as a potential response to the financial constraints of the temples, were seizing upon a role clearly based on the heroes of Egyptian literature but then developed as a Mediterranean cultural type through Roman culture's exoticism: the Egyptian *magos* and his superior powers.

Perhaps the best evidence for priests' entry into this Hellenistic cultural role of *magos* within Egypt itself comes from the ritual libraries of the third and fourth centuries. For these texts, while deeply ensconced within Egyptian priestly culture, show both a marked attention to self-presentation according to Hellenistic culture and a generally—or at least potentially—itinerant context for implementing the rites themselves. Indeed, they point to a world in which itinerant ritual experts with priestly training and culture were providing anywhere the ritual services once based in temples and temple priesthoods: healing, binding, repelling, divining, and assuring the fortune of a decision. "The locus of religious experience," one historian has proposed, "has been shifted from a permanent sacred center, the temple, to a place of temporary sacrality sanctified by a magician's power."[111] The historical clustering of the manuscripts in the second through fourth centuries C.E. suggests that the religious phenomenon the texts reflect coincided precisely with the economic decline of the temples.[112]

The so-called Magical Papyri, preserved in multiple manuscripts of Greek, Demotic Egyptian, and a form of transliterated Egyptian designated "Old Coptic," reflect above all an Egyptian priestly milieu; and it is as such priestly literature that I also return to them below (6.4). Ten

---

[109] *PGM* IV.2446–55, tr. O'Neil, in Betz 1986:83. See Kákosy 1995:2920.

[110] See De Salvia 1987.

[111] Smith 1978a:182; cf. idem 1995:23–27.

[112] See Kotansky 1994:xviii–xix. Note that the *latest* of three Egyptian amulets in this collection, #61 (third/fourth century), is exclusively Egyptian in formula and gods invoked.

manuscripts in both Egyptian and Greek, the Anastasi hoard, came as a bloc from Thebes, shared scribes and dialect, and thus seem to point us even closer to a priestly milieu of that region.[113] Certainly the presence of Demotic Egyptian itself in four of the Anastasi texts would have excluded anyone without traditional priestly scribal training by the third century C.E.; and the mix of Demotic and Old Coptic with Greek in several manuscripts, often from the same scribal hands, would imply scribes and readers proficient in both Greek and Egyptian. One grimoire in the Anastasi hoard, itself combining Greek, Demotic, and Old Coptic spells, is written on the back of an important Demotic manuscript of the "Myth of the Sun's Eye," hardly the typical fare of those outside the priesthood.[114]

The spells themselves reflect the ritual conventions and traditions of Egyptian temples and their scriptoria: the lector-priest's threats to return the world to chaos or to control through knowledge of secret names, his ritual claims of identity with series of Egyptian gods, his invocations of Re (Helios) and Seth (Typhon) and of Isis, Osiris, and Horus as efficacious paradigms, procedural necessities like priestly garments or writing materials, the sympathetic transfer of power through ingesting or applying written letters, and the ritual use of molded figurines and inscribed texts.[115]

Among the special interests of the Theban compilers of these Greek and Demotic grimoires, erotic spells and rituals for revelation and divination apparently predominated, comprising a large portion of the spells in each grimoire. Erotic spells (including both separation- and attraction-spells), are, of course, a perennial aspect of folk culture—"a kind of

---

[113] See Fowden 1986:168–76; Ritner 1995; and W. J. Tait, "Theban Magic," in Vleeming (ed.) 1995:169–82.

[114] *PGM* II = Leiden I 384v, ed. J. Johnson 1975. See J. Johnson 1986:lvi and Ritner 1995:3337–38.

[115] Use of secret names: *PGM* III.627–28; IV.885–86, 1167–1226; LVII.13; LXII.10–15. Identity with gods: I.250–53; III.652–85; V.247–54. Invocations of Re, Isis, and other gods as efficacious paradigms: *PGM* IV.1–25, 94–114, 661–75, 930–1114, 1471, 2373–440; XXXVI.141–45; LVII; and Kotansky 1994, #61—a third/fourth-century gold lamella with conception spell based on Isis/Osiris historiola. Priestly garments: *PGM* IV.3095–96. Priestly writing materials: *PGM* I.232; III.424–66. Power of written letters: *PGM* III.410–23; IV.789–90. Ritual figurines and texts: *PGM* IV.296–435; IV.296–435, with *P.Mich.* 6925 and other parallels in lead and papyrus (handbook) discussed in David G. Martinez, *P. Michigan XVI: A Greek Love Charm from Egypt (P. Mich. 757)*, ASP 30 (Atlanta: Scholars, 1991), 6–20. Note also P.Munich ÄS 6792, ed. William Brashear, "Ein neues Zauberensemble in München," *Studien zur altägyptischen Kultur* 19 (1992):79–109 + pls. 9–12. In general on the range of traditional techniques in Egyptian priestly "magic," see Sauneron 1966:36–49; Ritner 1993; and, on continuities in *PGM*, Jan Bergman, "Ancient Egyptian Theogony in a Greek Magical Papyrus," in *Studies in Egyptian Religion Dedicated to Professor Jan Zandee*, ed. by M. Heerma van Voss et al. (Leiden: Brill, 1982), 28–37.

sneak attack," as John Winkler put it, "waged in the normal warfare of Mediterranean social life."[116] Such spells appear in the most ancient Egyptian spell collections and testify to no unique level of superstition in their societies. What does stand out in the Greek and Demotic ritual grimoires, however, is the vast number of erotic spells as compared to obstetrical and gynecological spells. The impression one gets is that the priests responsible for these collections no longer held the same diversified function in local communities as had the priests behind ancient grimoires like Papyrus Leiden I 348, in which obstetrical and gynecological rituals are common.[117]

The revelation-spells are so elaborate, so pretentious, so evocative of early Christian and Jewish liturgies, that historians of the period have commonly used them as evidence of a broader Greco-Roman spiritual yearning for personal–divine encounter. This yearning, the argument inevitably goes, would be only satisfied by Christianity. And yet the roots of this fascination with various forms of private illumination lie in cultural trends within the priesthoods during the late pharaonic and Ptolemaic periods. In the process the archaic priestly ritual for consulting the will of the deity, the *pḥ-nt̠r,* becomes a quasi-mystical practice of direct encounter through dream and vision.[118]

Already in the second century B.C.E. the priest Hor is moving among a number of major temples in Lower Egypt following the directives of the goddess Isis as she revealed herself in dreams. Hor's own writings on ostraca record the contents and interpretations of these revelations and how he responded to them.[119] Among the stories of Setne Khamwas, which generally reflect Egyptian priestly imagination through the beginning of the Roman period, one describes the priestly hero's journey, led by his son, to the netherworld to view the fates of the righteous and unrighteous. The ability to impart such wisdom, the book implies, renders the son a "man of god" superior to all other priests and his father Setne blessed with exceptional illumination.[120] "What matters" in these materials, one Egyptologist has observed, "is that traditional Egyptian

---

[116] Jack J. Winkler, "The Constraints of Eros," in *Magika Hiera: Ancient Greek Magic and Religion,* ed. by C. Faraone and D. Obbink (New York: Oxford University Press, 1991), 233.

[117] Ed. Borghouts 1971 (see translations in Borghouts 1978, ##30–34, 60–69). See, in general, Ritner 1984 and Adolf Erman, *Zaubersprüche für Mutter und Kind* (Berlin: Königl. Akademie der Wissenschaften, 1901). This is not to imply that the *PGM/PDM* are entirely bereft of OB/GYN spells: see *PDM* xiv.953–84 (= P.Lond./Leiden, verso, v–vii); *PGM* VII.260–71. On OB/GYN ritual in the Greco-Roman world, see Aubert 1989.

[118] Ritner 1993:214–20. Assmann 1978 shows dream revelations as part of "personal piety" in the New Kingdom, but not rituals of actual incubation.

[119] See esp. Hor #13, in Ray 1976:55–57, 131.

[120] Setne II 23–27, tr. Lichtheim 1973/80, 3:141–42.

imagery, designed above all as a *ritual* symbolism, has become the object of revelation, of subjective religious experience."[121]

The culturally eclectic, or syncretistic, aspects of the revelation-spells in the Greek and Demotic grimoires do not in themselves require a provenance outside the priesthood. (Indeed, these eclectic details tend to be subsumed within traditional Egyptian structures.) But the individualistic character of the revelation-spells does seem to reflect circumstances when collectors were not, as in the case of "the temple literature, in the charge of institutions and hierarchies obliged to maintain traditional integrity."[122] Thus the revelation-spells may reflect a shift of private priestly revelation ritual to a wider clientele, a shift that would occur through priests themselves as they took their training and books beyond the temples, perhaps to well-paying Roman youths in search of new religious experiences.[123] Such a shift would also be evident in the synthesis of private Bes oracle spells from the literature of the Bes oracle at Abydos, discussed above (4.3.2). Here a temple's ritual is recast for use beyond the sacred precinct, as part of the repertoire of an itinerant hierophant.

The same mobilization of temple services is apparent in the synthesis and dissemination of oracle texts like the *Sortes astrampsychi* and a similar method found in one of the Anastasi grimoires, "Demokritos's Sphere," for divining the fate of a sick person.[124] The *Sortes astrampsychi* seemed to represent a shift of the locus of the oracle "rite" from temple to book, placing the ability to divine the future in the hands of the literate person who could operate the text, rather than in the god in his or her temple. Anyone with the ability to handle the *Sortes*'s instructions, presumably, could become an oracle-monger, and thus it has been suggested that expanded literacy had actually democratized religion itself in Roman

---

[121] Podemann Sørensen 1992:171–72, and *passim* on this trend.

[122] Podemann Sørensen 1992:177. The incubation rites of Hor, for example, appear far more circumscribed in form and goal than the revelation spells of the *PGM/PDM* (Ray 1976:130–36).

[123] This shift of priestly ritual forms into exoteric availability is well illustrated in a hematite amulet in the Louvre from the Roman period. Carved as a falcon, the amulet is covered in a Greek inscription much like the magical statues, statue bases, and statue heads of classical Egypt, invoking the power of Harpocrates to protect "-mon, *true priest,* for the time of life he has, from all evil, and wrath of the gods and *daimōnes,* and from all sorcerers [*baskanoi*]" (Inscr.Mus.Louvre 204 = *Suppl. Mag.* I.6). The original priestly owner's name was erased to allow the amulet's reuse. Compare magically inscribed heads published by László Kákosy and M. Cihó, "Fragment of a Magical Statue in Iasi (Roumania)," *Oriens Antiquus* 24 (1985):45–53; Bernard V. Bothmer, "Egyptian Antiquities," *Antiquities from the Collection of Christos G. Bastis* (Mainz am Rhein: Von Zabern, 1987), 67–69, and idem, "Egyptian Antecedents of Roman Republican Verism," *La ricerca scientifica* 116 (1988):60–62.

[124] *Sortes Astrampsychi:* see above, 4.4.1. Demokritos's Sphere: *PGM* XII.351–64.

Egypt.[125] But those in Egypt most traditionally viewed with the public role of advising in consultation with books were priests, and divination with books had been the province of the priesthood for millennia.

To the extent that priests might have been the developers, operators, and redactors of the *Sortes astrampsychi,* the text must imply a development not only in oracles (as we have seen) but also in priests. Certainly as a reference work for priests it has ample precedent and parallels in the various astrological guides compiled during the pharaonic period and copied profusely in Demotic and Greek during the Roman period.[126] But in putting the administration of oracles in the hands of a particular priest independently of his temple context the *Sortes* texts, like the ritual grimoires, seem to reflect a situation in which priests (among others, no doubt) were establishing themselves as private ritual consultants, gaining social status as itinerant ritual experts.

In this shift in context the whole significance and function of ritual expertise and its attendant charisma necessarily evolve. For through dislocation the priest changes from a cultic functionary addressing local concerns and crises in his or her professional capacity or an élite scribe preparing amuletic texts as an extension of the cult's ideology, to a freelance, expatriate hierophant like Heliodorus's Kalasiris, whose charisma rests to a great extent on exotic appeal.

Certainly in the small local cults the respective priests, thoroughly integrated as they were into communities, would have performed a variety of functions for those communities, including medical rites and the preparation of amulets, as an extension of their priestly status—this would evidently be the case in fifth-century Plewit, for example. The large "national" cult centers of Memphis and Thebes, however, assumed a sacred dichotomy between priesthood and populace that may also have affected the view of traditional Egyptian priests in the cities as well. With the decline of the temple infrastructure and the increasing need for additional sources of income, these priests shifted their base of authority into these wider worlds, offering their ritual expertise to a predominantly urban

---

[125] Beard 1991. See above, 4.4.1.

[126] Classical examples discussed in Lana Troy, "Have a Nice Day! Some Reflections on the Calendars of Good and Bad Days," in *The Religion of the Ancient Egyptians: Cognitive Structures and Popular Expressions,* Boreas 20, ed. by G. Englund (Uppsala: University of Uppsala, 1989), 127–47. Demotic examples in O. Neugebauer, "Demotic Horoscopes," *JAOS* 63 (1943):115–27; Parker 1959; O. Neugebauer and Richard A. Parker, "Two Demotic Horoscopes," *JEA* 54 (1968):231–35; Hughes 1951; O.Leiden.Dem. 333 (ed. M. A. A. Nur El-Din, *The Demotic Ostraca in the National Museum of Antiquities at Leiden* [Leiden: Brill, 1974], 264–65); and various unpublished texts in Copenhagen (Zauzich 1991:7). Greek examples: *P.Tebtunis* II.276; cf. *P.Oxy* XXXI.2554, which seems to be the written result *of* such an oracular consultation; and *P.Oxy* LXV.4173, 4471–72. See discussion in Jones 1994.

and ecumenical clientele. In this itinerant mode, penetrating an urbanized and Hellenized culture that distinguished itself culturally from the countryside, the traditional priest takes on the appearance of "magician," an ambiguously powered specialist in controlling fate and fulfilling individuals' most selfish desires.

The novelists' image of the Egyptian priest-*magos* therefore had some verisimilitude in the Roman period. It had become Hellenistic culture's offer of a desirable and profitable role to an impecunious priesthood. But it was also a role with a steady line of inheritance from the ritual texts and practices of classical Egypt. For Egypt the singular, heroic priest-thaumaturge was not a unique development of the Greco-Roman period, but very much a traditional type in the classical priestly literature.

### 5.3.4 The Revaluation of the Egyptian Priest in Roman Culture

With the entrance of the Egyptian priest into the character of the Greco-Roman *magos* there occurs a concomitant reevaluation of the traditional priestly rituals, not only those devoted to everyday safety or advantage but even those based in temple service, the normal cultic activities. As the Roman prefect of Egypt tries to proscribe traditional temple oracle procedures in 199 C.E. as "hazardous conjuring [*episphalous periergias*]," so in the fourth century a church historian can describe the ancient scriptorium of the Serapis temple in Canopus as a "public school of the *ars magica*" insofar as it taught "sacred letters—for thus in effect were called the ancient writings of the Egyptians."[127] Thus the most traditional of Egyptian priestly activities could fall under suspicion as dangerous, potentially subversive—as "magical."

The distinguishing of religious spheres seems to have begun as a conscious conceit of Egyptian priestly culture: "Lo, magic spells are divulged," imagines a text of the late Middle Kingdom as one more symptom of interregnal chaos: "Spells are made worthless through being repeated by people." A grimoire of the New Kingdom introduces one spell with a chief lector-priest's (*ḥry-tp*) admonition: "Do not reveal it to the common man [or: anyone else]—(it is) a mystery [or: secret] of the House of Life," the scriptorium.[128] The same institutional secrecy is recalled in a grimoire of the third or fourth century C.E.:

> Interpretations that the temple scribes employed, from the holy writings, in translation. Because of the curiosity of the masses [the scribes] inscribed the

---

[127] P.Coll.Youtie I.30 = P.Yale 299, ed. Rea 1977, on whose implications for Egyptian priestly ritual see Ritner 1993:217–19, and above, 4.2.1. Rufinus, *H.E.* 11.26, on whose polemical strategy see Thelamon 1981:224–43.

[128] Admonitions of Ipuwer (P.Leiden 344r) 6.5–6, tr. Lichtheim 1973/80, 1:155. P.Harris vi, 10, ed. Lange 1927:53–54, tr. Borghouts 1978:87, #126.

names of the herbs and other things that they had [typically] employed on the statues of the gods, so that [the masses], since they do not take adequate precaution, might not engage in conjuring [*periergazōntai*] due to the consequence of their misunderstanding.[129]

But at the time this frame was composed, in the cultural and economic complexity and, indeed, increasingly suspicious religious environment of late antique Egypt, there were many who would have received this traditional esotericism in quite different terms, as a dichotomy between a transcendent thaumaturgy and a base and dangerous "magic." The sentiments of the ancient grimoires, for example, take on a new and quite Roman flavor when Heliodorus puts them in the mouth of the priest Kalasiris. There is, Kalasiris asserts,

the common misapprehension that the wisdom of Egypt is all of one and the same kind. On the contrary: there is one kind that is of low rank and, you might say, crawls upon the earth; it waits upon ghosts and skulks around dead bodies; it is addicted to magic herbs, and spells are its stock-in-trade; no good ever comes of it; no benefit ever accrues to its practitioners; generally it brings about its own downfall, and its occasional successes are paltry and mean-spirited—the unreal made to appear real, hopes brought to nothing; it devises wickedness and panders to corrupt pleasures. But there is another kind, my son, true wisdom, of which the first sort is but a counterfeit that has stolen its title; true wisdom it is that we priests and members of the sacerdotal caste practice from childhood; its eyes are raised towards heaven; it keeps company with the gods and partakes of the nature of the Great Ones; it studies the movement of the stars and thus gains knowledge of the future; it has no truck with the wicked, earthly concerns of the other kind, but all its energies are directed to what is good and beneficial to mankind.[130]

Kalasiris distances himself, for example, from an old woman's necromancy (a rite for which, in fact, there is little real evidence in Egyptian religion), saying that

it was not proper for a priest either to take part in or to be present at such rites; the prophetic powers of priests proceeded from legitimate sacrifices and pure prayer, whereas those of the profane were obtained literally by crawling upon the ground and skulking among corpses.[131]

But if priests themselves were the primary ritual specialists in Egypt and responsible for, or at least capable of, providing the simplest amulet and the most effective curse-spell as well as performing temple service,

---

[129] *PGM* XII.401–44, tr. based on Betz, in Betz 1986:167. Cf. *PGM* IV.2967–3006.
[130] Heliodorus, *Aethiopica* 3.16, tr. Morgan 1989:421–22.
[131] Heliodorus, *Aethiopica* 6.14, tr. Morgan 1989:486–87.

how did such a dichotomy between ritual spheres develop? And how specifically did it affect the conception of the Egyptian priest in society?

Here it is useful to refer to comparative materials. The anthropologist Robert Redfield, in his 1941 study of culture in the Yucatan peninsula in Mexico, notes the differences in the way native Mayan tradition and Hispanic-Catholic Christianity are integrated at various levels of urbanization. In the most isolated rural village, he finds, the two traditions are completely harmonized, a synthesis of holidays, agricultural rituals, shamans, and lay Christian leaders. But as one moves closer to urban culture they become progressively juxtaposed, as a "religion" and a "paganism."

The critical contrast for our present purposes is between an isolated rural village and a small agricultural town on the train route. While the farmers in this town make continual use of traditional Mayan agricultural rites and expect the leadership of Mayan shamans in these rites, they view them in terms of their power, their efficacy. They don't understand the words or the character of the rites but respect them as necessary to ensure success. In the rural village, on the other hand, these same rites are conceived as part of an overall moral system, and villagers participate fully in them. Thus Redfield himself uses the term "magic" to denote how the traditional rites are viewed in the town; in the village the same rites comprise the performative aspects of religion as a whole, the binding dramas of the collectivity. In the village, that is, "the agricultural rituals are to a marked extent acts of piety. In [the town] they tend to be acts of safeguard."[132]

The important thing is how these dichotomous perceptions function vis-à-vis the ritual experts—in this case the shamans. In the village, Redfield observes,

> there is likely to be at least one [shaman], a relative and a close neighbor, who talks in the evenings with his fellows . . . about the significance of the ceremonies he performs. When the ceremonies are carried on, a group of men who truly represent the local community take part. [But in the agricultural town, where] there is no [shaman], nor has there been for many years[,] the [shaman is viewed as] a fellow with uncanny powers brought in from a more rustic settlement to do something which ought to be done lest harm come to the harvest. The [townspeople] are unaccustomed to his liturgical language and few of them understand it. "The [shaman] prays in Maya, [a townsperson explained to Redfield,] but we don't understand it. That's because he talks the true Maya and the Maya we talk isn't the real Maya."[133]

There are two lessons in Redfield's example. One is the interconnection of the health and safety rituals administered by the local Egyptian priest

---

[132] Redfield 1941:233.
[133] Redfield 1941:236.

with the rest of village religious life—that we should not assume that indigenous dichotomies between ritual spheres existed in the context of local religion (the separation of temple space notwithstanding). This lesson is apparent in Shenoute's crusade in the village of Plewit: while we have seen numerous indications that a priest or priests were responsible for leading the execration rituals supposed to repel Shenoute's monks, Besa's account of the episode regards it as a combined act of the villagers. The priest, the master of curses, is very much a member of the community.[134]

Second, one finds a progressive polarization or alienation of types of ritual and ritual expertise as one moves from the local village context into the orbit of urban culture. Thus a concept of "magic" disengaged from "religion" as well as a concept of "magician" whose ritual expertise is alien to his immediate environment both develop through the movement of the same phenomena out of their traditional environments.[135]

Historians of Greco-Roman Egypt have long observed the difference in economic and cultural complexity between Alexandria and "Egypt" proper and then between Alexandria's nodal cities like Panopolis and Oxyrhynchus and the small agrarian villages like Plewit. If anything there was more of a cultural spectrum in Roman Egypt than in 1940s Yucatan—between those areas thoroughly involved in the Mediterranean *oikoumenē* and those that lived according to millennia-old customs and worldviews. The biggest temple in the city of Oxyrhynchus might be that of the hippopotamus-goddess Thoēris; but the same town, as we have seen, was hiring Roman athletes for public events, collecting and commenting on Homer, staging Greek dramas, and generally cultivating a high Hellenistic tradition. Thus a traditional Egyptian priest in Oxyrhynchus would probably come off very much like the Mayan shaman: awesome and redolent of ancient tradition, able to work great miracles, a sine qua non of annual festivals—but also rather exotic, and thus just the person one might want to contact if one wanted to curse a rival's shop.

In moving, then, from Oxyrhynchus to Alexandria and then to Rome the Egyptian priest—or the image of an Egyptian priest—becomes ever more weird, an Oriental wise man constructed almost entirely according to the exoticist perspective of Roman culture.[136] In Roman times there is

---

[134] See 2.6.1 and 5.2.1.

[135] Redfield 1941:233–36. Karen McCarthy Brown notes the secrecy and aura of impropriety that shrouds voudou ritual among some Haitian immigrants living in New York City, requiring the ritual specialist to conceal images, shrines, and rites that in Haiti would have taken place in the open: *Mama Lola: A Voudou Priestess in Brooklyn* (Berkeley: University of California Press, 1991), 110.

[136] On the "magical" appeal of alien priests in foreign countries, see esp. Walter Burkert's work on the early, international circulation of Babylonian priests whose native methods of divination and spirit control contributed to an appearance at the same time traditional and alien—"magical" in the ancient Mediterranean sense: *Ancient Mystery*

no better historical example of Egyptian priests acquiring a "magical" role through itinerant service than Harnuphis, the priest who accompanied Marcus Aurelius in Germany and whom Cassius Dio describes specifically as a *magos*; but to their Mediterranean audiences the Egyptian priests in the works of Thessalos, Lucian, and Heliodorus conformed to the same *magos* stereotype. In such cases a thorough integration of ritual expert with local culture is completely lost; traditions that originally function in a total social and economic complex now become merely the hoary accoutrements of a foreign *magos*; and a priestly literary culture, the world of the temple scriptorium, becomes the fascinatingly incomprehensible "wisdom" of the Oriental guru.

---

*Cults* (Cambridge, Mass., and London: Harvard University Press, 1987), 31, 33–35, and *The Orientalizing Revolution: Near Eastern Influence on Greek Culture in the Early Archaic Age*, Revealing Antiquity 5, tr. by M. Pinder and W. Burkert (Cambridge, Mass.: Harvard University Press, 1992), 41–87. Burkert suggests that the icon shrine was an inevitable requirement for even the most peripatetic Egyptian priests, rendering them less as *magoi* as much as shrine servants (*Mystery Cults*, 38–39).

# 6

## THE SCRIPTORIUM AS CRUCIBLE

## OF RELIGIOUS CHANGE

### 6.1 The World of the Scriptorium

A N ANONYMOUS SCRIBE of the early Roman period, casting himself in the fictional role distinctive of the Egyptian romance genre, tells the story of an ancient book "full of divinity" that had been rediscovered by priests under Nectanebos, the last native Egyptian pharaoh and quintessential folk hero of later Egyptian writers. The book, so the scribe tells us, set out the full priestly services of the god (Imouthes-)Asclepius as the cult had taken place under an earlier pharaoh, who had lived in more peaceful times. The scribe then tells how he himself sought to render the book in Greek:

> Having often begun the translation of the said book in the Greek tongue, I learnt at length how to proclaim it, but while I was in the full tide of composition my ardour was restrained by the greatness of the story, because I was about to make it public; for to gods alone, not to mortals, is it permitted to describe the mighty deeds of the gods. . . . But if I did the god a service, both my life would be happy and my fame undying; for the god is disposed to confer benefits.[1]

His paralyzing awe is eventually resolved when the god himself appears. The theophany inspires the scribe's near-ecstatic proclamation of the glories of Imouthes-Asclepius, a popular healing god in the early Roman period whose cult at Deir el-Bahri (in association with Amenhotep I) is well attested in inscriptions.[2]

This text, preserved only on a piece of papyrus with little of the "book" itself, offers an engaging picture of the self-consciousness of the priestly scribe in the early Roman period. Ancient Egyptian literary motifs such as the royal patron of priestly service or the sacred book lost and rediscovered continue with great flexibility; translation into Greek has become a virtual duty in the literary maintenance of larger cults such as

---

[1] *P.Oxy* XI.1381, 32–52 (ed.'s trans.)
[2] See Kákosy 1995:2976–77 and above, 4.2.2.

this one of Imouthes-Asclepius-Amenhotep I, even while translation itself is occasionally presented as a problem, a betrayal of what should be restricted and divine. Finally and most important, we see the self-conscious piety of the priestly scribe engaged in these pursuits and problems. Far from being a mundane task, the scribe's endeavor involves the searching and interpreting of the most revered texts, in this case for the purpose of establishing a cult's authority by reference to literary tradition and promoting it according to the new values of Roman Hellenism. And it can, ideally, occasion a personal encounter with the deity served.

The Imouthes text is invaluable for its picture of the culture of that center of Egyptian literary and religious activity from ancient times, the temple scriptorium or "House of Life [Eg. *per-'nḫ*]." Documentation of the House of Life tends to be rare apart from the actual texts it produced (books of the dead, wall inscriptions) and, in earlier periods, ceramic models and tomb iconography of scribes in practice. Indeed, the best evidence that Egyptian scriptoria were actually operating into the fourth century comes from the church historian Rufinus, who describes an academy of sorts for the study of Egyptian sacred writings (*sacerdotalium litterarum*) operating in Canopus with an influence (he asserts) that surpassed that of Alexandria.[3]

An even more vivid picture of the priestly literary culture as it stood somewhat earlier is offered by Clement of Alexandria, who describes the book knowledge of different priestly ranks arranged as if in festival procession:

> First advances the Singer, bearing some one of the symbols of music. For they say that he must learn two of the books of [Thoth-]Hermes, the one of which contains the hymns of the gods, the second the regulations for the king's life. And after the singer advances the Astrologer, with a horologe in his hand, and a palm, the symbols of astrology. He must have the astrological books of [Thoth-]Hermes, which are four in number, always in his mouth. . . . Next in order advances the sacred Scribe [*hierogrammateus*], with wings on his head, and in his hand a book and rule, in which were writing ink and the reed, with which they write. And he must be acquainted with what are called hieroglyphics, and know about cosmography and geography, the position of the sun and moon, and about the five planets; and also the description of Egypt, and the chart of the Nile; and the description of the equipment of the priests and of the places consecrated to them, and about the measures and the things in use in the sacred rites. . . . There are also ten books which relate to the honour paid by [the *stolistes*] to their gods, and containing the Egyptian worship; as that relating to sacrifices, first-fruits, hymns, prayers, processions, festivals, and the like. And behind all walks the

[3] Rufinus, *H.E.* 2.26, on which see Thelamon 1981:225–29.

Prophet, with the water-vase carried openly in his arms; who is followed by those who carry the issue of loaves. He, as being the governor [*prostatēs*] of the temple, learns the ten books called "Hieratic"; and they contain all about the laws, and the gods, and the whole of the training of the priests. . . . There are then forty-two books of [Thoth-]Hermes indispensably necessary; of which the thirty-six containing the whole philosophy of the Egyptians are learned by the forementioned personages; and the other six, which are medical, by the *Pastophoroi*—treating of the structure of the body, and of diseases, and instruments, and medicines, and about the eyes, and the last about women.[4]

Although as stylized as a vase painting, Clement's picture of the Egyptian priesthood's sacred literature does condense some essential facts. The overall function of the priesthood was indeed the ordered preservation of the cosmos—earth, society, sky, gods—through the performance of rituals. These rituals were distributed throughout the calendar and set down in texts, some of them quite archaic. Thus the books with their sacred writing quite literally constituted the preservation of the cosmos: as the books set it down, so the priests performed or uttered, and so the cosmos continued according to *Ma'at*, order.

As an expression of the books' sacred function in maintaining the cosmos many were understood to be the writing of Thoth, the scribal god who "wrote" the cosmos in the beginning. In this sense the priestly rituals represented Thoth's compositions, choreography, and liturgy, not human beings', much in the way that Egyptian ritual spells traditionally present themselves as the words of gods, not people. Thoth had thus become by the Roman period the primary pseudonymous authority for diverse priestly texts, imbuing them with a kind of ultimate antiquity and secrecy: Setne Khamwas searches for a book full of spells "that Thoth wrote with his own hand" and that lay sunken beneath the Nile; scribes were still collecting an eclectic Wisdom of Thoth in Demotic Egyptian in the second century C.E.; and some shadowy conventicles of Greek-proficient priests composed the "Hermetic" corpus over the course of the second and third centuries C.E.[5]

Clement's assignment of different books to different priestly ranks and tasks is not so exact as emblematic, first of the way priestly roles were

[4] Clement, *Stromateis* 6.4.35.3–37.3 (ed. Otto Stählin and Ludwig Früchtel [Berlin: Akademie-Verlag, 1960], 2:449–50), tr. Wilson, *ANCL*, 2:323–24.

[5] Early Roman witnesses to the authority of Thoth-Hermes in priestly literature include I Setne (tr. Lichtheim 1973/80, 3:127–38); Diodorus 1.16.1–2; 43.6; Plutarch, *De Iside* 61 (375F); and in general Fowden 1986:57–74, with essential background in Patrick Boylan, *Thoth: The Hermes of Egypt* (London, 1922; repr. Chicago: Ares, 1987), 88–106. The Demotic Thoth texts were announced by Richard Jasnow and Karl-Theodor Zauzich at the Seventh International Congress of Egyptologists, Cambridge, 3–9 September 1995.

believed to be based in sacred writings, and second of the varieties of knowledge contained in the temples' scriptoria and the varieties of priestly expertise: not only sacred liturgy but astrology, geography, genealogy, anatomy, and healing.[6] Indeed, what bibliographies exist of the ancient temple libraries, preserved on walls of temples like that of Edfu, portray highly diverse, even idealized collections.[7] One gets the sense both of a temple culture that held the sacred book or manual in mythical esteem and, within that culture, a broadly literate and highly diversified priesthood.

Both this intellectual diversity and the mystique of the book that motivated that diversity become the essential background to a series of literary developments in the Roman period, all of which we can attribute to scriptoria such as Rufinus documents. For these developments reflect both the traditional archaism of Egyptian literature—the nostalgic and anachronistic appropriation of the past—and the energetic cultural syntheses typical of scribal cultures in the Hellenistic world.

## 6.2 Preservation and Syncretism

The activity of the House of Life consisted essentially of updating ancient materials. Scribes would revise ancient ritual texts to encompass new situations, record events in such a way as to reflect archaic paradigms, and recast a diversity of literary materials—oracles, spells, legends, mythography—in order to highlight certain essential themes, in particular, the kingship. In this last purpose Egyptian scribes were very much like those of Greco-Roman Judaism who rewrote or commented upon scripture in order to articulate present events, or turned folk legends into religious texts in order to clarify the activities of the one Hebrew god toward a self-defined elect.[8] And in as many ways as the Hebrew god's activities and intentions were spun in Jewish literature, so also the kingship appears in Egyptian and Greco-Egyptian literature of the same period.

In the Hellenistic period the kingship had been promoted through the use of several literary forms inherited from classical Egypt. *Königsnovellen* portrayed legendary kings as ideal types who make use of the various talents of their courtiers and manage to preserve their royal cha-

---

[6] See Deiber 1904:65–77; Sauneron 1960a:139–65.

[7] See Deiber 1904:73–76; Fowden 1986:57–58; and Alfred Grimm, "Altägyptische Tempelliteratur: Zur Gliederung und Funktion der Bücherkataloge von Edfu und et-Tôd," in *Akten des vierten internationalen ägyptologen Kongresses, München 1985* 3, ed. by S. Schoske (Hamburg: Buske, 1989), 159–69, on different types of bibliographical lists in traditional temples.

[8] See Daumas 1961.

risma despite adversity.[9] At the same time an ancient literature of "anti-kingship" promoted kingship through representing its antithesis in social and cosmic chaos or, following the Persian period, its opposite: the evil foreign king.

The *Demotic Chronicle*, an early Ptolemaic commentary on the oracular pronouncements of the god Harsaphes in his temple at Herakleopolis, is a convenient point of departure for understanding later developments because of its combination of local commitments, collected oracles, and broad political ambitions of the scribe or scribes. The text interprets the god's enigmatic phrases in connection with the Persian (and, implicitly, Greek) rulers of Egypt; and through these interpretations the text offers an ideal type of pharaoh based explicitly on the popular king Necta-nebos.[10] A central point of kingship in this text is the pharaoh's capacity to defend Egypt from foreigners; and indeed, Manetho, a priest of the same period, drew similarly from this point in applying a legend of the ancient pharaoh Amenophis to explain the Jewish Exodus story (evidently a point of cultural competition at the time). The pharaoh Amenophis, according to Manetho, had found an old book with a prophecy of an imminent invasion of Jews, portrayed as an impure and chaotic people; he safeguarded Egypt's sacred images from their temporary dominion; and then he returned to expel them.[11]

Both Amenophis and Nectanebos are central heroes of numerous Egyptian works of the Ptolemaic period. Amenophis is the king before whom the god Khnum appears in his oracular guise of Potter in the Oracle of the Potter.[12] Nectanebos is portrayed in one story receiving a prophetic dream from Isis, and in the *Alexander-Romance* he uses a priestly divination procedure to discover the Egyptian gods' intention to hand the country over to Persia for a period. The same text actually reveals Nectanebos to be the sire of Alexander the Great, rendering the Macedonian conqueror a legitimate king in the very dynasty of Nectanebos. In such diverse ways scribes returned time and time again to the same legendary kings, models of royal power and order, to ground the institutions, circumstances, hopes, and values of the present.[13]

[9] See Alfred Hermann, *Die ägyptische Königsnovelle*, Leipziger ägyptologische Studien 10 (Glückstadt: Augustin, 1938); Koenen 1985:172–73; and Antonio Loprieno, "The 'King's Novel'," in Loprieno (ed.) 1996:277–95.

[10] Janet H. Johnson, "The Demotic Chronicle as a Statement of a Theory of Kingship," *JSSEA* 13 (1983):61–72.

[11] Manetho fr. 54 = Josephus, *Against Apion* 227–87, on which see Weill 1918:120–45 and Yoyotte 1963:133–43.

[12] Koenen 1968:182–86.

[13] Amenophis texts: *P.Oxy* XLII.3011; Manetho fr. 54 = Josephus, *Against Apion* 236–50; Weill 1918:77–78, 118–20. Nectanebos texts: Martin Braun, *History and Romance in Graeco-Oriental Literature* (Oxford: Blackwell, 1938), 19–25; B. E. Perry, "The Egyptian

The same royal models served the literary imagination of "anti-kingship." Protracted tableaux of chaos (*Chaosbeschreibung*) appear already in the second millennium B.C.E. as prophecies delivered to legendary kings from a god or a priest. By portraying in lurid detail the consequences of a lapse of kingship on the land of Egypt—the Nile running with blood from civil strife, heavenly bodies out of order, Egypt's boundaries open to foreign hordes and dangerous animals, inversion of the social order—texts would thus point to the salvific nature of the royal presence or accession. Manetho and the author of the *Alexander-Romance,* for example, promote Amenophis and Nectanebos (respectively) by describing the fate of Egypt in their absence.

The earliest of the full-blown tableaux of chaos, the *Prophecy of Neferti,* casts the images of catastrophe as the prophecy of a "great lector-priest of Bastet" before the legendary king Snefru. Later texts like the Oracle of the Potter (second century B.C.E., recopied in the third century C.E.) follow this scribal custom of linking the *Chaosbeschreibung* discourse to a narrative frame from the tradition of royal legends. Such a frame would imbue any "enclosed" text—an oracle, prediction, or teaching delivered—with an archaistic authority: the text becomes the words of a great sage to an ancient king, preserved or "discovered" through the meritorious activities of scribes and even translated into Greek by the favor of the god and the patronage of the king. Even when we lack the more elaborate *Königsnovellen* in manuscript form, the frames by themselves are strong evidence that the longer texts existed in temple libraries, much in the way Herodotus found them in the fifth century B.C.E.[14]

Another way of articulating "anti-kingship" evolved in the early Ptolemaic period out of the royal legend itself: legends of evil kings, the Persian Cambyses in particular. Much like Manetho's image of impure settlers who are finally expelled by King Amenophis, the legend of Cambyses's invasion and dominion (still being developed in the fifth or sixth century C.E.) emphasized the chaos arising in Egypt under the Persian king's dominion.[15]

Texts like the Cambyses saga and the prophecies of Egypt's ruin under Persian-like foreigners were clearly based in the ancient kingship ideol-

Legend of Nectanebus," *TPAPA* 97 (1966):327–33; Merkelbach 1977:77–88; Lloyd 1982:46–50; Koenen 1985.

[14] Herodotus 2.99.2–141.1. In general on *Chaosbeschreibung* traditions in Egyptian literature, see Weill 1918:22–145; Lichtheim 1973/80, 1:134–35, 139, 149–50; Assmann 1983; Frankfurter 1993:168–85.

[15] Cambyses texts: H. Ludin Jansen, *The Coptic Story of Cambyses' Invasion of Egypt,* Avhandlinger utgitt af det Norske Videnskaps-Akademi i Oslo 2, Hist.-Filos. Klasse 1950, 2 (Oslo: Dybwad, 1950), and Leslie S. B. MacCoull, "The Coptic Cambyses Narrative Reconsidered," *GRBS* 23 (1982):185–88.

ogy and served fundamentally to articulate the pharaoh's preservation of borders and safety. Yet by the end of the Ptolemaic period this repeated literary emphasis had gained almost nationalistic overtones, and the consequent images of an Egypt revived under a new, ideal pharaoh grew increasingly ahistorical and fantastic. An ideology that had once exalted specific kings had become a rationale for an ultimate king.

The texts, perhaps ironically, were increasingly disseminated in Greek, their idealistic propaganda directed in support of Ptolemaic and Roman rulers; hence one would be mistaken to find a revolutionary nativism in the literature's overtones of xenophobia.[16] Likewise, despite the foundations of the literature in the archaic kingship ideology, it would be incorrect to limit the scribal task to political propaganda. The recurring emphasis in the Greek and Demotic texts on the sacred book, on the cultic charters, spells, or prophecies it holds, and on its circumstances of composition and rediscovery under legendary kings shows the self-conscious presence of the House of Life as an institution in its own right. The theme of the sacred book combines, on the one hand, the House of Life's perennial plays for royal patronage, and on the other hand its self-interested assertion that even kings must submit to the wisdom of the scriptorium's ancient books. Thus scribes inevitably promoted their own authority by means of the kingship ideology and its literary themes.

In its continuous output this mass of literature sheds important light on the culture of the scriptorium as a whole in the Greco-Roman period. The enterprise of interpreting old traditions was at the same time *archaistic,* in the sense of continually reinforcing the paradigmatic significance of ancient legends and their characters, and *synthetic,* in the sense of articulating the archaic models as contemporary propaganda of immediate historical relevance. This fundamental drive to synthesize was largely responsible for Egyptian priestly culture's tremendous capacity to assimilate foreign words, gods, and ritual methods like astrology, and ultimately to transform "Hellenism," its language, ideas, and mythologies, into a thoroughly Egyptian discourse.

Indeed, we would know little about the literary world just described if it were not for manuscripts and fragments of the Roman period, particularly the first through third centuries C.E. The literary remains of these later scriptoria show a continuing devotion to the composition and translation of *Königsnovellen,* recounting the adventures of such paradigmatic Egyptian royal or priestly figures as Tinouphis, Sesonchosis, Petubastis, Setne-Khamwas, and especially Amenophis and Nectanebos.[17] While

---

[16] See Lloyd 1982; Koenen 1983.

[17] Setne narratives: F. Ll. Griffith, *Stories of the High Priests of Memphis* (Oxford:

many of these texts were still being copied in Demotic Egyptian, we find them increasingly translated into Greek or composed in Greek along Egyptian models, or even, as Demotic Egyptian documents are increasingly making clear, composed in Demotic according to Greek models.[18] This was no vain and hurried effort at cultural preservation in the face of inevitable decline, but rather the lively continuation of an indigenized literary Hellenism, one that involved experimenting with both Greek and Egyptian ways of expression.[19] The Demotic literature alone from this period includes "nearly every genre of the classical pharaonic literature."[20] Even a mythological text, the "Myth of the Sun's Eye," appears in both second-century Demotic papyri and third-century Greek translation, together reflecting a living tradition in which scribes might recast the stories of gods in Greek guise.[21]

In this Egyptian context the fragmentary text discussed above about Nectanebos and the Imouthes-Asclepius cult appears thoroughly steeped in the tradition of the Egyptian *Königsnovelle*. Nectanebos "enriched [Imouthes-]Asclepius himself with three hundred and thirty arurae more of corn-land, especially because he had heard through the book that the god had been worshipped with marks of great reverence by [the ancient king] Mencheres." But the scribe's own story reflects the kind of new developments we saw in the case of divination and revelation spells, that increased emphasis in priestly culture on the direct revelation. Here the scribe, awe-struck at the prospect of translating a sacred Egyptian book into Greek, is graced with the god's personal visitation, an epiphany lead-

---

Clarendon, 1900); Lichtheim 1973/80, 3:125–51; Tait 1991. Petubastis narrative: Spiegelberg 1910; Lichtheim 1973/80, 3:151–56. Tinouphis narrative: *P.Turner* 8 (second century C.E.). Sesonchis narrative: *P.Oxy* XV.1826; XXVII.2466, 6–24; XLVII.3319 (third to fourth century C.E.). Amenophis narrative: *P.Oxy* XLII.3011.

[18] Spiegelberg 1933:47–50, 55–61; Barns 1956; Merkelbach 1977:77–78; Reymond 1983:47; Tait 1994a. On Greek influence on Egyptian texts, see Thissen 1992.

[19] Reymond 1983:48 and Friedhelm Hoffmann, *Ägypter und Amazonen: Neubearbeitung zweier demotischer Papyri P.Vindob. D 6165 und P.Vindob. D 6165 A*, MPN 24 (Vienna: Hollinek, 1995), 22–26, 29–30, on the implications of Vienna Demotic texts, with similar observations about priestly "projects" by Zauzich on Carlsberg library (1991:5) and Tait 1994b:191.

[20] Jan Mertens, "Bibliography and Description of Demotic Literary Texts: A Progress Report," in J. Johnson (ed.) 1992:233–35. See also E. A. E. Reymond, "From the Contents of a Temple Library," *Das römisch-byzantinische Ägypten,* Aegyptiaca Treverensia 2 (Mainz am Rhein: Philipp von Zabern, 1983), 81–83, and Karl-Theodor Zauzich, "Demotische Texte römischer Zeit," *Das römisch-byzantinische Ägypten,* 77–80.

[21] Stephanie West, "The Greek Version of the Legend of Tefnut," *JEA* 55 (1969):161–83, and Françoise De Cenival, *Le mythe de l'oeil du soleil,* Demotische Studien 9 (Sommerhausen: Zauzich, 1988). Zauzich reports a Demotic fragment with Greek reference numbers among unpublished Carlsberg texts (1991:6). In general, see Tait 1994a:212–13.

ing him to rejoice that "every Greek tongue will tell thy story, and every Greek man will worship the son of Ptah, Imouthes! . . . For every place has been penetrated by the saving power of the god."[22]

Motifs of the *Königsnovelle* about kings and priests, or priests and books, or the wisdom found in temples, are still current enough in priestly culture by the end of the third century that they are drawn upon as frames for ritual spells. Spells that appeal to the priest Panchrates in his intimacy with the emperor Hadrian, to the priest Nephotes writing to Psammetichos, king and "leader of *magoi*," to texts inscribed in temples, and to now-unknown figures of renown like Pibechis, Jeu the hieroglyphist, and King Ostanes, all draw on the wider literary traditions of the House of Life. The spell-manuals, or grimoires, thus offer, if not a "last stage" in such literature, at least proof of the abiding value of the literature—its ability still to reflect images of authority and ideal ritual service.[23]

Not only the royal legends retained value in their capacity as narrative frames. It is also in the context of the expanding priestly literature of the Roman period that we find the uses of the *Chaosbeschreibung* discourse expanding, changing from symbolic kingship acclamation to an actual prophecy of imminent catastrophe. From earliest times a scribe could, of course, spin these tableaux of disorder in different ways according to the narrative frame in which he placed it. When the "great lector-priest of Bastet" issues it as a monologue before King Snefru in the ancient *Prophecy of Neferti* it is a prophecy, but issued well before the time of the text's own author and audience. It is the same in the Ptolemaic era Oracle of the Lamb to King Bocchoris and the Oracle of the Potter before King Amenophis: images of chaos constitute prophecy delivered in ancient times about the author's present, the mid-second century B.C.E.[24]

But as these same texts continue to circulate and to be invoked even after the Ptolemaic period—even, indeed, as late as the third century C.E.—the prophecy itself begins to assume the same paradigmatic impor-

---

[22] *P.Oxy* XI.1381, ii, 26–32; ix.198–202, x.215–18 (ed.'s tr.).

[23] *PGM* IV.154 (Nephotes to Psammetichus), 885–88 (hieroglyphic names written by Thoth-Hermes), 2006 (letter to King Ostanes), 2446ff (spell that Panchrates, "prophet of Heliopolis," revealed to Hadrian), 3007 (tested charm of Pibechis); V.96 ("stele of Jeu the Hieroglyphist"); XII.121 (dream-revelation spell of Zminis of Dendara), 401–44 (secret priestly ingredients); XIII.229–34 (hiding a text); *PDM* xiv.232 (Paysakh, priest of Cusae); cf. IV.2967–3006 (priestly herb-picking rite); *C.H.* XVI.1; *Discourse on the Eighth and Ninth* (NHC VI, 6, 61–63). In general, see Hans Dieter Betz, "The Formation of Authoritative Tradition in the Greek Magical Papyri," in *Jewish and Christian Self Definition*, vol. 3, *Self-Definition in the Greco-Roman World*, ed. by B. F. Meyer and E. P. Sanders (Philadelphia: Fortress, 1982), 161–70, 236–38.

[24] Koenen 1968, 1970, 1974, 1984; Zauzich 1983. See also C. C. McCown, "Hebrew and Egyptian Apocalyptic Literature," *HTR* 18 (1925):392–401; Assman 1983:362–64.

tance for the present traditionally borne only by the "framing" legends of Amenophis, Bocchoris, and Nectanebos.[25] *Chaosbeschreibung* begins to function as a kind of cosmic eschatology, integrating broader Mediterranean motifs of cosmic destruction and world renewal (and no doubt reflecting to some degree many scribes' feelings of disenfranchisement under Roman rule).[26] It is to stress the cosmic implications of that chaos that some priest of the third century C.E. composed a new tableau, framed as Thoth's own "Perfect Discourse" to his disciple Asclepius:

> Egypt will be widowed; it will be abandoned by the gods. For foreigners will come into Egypt, and they will rule it. Egypt! . . . No longer will it be full of temples, but it will be full of tombs. Neither will it be full of gods but (it will be full of) corpses. Egypt! Egypt will become like the fables. And Egypt will be made a desert by the gods and the Egyptians. And as for you, River, there will be a day when you will flow with blood more than water. . . . And he who is dead will not be mourned as much as he who is alive.[27]

The image of Egypt's decline in this case, linked with no king or quality of kingship, becomes an oracle of sorts, a quasi-divine revelation to an insider, meant to stand alongside the other revelations and teachings in the Egyptian Hermetic tradition.[28] It would not have struck its initial audiences as predictive of actual disasters so much as reinforcing of the boundaries around those insiders privileged enough to have such lore revealed to them—it restored the traditional literary form within the Hermetic milieu.[29]

It is with a similarly cosmic eschatological sense that a third-century Christian, evidently well-versed in such priestly discourse, applied the

[25] Potter's Oracle ms. P1 = P.Graf 29787 (second century C.E.); ms. P2 = P.Rainer 19 813 (third century C.E.); ms. P3 = *P.Oxy* 2332 (late third century C.E.), all ed. Koenen 1968. Oracle of the Lamb to Bocchoris: P.Rainer 10 000 (third to fourth century C.E.), ed. Zauzich 1983.

[26] Koenen 1970; Dunand 1977; and Jonathan Z. Smith, "Wisdom and Apocalyptic," in Smith 1978:67–87.

[27] *Perf. Disc.* = *Ascl* 24 = NHC VI, 8.70–71, tr. Brashler/ Dirkse/Parrott, *NHLE*, 334–35. On relationship to classical Egyptian *Chaosbeschreibung*, see Mahé 1982:47–113 and Fowden 1986:38–44.

[28] See Fowden 1986:155–95, with Richard Valantasis, *Spiritual Guides of the Third Century,* HDR 27 (Minneapolis: Fortress, 1991) on the narrative conceit of the master and disciple. The newly collated Demotic Thoth texts (see above, n. 5) seem to depend on the same Thoth/disciple dialogue structure.

[29] A more narrow stream of scholarship has tended to view the *Perf.Disc.* as *vaticinium ex eventu* related either to the Palmyrene invasion of Egypt in the later third century (W. Scott 1924/36, 1:61–76) or to the Christian iconoclastic riots and the destruction of the Alexandrian Serapeum at the end of the fourth century (Athanassiadi 1993a:15–16). On problems with the assumption of *ex eventu* references, see Mahé 1982:69–72; Fowden 1986:38–39; Frankfurter 1993:195–200.

traditional Egyptian *Chaosbeschreibung* form to the imminent last days that would precede the second coming of Christ. But here, in the *Apocalypse of Elijah,* whose immediate translation into Coptic from Greek reflects an appeal to indigenous Egyptians, the author has actually returned to a far more ancient scribal tradition, the linking of disorder to either an interregnal period or bad kingship. The text portrays a series of premillennial rulers whose alternating malevolence and beneficence is symbolized by, respectively, the chaos or fruitfulness of the cosmos— amounting to a kind of eschatological kingship chronicle. The series culminates in a Christ-figure who himself performs many ideal pharaonic functions, like restoring fertility and protecting the sun from a demonic figure. The *Apocalypse of Elijah* provides a glimpse of the priestly culture's strong legacy even as its members left the temple scriptorium for other religious worlds and applied their traditional discourse to new ideologies.[30]

By the end of the third century the outpouring of Egyptian literature in Greek seems to have virtually halted. But the decline in the literary production of *Königsnovellen* and their offshoots does not signal the demise of the Houses of Life, as Rufinus makes clear. For the same endeavors of archaism and synthesis are still devoted to other types of texts, especially to the collecting and framing of spells and oracles, literary forms closely linked to the priestly role of ritual expert.

## 6.3 The Holiness of Languages and the Evolution of Coptic Script

By the third century "Egyptian" as a spoken language was a thorough amalgamation of Greek and Egyptian words, while the written language, pretending an archaic purity, could still be used in its Demotic, hieratic, and, more rarely, hieroglyphic forms. Some knowledge of the traditional writing systems was still required for priestly service, as we find in a certificate of 162 C.E., attesting that "Marsisouchos . . . and Thenkebkios have demonstrated a knowledge of hieratic and Egyptian letters from a hieratic book from those that the sacred scribes produced." But already in the early second century a guild of hieroglyph-carvers in Oxyrhynchus swears to a Roman official that its members number no more than five, "there being neither apprentices nor strangers continuing the craft to the present day." And by the time Esmet-Akhom the scribe leaves his votive

---

[30] See Dunand 1977:54–56; Frankfurter 1993:195–238. On the author's possible background in priestly culture, see Frankfurter 1993:101–2.

graffito at Philae in August 394, hieroglyphic facility is virtually dead: his is the last dated hieroglyphic inscription.[31]

Hieroglyphs themselves traditionally bore the numinous importance of being the actual writing of the gods and through the third century appear in such symbolic or even "magical" contexts as amulets, ritual texts (as on the wall of the temple of Esna), and even the names of beneficent emperors.[32] But by this time the corpus of hieroglyphs had multiplied into a sprawling and often indecipherable assortment of characters, as priests sought to exploit the symbolic potential of the medium. Now released from scribal serviceability by the rise of Demotic script, hieroglyphs could develop as an art form. At the same time some uses of hieroglyphs, especially those inscribed on the protective *cippi* of Horus, reflect an almost exclusively efficacious (as opposed to communicative) function: they have become for all intents and purposes magical symbols.[33] Both developments suggest an idealization, even a veneration, of the ancient writing system. And if that idealization was the practical result of the dwindling number of priests capable of using hieroglyphs in their traditionally phonetic senses, the sentiment nevertheless served to guard hieroglyphs' allure and importance in priestly circles beyond the fourth century.

With the technical decline of the hieroglyphic and hieratic systems it was Demotic writing, a shorthand system originally developed for record-keeping, that came into the service of literary and ritual texts. And true to the spirit of Egyptian writing, which had always signified more than simple transliteration of the spoken word, Demotic preserved texts of the Roman era in a state of sacred isolation from a common tongue that was steeped in Greek loanwords.[34]

---

[31] Priestly examination: *P.Tebtunis* II.291, 40–43, on which see Sauneron 1962b. Hieroglyphic inscribers: *P.Oxy* VII.1029, 24–26. Esmet-Akhom at Philae: IDemPhilae 436, ed. Griffith 1937:126–27, and see also Kákosy 1984:72–73.

[32] In choosing to date the last sacred bull of the Bucheum (d. 340 C.E.) by the reign of Diocletian instead of the current, Christian emperor Constantius II, Jean-Claude Grenier has argued, the priests of Hermonthis adhered to a long tradition of memorializing beneficent emperors and erasing the memory of bad ones (Grenier 1983). The intrinsic connection between the Buchis bulls and the kingship in general would cast a particularly "eternal" value on the words of the stela's inscription and the hieroglyphs that bore it. Sauneron 1952 discusses the mutilation of emperors' cartouches, again based on ancient traditions of memorial, erasure, and the power of the written name.

[33] See Sternberg-El Hotabi 1994. To her discussion of Horus-*cippi* as important data on the later use of hieroglyphs one might add the magical name written in hieroglyphs in *PDM* xiv.126, 176a (= P.Lond./Leiden V.8; VI.25), on which see Griffith/Thompson 1904:54–55n.

[34] See Gallo 1992:119; Tait 1992, 1994a, 1994b.

To preserve or compose a text in Demotic rather than Greek was essentially scribal conceit, an expression of tradition, rather than some protonationalist impulse toward linguistic purity. There is now abundant evidence that by the second century C.E. even the most insular, conservative priesthoods commonly used and conversed in Greek.[35] Like Hellenistic art in its effect on the representation of Egyptian gods, the Greek language had become a common means for native expression already in the Ptolemaic period, with the Oracle of the Potter as the case in point: militantly anti-Greek yet composed in Greek. While composition in Greek might well entail an author's deep involvement with Hellenistic literary style and ideas, Greek had become for most simply a neutral lingua franca, the medium of broadest circulation. The Hellenization of the priesthoods did not, then, render them "Greek" in any sense distinct from "Egyptian": one might still find a chief priest, whom we would expect to have facility with written Egyptian, unable to read or write Greek in the early fourth century. But Hellenization was thorough: a large number of bilingual (Greek and Egyptian) texts from the Roman period, covering financial accounts and contracts, funerary stelae, and ritual grimoires, gives the impression that a solidly bilingual scriptorium was the norm in many regions.[36]

It is to this complex native scriptorial culture of translation and synthesis, of archaism and preservation, and of professional interest in the effectiveness of propaganda and ritual that we may now ascribe the origins of Coptic writing, the standardized Greek transliteration of spoken Egyptian (complete with Greek words) that came to particular efflorescence in the Christian monasteries. The earliest forms in which scribes applied Greek letters—with some Egyptian characters—to the transliteration of Egyptian speech come from the first three centuries C.E., and all concern what we may broadly designate ritual contexts: a horoscope, an appeal to a god, and, especially, "magical" grimoires. In such contexts we would be accustomed to see some special efficacy attached to speech. And indeed, these texts have long been taken as evidence that the Coptic script itself was invented for liturgical precision in ritual spells. These Old Coptic texts apparently signal a coordinated endeavor, initiated in the north by the first century C.E., to preserve the spoken Egyptian for the

---

[35] See Tait 1992:309–10.

[36] Greek-illiterate priest: *P.Oxy* I.71, i, 11. Bilingual texts: *PGM/PDM* XII, LXI (on which see Harold Idris Bell, Arthur Darby Nock, and Herbert Thompson, "Magical Texts from a Bilingual Papyrus in the British Museum," *Proceedings of the British Academy* [1931]:235–87), and Dorothy J. Crawford and P. E. Easterling, "Three Greek Papyri in Westminster College, Cambridge," *JEA* 55 (1969):184–90. See also Yoyotte 1969 and Willy Clarysse, "Egyptian Scribes Writing Greek," *CdÉ* 68 (1993):186–201, for Ptolemaic period and Tait 1992 for early Roman times.

specific purpose of controlling ritual pronunciation, often in order to augment Demotic texts.[37]

This ritual function of Old Coptic script is most apparent in the third- or early-fourth-century C.E. Demotic ritual texts found in Thebes, part of the Anastasi hoard that includes many of the Greek grimoires. In these texts the transliteration in Greek letters often appears above the Demotic text as a gloss or in the text to spell a foreign word.[38] In another text, from the mid-second century, Greek letters are used simply to transliterate an Egyptian obstetrical ritual; but the text is archaistically "pure," lacking the Greek loanwords typical of Demotic ritual texts much as other Demotic texts of the period kept a pristine "Egyptian" separate from what was commonly spoken.[39] A horoscope from the second century also excludes Greek words from the Old Coptic transliteration; yet it uses Greek headings to designate the astrological periods and it is appended to another horoscope in Greek. For some reason the scribe viewed Egyptian as proper to the astrological predictions, while the period-headings, as frames, could be Greek.[40] We begin to get a sense of some incipient dichotomy within the scriptorium between the nature or facility of the two languages as they were perceived by many priests.

The Schmidt papyrus (ca. 100 C.E.), in which one Esrmpe appeals to the local mortuary god Osiris of Hasro for a child, resembles an archaic literary genre of popular religious appeal, the "letter to the dead," by which Egyptians had long communicated their woes to deceased relatives or to mortuary deities with the hope of some resolution.[41] These letters seem to have developed as a concrete, formulaic representation of a far

---

[37] Among the best discussions of these "ritual" origins of Coptic script are Paul E. Kahle, *Bala'izah: Coptic Texts from Deir El-Bala'izah in Upper Egypt* 1 (Oxford: Griffith Institute, 1954), 252–57; Walter Till, "Coptic and Its Value," *BJRL* 40 (1957):229–30; A. F. Shore, "Christian and Coptic Egypt," in *The Legacy of Egypt,* 2nd ed., ed. by J. R. Harris (Oxford: Clarendon, 1971), 420; Jan Quaegebeur, "De la préhistoire de l'écriture copte," *OLP* 13 (1982):129–30; Satzinger 1984:137–46; J. Johnson 1986:lvi; and McBride 1989:93–94.

[38] See J. Johnson 1986 and hand-copy of text in Griffith/Thompson 1905.

[39] P. B.M. 10808, ed. Jürgen Osing, *Der spätägyptische Papyrus BM 10808,* Ägyptologische Abhandlungen 33 (Wiesbaden: Harrassowitz, 1976). Cf. W. E. Crum, "An Egyptian Text in Greek Characters," *JEA* 28 (1942):20–31, and Aksel Volten, "An Egyptian Text in Greek Characters," *Studia Orientalia Ioanni Pedersen* (Copenhagen: Munksgaard, 1953), 364–76.

[40] Griffith 1900. Among other extant "oracular" horoscopes *P.Oxy* XXXI.2554 alone is in Greek, while Hughes 1951 and Parker 1959, a manual for divining by eclipse- and lunar-omina, are in Demotic.

[41] P.Schmidt, ed. Satzinger 1975, on which see esp. idem 1984:140–41. On letters to mortuary gods, see George R. Hughes, "A Demotic Letter to Thoth," *JNES* 17 (1958):3–5, and idem, "A Demotic Plea to Thoth in the Library of G. Michaelides," *JEA* 54 (1968):176–82 (with particularly colloquial phraseology).

more ancient (and cross-cultural) tradition, the oral appeal at tombs or shrines. The letters to the dead were themselves often designed for oral recitation before the tombs: one letter contains the instruction on the verso to "read it aloud [Eg. *š.sw*] before him (at) the tomb."[42] The choice to write Esrmpe's letter in Greek characters must have been connected to the custom of reading such letters aloud before tombs and shrines. Old Coptic fixed the pronunciation of a plea to a god, whether formulaic or (as this letter appears) colloquially phrased, and ensured that the same text that was deposited at the shrine could be read aloud before it.[43]

To be sure, the paucity of Old Coptic texts suggests the writing system's experimental nature. In most cases we can see a scribe self-consciously extending Demotic or Greek materials, whether to facilitate the transition from the written text to the spoken word or to designate the sacred ritual utterances in more pronounceable written form. But in the broader context of continuing Demotic preservation and Greek translations these linguistic experiments reveal the priesthoods actively negotiating the traditional efficacy of Egyptian writing within the phonetic efficiency of the Greek alphabet.

The priesthoods among whom Coptic developed clearly viewed Egyptian itself as sacred, with sounds that could only be sharpened in efficacy by the addition of the Greek vowels. This veneration of Egyptian appears vividly in a passage in the Greek Hermetic literature. The passage opens, like so many frames in the tradition of Egyptian *Königsnovellen*, as a letter from Asclepius to a King Ammon, reporting the revelations he had received from Thoth-Hermes himself:

> [The teachings of Thoth] will be thought more obscure in time to come, when the Greeks think fit to translate these writings from our tongue into theirs. Translation will greatly distort the sense of the writings, and cause much obscurity. Expressed in our native language, the teaching conveys the sense of the words; for the very quality of the sounds and the intonation of the Egyptian words carry in themselves the power of the things said. There-

[42] P.Brooklyn 37.1799Ev, ed. Richard Jasnow and Günter Vittmann, "An Abnormal Hieratic Letter to the Dead (P.Brooklyn 37.1799E)," *Enchoria* 19/20 (1992/93):23–43. On the oral background of letters to the dead, see Baines 1991:153–55.

[43] It is conceivable that a scribe produced this text in Greek letters in order that Esrmpe herself, who presumably could not read Egyptian script but might have been literate in Greek, could read her own plea before the shrine. In that case the requirement of depositing at the shrine the exact same text that was read aloud (instead of delivering a Demotic text and improvising an oral plea) would still point to some sacred importance in maintaining a connection between the oral and written media. Compare P.Carlsberg 67 (5 B.C.E.), in which a woman's plea to Sobek of Tebtunis for healing is inscribed in careful Demotic script and with formulaic imprecations (ed. J. D. Ray, "Papyrus Carlsberg 67: A Healing-Prayer from the Fayûm," *JEA* 61 [1975]:181–88).

fore, my king, as far as it is in your power (and you are all-powerful), keep the teaching untranslated, in order that secrets so holy may not be revealed to Greeks, and that the Greek mode of speech, with its arrogance and feebleness, and showy tricks of style, may not reduce to impotence the holiness and strength and efficacious power [*energetiken*] of the words. For the speech of the Greeks, my king, is devoid of power to convince; and the Greek philosophy is nothing but a noise of talk. But our (own) speech is not mere talk; it is an utterance replete with workings.[44]

The rejection of Greek is ironic: Asclepius's "letter" is itself a Greek composition (as is the entire Hermetica).[45] But it presents the efficacious power of Egyptian writing and ritual speech as if from an insular and pure milieu committed to Egyptian discourse and therein preserving the genuine teachings of Thoth. In this way the Hermetic passage does reliably report a priestly view of Egyptian language and writing in contrast to Greek. That contrast, Asclepius says, pivots on the "oral" power, the concrete efficacy, of Egyptian ritual speech; and Coptic seems to have been conceived for, or at least quickly applied to, the preservation of this power in a more precise vocalic form.[46]

This transformation of Egyptian language into efficacious sounds, "replete with workings," naturally corresponds to a view of hieroglyphs themselves as more of an ideal than a practical writing system. This reverence for hieroglyphs as the quintessential sacred writing continues most vividly in the priestly family of Horapollo, author of the *Hieroglyphica*. Like many priestly families of the fourth century, that of Horapollo and his father Asklepiades sought in vain to preserve various traditions and skills at the same time as achieving a unique degree of Hellenistic education. Indeed, by Horapollo's own generation the "traditions" themselves may well have been accessible only in such Greek forms as the Hermetica, or orally as the family stories of a golden age of priestly authority. Thus a practical literacy in hieroglyphic writing had become, over the generations, subordinated to a vague sense that proper cult requires hieroglyphs. When Asklepiades entombs his brother, Heraiskos, the once-obligatory mortuary spells in hieroglyphic appear miraculously on the shroud only as "hieroglyphs."[47] One might compare these miraculous

[44] *C.H.* 16.1–2, ed. Festugière 1950, 2:232, trans. modified from W. Scott 1924/36, 1:262–5.

[45] The new Demotic "Books of Thoth" being assembled from among European collections give no evidence of Egyptian sources for extant Greek Hermetica.

[46] On the Egyptian perspective of the *C.H.* passage, see Jørgen Podemann Sørensen, "Ancient Egyptian Religious Thought and the XVIth Hermetic Tractate," in *The Religion of the Ancient Egyptians: Cognitive Structures and Popular Expressions*, Boreas 20, ed. by G. Englund (Uppsala: University of Uppsala, 1989), 41–57.

[47] Damascius, fr. 174, on which see Athanassiadi 1993a:20.

hieroglyphs to the meaningless assortments found on many mummy-cases of the Roman period: it was the concept of the hieroglyph in its mortuary function, rather than the semantic replication of a particular spell in hieroglyphs, that increasingly determined the use of Egyptian characters.[48]

Horapollo's essay on the meaning of the hieroglyphic signs, read devoutly in Europe after its fifteenth-century discovery in Greece, manifestly continues this veneration for the concept of pictographic writing. The *Hieroglyphica* attempts to explain why certain meanings or concepts are represented by specific images. But while Horapollo often seems to understand a hieroglyph's general determinative meaning, his recourse to popular animal legends and the like to derive such meanings is imaginary, the vain retrospection of a man steeped in Aesop and Aristotle toward the rational basis of his own past. Hieroglyphic writing had evolved out of the phonetic resemblances between the images represented and the sounds the images designated. But in Horapollo's *Hieroglyphica* a duck means "son" not for the correct reason that "son" and "duck" were phonetically cognate in ancient Egyptian but because of the species' overwhelming concern for its young; a falcon is a divine symbol not because it was the traditional symbol of Horus but because of the mysterious nature of the falcon (1.6); and a vulture signifies a mother "since there is no male in this species of animal" (1.11).[49]

Still, Horapollo's endeavor shows that the respect for the hieroglyph's symbolism, even its romantic allure as a system of otherworldly characters, was an intra-Egyptian tradition, not simply the exoticism of outsiders. A text like the Coptic Gnostic *Gospel of Truth* could thus project an informed notion of hieroglyphs' "logographic" function into the broader Mediterranean image of the heavenly book, in this case,

> the living book which [the Father] revealed to the aeons, at the end, as [his letters], revealing how they are not vowels nor are they consonants, so that one might read them and think of something foolish, but they are letters of the truth which they alone speak who know them. Each letter is a complete thought like a complete book, since they are letters written by the Unity, the Father having written them for the aeons in order that by means of his letters they should know the Father.[50]

[48] For example, British Museum mummies ##29583, 29588, and 54057 (Rm 60). On the development of this view of hieroglyphs in Egypt, see Sternberg-El Hotabi 1994.

[49] Horapollo, *Hieroglyphica* 1.6, 11, 53, on which symbols see Alan H. Gardiner, *Egyptian Grammar*, 3rd ed. (London: Oxford University Press for Griffith Institute, 1957), 468–71, sign ##G7, G14, G39. On Horapollo's approach to hieroglyphs, see Iversen 1961:47–49 and George Boas, *The Hieroglyphics of Horapollo*, Bollingen Series 23 (Princeton, N.J.: Princeton University Press, 1950; repr. 1993).

[50] NHC I, 3 (= XII, 2), 22.39–23.18, tr. Attridge/MacRae, *NHLE*, 43, on which see

The author, probably of the second or third century, knows in the most general terms of the difference between hieroglyphic and Greek writing systems, enough to distinguish what seem to be hieroglyphs from Greek vowels and consonants and to point out the "complete thought" involved in the Egyptian determinative signs (which clarified the sense of phoneticized words in Egyptian writing). But there is a distance, an idealization born of ignorance, perhaps not to the degree of an Asclepiades or Horapollo but certainly of a time when few could read and write the traditional signs. This Egyptian Gnostic scribe is then applying his sense of hieroglyphic characters to the synthesis of an idea, the letters of a heavenly book in their transcendent incomprehensibility. Hieroglyphs, it seems, were beginning to serve a broader idea in the Roman world, one certainly continuous with Egyptian literature but which was now capturing the imagination of multiple new religions: the image of a secret holy writing preserved in a heavenly book to which only the pure could be privy.[51]

One can see the priestly contribution to this kind of marketing of the hieroglyph: when a spell announces, "I speak your names which Hermes Trismegistus wrote in Heliopolis with hieroglyphic letters," there is a kind of deliberate, explanatory exoticism in pointing out the medium of those names.[52] But in a world of fascinated outsiders, whose ignorance of Egyptian writing made it all the more alluring, hieroglyphs provided an immediate inspiration for new sacred writing "systems." When the Roman author Apuleius describes an Egyptian book "brought out from the hidden quarters of" an Isis shrine in the city of Rome, he sees not only "forms of all kinds of animals"—the popular image of hieroglyphs that Horapollo addressed—but also a peculiar system that, to the author's eye, "barred the possibility of being read from the curiosity of the profane, in that their extremities were knotted and curved like wheels or closely intertwined like vine-tendrils."[53]

These are certainly not hieroglyphs, and it would be difficult to relate Apuleius's description to hieratic or Demotic writing either. Indeed, it is far less likely that Apuleius here describes actual Egyptian books than that he is associating those books with an innovative "magical letter" tradition then widespread in the Mediterranean world. On gems, amulets, and instructions for amulet manufacture one finds *kharaktēres*, ring-tipped combinations of lines, asterisks, even versions of Greek letters.

Laurent Motte, "L'hiéroglyphe, d'Esna à l'Évangile de Vérité," *Deuxième journée d'études coptes,* Cahiers de la bibliothèque copte 3 (Louvain: Peeters, 1986), 111–16.

[51] See Sternberg-El Hotabi 1994 and, on outsiders' views of hieroglyphs, Iversen 1961:45.

[52] *PGM* IV.885–87, tr. Grese in Betz 1986:55.

[53] Apuleius, *Metamorphoses* 11.22, tr. Griffiths 1975:96–97.

Their application in spells as a distinctive kind of unintelligible sacred letter seems very much to draw on the idea of Egyptian hieroglyphs (which themselves appear throughout the Egyptian grimoires and amulets); and their origin (or initial promulgation) may derive from the ritual innovations of priestly ritual experts before becoming generalized as part of the common amulet craft of the Mediterranean world. *Kharaktēres,* as they appear in spells and gems, seem to replicate the efficacious and symbolic roles of hieroglyphs. Inscribed within a frame shaped like a stela, the overall arrangement of the *kharaktēres* recalls the *cippi* of Horus (and other ritual stelae) that stood by temples and "worked" contagiously through water poured over the very hieroglyphs of the spells. Many gems and amulets are actually designed in explicit imitation of stelae, their *kharaktēres* surrounding hybrid divinities in the same way that protective images of Horus, Bes, or Amun were commonly surrounded with hieroglyphic spells.[54]

The *kharaktēr* garnered such popularity among the ritual grimoires—of Egypt especially, but also throughout the Roman world—because it represented precisely that sacred writing system idealized (if no longer understood) in hieroglyphs. In the ritual spells they are logograms, albeit incomprehensible; they are "seals," efficacious through their wearing; they are "words of power," even if unpronounceable. There is a pretentious secrecy to their deployment reminiscent of the ancient Egyptian notion that ritual spells and the secret names that drove them came from the mouth of Thoth or Re. And yet there was a sense of international currency to *kharaktēres:* everybody was familiar with them. Through *kharaktēres,* then, a functional (if idealized and symbolic) sense of hieroglyphs could continue well beyond the third century even while the meaning and use of the traditional phonetic hieroglyphic writing had died. The creativity that developed and to some extent systematized *kharaktēres* recalls milieus like the family of Horapollo, yearning for archaic traditions lost but also developing them anew within the media and culture at hand. In other contexts as well, a notion of magically symbolic writing governed various scribal developments in Coptic monastic culture: graffiti, iconography, the writing of sacred names, and even the mystical interpretation of Greek letters.[55]

---

[54] See Delatte/Derchain 1964, ##178–79, 183–86, 202, 376–77. In general on the relationship between *kharaktēres* and hieroglyphs, see Frankfurter 1994b:205–10.

[55] See Frederik Wisse, "Language Mysticism in the Nag Hammadi Texts and in Early Coptic Monasticism, I: Cryptography," *Enchoria* 9 (1979):101–20 (re: graffiti); Colin H. Roberts, *Manuscript, Society, and Belief in Early Christian Egypt* (London: British Museum, 1979), 26–47 (re: sacred names); A. Hebbelynck, *Les mystères des lettres grecques* (Louvain: Istas; Paris: Leroux, 1902); and Nicole Gourdier, "Le vêtement et l'alphabet mystique chez les coptes," in *Actes du IVᵉ congrès copte* 1, ed. by M. Rassart-Debergh and

## 6.4 From House of Life to Coptic Scriptorium

Socially, self-consciously, by their skill and capacity as scribes, Egyptian priests maintained authority and even legacy in the domain of ritual expertise, "magic," a phenomenon that in Egypt traditionally revolved around the sacred text, its writing, its origin, its habitat in the temple's House of Life. Through the fourth century we have seen grimoires carrying on archaic literary motifs of kings and priests, priests and books, and the sacred space of temples. With the closing of the temple scriptoria a once deeply privileged body of tradition became dispersed among those of priestly education as a practical lore that could be invoked and applied in a diversity of ritual situations, to reinforce the authority of the old traditions in the village environment as well as the authority of the ritual expert in his (or her) itinerant charisma. Some priests, it seems, shifted their locus of service from declining temples to the town or village; others carried their ritual training and priestly affiliation well beyond the temple precincts, becoming itinerant ritual specialists, "magicians," part of a network of itinerant poets, performers, and intellectuals in late antique Egypt with only marginal or gratuitous identification with particular temples or places (see 5.3.3).

Over the course of the fourth century the monopoly on ritual expertise fell increasingly to Christian holy men and shrines, both proffering nearly the same services as Egyptian temples and priests. This much we have seen (4.4.2; 5.2.3); but additional facets of the shift to Christianity emerge when we understand the nuances of the traditional scribal culture of the Egyptian priesthood and its relationship to popular ritual expertise. As the shift can be documented through the large body of Coptic (Christian) grimoires and amulets, for example, the ritual experts of post-fourth-century Christian Egypt seem to have inherited a social role similar to those of much earlier times. Most important, these grimoires reflect no more of a distinction between "religious" and "practical" spheres than do those of Greco-Roman or pharaonic times. More than the Greek and Demotic grimoires, the Coptic spell collections (often consisting of a number of loose-leaf scraps with master-spells) devote enormous attention to issues of health (including obstetrical and gynecological domains of practice), financial and agricultural concern, apotropaic needs, and such exigencies of social competition as curses and aphrodisiacs.[56] Assembled together in the same manuals and hoards of scraps, the spells

---

J. Ries (Louvain-la-neuve: Institut orientaliste, 1992), 135–40 (re: Greek letters). In general on the legacy of the hieroglyph in Coptic scribality, see Frankfurter 1994b:210–11.

[56] See Meyer/Smith (eds.) 1994 and Sergio Pernigotti, "La Magia copta: I Testi," *ANRW* II.18.5 (1995):3685–3730.

imply at the very least the owners' centralization of ritual functions—their service to a diversity of problems.

But among whom did the Coptic ritual texts arise? In what part of late antique Egyptian society does one place them? Three subcultures appear in our various sources, all distinctive for their passionate book culture in a society of sparse literacy. One such subculture is revealed in a letter about a separation-spell that was found in a fourth-century Manichaean house in the oasis town of Kellis. Literary conventicles such as Manichaeism promoted lent themselves to the active exchange of spells and perhaps their compilation into grimoires.[57] A second subculture would be that small, élite world of literate landowners represented by the sixth-century poet Dioscorus of Aphrodito, for an apotropaic prayer from his pen betrays considerable familiarity with the typical discourse of the Coptic ritual texts.[58] But the main locus in Coptic society for ritual expertise was the monastic scriptorium and the ecclesiastical apparatus of Coptic shrines.[59]

There is some documentary evidence of this link between monasteries and "magic," although it appears only sporadically. One finds, for example, a special category of penance prescribed for any "of the clergy consulting books of *magia*" in a fourth-century Coptic canon, and an extensive grimoire of the sixth or seventh century was unearthed from a monk's cell at the monastery of Epiphanius of Thebes.[60] These materials offer a decisive but limited context for ritual texts, and they lead one to assume that the use of such manuals was usually a secret endeavor. But a long master-spell in the Berlin Museum, designed for healing, offers a

[57] P. Kell. Cop. 35, edited with extensive commentary in Paul Mirecki, Iain Gardner, and Anthony Alcock, "Magical Spell, Manichaean Letter,"in *Emerging from Darkness: Studies in the Recovery of Manichaean Sources*, NHS 43, ed. by Paul Mirecki and Jason BeDuhn (Leident: Brill, 1997), 1–32.

[58] P.Cair.Maspero II.67188v, in Leslie S. B. MacCoull, "P. Cair. Masp. II 67188 Verso 1–5: The *Gnostica* of Dioscorus of Aphrodito," *Tyche* 2 (1987):95–97 (= *PGM* P13a, Meyer/Smith [eds.] 1994, #22). On the literary culture of Dioscorus, see Leslie S. B. MacCoull, *Dioscorus of Aphrodito: His Work and His World* (Berkeley: University of California Press, 1988), 17–19. There is no evidence of Dioscorus's ownership of grimoires, however.

[59] C. Detlef G. Müller, "Wie arbeitete der koptische Zauberer?" in *Proceedings of the XIXth International Congress of Papyrology* 1, ed. by A. H. S. El-Mosalamy (Cairo: Ain Shams University, 1992), 651–52.

[60] "Clergy consulting books of *magia* [Copt. *nneklērikos efkōte hi henjōōme mmagia*]": *Canon of Pseudo-Athanasius* 71–72, ed. Riedel/Crum 1904:108, 135. The text assumes that these books are the personal property of the *klērikos:* he must burn "his books [Copt. *nefjōōme tērou*]" (72). The *Life of Theodore of Sykeon* includes in its general picture of sixth-century rural Asia Minor a *klērikos* who was also a *pharmakeias* (ch. 159). Grimoire of Monastery of Epiphanius: Cairo 45060 (ed. Kropp 1930/31, 1:50–54; 2:31–40; tr. Meyer/Smith [eds.] 1994, #128); on the character of the find, see W. E. Crum, *The Monastery of Epiphanius at Thebes* 2 (New York: MMA, 1926), 21, 207.

more exoteric context. Invoking a great variety of heavenly powers loosely based in Christian apocalyptic tradition (seven archangels, twenty-four Elders, four Incorporeal Creatures, all named individually), the spell concludes with the reminder that "Apa Anoup has sealed this oil, Michael is the one who intercedes, Jesus Christ is the one who gives healing."[61] The orthodoxy is deliberate, as one might expect from a spell's narrative frame; but Apa Anoup certainly had the immediate role as ritual specialist.

A broader connection is the demographics of literacy in Coptic script. The hands and the grammar of the ritual spells may not equal the beautiful Coptic gospels and translations that were being produced at the same time, but Coptic writing in the era of these texts was for the most part a monastic system. That one hoard of grimoires displays the interaction of at least five different scribes, of various levels of training, virtually requires the context of a monastic scriptorium.[62]

Then there is the idiom of the spells: the invocations in Coptic spells for sex, cursing, healing, protection, and the rest continue the angelology, liturgical cadences, and formal details of the ecclesiastical cult, suggesting some demographic continuity as well between Christian cult and local ritual expertise.[63] Like Apa Anoup's healing spell, one finds an amuletic papyrus in Greek repelling "every sting of the devil's beasts . . . through the oil of the s[acred b]apt[ism]" and a later Coptic spell that advises the following invocation before one repeats the names of an obscure set of alphabetic powers:

> send me today Gabriel, the archangel who has received the good news of the son of the almighty until today, so that he might come down on this water and this oil [ . . . ] and this honey, and mark the water and fill it with healing and favor and peace and uprightness and salvation and [ . . . ] my soul, so that if a wicked person [ . . . ] my heart and my [ . . . ] soul [ . . . ].[64]

We have seen how Christian shrines were deeply engaged in filling the same needs for oracular divination and healing by incubation that Egyp-

---

[61] Berlin 11347, ed. Walter Beltz, "Die koptischen Zauberpapiere und Zauberostraka der Papyrus-Sammlung der Staatlichen Museen zu Berlin," *Archiv* 31 (1985):32–35; tr. Meyer/Smith (eds.) 1994, #63, and see Kropp 1930/31, 2:113–17.

[62] *P. Mich.* 593 (fourth to fifth century), on which see Mirecki in Meyer/Smith (eds.) 1994:295.

[63] Examples: Meyer/Smith (eds.) 1994, ##70–71, 113, 122, 133; cf. Kropp 1930/31, 3:180–97. *P.Oxy* XI.1384, a fifth-century medical miscellany, reinforces the link between the monastery and ritual expertise in its combination of simple remedies with magical legends of Jesus and angels.

[64] Vienna Rainer 5 (13b) = *PGM* P12 = Meyer/Smith (eds.) 1994, #17. London Or. ms. 5899 (1), ed. W. E. Crum, *Catalogue of the Coptic Manuscripts in the British Museum* (London: British Museum, 1905), 417–18, tr. Meyer/Smith (eds.)1994, #57 (pp. 103–4).

tian shrines had filled (4.4.3); and one would suspect that the ecclesiastical functionaries of these shrines, as representatives of a great tradition imbued with the power of speech and pen, provided the same "additional" services to pilgrims that priests of the native shrines had provided. Ethiopian *debteras* and local Coptic priests in modern Egypt themselves serve also as amulet manufacturers, exorcists, diviners, and supernatural healers for village communities.[65] Such popular roles of ritual expert would inevitably offer a vital income.

Given this monastic or ecclesiastical context for the compilation of the Coptic ritual texts it is remarkable the degree to which these texts (which tend to cluster paleographically in the fifth through seventh centuries) actually preserve ritual traditions—methods, themes, characters, literary structures—from pre-Christian culture.[66] Three seventh-century love-spells draw upon the same myth of the ailing Horus and the healing Isis that motivated the Horus-*cippi*.[67] Another text invokes this myth to cure abdominal pain—on the same papyrus strip as a spell referring to Michael and the Mount of Olives. And other texts invoke Isis, Osiris, and Horus in their various mythic capacities for other types of healing and erotic union.[68] Coptic spells and amulets list a wide range of environmental demons repelled—"every doom and every devil and every Apalaf and every Aberselia . . . and every evil eye and every eye-shutter"—according to the same form that Egyptian apotropaic amulets had used from the classical through Roman periods.[69]

Certainly Egypt's supernatural landscape could not have changed substantially: demons were still responsible for divorce in Christian villages

[65] See Kropp 1930/31, 3:197–216. Shenoute was revered both pre- and posthumously as having power over the Nile surge: see above, 2.2. On modern Coptic priests, see W. Blackman 1927:230–34; on *debteras,* see above, 5.2.2 with sources cited.

[66] On dates of Coptic ritual texts, see W. E. Crum, "Foreword," in Kropp 1930/31, 1:ix–xii. In general on formal continuities in Coptic ritual texts, see Lexa 1925, 1:139–47.

[67] Coll.Schmidt 1–2, ed. Kropp 1930/31, 1:11–14; tr. Meyer/Smith (eds.) 1994, ##48, 72; Berlin 5565, ed. Beltz 1983:61–63, tr. Meyer/Smith (eds.) 1994, #47. See above, 2.3, on mythology of *cippi*.

[68] Berlin 8313, ed. Beltz 1983:65–67; tr. Meyer/Smith (eds.) 1994, #49. Cf. Michigan 136, 2.17–3.34, ed. Worrell 1935:18 (iv), tr. Meyer/Smith (eds.) 1994, #43; and Michigan 4932r, 3–4, ed. Worrell 1935:184 (v), tr. Meyer/Smith (eds.) 1994, #82.

[69] Apotropaic demon lists: *PGM* VII.579–90; London. Or. Ms. 5525, ed. Kropp 1930/31, 1:15–21, tr. Meyer/Smith (eds.) 1994, #64; Leiden Anastasi 9, ed. W. Pleyte and P. A. A. Boeser, *Manuscrits coptes du Musée d'Antiquités des Pays-Bas à Léide* (Leiden: Brill, 1897), 441–54, tr. Kropp 1930/31, 2:161–71. On their liturgical context, see Henry Ansgar Kelly, *The Devil at Baptism* (Ithaca, N.Y., and London: Cornell University Press, 1985), 199. Precedents include oracular amuletic decrees (Third Intermediate Period): Edwards 1960; self-dedication amulets (Ptolemaic): Herbert Thompson, "Self-Dedications," *Actes du V^e congrès international de papyrologie* (Brussels: Fondation égyptologique Reine Élisabeth, 1938), 497–504. The demon list form becomes standardized in medieval Jewish amulets of Egyptian provenance: TS K1. 18, 30, ed. Schiffman/Swartz 1992:69–82.

no less than beforehand, in traditional villages.[70] And these kinds of realities must have been in some way responsible for the continuity of tradition in the Coptic rituals. Whether composed out of remembered tradition or copied from a more ancient grimoire, the Coptic spells suggest that the social world of Coptic ritual expertise was able to preserve to a remarkable degree the ritual idiom—mythic characters, *historiolae,* invocational forms—traditional to Egyptian priestly lore.[71]

The monks and ecclesiastical functionaries must themselves have been the means by which traditional divine names and priestly themes could continue into the scribal world of Christianity. We might indeed wonder what Shenoute's monks did with the "books full of magic"—undoubtedly in Greek by his time—that they ransacked from the temple of Plewit in the early sixth century.[72] And yet the notion of demographic continuity between the ancient House of Life and the monastery requires only that among those who entered the monastic environments were individuals who had been originally trained in priestly traditions and who thus would carry the ritual idiom and traditions with them, perhaps even already in Coptic.

One argument for this demographic continuity, of course, is the Coptic medium itself: while systematized for Christian literature in the fourth century, the writing system, we have seen, probably originated in the temples for ritual purposes. Thus some early Coptic scribes may well have carried traditional assumptions about the power of writing and vocalized sacred texts into monasteries along with their skill in Coptic translation. The evidence most encouraging of this notion is the third- or fourth-century Gnostic text, the *Books of Jeu,* whose author has constructed rituals of heavenly ascent according to models of Egyptian mortuary texts, all framed as a dialogue between Jesus and the apostles. Classical Egyptian mortuary "guides," which protected the soul in its passage through the underworld, are well represented into the second century C.E.[73] And likewise the *Books of Jeu* present the passage for a soul's ascent as a sequence of doors, each held by a guardian figure whose name must be known and to whom one must display a "seal" and utter a spell.

---

[70] Divorce demons: *P.Lond.* V.1713 (569 C.E.); cf. *P.Grenfell* II.76 (305–6 C.E.).

[71] See Kropp 1930/31, 3:5–11. On *historiolae,* brief accounts of successful supernatural interventions supposed to produce the same effect when spoken or written, see David Frankfurter, "Narrating Power: The Theory and Practice of the Magical *Historiola* in Ritual Spells," in *Ancient Magic and Ritual Power,* RGRW 129, ed. by M. Meyer and P. Mirecki (Leiden: Brill, 1995), 457–76.

[72] Shenoute, "Only I Tell Everyone Who Dwells in This Village" (= Leipoldt 3:89.15–16, #26).

[73] See François René Herbin, *Le Livre de parcourir l'Éternité,* OLA 58 (Leuven: Peeters, 1994), discussing a hybrid of the Egyptian *Book of Gates* (originating in the Ptolemaic period) that leads the owner through the various realms of the underworld.

Like a passport through the heavens, *Jeu* contains the drawings of these seals, which consist of none other than *kharaktēres*, discussed above as heirs to the idea of hieroglyphs.[74]

*Jeu* is certainly Christian in its choice of literary characters, and the instructions for ascent ritual in *Jeu* ultimately became broadly diffused in late antique religions. But *Jeu*'s proximity to the ancient mortuary "guides" and the apotropaic rites and symbols that tradition involved point to a scribe well-versed in the traditions of such mortuary texts.[75] The shift from a traditional priestly to a Christian-Gnostic milieu is then no more radical than the shift from temple to Hermetic conventicle that Garth Fowden described so cogently.[76] Of course, one must take the concept of "shift" in its loosest sense, since the mere fact of conserved tradition in texts like the Hermetica, the *Books of Jeu*, and the Coptic grimoires implies more of a reassertion than a transformation of scribal self-definition.

Coptic literature itself provides suggestive evidence for the conversion of Egyptian priests and their recruitment to monasteries. An elderly Theban monk describes his childhood as the son of an Egyptian priest. Macarius the Great was credited with converting a priest merely through his wise words and thereby inspiring the conversion of many villagers (a demonstration of priests' ideological leadership). In Paphnuti's *History of the Monks of Upper Egypt* one Apa Macedonius describes how he won over the two sons of a priest of Horus at Philae in the mid-fifth century, successfully baptized them with biblical names, and then converted their father as well. The story of Apa Moses's late-fifth-century destruction of cultic worship around Abydos concludes with "the sons of priests" becoming Christian. Nor was this shift from temple to monastery understood as radical in all cases: Apa Olympius credits the wisdom of one Egyptian priest who visited him in his cell and observed that impure thoughts were hindering him (Olympius) from receiving revelations. One cannot, of course, assume the historicity of all such reports. But they

---

[74] *1, 2 Jeu* (esp. *2Jeu* ch. 52), ed. Carl Schmidt and Violet MacDermot, *The Books of Jeu and the Untitled Text in the Bruce Codex*, NHS 13 (Leiden: Brill, 1978). On continuities with the *Book of the Gates* literature, see Scott-Moncrieff 1913:192; László Kákosy, "Gnosis und ägyptische Religion," *Le Origini dello Gnosticismo: Colloquio di Messina 13–18 Aprile 1966*, Numen Supplements 12 (Leiden: Brill, 1970), 240–44. On the concrete efficacy of traditional mortuary spells and inscriptions, see Richard Caminos, "Magic for the Dead," in Roccati and Siliotti (eds.) 1987:147–59.

[75] See McBride 1989:97–98 on the potential scribal milieu of *1,2 Jeu*. Examples of the diffusion of the *Gates* tradition include the "Mithras Liturgy" of *PGM* IV.475–829 (esp. ll.555–628), which incorporates ritual details from many Greco-Roman traditions, and Jewish *Hekhalot* literature, on which see Martha Himmelfarb, "Heavenly Ascent and the Relationship of the Apocalypses and the *Hekhalot* Literature," *HUCA* 59 (1988):80–84.

[76] Fowden 1986.

do cumulatively give reason to believe that monastic and ecclesiastical recruits, many of whom we know to have come from élite backgrounds, did occasionally arrive with various degrees of priestly education (and various degrees of commitment to traditional lore).[77] Moreover, this Egyptian evidence matches reports from other late antique and medieval cultures undergoing Christianization, in which traditional religious specialists joined the monastic ranks, whether by virtue of their roles as synthesizers, as heralds of new idioms and graspers of new problems, or through their personal interests in new cosmic speculation.[78]

That monks with traditional priestly backgrounds might continue to articulate their traditional literary and ritual sensibilities in the new idiom merely extends an observation often made about the eclecticism of early Coptic monastic culture. The multiple Coptic codexes of Gnostic, Hermetic, and other texts found buried in Nag Hammadi (south of Abydos), near a Pachomian monastery, seem to reflect an early period of literary and ideological diversity that may have been brought to a halt by proponents of an orthodoxy.[79] The integration of Egyptian with Jewish and Christian literary forms in the *Apocalypse of Elijah* in the late third

[77] Son of Egyptian priest: *Apophth.Pat.* (anon.) 190, ed. Nau 1908:274–75. Macarius: *Apophth.Pat.*: Macarius 39, *PG* 65:280–82. Macedonius and the priest's sons: Paphnutius, *History of the Monks in Upper Egypt* 31–50 (tr. Vivian 1993:87–95). Apa Moses and the sons of priests: *Life of Moses of Abydos,* ed. Amélineau 1888/95:687 = Till 1936:50.2–3, 68. Olympius's admiration for priest: *Apophth.Pat.*: Olympius 1, *PG* 65:313. In general on monks' backgrounds, see Lucien Regnault, *La vie quotidienne des pères du désert en Égypte au IV$^e$ siècle* (Paris: Hachette, 1990), 32–33, and Wipszycka 1992:115–19.

[78] See, on medieval Ethiopia, Steven Kaplan, *The Monastic Holy Man and the Christianization of Early Solomonic Ethiopia,* Studien zur Kulturkunde 73 (Wiesbaden: Steiner, 1984), 115–16, and on modern Nigeria, J. D. Y. Peel, "The Pastor and the *Babalawo:* The Interaction of Religions in Nineteenth-Century Yorubaland," *Africa* 60 (1990):350–59. Canons 1–4 of the early-fourth-century Synod of Elvira wrestle with the apparently common situation of Roman priests, *flamines,* who continue to fulfill their traditional cultic functions even after Christian baptism (see Alan Wardman, "Pagan Priesthoods in the Later Empire," *Pagan Gods and Shrines of the Roman Empire,* OUCA Monograph 8, ed. by M. Henig and A. King [Oxford: OUCA, 1986], 1986:258–59, and Henri Leclerq's energetic argument against any religious significance to *flamen* in these cases, *DACL* 5, 2 [1923]:1643–51). In the mid-fourth century one Heraclius, a "priest of Hercules" in Tyre, is ordained deacon by Eleusius, bishop of Cyzicus (Sozomen, *H.E.* 4.24). Socrates Scholasticus repeats a tradition that priests of Serapis became Christian at the Serapeion's destruction (*H.E.* 5.17), and Jerome mentions the conversion of a priest of "Venus" in Palestine (*V.Hil.* 25). Bede describes the conversion of Coifi, the traditional high priest of King Edwin of Northumbria (627 C.E.): *History of the English Church* 2.13.

[79] Frederik Wisse, "Gnosticism and Early Monasticism in Egypt," in *Gnosis: Festschrift für Hans Jonas,* ed. by B. Aland (Göttingen: Vandenhoeck & Ruprecht, 1978), 431–40, although noting the provocative critiques of Armand Veilleux, "Monasticism and Gnosis in Egypt," in Pearson/Goehring (eds.) 1986:271–306. Gedaliahu G. Stroumsa ("The Manichaean Challenge to Egyptian Christianity," in Pearson/Goehring [eds.] 1986:307–19) gives a compelling image of monastic diversity in the fourth century.

century, its rapid copying in Coptic during the fourth and fifth centuries, and its addition to the library of Shenoute's own monastery also seem to mark this kind of early ecumenism of traditions, as does the Coptic preservation of the legend of the Persian invader Cambyses. Those ecclesiastical ritual specialists reported by Shenoute and the Jacobite Synaxarium (5.2.3) certainly understood no dogmatic contradictions between their everyday ritual services and the institutions that they represented; but at the point we find them they have come under the censorship of certain figures promoting orthodoxy. Both within and without Egypt one can see the exceptional diversity of literature read, copied, composed, and valued in monastic scriptoria, as reflected in manuscripts, book lists, and patristic testimony that was often quite polemical. One can only surmise that the scribal enterprise itself in Coptic monasticism—the interest among literate monks in books of any sort—was voracious.[80] And at least initially (in many places continually) that voracious enterprise held to dogmatic boundaries as little as the priestly scribes of the temple libraries had held to ethnic boundaries. Even when orthodoxy movements blew through particular monasteries or regions it does not seem that the types of traditions one finds in the Coptic ritual corpora fell under censure. Indeed, the archaic practices of ritual healing and protection in the Coptic corpora, practices essential to traditional temple "magic," were by the sixth century so basic to the Coptic pilgrimage cults as to be inseparable from the rest of ecclesiastical service.

[80] See David Frankfurter, "The Legacy of the Jewish Apocalypse in Early Christian Communities: Two Regional Trajectories," in *The Jewish Apocalyptic Heritage in Early Christianity*, CRINT 3.4, ed. by J. VanderKam and W. Adler (Assen/Maastricht: Van Gorcum; Minneapolis: Fortress, 1996), 185–200. Behlmer 1996b provides the best survey to date of Egyptian "survivals" in Coptic literature.

# 7

# IDIOM, IDEOLOGY, AND ICONOCLASM:

# A PROLEGOMENON TO THE CONVERSION

# OF EGYPT

O N A DAY in the fifth century Abbot Shenoute of Atripe stood before a mixed audience of monks and villagers and spoke of what he had just done with a local temple:

At the site of a shrine to an unclean spirit, it will henceforth be a shrine to the Holy Spirit. And at the site of sacrificing to Satan and worshipping and fearing him, Christ will henceforth be served there, and He will be worshipped, bowed down to and feared. And where there are blasphemings, it is blessings and hymns that will henceforth be there.

Shenoute then turned to the hieroglyphic symbols, still imbued with power, which covered the walls in this converted temple:

If previously it is prescriptions for murdering man's soul that are in there, written with blood and not with ink alone—[indeed,] there is nothing else portrayed . . . except the likeness of the snakes and scorpions, the dogs and cats, the crocodiles and frogs, . . . the likeness of the sun and moon . . .— where these are, it is the soul-saving scriptures of life that will henceforth come to be in there . . . and His son Jesus Christ and all His angels, righteous men and saints [will be portrayed on these walls].[1]

Here is one of the rare instances of early Christian literature in which we can almost experience the converting of a traditional temple in order to house the new religion of Christianity. But the gutting and conversion of traditional Egyptian temples, often still functioning, was a widespread phenomenon in Egypt during the fourth, fifth, and sixth centuries. Still today the visitor can see the crosses gouged into the pillars of one temple's antechamber; the portraits of saints and martyrs, much as Shenoute describes, fading on the pillars of another temple (see pl. 23); and pious graffiti decorating a sanctified portion of a third. They were important temples, places of tremendous regional renown in classical Egypt: Karnak, Philae, Dendara, and the great Amun temple of Luxor with no less

---

[1] Michigan ms. 158, ed. and tr. D. Young 1981:353–54. See Emmel 1993:639, 1005 (Acephalous Work A6).

than five churches built into or beside it (and a mosque still thriving in the Ramses courtyard). Clearly something powerful, something axial, was being maintained in putting churches in temples, the Christians in a way grafting themselves to what was already long-sacred in the Egyptian world.[2]

These scenes of ancient temples turned into churches capture, perhaps more than any other single phenomenon, the tenacity of tradition in the ongoing religious life of an area. To be sure, they involved more than a simple transfer of authority. But the turning of a temple into a church does point to the mode in which Christian authority and institution presented itself and, even more, placed itself in the Egyptian landscape.

What would these temples have represented to an ordinary Egyptian in the century following 324, when the emperor embraced Christianity? Libanius of Antioch's sensitive (if patronizing) image of the fourth-century temple as "the soul of the countryside" has provided a useful theme over the course of this book, bringing together a great variety of evidence for popular religion around temples in the Roman period. As we have fleshed out his words we have found temples providing, above all, a sense of axis and supernatural stability in their structural antiquity, archaic rituals, and interplay with the rhythms of agricultural life. Temples also evoked a sense of authority in the person of their priests, the magical writing that the priests controlled and the temple displayed, and the holy objects and gods that lay within the temple. And most important for the vicissitudes and crises of late antique rural life, the temples provided supernatural power accessible in the spoken words and images carried by the priests, in the amulets and incantations the priests provided for all quarters of life, and in the very stones of the temple itself: the inscribed hieroglyphs, the folk altars, the protective stelae that could be touched or soaked up at the exterior of the temple. In all these ways temples were very much the souls of the countryside, expressing the basic social and supernatural needs of local Egyptian religion.

Even when Shenoute was inaugurating his new temple-church, this kind of temple-centered religion was continuing all over the land, despite profound financial straits. And one thing our sources show, whether papyri, inscriptions, or saints' lives, is that adherence to traditional religion was not an individual affair of personal salvation but a community affair, something that inspired the participation and often active defense of villagers. To put it in Durkheimian terms, it was an adherence to the sacredness of the community itself and its environment. As much as they could, villages held onto their cults, their festivals, their priests, and their broader

[2] See Jullien 1902; Munier 1938; O'Leary 1938; Nautin 1967; Coquin 1972:169–78; and, on Luxor, Peter Grossmann, "Eine vergessene frühchristliche Kirche beim Luxor-Tempel," *MDAIK* 29 (1973):167–68, and Kákosy 1995:2971–72.

religious traditions, resisting exterior change as disruptive to cosmic, social, and individual order. So the shift to embrace Christianity would be in Egypt, as elsewhere in the Roman Empire, most commonly also a community affair, made according to collective concerns and needs.[3]

But then, given the fact that traditional local religion continued to be a viable—indeed a vital—system of community and action in late antique Egypt, what impelled communities to embrace Christianity, and in what forms did they embrace it?

## 7.1 Real Power

The first answer would have to be that Christianity presented more efficient, or integrated, or coherent fonts of supernatural power than could at that time be negotiated through most village temples.[4] In what ways did Christianization specifically compete through the supplying of supernatural power?

The earliest and perhaps most basic form of Christian power lay in the integrating charisma of the Christian holy man. Figures like Antony, Paul of Thebes, John of Lycopolis, Elias of Antinoë, the virgin Piamoun, all seem to communicate with their visitors primarily by delivering a verbal charm, a charmed substance, or practical advice much in the order of a temple's oracle or a temple priest's word.[5] Antony, in his famous biography, is remembered for his powerful *apotropaia* against demons. Elias and John are famous for healing powers gained by virtue of "prophetic spirits" and transmitted through such media as oil and dust. Piamoun's clairvoyance resolves a dispute over water rights much in the way temple oracles had served communities. People in Shenoute's vicinity know of a "great monk" who handed out amuletic fox claws. Peering past the theological lenses of their biographers we can see these various desert saints repeating the local functions of temples and their priesthoods quite closely.

Despite hagiographers' imputations of pious asceticism and even Christian orthodoxy to these desert prophets, we can in no way be certain of the ideological, "Christian" coherence of this movement into the desert and its phenomenal growth during the fourth century, nor indeed of the singularity of one "movement." In placing themselves on the periphery of civilization, requiring pilgrimage and a kind of supralocal devotion untypical of local cults, the desert saints resemble more the

---

[3] See MacMullen 1984:80–81 and Wipszycka 1988:121–22.

[4] This "magical" explanation for Christianity has also been advanced in various forms by Brown 1975, MacMullen 1984, and Flint 1991.

[5] See above, 4.4.2, 5.2.3, and in general Lexa 1925, 1:151–53, 2:207–16; Dunand 1991a; and Brown 1982.

prophet cults that have periodically swept up regions of Africa than Christian scripture.[6] Other scholars have found glimmers of a more radical or a more indigenous prophetism behind the saintly lives of these desert holy figures.[7] Despite their apparently uniform commitment to Christian ideology they must have represented a far more autochthonous phenomenon, born of regional as opposed to scriptural tendencies, than we have been led to believe by their biographers. It is certainly possible, as modern parallels show, that ritual specialists of renown might consolidate their authority under Christianity's dominance by employing Christian symbols and terms without in any way converting to a new ideological position.[8] And yet, to whatever degree the desert holy men in Egypt proffered the same Christianities as did the bishops, their charismatic appeal to villagers over broad regions seems to have provided a major entrée for the Christian institution during the fourth century. And as such they show that people had found a dramatic new source for the supernatural power required for daily living.[9]

Scripture itself was a means of conveying Christian power—but not "scripture" in the abstract sense. Rather, what fascinated people lay in the concrete representation of holy words on papyrus or parchment, whose numinous power among nonliterate cultures is well known to those who study the local use of the Bible or Qur'an in traditional societies. While Egypt did not exceed any other area of the Roman Empire in general literacy, Egypt had an exceptionally long tradition of sacred letters, hieroglyphs, that were easily and traditionally drawn into service for protection or healing. One could rub dust from inscribed hieroglyphs, one could acquire a hieroglyph-amulet, one could pour water over inscribed spells. As much as hieroglyphic writing (and its derivatives, hieratic and Demotic) had been practical writing systems for the most mundane record-keeping, in a religious sense they and the spells and images they formed were believed at every level of society to carry great power, applicable to any purpose. The locus of this power in Egyptian religion was, of course, the temple; and the authorities over the hieroglyphs and their applications were the priests. The concept of supernatural power in Egypt was strongly tied to the notion of writing.[10]

[6] See Garbett 1977, Colson 1977, Ranger 1993:72–80; D. H. Johnson 1994; and above, 4.4.2.

[7] See Michael A. Williams, "The *Life of Antony* and the Domestication of Charismatic Wisdom," *Charisma and Sacred Biography, JAARTS* 48, 3–4, ed. by M. Williams (Chico, Calif.: Scholars, 1982), 23–45; Brown 1995:67–68. Cf. Frankfurter 1990 on indigenous elements in fifth-century Syrian charisma.

[8] See Werbner 1989:277–78.

[9] See Fisher 1985:158–59.

[10] On Egyptian literacy, see Baines 1983; Harris 1989:29, 276–80; and Bagnall 1993:240–51. On the conceptualization of hieroglyphs in the Roman period, see Sternberg-El Hotabi 1994 and above, 6.3.

The economic decline of the temples after the third century did not of course lead to any concomitant decline in the popular need for or receptivity to the empowered word or letter. And this is why the Christians' emphasis on text, an emphasis reflected as much in the papyrus remains as the ancient church writers, would have been received with particular interest. Indeed, many of the scraps of papyrus on which biblical and New Testament verses were written in the third and fourth centuries, which have often been assumed to be mere parts of complete lectionaries, now seem to have been intended as amulets.[11] That is, Christian scripture was being received and employed from a quite early point as an efficacious substance. Of course, this is hardly unique to Egypt, for there is extensive evidence for amuletic scripture in Judaism and Christianity of this period. Over in Antioch John Chrysostom complains that "women and little children suspend gospels from their necks as a powerful amulet and carry them about in all places wherever they go."[12] The crucial element in these cases is the appearance of a "book religion" to people whose understanding of sacred text had long been associated with the concrete efficacy of the letters. It becomes another way by which the Christian institution plugged into indigenous expectations of supernatural power.[13]

Even the notion of a Christian scriptural canon, a fixedness to the sacred text, was received and even promulgated in fourth-century Egypt much in the way texts of Homer and the *Sortes Astrampsychi* were being used at this time and in the way that written oracles of Harsaphes and Khnum had been scrutinized in some temples throughout the Greco-Roman period.[14] They became media for divination, sacred devices whose literate owners could be consulted on all manner of hopes and crises and then could extract the truths from the text as if from an attentive temple god. In a culture of oracular texts another volume with even higher claims to divinity and to relevance in everyday issues would be quickly respected as such.[15]

---

[11] E. A. Judge, "The Magical Use of Scripture in the Papyri," in *Perspectives on Language and Text: Essays and Poems in Honor of Francis I Andersen's Sixtieth Birthday*, ed. by E. Conrad and E. Newing (Winona Lake, Ind.: Eisenbrauns, 1987), 339–49.

[12] Chrysostom, *Hom.* 19.14 (PG 49:196).

[13] Wolfgang Speyer, "Das Buch als magisch-religiöser Kraftträger im griechischen und römischen Altertum," in *Das Buch als magisches und als Repräsentationsobjekt*, Wolfenbütteler Mittlealter-Studien 5, ed. by P. Ganz (Wiesbaden: Harrassowitz, 1992), 59–86; Robin Lane Fox, "Literacy and Power in Early Christianity," in *Literacy and Power in the Ancient World*, ed. by A. Bowman and G. Woolf (Cambridge: Cambridge University Press, 1994), 139–41; Frankfurter 1994b:190–99; Harris 1989:298–300; and on the typically "magical" reception of scripture among oral cultures, Jack Goody, *The Interface between the Written and the Oral* (Cambridge: Cambridge University Press, 1987), 129–32.

[14] See above, 4.4.1. On the interpretation of written oracles, see Daumas 1961.

[15] See Brakke 1994:416–17.

The literate clerics who had the ability to copy scripture, write prayers, and divine proper action from the text, consequently, would have held a position of authority over sacred power very akin to that of Egyptian priests. And this leads to a third phenomenon in the Christian delivery of supernatural power: ritual expertise itself. In modern Sudan and Ethiopia the figures most responsible at the village level for "magic"—for supernatural healing, exorcising, and protecting—are functionaries of the Muslim or Christian religious institutions. And they carry their scribal training and authority from the "official" institution into the village. They are the intermediaries between the great and the little traditions.[16]

Into the fourth century in Egypt the main local ritual expert was a rank of temple priest; and his "charisma" in making amulets and healing certainly came from his authority over the sacred word. During the fourth century, as we saw in the hoards of "magical" texts (usually ritual manuals) written in Coptic, ritual expertise multiplied in communities, and in many places the role was taken over by Christian clerics and monks. These grimoires contain as diverse a selection of spells and remedies as those found in Egyptian temples, showing that the books' owners covered the gamut of local crises: from childbirth to snakebite to love to cursing to specific diseases. This phenomenon places the role of church, monastery, and cleric in the life of early Egyptian Christians in a somewhat different light.[17]

It would be easy to say that this accretion of "magic" in official Egyptian Christianity was a natural part of the steady departure any regional Christianity is said to make from its allegedly pure scriptural origins. This is the nineteenth-century Protestant perspective, that an originally pure message of Jesus was gradually distorted, paganized, transformed into the whitewashed heathenism of the Catholic and Orthodox churches. It is a view that reeks of sectarian bias, but tends still to influence discussion of late antique religion. In the case of these Coptic grimoires and amulets, however, we can take a more sympathetic approach to the phenomenon. Monks and clerics were evidently continuing the same attention to local needs for supernatural power and authority that had allowed the Christian institution first to present itself in minimally attractive terms. They fulfilled that necessary role of traditional ritual expert, preparing amulets and uttering spells and invoking the "official" language of Christian liturgy as the new authority over the supernatural.

Certainly by the end of the fourth century there were ritual experts, "magicians," who were able to write a spell but who were not at all members of the Christian institution. Still, we cannot expect that these

[16] See above, 5.2.2, with El-Tom 1985 (Sudan) and A. Young 1975 and Mercier 1979 (Ethiopia).
[17] See above, 5.2.3 and 6.4.

ritual services had therefore become the exclusive domain of freelance "magicians." Monks and clerics continued to prepare amulets and consult ritual texts in their official capacities; and this official attention to everyday needs is most evident in the practices of Christian pilgrimage shrines.

As we saw in 4.4.3, these shrines operated according to highly traditional—one might even say archaic—ritual practices. In the year 484, for example, that particularly resilient temple of the goddess Isis in the town of Menouthis was converted to a shrine of Saints John and Cyrus. The Isis temple, we know from eyewitness sources, had long been a recourse for healing and for conception, blessings achieved through incubation in the shrine and consultation with a priest.

And so also did the John and Cyrus shrine advertise itself. One healing shrine simply superseded another. And we find pilgrimage centers throughout Egypt in which supplicants could sleep and receive dream-visions pertaining to health or other mundane concerns. Shenoute himself mentions "those who sleep in tombs to receive dreams and who question the dead about the living." People were flocking to sleep at the shrine of Apa Mena, west of Alexandria. Both supplicants and monks were putting great store in the instructions and revelations of dreams.[18] In this major context for religious pilgrimage, healing, we can see the Christian institution itself assuming native practice in a fairly wholesale manner.

Not only did Christian shrines take over the dream-incubation ritual; they also assumed the practice of delivering personal written oracles. The piles of oracle "tickets" from the Ptolemaic and Roman periods that provide such critical documentation of the temples' activities in the realms of justice, crisis resolution, and personal advice are beginning to be equalled by the collections of such tickets from the shrines of Saint Philoxenus in the Fayyum, Saint Colluthos in Antinoë, and others, requesting or rendering the saints' decisions on various mundane matters, all according to scribal formulations identical to those used in traditional temples.

What we have in all these cases—the services of the holy man, the power of the text, the "magical" services of the monks, and the healing and oracular practices of Christian pilgrimage shrines—is a continuing focus on the local, everyday need for supernatural power, so much so that even the very rituals for transmitting this power continue. Popular religion represents a virtual framework of necessity and accessibility. And for this framework Christianization presented a new idiom for supernatural power: a new authority, a new scheme, with new locations, to

---

[18] Shenoute, Discourses 8: "Those Who Work Evil," ed. Amélineau 1909:219–20, in Lefort 1954:230, with Emmel 1993:384, 637, 979–80). On Apa Mena, see Drescher 1946:xi, xx–xxi, 30–32, 64–65, 119, 123; and Grossman/Jaritz 1980, with archaeological light on the pilgrimage cult. In general, see MacCoull 1991.

be sure, but laid upon an indigenous, archaic, and surprisingly determin-
istic religious framework.

Nor could Christianization be absolute in this dimension of power. It
is in this context of Christian idiom that all the "crossovers," the syncre-
tisms, between Christian and native idioms occurred: the Horus-Christs,
the Christ-Re's, the Ankh-crosses, the saints and angels and Mary images, modeled explicitly upon local images of power that still dominated
the sensibilities of craftspeople, consumers, and supplicants, participants
in that endless search for effective cures and protections.[19]

So we begin to see the precise points on which local communities could
have abandoned their traditional religious forms—their authorities and
centers—and flocked to churches and saint shrines. They were not choosing an ideology, a definition of spirituality or morality, but an idiom: a
language, a map, a prosopography of power.[20]

From this point of collectively accepting a Christian scheme of supernatural power, a community will naturally undergo some change in self-
definition. But we will never really be able to grasp the mechanics or
character of this change as it would have played itself out among local
communities occupied with all manner of needs and crises. It is difficult
to posit, for example, that people embracing Christianity thereby felt
part of a larger cosmos of Christendom. A larger cosmos had already
been thrust upon Egypt, at almost every level and domain, with the beginning of Hellenism. Consequently for centuries the large proportion of
Egyptian communities had been negotiating the tension between the ecumenical and the local in issues of language, naming, and especially religion. On the other side, the Christian leaders, shrines, and practices for
which we have evidence were all highly localized: they did not necessarily
evoke a broad cosmos.[21]

[19] Among the most useful studies of these crossovers in Coptic Egypt are Michailides
1950; Jean Doresse, *Des hiéroglyphes à la croix* (Istanbul: Nederlands Historisch-
Archaeologisch Instituut, 1960); Krause 1983; Behlmer 1996b. On Horus-Christ or -saints,
see also Clermont-Ganneau 1876; Barb 1964:10–17. On late antique native/Christian
syntheses outside Egypt, see G. F. Hill, "Apollo and St. Michael: Some Analogies," *JHS* 36
(1916):134–62; Trombley 1985; Frankfurter 1990; Limberis 1994; and MacMullen 1997,
ch. 4.

[20] See MacMullen 1984:21–23, 40–41; Flint 1991; with comparative discussions by
White 1988:23–24 and, in general, J. Scott 1977:28. Schoffeleers 1994 notes that both
Christ and Christian pastors have been generally understood among many African peoples
as forms of ritual expert (in Bantu, *nganga*). Sabine MacCormack notes that "Christianization [in the sixteenth-century Andes] had amounted to a reorganization of space," although
that reorganization is itself kept in tension with local religion and at some points explicitly
rejected by the villagers (" 'The Heart Has Its Reasons': Predicaments of Missionary Christianity in Early Colonial Peru," *HAHR* 65 [1985]:459).

[21] See Ranger 1993:65–98 on the cross-cultural implications of a new religion's wider
cosmos for its popular appeal.

## 7.2 Demons

Abbot Shenoute has appeared throughout this study as an opponent of popular, traditional religious practices in fifth-century Egypt. Does he not point to a more ideological form of Christianity and Christianization? Given his perspective on native religion and his influence among monks and villagers, is it not apparent that Christianization did represent a deeper change in the popular understanding of the world and its powers?

Shenoute's sermons return repeatedly to the issue of the devil's power. Satan stands behind everything indigenous or heretical; but Shenoute argues the devil's fundamental impotence, his utter dependence upon human weakness and his eventual downfall. This point, meant to be reassuring, requires the audience's prior terror of demonic threat; and it caps an already pronounced tradition in Egyptian Christianity that put an obsessive focus on demons, their whereabouts, appearances, effects, and manner of exorcism. The best-known life of an Egyptian desert saint, the *Life of Antony,* gives far more attention to Antony's power over demons than to any other subject.[22] Other biographies of desert saints and monastic founders present their exorcistic powers as crucial to the saints' charisma. Even more, it is their ability to *recognize* demonic activity around them that is basic to these figures' popular authority. In such ways Egyptian Christian literature almost surpasses that of any other regional Christianity in its concern with demons.[23]

Holy men, the monks, the abbots, the bishops thus all become heroes of a dualistic universe presented in Egyptian Christian literature and preaching. And much of their deep appeal to local communities would

[22] See Norman H. Baynes, "St. Antony and the Demons," *JEA* 40 (1954):7–10, and on theological background, Jean Daniélou, "Les démons de l'air dans la 'Vie d'Antoine'," in *Antonius Magnus Eremetia 356–1956,* Studia Anselmiana 38, ed. by B. Steidle (Rome: Pontifical Institute of St. Anselm, 1956), 136–47. Samuel Rubenson notes a significant difference between the demonology of Athanasius's *Life of Antony* and that in Antony's own letters (1995:86–88, 139–40, with *Ep.* 6, pp. 216–24); yet both sources exhibit an overwhelming interest in demons.

[23] See A.-J. Festugière, *Les moines d'Orient,* vol. 1, *Culture ou sainteté* (Paris: Éditions du Cerf, 1961), ch. 1; Janet Ann Timbie, "Dualism and the Concept of Orthodoxy in the Thought of the Monks of Upper Egypt" (Ph.D. dissertation, University of Pennsylvania, 1979), 113–59; Jacques van der Vliet, "Demons in Early Coptic Monasticism: Image and Reality," in *Coptic Art and Culture,* ed. by H. Hondelink (Cairo: Shouhdy, 1990), 135–57, and idem, "Chénouté et les démons," in *Actes du IVᵉ congès copte* 2, ed. by M. Rassart-Debergh and J. Ries (Louvain: Institut orientaliste, 1992), 41–49. For the distinctively monastic development of an ascetic demonology, "mapping" the misfortunes one might encounter during ascetic concentration, see Richard Valantasis, "Demons and the Perfecting of the Monk's Body: Monastic Anthropology, Daemonology, and Asceticism," *Semeia* 58 (1992):47–79.

have required that these communities buy into that dualistic universe, that they accept a cosmos polarized with demons as an everyday reality: "By the life of the religion," promises the hero in a Coptic legend, "you will drive away the demons!"[24]

But how would they accept such a cosmos? They would do so in the course of embracing that very charisma of the Christian holy man, choosing him as the locus of supernatural power in the landscape, the arbiter of social tensions. The exorcisms and healings performed by the holy men had, then, a demonstrative role in explicating a new ideology. More than simply a compelling faucet for supernatural power, these Christian thaumaturges dramatized a cosmos in which they alone were pitted against a storm of evil beings. Their "charisma" lay precisely in their ability to gain the adherence of visitors not only to their own supernatural powers but also to the very cosmos in which those powers took on that particularly heroic sense.[25]

There is little doubt that the ancient world knew demonic powers of various sorts before Christianity arrived. And thus we are led to ask in the Egyptian case how much this polarizing ideology actually revolutionized Egyptian mentality and life. What was it in the life of Egyptians that became polarized? The absolutist ethical cast in Christian demonology always made it quite distinct among cultural mentalities, something difficult to reconcile with the ambiguities of local experience. And so the articulation of demonology on the part of the missionary was always an imposition from without and a distortion of experience and misfortune according to an ideology inherited from remote apocalyptic sects, in which life could be divided between the all-good and the all-evil. It is then what falls under this ideology that becomes highly important for analyzing the process of Christianization.

There is hardly a small culture on earth that does not spend its life in complex and dynamic interaction with a range of capricious spirits or powers capable of causing gross misfortune.[26] In Egypt of the Greco-Roman period we find a spate in the production of divine images, even a rise of protective deities, meant specifically to avert malevolent spirits.[27] Could this fact point to an increased concern at the local level for the malevolence of supernatural forces? For when local cultures begin to un-

---

[24] *Testament of Jacob,* tr. W. J. Stinespring, *OTP* 1:917. The speaker is the biblical patriarch Jacob on his deathbed; the text was composed before the ninth century C.E.

[25] On this aspect of charisma, see Geertz 1973:218–20 and Goody 1975:100. On the significance of exorcistic drama, see Brown 1975:25, 74–75 and MacMullen 1984:18–19, 27–29.

[26] See J. Scott 1977:22–25; White 1988:14, 23–24.

[27] See above, 3.4, and further: Moret 1915; Sauneron 1960b; Koenig 1994:100–129; Sternberg-El Hotabi 1994:242–44.

derstand themselves within a *supralocal* cosmos (such as Hellenism of-fered) they often find more value in gods capable of embracing that larger cosmos and correspondingly less value *and more threat* from the gods and spirits of the local environment.[28] Had the establishment of Hellenis-tic culture already created this increased fear of local spirits? And did Coptic demonology pick up on this theme to push it further? Indeed, the remarkable attribution of a (non-Christian) couple's divorce in the early fourth century to "a certain evil demon" seems to anticipate the identical etiology in a (probably Christian) sixth-century contract, as if the native religion had found a sense of distinctly evil demons before Christianity imposed it.[29]

It is an intriguing notion, but perhaps too easy. For even before the onset of the Hellenistic macrocosm Egyptian amulets already betrayed a marked sense of the dangers of the landscape: not only are there demons of disease, of terror, of unhappy dead, of scorpions, of lakes, but even the epiphanies of great gods, like Isis and Amun, are viewed as potentially dangerous. Far from reflecting some sort of cultural paranoia these an-cient amulets offer only a kind of baseline catalogue of all possible mis-fortunes, which is hardly surprising considering that amulets are in-tended to protect in the broadest possible manner.[30]

If we cannot conclude that there was already a "demonization" of local spirits in the centuries preceding Christianization, we can neverthe-less assume that the demonically polarized universe of Christianity en-gulfed precisely the spirits inhabiting the immediate environment of communities—spirits that had been alternately propitiated and averted since time immemorial. They all suddenly became uniformly evil with the embracing of the Christian cosmos.[31]

What is the attraction in all of this? When one's livelihood and social nexus are rooted in the local milieu and its particular layout of super-natural forces, for what possible reason would one demonize the lot? What is the conceivable practicality of a dualistic cosmos?

The attraction may well have been polarization itself. E. R. Dodds

[28] As Robin Horton noted in cases of African conversion ("African Conversion," *Africa* 41 [1971]:85–108, esp. 102).

[29] *P.Grenfell* II.76, 3–5; *P.Lond.* V.1713, 18–21.

[30] Edwards 1960. See also L. Keimer, "L'horreur des égyptiens pour les démons du désert," *BIE* 26 (1944):135–47; Meeks 1971:25–26, 45–49.

[31] Thus Birgit Meyer has described the demonization and polarization of the normative supernatural powers among the Ewe of Ghana: " 'If You are a Devil, You Are a Witch and, If You Are a Witch, You Are a Devil.' The Integration of 'Pagan' Ideas into the Conceptual Universe of Ewe Christians in Southeastern Ghana," *JRAf* 22 (1992):98–132, and "Beyond Syncretism: Translation and Diabolization in the Appropriation of Protestantism in Afri-ca," in *Syncretism/Anti-Syncretism: The Politics of Religious Synthesis,* ed. by C. Stewart and R. Shaw (London and New York: Routledge, 1994), 45–68.

once suggested that "in an age of anxiety any 'totalist' creed exerts a powerful attraction," and Ramsay MacMullen too felt that "the empire seemed positively to invite a sharply focused and intransigent creed." Indeed, Christianity in its various forms has often carried such an absolutist appeal into African cultures.[32]

It was not just the cultural disintegrations of third- and fourth-century Egypt that made Christian absolutism so appealing. No doubt the decline of the traditional religious infrastructure and the decentralization of society by the middle of the fourth century lent this "sharply focused and intransigent creed" an exhilarating newness, a certainty, especially coming as it did coupled with its own infrastructure of bishops and monasteries.[33] But the examples of twentieth-century African conversion show that people's attraction to polarization and absolutism does not merely or even usually depend on some prior religious crisis or cultural decadence or "anxiety." It is the absolutism itself that attracts. And thus also in fourth-century Egypt, what captured local religious imaginations was the abjectly polarized cosmos, an ideology of sweeping relevance. The demonology promoted by Christianization set all the capricious spirits of the village along one battle line, to be vanquished by some desert prophet and then kept at bay, hopefully, by the society of the churches and monasteries.

Indeed, one can see the very ritual process of repelling these forces for the Christian audience's behalf: verbal execrations. A third-century prophecy describes in performative "curse" style the demise of the Lawless One: "You are an enemy of the angels and Thrones," shout Enoch and Elijah, "You are always a stranger! You have fallen from heaven like the morning star. You changed (and your lineage) became dark to you! Are you not indeed ashamed, as you establish yourself against God—you, O Devil!" And then, this prophecy describes, "They will kill him without his being able to utter a word. In that time he will dissolve in their presence as ice dissolves in water. He will perish like a serpent with no breath in it. They will say to him, Your time has passed by! Now indeed you will perish with those who believe in you!" Shenoute's own apostrophic sermon against the devil renders the latter impotent through a kind of efficacious accusation: You are fundamentally impotent due to your dependence on illusory forms, Shenoute berates, and so you are nothing! As I label you, so you become for my audience. Christian liturgy thereby became a repeated drama of assault on and victory over a vividly monolithic enemy.[34]

---

[32] Dodds 1965:133–34; MacMullen 1984:16, 19. Fisher ascribes Islam's appeal in Africa to "the idea of an exclusive religious allegiance" (1985:165–66).

[33] Cf. Bagnall 1988.

[34] *Apocalypse of Elijah* 4.10–12; 5.32–34 (tr. Frankfurter 1993:317–18, 327–28);

But how resilient is such a polarized worldview in the realities and constraints of ordinary life? After all, Christianization did not mean joining a sectarian utopia, in which polarization reflects a lived social structure. What is distinctive about Egyptian Christianity's dualism, again, is that it served to "fix" supernatural forces and charismatic leadership in a polarity both cosmic and ethical. Spirits and religious leaders were either uniformly salvific or utterly evil. Traditional cultures, on the other hand, tend to view supernatural forces and people in more ambiguous terms: terms of greater or lesser power or greater or lesser danger. It is a question of negotiating the ambivalent, not cleaving to the absolute. What is practical, accessible; what can backfire; what always works; who can help; who to avoid; who should be consulted only in dire circumstances—these are the questions that people in local cultures return to inevitably.[35]

And in fact Christianity also began to allow this ambiguous approach to supernatural powers from at least the fourth century. Demons exorcised at martyrs' shrines, Bishop Athanasius complains in 370, had already become the objects of oracular consultation.[36] The religious system as lived resists polarization. And so also in the Christian saints and leaders who killed, cursed, or crafted amulets, in the magical spells that invoked esoteric angels, Egyptian Christianity assimilated a universe of ambiguous powers.

## 7.3 Rites of Demolition

But for some the ideology of saints versus demons was so captivating that it begged for action, for making some decisive change that would symbolize the change in the cosmos, for working that polarization into the landscape. Thus we arrive at the actual attacks on native religion—its temples, its sacred images, its priests: the most extreme form of Christianization. As Libanius of Antioch describes the rampages of monks during the 380s, their "black-robed tribes" would

hasten to attack the temples with sticks and stones and bars of iron. . . . Then utter desolation follows, with the stripping of roofs, demolition of walls, the tearing down of statues and the overthrow of altars, and the priests must either keep quiet or die. After demolishing one, they scurry to

---

Shenoute, "Sermon on the Devil" (ed. Pierre du Bourguet, "Diatribe de Chenouté contre le démon," *BSAC* 16 [1961/62]: 17–72). On the nature of Coptic liturgical cursing of the devil, see Frankfurter 1993:127–40.

[35] See, for example, C. Stewart 1991 and Walter E. A. van Beek, "The Innocent Sorcerer: Coping with Evil in Two African Societies," in Blakely et al. (eds.) 1994:196–228.

[36] Athanasius, Festal Letter 42 (370), ed. Lefort 1955:65–66.

another and to a third, and trophy is piled on trophy. Such outrages occur even in the cities, but they are most common in the countryside.[37]

By the end of the fourth century such militant destruction of native shrines and images had become epidemic around the Mediterranean world. By the middle of the fifth century monastic leaders like Shenoute, Makarios of Tkôw, and Moses of Abydos were gaining a modest fame for burning temples, killing priests, and invading homes to destroy private shrines. And indeed, the impetus for such havoc came not from Roman edicts against "paganism" but rather from the whims and machinations of bishops. It was a matter of charismatic leadership, mobilization, and systematic iconoclasm, occurring outside governmental direction.[38]

The main participants, both outsiders and insiders seem to agree, were monks—hardly surprising in that they led lives of somewhat greater application to that polarizing ideology than those outside the monasteries. And in many, perhaps most, aspects the active involvement of monks in the destruction of sacred things is understandable on these ideological grounds: in their rampages they were extirpating heathenism according to biblical precepts, waging a kind of Holy War, purifying the landscape for the presence of Christ. Perhaps too they were avenging those bygone martyrs, the lurid accounts of whose tortures were avidly read in the monasteries.[39]

But what specific factors impel a band of monks to enter villages at some remove from the monastery and burn down shrines and divine images, particularly if a good portion of those monks had shared the culture of the villagers in some fundamental ways? What factors led laypeople to join in the iconoclastic fervor? For these questions we have to think more seriously, more comparatively, about what it means to destroy religious objects, whether someone else's or one's own.

The comparative study of violence, destruction, and iconoclasm reveals an extensive vocabulary of destructive acts all distinctly meaningful to the actors' senses of identity and social change. In the religious wars of the Reformation, for example, the Protestants destroyed images while the Catholics killed Protestants: each located a cosmic impurity in a different point of the enemy's culture. In the Chinese cultural revolution one district ate its counter-revolutionaries. In 1930s Spain *milicianos* exhumed sacred corpses and dragged them outside churches. Large-scale, systematic rape was a crucial tactic in the Serbian war on Bosnian Muslim cul-

---

[37] Libanius, *Or.* 30.8–9, tr. Norman, LCL, 2:109.

[38] See Fowden 1978; MacMullen 1984:99–100 and 1997:51–53; Frend 1990; and esp. Brown 1995:49–51, who notes an important rhetorical element to Libanius's claims.

[39] The Abydos Osireion contains a Christian graffito of martyrs undergoing torture, suggesting that such images were often on the monks' minds (Piankoff 1958/60:134–37).

ture in the early 1990s.[40] And thus Peter Brown reconstructs the lynching of the Alexandrian philosopher Hypatia in 415 C.E.:

> A Christian mob, led by a lay reader and almost certainly reinforced by the dread *parabalani* of the patriarch, stoned her to death in the courtyard that opened up in front of a major church. Her body was hacked to pieces with shards of pottery, and what was left was burned in a public square. It was a deliberate act of total annihilation, a "cleansing" of the land, similar to that achieved through the burning of the statues of the gods. To supporters of [the bishop,] Cyril, Hypatia, the public-spirited philosopher, was the last of the idols.[41]

Violence and iconoclasm quite clearly involve a high degree of symbolism, of the ritual negation and creation of sacred order. Thus the Egyptians' destruction of their own sacred shrines and images as a symptom of Christianization begs for interpretation beyond simply ascribing it to a biblical fundamentalism.

One clear impetus to the destruction of shrines, images, and personnel of traditional cults was exorcism, the extirpation of demons and hostile powers. We have seen some, if incomplete, evidence that the Roman period might already have incurred a progressive "demonization" of local spirits—that the typical village might have felt an increased sense of danger in the landscape. For those like monks who were constantly subject to Christian demonology this supernatural danger became fixed not only to wells and deserts but to the sacred shrines as well. Thus one must eradicate the evil powers in the shrines.[42]

But how does one accomplish this in an enormous stone temple? Egyptian monks, supported increasingly by the large-scale military resources of the Roman authorities, chose a method as old as the pharaohs for handling the maleficent powers that dwelled in certain images. Lest a demonic snake portrayed on a wall escape, lest the spirit of a repudiated king dwell in the hieroglyphs of his name, Egyptians would quite literally erase all or part of the inscription—to render it impotent. This "apo-

---

[40] See Natalie Zemon Davis, "The Rites of Violence," *Society and Culture in Early Modern France* (Stanford, Calif.: Stanford University Press, 1975), 152–87, 315–26; Trexler 1980:118–28; Lincoln 1989:89–127; Lee Palmer Wandel, *Voracious Idols and Violent Hands: Iconoclasm in Reformation Zurich, Strasbourg, and Basel* (Cambridge: Cambridge University Press, 1995); and the more impressionistic analysis of Freedberg (1989:385–428). On China, see Liu Binyan, "An Unnatural Disaster," *New York Review of Books* (April 8, 1993):3–6. Note that I construe "iconoclasm" here in broader terms than simply opposition to iconographic representation itself.

[41] Brown 1992:116, based on Socrates, *H.E.* 7.15. Cf. Trexler's discussion of a similar episode in Renaissance Florence (1980:125–26).

[42] Brown 1995:5 notes the ideological significance of reconstructing past local conversions in terms of exorcism.

tropaic mutilation" could be done with immense precision, cutting the legs of a human- or bird-figure on the wall. In the third century priests in temples still benefiting from imperial munificence followed this tradition in chipping the cartouches of hated imperial precursors off the temple walls.[43] And thus we find in the fourth and later centuries that monks, the soldiers assisting them on scaffolds, and the bishops in charge paid particular attention to the faces of gods in their endeavors to neutralize temples.[44] Indeed, if one visits Egyptian temples today one finds scarcely a divinity that has not been meticulously hacked at. This kind of iconoclasm bears little connection to biblical stories of overturning altars of Baal. It is a pragmatic, traditional act that recognizes the abiding power in religious images and neutralizes that power for the safety of all. Safety itself becomes the paramount issue more than repudiation.

But the rationality of chipping off a god's face pales before the frenzy of a group of monks and villagers throwing wooden images onto a bonfire. What brings people to destroy the images that maintained the cycles of life over generations? The Protestant model of a postconversion rebirth would be anachronistic here: societies simply do not get "born again" and disregard their past in one fell swoop. The closest parallels to this wild destruction of one's own sacred objects have been documented in Pacific cultures following intimate colonial contact in the eighteenth and nineteenth centuries. In 1819 the traditional priests of Hawaii led the people in a mass destruction of traditional images and shrines after the royalty had embraced Christianity.[45] In the early twentieth century "cargo cults" arose throughout the Pacific islands: "In an orgy of destruction," describes one anthropologist, "the islanders themselves razed their temples, smashed their sacred structures and images."[46]

These examples begin to reveal the relationship between enthusiasm and the destruction of one's own icons, the idea that iconoclasm itself, the destruction of the sacred, can throw people into a state of frenzy. And that frenzy, that enthusiastic collective action, in itself functions at least

---

[43] See Pierre Lacau, "Suppressions et modifications des signes dans les textes funéraires," *ZÄS* 51 (1913):1–64; Ritner 1993:157, 164–65; and Sauneron 1952 on imperial names. On the broader appearance of the same mutilations, see Freedberg 1989:415–16 and Trexler 1980:118–28 on similar customs of execratory iconoclasm in Renaissance Florence.

[44] Nautin 1967:25–27. Cf. sources in MacMullen 1997:189n.68.

[45] See William Davenport, "The 'Hawaiian Cultural Revolution': Some Political and Economic Considerations," *American Anthropologist* 71 (1969):1–20.

[46] Kenelm Burridge, *New Heaven, New Earth: A Study of Millenarian Activities* (Oxford: Blackwell, 1980), 37; see also Goody 1991:1246–48. In seventh-century England the chief priest in the retinue of King Edwin of Northumbria took up military accoutrements hitherto profane to his office and led the demolition of his cult sanctuary (Bede, *History of the English Church* 2.14).

temporarily to inaugurate a new ideological order of things, a new cosmos. The symbolism of iconoclasm lies therefore not so much in the eventual replacement as in the immediate loosening of people's most vital connections to land, family, generations, society. The participants, the destroyers, thereby move as a body out of their quotidian lives, past the occasional effervescence and reversals of a festival, into a status that is vividly disconnected from the normal world, into what Victor Turner labeled "communitas" in its most radical form.[47]

Late antique Christianity often presented itself in hagiography as a religion of mass enthusiasm and solidarity—around saints, around relic translations, around charismatic bishops.[48] And there appears a persistent scenario in the sources whereby observers get swept up into enthusiastic participation after witnessing some dramatic act of destruction committed by a holy man or monk. "On beholding the objects of their former reverence and fear boldly cast down," says Sozomen about the destruction of holy sites in Constantinople, "the people were led to despise what they had previously venerated."[49] The same happens at the destruction of the Alexandrian Serapeum and then at a Serapeum in the nearby town of Canopus: people watch the actions of soldiers and monks and, in their experience of gross destruction, choose to engage in it even more.[50] Shenoute is actually hauled into court for plundering shrines and destroying images; but by these acts he apparently has galvanized a fair number of locals, for they start shouting "Jesus! Jesus!" at his arraignment.[51] And near the end of the fifth century iconoclastic strife again hits the region of Atripe, as a new generation of Christians, seeking to remove all traces of the old customs, antagonizes traditionalists, and a mélée ensues. This situation (and its modern African parallels), I would suggest, best explains the then-abbot's need to upbraid Christians "not to fight for nothing over a piece of wood"—that is, a mere idol.[52]

---

[47] Turner 1974:294–95; see also Jean Guiart, "The Millenarian Aspect of Conversion to Christianity in the South Pacific," in *Millennial Dreams in Action,* ed. by S. Thrupp (New York: Schocken, 1970), 122–38, and White 1988. Following a series of epidemics and cultural catastrophes in early-twentieth-century Nigeria, so J. D. Y. Peel has noted, several prophets appeared and "initiated a series of massive popular revivals, which caused wholesale conversion among large numbers of pagan farmers" ("Syncretism and Religious Change," *Comparative Studies in Society and History* 10 [1967/68]:130).

[48] See Brown 1981:93–105. These images are, of course, somewhat stylized in the hagiographical sources (see also Brown 1995:68–69, 73–77).

[49] Sozomen, *H.E.* 2.5.6, tr. Hartranft, *NPNF* 2:262.

[50] Eunapius, *V.P.* 472 = 6.10–11. On the instigation of the crowds, see esp. Thelamon 1981:255–57; Wipszycka 1988:142; Kákosy 1995:2938–39.

[51] "Only I Tell Everyone Who Dwells in this Village" (ed. Leipoldt #26), with Emmel 1993:891, on historical aspects of the event. Cf. MacMullen 1997:51–52, discussing Augustine of Hippo's iconoclastic demagoguery (*Ep. 50* and *Sermon 24.6*).

[52] Besa, "To the Dignitaries and People of the Village" 2 = Paris copte 1305, 127v, ed.

We have to recognize the "drama" in all of this: there is a destructive act of such public, symbolic force that people feel collectively enraged and enthused at the same time and choose to engage not in defense and "world reconstruction" but in further cosmic destruction. The destruction of the Serapeum itself is preceded by the exposure of sacred images from other shrines, caricatured in a highly ceremonial manner: the bishop "paraded around [*epompeue*] publicly with the objects of the Mithraeum's bloody mysteries. . . . He exposed them to laughter, ordering the (sacred) phalluses to be carried through the marketplace."[53] It is not that the images are thereby proven impotent, as the ancient apologists explained the effect of such performances, but that the most critically placed things are put out of place. The world is turned upside-down. And here the effect on the populace was telling. The initial exposure of sacred things incited a riot of anger against Christians, which allowed the bishop to call in military support. A portion of the anti-Christian mob retreated to the Serapeum; and it is then, when the soldiers attacked the Serapeum and its exterior images and Theophilus hauled out the sequestered images, that the mobs joined in the iconoclastic fray.

Christian leaders were evidently highly skilled at such negative dramaturgy. And immediately behind them stood not random passersby but Christian confraternities devoted to the leader's authority and primed to respond to his charismatic displays, who would gather, serve, chant, and riot by avocation. Whether in Alexandria or Panopolis, popular iconoclasm meant joining a pre-set mob.[54] But the *dramatistes* most inclined to make such public acts were the holy men and desert prophets. Well before the destruction of the Serapeum we find Apa Macedonius destroy-

---

Kuhn 1956, 1:129. On the interpretation of this dispute as an iconoclastic "purge" movement on the part of Christians, I am indebted both to Goody 1991 and to an unpublished paper by Mary Douglas, "The Problem of Evil among the Lele: Sorcery, Manicheeism, and Christian Teaching in Africa" (1987), developed in preliminary published form in "An Anthropology of the Afterlife" (Ingersoll Lecture), *Harvard Divinity Bulletin* 26, no. 4 (1997):20–23.

53 Socrates, *H.E.* 5.16 (*PG* 67:604). See Thelamon 1981:254–55. Jacques Schwartz ("La fin du Serapeum d'Alexandrie," in *Essays in Honor of C. Bradford Welles*, ASP 1 [New Haven, Conn.: American Society of Papyrologists, 1966], 97–111, esp. 109) has argued that this scene is invented as a doublet to events of 363 (Socrates, *H.E.* 3.2; cf. Sozomen, *H.E.* 5.7); but it is not unlikely that the events themselves were similar (both iconoclastic events trigger a mob response).

54 Lüddeckens 1968; Ewa Wipszycka, "Les confreries dans la vie religieuse de l'Égypte chrétienne," in *Proceedings of the Twelfth International Congress of Papyrology*, ASP 7, ed. by D. H. Samuel (Toronto: Hakkert, 1970), 511–25; and Ramsay MacMullen, "The Historical Role of the Masses in Late Antiquity," *Changes in the Roman Empire: Essays in the Ordinary* (Princeton, N.J.: Princeton University Press, 1990), 271–75. See also Bowersock 1986:312–14 and, for an early Roman witness to such confraternities, Philo, *In Flaccum* 135–37.

ing a sacred falcon statue at the temple of Philae and Apa Apollo of Hermopolis with a reputed commission from God to destroy all traces of native religion, who succeeds in inciting a village to burn its processional image. Apa Ammonius of Nitria, in Alexandria with a host of his brethren to oppose current religious policies (414 C.E.), instigates a riot by throwing a stone at the prefect (and subsequently earns for his own tattered corpse the name *thaumasios,* "miraculous one," aligning him with the martyrs of old).[55] Iconoclastic acts seem to have been part of the discourse of prophetic charisma during the fourth century.

But it was really the monks and their abbots who inspired the most drastic demolitions. And here the force of the drama came not from one prophet but a phalanx of "black-robes" already captivating to audiences by the intensity of their ideological conviction. The church historian Sozomen could not have been altogether exaggerating when he asserted that monks held ideological sway over the people.[56] A gang of monks could raze a local temple and its village, and assassinate the inhabitants as well, so the observer could only choose between traumatized passivity or an active leap into the strange, polarized world that the monks were enforcing on the landscape. It was not Christianity per se but the dramatic (and inevitable) force of the ideologically inspired that incited people to iconoclasm.

Let us return to Abbot Shenoute, christening his new chapel inside the Egyptian temple. His sermon captured at least two essential aspects of Christianization as it developed in late antique Egypt: the maintaining of sacred places, the demonization of traditional powers and their figural representations, and presumably iconoclasm itself—one assumes Shenoute's monks did their bit to "neutralize" the space beforehand. Shenoute's words *might* be taken as mirrors of contemporary Christian discourse and its retrospective sense of triumph over "paganism." But the dynamics of conversion in Egypt were internal, autochthonous phenomena, even forms of native religious revitalization.

Without a doubt Christianization brought a novel ideology, or ideologies; but was it ideology that distinguished the Christianity that resulted? We have seen numerous examples of custom, of local identity, of traditional expression, of the life-constituting practices of village society asserting themselves through or despite ideology. Christianity, like any ideal great tradition, was only realized in cultures through the appropriation of its idioms. In late antiquity, as in the sixteenth-century Americas

[55] Macedonius: Paphnutius, *Histories of the Monks of Upper Egypt,* 31 (tr. Vivian 1993:87). Apollo: *Historia Monachorum in Aegypto* 8.3, 24–29. Ammonius: Socrates, *H.E.* 7.14.

[56] Sozomen, *H.E.* 4.10.12; 6.20.5. See also Lüddeckens 1968:204–5.

and twentieth-century Africa, "conversion" was an idiosyncratic process that involved even at the highest levels a protracted scrambling for definition and ideological authority, but at the local level the assimilation of an ideology (whether seductive or forced) to the realities of success, hierarchy, disease, harvest, and population. As Christian demons and saints became oracles in the Egyptian mold, so it is not so unimaginable, as a late-fourth-century Alexandrian author asserted satirically, that "those who worship Serapis are, in fact, Christians, and those who call themselves bishops of Christ are, in fact, devotees of Serapis."[57] After the initial violence, after the shift in mapping demonic powers, Christianity settled back to function as an idiom for supernatural authority. And that, we may conclude, speaks to the resilience, indeed the triumph, of local culture.

[57] *Scriptores Historia Augustae:* Vopiscus, *Vita Saturnini* 8, tr. Magie, LCL, 3:399. Important discussions of these assertions include Wolfgang Schmid, "Die Koexistenz von Sarapiskult und Christentum im Hadrianbrief bei Vopiscus," *Bonner Historia-Augusta-Colloquium 1964/65* (1966):153–84, and Reinhold Merkelback, "Astrologie, Mechanik, Alchimie und Magie im griechish-römischen Ägypten," *Begegnung von Heidentum und Christentum im spätantiken Ägypten*, Riggisberger Berichte 1 (Riggisberg: Abegg-Stiftung, 1993), 56–59. Scholars commonly point to a fifth-century legend that crosslike *ankh*s were found inscribed on the interior walls of the Serapeum and were in their time taken as proof of the common basis of Christianity and the Serapis cult: Rufinus, *H.E.* 11.29; Socrates, *H.E.* 5.17; Sozomen, *H.E.* 7.15.10; with useful remarks by Thelamon 1981:267–73.

# SELECT BIBLIOGRAPHY

*Note:* Sources appearing here are cited more than once in the notes; all others receive full entries in the notes.

Adriani, Achille 1933/35 "La nécropole de Moustafa Pacha." *Annuaire du Musée Gréco-Romain* 2:1–189.

———. 1935/39 "Sanctuaire de l'époque romaine à Ras el Soda." *Annuaire du Musée Gréco-Romain* 3:136–48, pls. I, L–LIX.

Aly, Azza Shaaban 1987 "Eight Greek Oracular Questions in the West Berlin Collection." *ZPE* 68:99–104.

Amélineau, Émile 1888/95 *Monuments pour servir à l'histoire de l'Égypte chrétienne aux IVᵉ et Vᵉ siècles.* Mémoires publiés par les membres de la mission archéologique française au Caire 4. Paris: Leroux.

———. 1909 *Oeuvres de Schenoudi,* vol. 1. Paris: Leroux.

Assmann, Jan 1978 "Eine Traumoffenbarung der Göttin Hathor: Zeugnisse 'Persönlicher Frömmigkeit' in thebanischen Privatgräbern der Ramessidenzeit." *RdÉ* 30:22–50.

———. 1983 "Königsdogma und Heilserwartung. Politische und kultische Chaosbeschreibung in ägyptischen Texten." In *Apocalypticism in the Mediterranean World and the Near East,* pp. 345–77. Ed. by David Hellholm. Tübingen: Mohr (Siebeck).

Athanassiadi, Polymnia 1993a "Persecution and Response in Late Paganism: The Evidence of Damascius." *JHS* 113:1–29.

———. 1993b "Dreams, Theurgy and Freelance Divination: The Testimony of Iamblichus." *JRS* 83:115–30.

Aubert, Jean-Jacques 1989 "Threatened Wombs: Aspects of Ancient Uterine Magic." *GRBS* 30:421–49.

Bagnall, Roger 1988 "Combat ou vide: christianisme et paganisme dans l'Égypte romaine tardive." *Ktema* 13:285–96.

———. 1993 *Egypt in Late Antiquity.* Princeton, N.J.: Princeton University Press.

Baines, John 1983 "Literacy and Ancient Egyptian Society." *Man* 18:572–99.

———. 1987 "Practical Religion and Piety." *JEA* 73:79–98.

———. 1991 "Society, Morality, and Religious Practice." In Shafer (ed.) 1991:123–200.

Ballet, Pascale, and Mahmoud, Fatma 1987 "Moules en terre cuite d'Éléphantine (Musée copte): Nouvelles données sur les ateliers de la région d'Assouan, à l'époque byzantine et aux premiers temps de l'occupation arabe." *BIFAO* 87:53–72, pls. IX–XIV.

Barb, A. A. 1964 "Three Elusive Amulets." *Journal of the Warburg and Courtauld Institutes* 27:1–22.

Barnes, T. D. 1987 "Christians and Pagans in the Reign of Constantius." In *L'Église et l'empire au IVᵉ siècle*. Entretiens sur l'antiquité classique 34, pp. 301–37. Ed. by Albrecht Dihle. Geneva: Vandoeuvres.

Barns, John Wintour Baldwin 1949 "The Nevill Papyrus: A Late Ramesside Letter to an Oracle." *JEA* 35:69–71, pl. VI.

———. 1956 "Egypt and the Greek Romance." *Mitteilungen aus der Papyrussammlung der österreichischen Nationalbibliothek* 5:29–36.

———. 1964 "Shenute as a Historical Source." In *Actes du Xᵉ congrès international de papyrologues*, pp. 151–59. Ed. by Józef Wolski. Wroclaw/Warsaw/Cracow: Polish Academy.

Bataille, André 1951 *Les inscriptions grecques du temple de Hatshepsout à Deir el-Bahari*. Textes et documents 10. Cairo: IFAO.

———. 1952 *Les memnonia: Recherches de papyrologie et d'épigraphie grecques sur la nécropole de la Thèbes d'Égypte aux époques hellénistique et romaine*. Cairo: IFAO.

Baumeister, Theofried 1972 *Martyr Invictus: Der Martyrer als Sinnbild der Erlösung in der Legende und im Kult der frühen koptischen Kirche*. Forschungen zur Volkskunde 46. Münster: Regensberg.

Beard, Mary 1991 "Writing and Religion: Ancient Literacy and the Function of the Written Word in Roman Religion." In *Literacy in the Roman World*. JRA Supp. 3, pp. 35–58. Ann Arbor, Mich.: JRA.

Beaujeu, Jean 1976 "Cultes locaux et cultes d'empire dans les provinces d'Occident aux trois premiers siècles de notre ère." In *Assimilation et résistance à la culture gréco-romaine dans le monde ancien: Travaux du VIᵉ Congrès international d'Études classiques*, pp. 433–43. Ed. by D. M. Pippidi. Bucharest: Academiei; Paris: Les Belles Lettres.

Behlmer, Heike 1993 "Historical Evidence from Shenoute's *De extremo iudicio*." In *Sesto Congresso internazionale di Egittologia: Atti*, vol. 2, pp. 11–19. Turin: Società Italiana per il Gas p.A.

———. 1996a *Schenute von Atripe: De iudicio (Turin, Museo Egizio, Cat. 63000, cod. IV)*. Turin: Museo Egizio.

———. 1996b "Ancient Egyptian Survivals in Coptic Literature: An Overview." In Loprieno (ed.) 1996:567–90.

Beidelman, T. O. 1971 "Nuer Priests and Prophets: Charisma, Authority, and Power among the Nuer." In *The Translation of Culture: Essays to E. E. Evans-Pritchard*, pp. 375–415. Ed. by T. O. Beidelman. London: Tavistock.

Bell, David N. 1983 *Besa: The Life of Shenoute*. CSS 73. Kalamazoo, Mich.: Cistercian Publications.

Bell, Harold Idris 1953 *Cults and Creeds in Graeco-Roman Egypt*. Liverpool: University of Liverpool Press; repr. Chicago: Ares, 1975.

Beltz, Walter 1983 "Die koptischen Zauberpapyri der Papyrus-Sammlung der Staatlichen Museen zu Berlin." *Archiv* 29:59–86.

Bernand, André 1970 *Le delta égyptien d'après les textes grecs*, vol. 1, *Les confins libyques*. MIFAO 91. Cairo: IFAO.

Bernand, Étienne 1969a *Inscriptions métriques de l'Égypte gréco-romaine*. Annales littéraires de l'université de Besançon 98. Paris: Les Belles Lettres.

———. 1969b  *Les inscriptions grecques et latines de Philae.* 2 vols. Paris: CNRS.

———. 1975  *Recueil des inscriptions grecques du Fayoum,* vol. 1. Leiden: Brill.

———. 1981  *Recueil des inscriptions grecques du Fayoum,* vols. 2–3. Bibliothèque d'étude 79–80. Cairo: IFAO.

———. 1984  "Epigraphie grecque et architecture égyptienne à l'époque imperiale." In *Hommages à Lucien Lerat,* vol. 1. Centre de recherches d'histoire ancienne 55, pp. 73–89. Ed. by Hélène Walter. Paris: Les Belles Lettres.

———. 1988  *Inscriptions grecques et latines d'Akôris.* Bibliothèque d'étude 103. Cairo: IFAO.

———. 1992  *Inscriptions grecques d'Égypte et de Nubie au Musée du Louvre.* Paris: CNRS.

Bertrand, Jean-Marie 1988  "Les boucôloi ou le monde à l'envers." *Revue des études anciennes* 90:139–49.

Betz, Hans Dieter (ed.) 1986  *The Greek Magical Papyri in Translation, Including the Demotic Spells,* vol. 1. Chicago: University of Chicago Press.

Blackman, Aylward M. 1925  "Oracles in Ancient Egypt." *JEA* 11:249–55.

———. 1926  "Oracles in Ancient Egypt." *JEA* 12:176–85.

Blackman, Winifred 1927  *The Fellahin of Upper Egypt.* London: Harrap.

Blakely, Thomas D.; Van Beek, Walter E. A.; and Thomson, Dennis L. (eds.) 1994  *Religion in Africa: Experience and Expression.* London: James Currey; Portsmouth, N.H.: Heinemann.

Blockley, R. C. 1981/82  *The Fragmentary Classicising Historians of the Later Roman Empire.* 2 vols. Liverpool: Cairns.

Boak, Arthur E. R. (ed.) 1933  *Karanis: The Temples, Coin Hoards, Botanical and Zoölogical Reports, Seasons 1924–31.* Ann Arbor: University of Michigan Press.

Bonneau, Danielle 1964  *La crue du Nil, divinité égyptienne, à travers mille ans d'histoire.* Études et commentaires 52. Paris: Klincksieck.

———. 1971  "Les fêtes de la crue du nil: Problèmes de lieux, de dates et d'organisation." *RdÉ* 23:49–65.

———. 1974  "Les fêtes Amesysia." *CdÉ* 49:366–79.

———. 1984/85  "Les fêtes Amesysia et les jours épagomènes (d'après la documentation papyrologique et égyptologique)." *ASAE* 70:365–70.

———. 1995  "La divinité du Nil sous le principat en Égypte." *ANRW* II.18.5:3195–3215.

Borghouts, J. F. 1971  *The Magical Texts of Papyrus Leiden I 348.* OMRO 51. Leiden: Brill.

———. 1978  *Ancient Egyptian Magical Texts.* Nisaba 9. Leiden: Brill.

Borkowski, Zbigniew 1975  *Une description topographique des immeubles à Panopolis.* Warsaw: Panstwowe Wydawnictwo Naukowe.

———. 1990  "Local Cults and Resistance to Christianity." *JJP* 20:25–30.

Bowersock, Glen W. 1984  "The Miracle of Memnon." *BASP* 21:21–32.

———. 1986  "The Mechanics of Subversion in the Roman Provinces." In *Opposition et résistances à l'empire d'Auguste à Trajan.* Entretiens sur l'antiquité classique 33, pp. 291–317 + discussion, pp. 318–20. Geneva: Vandoeuvres.

―――. 1990　*Hellenism in Late Antiquity*. Ann Arbor: University of Michigan Press.

―――. 1994　*Fiction as History: Nero to Julian*. Sather Classical Lectures 58. Berkeley: University of California Press.

Bradbury, Scott 1994　"Constantine and the Problem of Anti-Pagan Legislation in the Fourth Century." *CP* 89:120–39.

Brakke, David 1994　"Canon Formation and Social Conflict in Fourth-Century Egypt: Athanasius of Alexandria's Thirty-Ninth *Festal Letter*." *HTR* 87:395–419.

Breccia, E. 1930/34　*Terrecotte figurate greche e greco-egizie del museo di Alessandria*. 2 vols. Monuments de l'Égypte gréco-romaine 2. Bergamo: Istituto Italiano d'Arti Grafiche.

Bresciani, Edda 1975　*L'Archivo demotico del tempio di Soknopaiu Nesos nel Griffith Institute di Oxford*. Milan: Cisalpino-La Goliardica.

Brovarski, Edward 1984　"Sobek." *LexÄg* 5:995–1031.

Brown, Peter 1975　*The Making of Late Antiquity*. Cambridge, Mass.: Harvard University Press.

―――. 1981　*The Cult of the Saints: Its Rise and Function in Latin Christianity*. Chicago: University of Chicago Press.

―――. 1982　"The Rise and Function of the Holy Man in Late Antiquity." In Peter Brown, *Society and the Holy in Late Antiquity,* pp. 103–52. London: Faber & Faber.

―――. 1992　*Power and Persuasion in Late Antiquity: Towards a Christian Empire*. Madison: University of Wisconsin Press.

―――. 1995　*Authority and the Sacred: Aspects of the Christianisation of the Roman World*. Cambridge: Cambridge University Press.

Browne, Gerald M. 1974　*The Papyri of the Sortes Astrampsychi*. Beiträge zur klassischen Philologie 58. Meisenheim: Hain.

―――. 1977　"Harpocration Panegyrista." *ICS* 2:184–96.

―――. 1983　*Sortes Astrampsychi* 1. Leipzig: Teubner.

―――. 1987　"The Sortes Astrampsychi and the Egyptian Oracle." *Texte und Textkritik: Eine Aufsatzsammlung*. TU 133, pp. 67–71. Ed. by Jürgen Dummer. Berlin: Akademie.

Bruyère, Bernand 1939　*Rapport sur les fouilles de Deir El Médineh*, pt. III, *Le village, les décharges publiques, la station de repos du col de la vallée des rois*. Fouilles de l'IFAO 16. Cairo: IFAO.

Budge, E. A. Wallis 1915　*Miscellaneous Coptic Texts in the Dialect of Upper Egypt*. Coptic Texts 5. London: British Museum; repr. New York: AMS, 1977.

Burkhardt, Adelheid 1984　"Zu späten heidnischen Priestern in Philae." In Nagel (ed.) 1984:77–83.

Cameron, Alan 1965　"Wandering Poets: A Literary Movement in Byzantine Egypt." *Historia* 14:470–509.

Cameron, Averil 1993　*The Mediterranean World in Late Antiquity, AD 395–600*. London and New York: Routledge.

Castiglione, Ladislas 1957　"Greichisch-ägyptische Studien: Beitrag zu dem griechisch-ägyptischen Privatkult." *Acta antiqua hungaricae* 5:220–27.

―――. 1970　"Diocletianus und die Blemmyes." *ZÄS* 96:90–102.

Černý, Jaroslav 1935 "Questions adressées aux oracles." *BIFAO* 35:41–58.
———. 1941 "Le tirage au sort." *BIFAO* 40:135–41.
———. 1962 "Egyptian Oracles." In Parker 1962:35–48.
Christian, William A., Jr. 1981 *Local Religion in Sixteenth-Century Spain.* Princeton, N.J.: Princeton University Press.
Chuvin, Pierre 1990 *A Chronicle of the Last Pagans.* Revealing Antiquity 4. Cambridge, Mass.: Harvard University Press.
Clarysse, Willy 1984 "Bilingual Texts and Collaboration between Demoticists and Papyrologists." In *Atti del XVII Congresso internazionale di Papirologia,* vol. 3, pp. 1345–53. Naples: CISP.
Clermont-Ganneau, Charles 1876 "Horus et Saint Georges." *Revue archéologique* n.s. 32:196–204, 372–99.
Coles, Revel A. 1967 "More Papyri from the British Museum." *JEA* 63:121–30 + pl. XVII.
Colson, Elizabeth 1977 "A Continuing Dialogue: Prophets and Local Shrines among the Tonga of Zambia." In Werbner (ed.) 1977:119–40.
Coquin, René-Georges 1972 "La christianisation des temples de Karnak." *BIFAO* 72:169–78.
———. 1986 "Moïse d'Abydos." *Deuxième journée d'études coptes, Strasbourg 25 mai 1984.* Cahiers de la bibliothèque copte 3, pp. 1–14. Louvain: Peeters.
Creel, Margaret Washington 1988 *"A Peculiar People": Slave Religion and Community-Culture among the Gullahs.* New York and London: New York University Press.
Crum, W. E. 1939 *A Coptic Dictionary.* Oxford: Clarendon.
Daressy, M. G. 1903 *Textes et dessins magiques.* Catalogue général des antiquités égyptiennes du Musée du Caire, nos. 9401–9449. Cairo: IFAO.
Dasen, Véronique 1993 *Dwarfs in Ancient Egypt and Greece.* Oxford: Clarendon.
Daumas, François 1957 "Le sanatorium de Dendara." *BIFAO* 56:35–57, pls. I-XIV.
———. 1958 *Les mammisis des temples égyptiens.* Annales de l'université de Lyon, ser. 3, Lettres 32. Paris: Les Belles Lettres.
———. 1961 "Littérature prophétique et exégétique égyptienne et commentaires esséniens." In *A la rencontre de Dieu (Mémorial Albert Gelin).* Bibliothèque de la faculté catholique de théologie de Lyon 8, pp. 203–21. Le Puy: Mappus.
———. 1969 *Dendara et le temple d'Hathor.* Cairo: IFAO.
D'Auria, Sue; Lacovara, Peter; and Roehrig, Catharine H.
———. 1992 *Mummies and Magic: The Funerary Arts of Ancient Egypt.* 2nd ed. Dallas: Museum of Art.
Dawes, Elisabeth, and Baynes, Norman H. 1977 *Three Byzantine Saints.* Crestwood, N.Y.: St. Vladimir's Seminary.
De Cenival, Françoise 1987 "Le Papyrus Dodgson (P. Ashmolean Museum Oxford 1932–1159): Une interrogation aux portes des dieux?" *RdÉ* 38:3–11.
De Nie, H. 1942 "Een koptisch-christelijke Orakelvraag." *Jaarbericht van het voorazÍatisch-egyptisch Gezelschap: Ex Oriente Lux* 8:615–18.

De Salvia, Fulvio 1987 "La Figura del Mago Egizio nella Tradizione Letteraria Greco-Romana." In Roccati and Siliotti (eds.) 1987:343–65.

De Vis, Henri 1990 *Homélies coptes de la Vaticane*. 2 vols. Cahiers de la Bibliothèque copte 5–6. Louvain: Peeters.

Deiber, Albert 1904 *Clément d'Alexandrie et l'Égypte*. MIFAO 10. Cairo: IFAO.

Delatte, A., and Derchain, Philippe 1964 *Les intailles magiques gréco-égyptiennes*. Paris: Bibliothèque nationale.

Derchain, Philippe 1963 "Pseudo-Jamblique ou Abammôn?" *CdÉ* 76:220–26.

———. 1965 *Le papyrus Salt 825 (B.M. 10051): Rituel pou la conservation de la vie en Égypte*. Mémoires de l'Académie royale de Belgique 58, 1. Brussels: Palace of the Academies.

Derda, Tomasz 1991 "Necropolis Workers in Graeco-Roman Egypt in the Light of the Greek Papyri." *JJP* 21:13–36.

Desroches Noblecourt, Christiane 1985 "Les zélateurs de Mandoulis et les maîtres de Ballana et de Qustul." In *Mélanges Gamal Eddin Mokhtar*, vol. 1, pp. 199–218. Ed. by Paule Posener-Kriéger. Cairo: IFAO.

Dodds, E. R. 1965 *Pagan and Christian in an Age of Anxiety*. New York: Norton.

Douglas, Mary (ed.) 1970 *Witchcraft Confessions and Accusations*. ASA Monographs 9. London: Tavistock.

Drescher, James 1946 *Apa Mena: A Selection of Coptic Texts Relating to St. Menas*. Cairo: Société d'archéologie copte.

Duchesne, L. 1910 "Le sanctuaire d'Aboukir." *BSAA* 12:3–14.

Dunand, Françoise 1976 "Lanternes gréco-romaines d'Égypte." In *Dialogues d'histoire ancienne 1976*. Annales littéraires de l'Université de Besançon 188, pp. 71–95 + pls. I–XVI. Paris: Les Belles Lettres.

———. 1977 "L'Oracle du Potier et la formation de l'apocalyptique en Égypte." In *L'Apocalyptique*. Études de l'histoire des religions 3, pp. 41–67. Ed. by Marc Philonenko. Paris: Geuthner.

———. 1978 "Le statut des *hiereiai* en Égypte romaine." In *Hommages à Maarten J. Vermaseren*, vol. 1, pp. 352–74. EPRO 68. Ed. by Margreet B. de Boer and T. A. Edridge. Leiden: Brill.

———. 1979 *Religion populaire en Égypte romaine*. EPRO 77. Leiden: Brill.

———. 1981 "Le petit Serapieion romain de Louqsor, III. Le culte au Sarapieion de Louqsor." *BIFAO* 81:135–48.

———. 1982 "Les 'têtes dorées' de la nécropole de Douch." *BSFE* 93:26–46.

———. 1984 "Religion populaire et iconographie en Égypte hellénistique et romaine." *Visible Religion* 3:18–42.

———. 1985 "Les nécrotaphes de Kysis." *Cahier de recherches de l'Institut de papyrologie et d'égyptologie de Lille* 7:117–27.

———. 1990 *Catalogue des terres cuites gréco-romaines d'Égypte*. Paris: Réunion des musées nationaux.

———. 1991a "Miracles et guérisons en Égypte tardive." In *Mélanges Étienne Bernand*, pp. 235–50. Ed. by Nicole Fick and Jean-Claude Carrière. Paris: Les Belles Lettres.

———. 1991b "L'Égypte ptolémaïque et romaine." In Françoise Dunand and

Christiane Zivie-Coche, Ḏieux et hommes en Égypte, 3000 av. J.-C. [-] 395 apr. J.C.: Anthropologie religieuse, pp. 199–329. Paris: Colin.

———. 1992 "Pratiques funéraires." In La nécropole. Douch 1, pp. 247–66. Cairo: IFAO.

———. 1997 "La consultation oraculaire en Égypte tardive: l'Oracle de Bès à Abydos." In Heintz (ed.) 1997:65–84.

Eddy, Samuel K. 1961 The King Is Dead: Studies in the Near Eastern Resistance to Hellenism, 334–31 B.C. Lincoln: University of Nebraska Press.

Edwards, I. E. S. 1960 Oracular Amuletic Decrees of the Late New Kingdom. 2 vols. Hieratic Papyri in the British Museum 4. London: British Museum.

El-Tom, Abdullahi Osman 1985 "Drinking the Koran: The Meaning of Koranic Verses in Berti Erasure." In 'Popular Islam' South of the Sahara (Africa 55, 4), pp. 414–31. Ed. by J. D. Y. Peel and C. C. Stewart. Manchester: Manchester University Press.

Emmel, Stephen Lewis 1993 "Shenoute's Literary Corpus." Ph.D. dissertation, Yale University.

———. 1994 "Ithyphallic Gods and Undetected Ligatures: Pan Is Not 'Ours,' He Is Min (Rectification of a Misreading in a Work of Shenute)." GM 141:43–46.

Evans, J. A. S. 1961 "A Social and Economic History of an Egyptian Temple in the Greco-Roman Period." YCS 17:143–283.

Fairman, H. W. 1954 "Worship and Festivals in an Egyptian Temple." BJRL 37:165–203.

Fakhry, Ahmed 1944 Siwa Oasis: Its History and Antiquities. Cairo: Government Press.

Festugière, A.-J. 1939 "L'expérience religieuse du médecin Thessalos." Revue Biblique 48:45–77.

———. 1950 La révélation d'Hermès Trismégiste. 3 vols. 2nd ed. Paris: Les Belles Lettres.

———. 1971 Historia Monachorum in Aegypto: Édition critique du texte grec et traduction annotée. Subsidia Hagiographica 53. Brussels: Société des Bollandistes.

Feuchtwang, Stephan 1974 "Domestic and Communal Worship in Taiwan." In Religion and Ritual in Chinese Society, pp. 105–29. Ed. by Arthur P. Wolf. Stanford, Calif.: Stanford University Press.

Fisher, Humphrey J. 1985 "The Juggernaut's Apologia: Conversion to Islam in Black Africa." Africa 55:153–73.

Flint, Valerie I. J. 1991 The Rise of Magic in Early Medieval Europe. Princeton, N.J.: Princeton University Press.

Fögen, Marie Theres 1993 Die Enteignung der Wahrsager: Studien zum kaiserlichen Wissensmonopol in der Spätantike. Frankfurt: Suhrkamp.

Fowden, Garth 1978 "Bishops and Temples in the Eastern Roman Empire, A. D. 320–435." JTS 29:53–78.

———. 1982 "The Pagan Holy Man in Late Antique Society." JHS 102:33–59.

———. 1986 The Egyptian Hermes: An Historical Approach to the Late Pagan Mind. Cambridge: Cambridge University Press.

Frankfurter, David 1990 "Stylites and Phallobates: Pillar Religions in Late Antique Syria." VigChr 44:168–98.

————. 1992   "Lest Egypt's City Be Deserted: Religion and Ideology in the Egyptian Response to the Jewish Revolt (116–117 C.E.)." *JJS* 43:203–20.

————. 1993   *Elijah in Upper Egypt: The Apocalypse of Elijah and Early Egyptian Christianity.* Minneapolis, Minn.: Fortress.

————. 1994a   "The Cult of the Martyrs in Egypt before Constantine: The Evidence of the Coptic *Apocalypse of Elijah.*" *VigChr* 48:25–47.

————. 1994b   "The Magic of Writing and the Writing of Magic: The Power of the Word in Egyptian and Greek Traditions." *Helios* 21:189–221.

Freedberg, David 1989   *The Power of Images.* Chicago and London: University of Chicago Press.

Frend, W. H. C. 1990   "Monks and the End of Greco-Roman Paganism in Syria and Egypt." *Cristianesimo nella Storia* 11:469–84.

Friederich, Hans-Veit 1968   *Thessalos von Tralles.* Beiträge zur klassischen Philologie 28. Meisenheim: Hain.

Froidefond, Christian 1971   *Le mirage égyptien dans la littérature grecque d'Homère à Aristote.* Paris: University of Paris.

Gallo, Paolo 1992   "The Wandering Personnel of the Temple of Narmuthis in the Faiyum and Some Toponyms of the Meris of Polemon." In J. Johnson (ed.) 1992:119–31.

Garbett, Kingsley 1977   "Regional and Non-Regional Alternatives: The Waxing and Waning of Cults." In Werbner (ed.) 1977:55–92.

Gazda, Elaine K. 1978   *Guardians of the Nile: Sculptures from Karanis in the Fayoum (c. 250 BC–AD 450).* Ann Arbor, Mich.: Kelsey Museum of Archaeology.

————. 1983   (ed.) *Karanis: An Egyptian Town in Roman Times.* Ann Arbor, Mich.: Kelsey Museum of Archaeology.

✓ Geertz, Clifford 1973   "Ideology as a Cultural System." In idem, *The Interpretation of Cultures,* pp. 193–233. New York: Basic.

Geffcken, Johannes 1978   *The Last Days of Greco-Roman Paganism.* Tr. by Sabine MacCormack. Europe in the Middle Ages, Selected Studies 8. Amsterdam: North-Holland.

Gilliam, Elizabeth H. 1947   "The Archives of the Temple of Soknobraisis at Bacchias." *YCS* 10:181–281.

Glare, Penelope 1993   "The Temples of Egypt: The Impact of Rome." Ph.D. dissertation, Cambridge University.

Golvin, Jean-Claude, and 'Abd el-Hamid, Sayyed 1981   "Le petit Sarapieion romain de Louqsor, I. Étude architecturale." *BIFAO* 81:115–28.

Goody, Jack 1975   "Religion, Social Change and the Sociology of Conversion." In *Changing Social Structure in Ghana,* pp. 91–106. Ed. by Jack Goody. London: International African Institute.

————. 1991   "Icônes et iconoclasme en Afrique." *Annales ESC* 46:1235–51.

Goyon, Jean-Claude 1981   "L'Eau dans la médecine pharaonique et copte." In *L'homme et l'eau en Méditerranée et au proche orient,* vol. 1, pp. 143–50. Travaux de la Maison de l'Orient 2. Lyon: GIS—Maison de l'Orient.

Gregory, Timothy E. 1986   "The Survival of Paganism in Christian Greece: A Critical Essay." *AJP* 107:229–42.

Grenier, Jean-Claude 1978   "L'Anubis cavalier du Musée du Louvre." In *Hommages à Maarten J. Vermaseren,* vol. 1, pp. 405–8. EPRO 68. Ed. by Margreet B. de Boer and T. A. Edridge. Leiden: Brill.

———. 1983   "La stèle funéraire du dernier taureau Bouchis." *BIFAO* 83:197–208, pl. XLI.

———. 1988   "Notes sur l'Égypte romaine (I, 1–7)." *CdÉ* 63:57–76.

Griffith, F. Ll. 1900   "The Old Coptic Magical Texts of Paris." *ZÄS* 38:85–93.

———. 1909   "Papyrus Dodgson." *PSBA* 31:100–109.

———. 1937   *Catalogue of the Demotic Graffiti of the Dodecaschoenus,* vol. 1. Oxford: Oxford University Press/Service des antiquités de l'Égypte.

Griffith, F. Ll., and Thompson, Herbert 1904   *The Demotic Magical Papyrus of London and Leiden,* vol. 1. London: Grevel. Repr.: *The Leyden Papyrus: An Egyptian Magical Book.* New York: Dover, 1974.

———. 1905   *The Demotic Magical Papyrus of London and Leiden,* vol. 2. London: Grevel. Repr.: Milan: Cisalpino-La Goliardica, 1976.

Griffiths, John Gwyn 1970   *Plutarch: De Iside et Osiride.* Cardiff: University of Wales Press.

———. 1975   *Apuleius of Madauros: The Isis-Book (Metamorphoses, Book XI).* EPRO 39. Leiden: Brill.

Griggs, C. Wilfred 1990   *Early Egyptian Christianity: From Its Origins to 451 CE.* Coptic Studies 2. Leiden: Brill.

Grossmann, Peter, and Jaritz, Horst 1980   "Abu Mina: Neunter vorläufiger Bericht. Kapagnen 1977, 1978, und 1979." *MDAIK* 36:203–27.

Guéraud, Octave 1935   "Notes gréco-romaines, I. Le monument d'AGRIOS." *ASAE* 35:1–24 + pls. 1–2.

Hamilton, Walter (tr.) 1986   *Ammianus Marcellinus: The Later Roman Empire (A.D. 354–378).* Harmondsworth: Penguin.

Harl, K. W. 1990   "Sacrifice and Pagan Belief in Fifth- and Sixth-Century Byzantium." *Past and Present* 128:7–27.

Harris, William V. 1989   *Ancient Literacy.* Cambridge, Mass.: Harvard University Press.

Hart, Laurie Kain 1992   *Time, Religion, and Social Experience in Rural Greece.* Lanham, Md.: Rowman & Littlefield.

Heintz, Jean-Georges (ed.) 1997   *Oracles et prophéties dans l'antiquité: Actes du colloque de Strasbourg 15–17 juin 1995.* Paris: De Boccard.

Hengel, Martin 1974   *Judaism and Hellenism.* Tr. by J. Bowden. Philadelphia: Fortress.

Henrichs, Albert 1973   "Zwei Orakelfragen." *ZPE* 11:115–19.

Herzog, Rudolf 1939   "Der Kampf um den Kult von Menuthis." In *Pisciculi: Studien zur Religion und Kultur des Altertums,* pp. 117–24. Ed. by Theodor Klauser and Adolf Rücker. Münster: Aschendorff.

Hobson, Deborah W. 1984   "Agricultural Land and Economic Life in Soknopaiou Nesos." *BASP* 21:89–109.

Hoogendijk, F. A. J., and Van Minnen, P. 1991   *Papyri, Ostraca, Parchments and Waxed Tablets in the Leiden Papyrological Institute.* P. Lugd.-Bat. 25. Leiden: Brill.

Hope, Colin A. 1994   "Isis and Sarapis at Kellis: A Brief Note." *BACE* 5:37–42.

Hope, Colin A.; Kaper, Olaf E.; Bowen, Gillian E.; and Patten, Shirley F. 1989   "Dakhleh Oasis Project: Ismant el-Kharab 1991–92." *JSSEA* 19:1–26.

Hughes, George R. 1951   "A Demotic Astrological Text." *JNES* 10:256–64.

Hussein, Adel, and Wagner, Guy 1994   "Une dédicace grecque du grand temple d'Esment El-Kharab." *ZPE* 101:109–12.

Ikram, Salima 1989   "Domestic Shrines and the Cult of the Royal Family at Tel-'Amarna." *JEA* 75:89–101.

Iversen, Erik 1961   *The Myth of Egypt and Its Hieroglyphs in European Tradition.* Copenhagen: GEC GAD; repr. Princeton, N.J.: Princeton University Press, 1993.

Jelínková-Reymond, E. 1956   *Les inscriptions de la statue guérisseuse de Djed-Her-le-Sauveur.* Cairo: IFAO.

Johnson, David W. 1980   *A Panegyric on Macarius, Bishop of Tkôw, Attributed to Dioscorus of Alexandria.* 2 vols. CSCO 415–16, S. Coptici 41–42. Louvain: Sécretariat du CSCO.

Johnson, Douglas H. 1992   "On Disciples and Magicians: The Diversification of Divinity among the Nuer during the Colonial Era." *JRAf* 22:2–22.

———. 1994   *Nuer Prophets: A History of Prophecy from the Upper Nile in the Nineteenth and Twentieth Centuries.* Oxford: Clarendon.

Johnson, Janet H. 1975   "The Demotic Magical Spells of Leiden I 384." *OMRO* 56:29–64.

———. 1977   "Louvre E3229: A Demotic Magical Text." *Enchoria* 7:55–102.

———. 1986   "Introduction to the Demotic Magical Papyri." In Betz (ed.) 1986:lv–lviii.

———. 1992   (ed.). *Life in a Multi-Cultural Society: Egypt from Cambyses to Constantine and Beyond.* SAOC 51. Chicago: Oriental Institute.

Joly, Henri 1982   "Platon égyptologue." *Revue philosophique* 2:255–66.

Jones, Alexander 1994   "The Place of Astronomy in Roman Egypt." In *The Sciences in Greco-Roman Society (Apeiron* 27, 4), pp. 25–51. Ed. by T. D. Barnes. Edmonton, Alberta: Academic Printing & Publishing.

Jullien, Michel 1902   "Le culte chrétien dans les temples de l'antique Égypte." *Études* 92:237–53.

Kákosy, László 1964   "Reflexions sur le problème de Totoès." *Bulletin du Musée hongrois des Beaux-Arts* 24:9–16.

———. 1966a   "Der Gott Bes in einer koptischen Legende." *Acta antiqua academiae scientiarum Hungaricae* 14:185–96.

———. 1966b   "Prophecies of Ram Gods." *AOH* 19:341–58.

———. 1984   "Das Ende des Heidentums in Ägypten." In Nagel (ed.) 1984:61–76.

———. 1995   "Probleme der Religion im römerzeitlichen Ägypten." *ANRW* II.18.5:2894–3049.

Kaper, Olaf E. 1987   "How the God Amun-Nakht Came to Dakhleh Oasis." *JSSEA* 17:151–56.

———. 1991   "The God Tutu (Tithoes) and His Temple in the Dakhleh Oasis." *BACE* 2:59–67.

———. 1997   "Temples and Gods in Roman Dakhleh: Studies in the Indigenous Cults of an Egyptian Oasis." Ph.D. dissertation, Rijksuniversiteit Groningen.

Knipfing, John R. 1923   "The Libelli of the Decian Persecution." *HTR* 16:345–90.

Koenen, Ludwig 1968 "Die Prophezeiungen des 'Töpfers.'" *ZPE* 2:178–209.

———. 1970 "The Prophecies of a Potter: A Prophecy of World Renewal Becomes an Apocalypse." In *Proceedings of the XIIth International Congress of Papyrology*. ASP 7, pp. 249–54. Ed. by Deborah H. Samuel. Toronto: Hakkert.

———. 1974 "Bemerkungen zum Text des Töpferorakels und zu dem Akaziensymbol." *ZPE* 13:313–19.

———. 1983 "Die Adaptation ägyptischer Königsideologie am Ptolemäerhof." In *Egypt and the Hellenistic World*. Studia Hellenistica 27, pp. 143–90. Ed. by E. Van't Dack, P. Van Dessel, and W. Van Gucht. Louvain: Studia Hellenistica.

———. 1984 "A Supplementary Note on the Date of the Oracle of the Potter." *ZPE* 54:9–13.

———. 1985 "The Dream of Nektanebos." *BASP* 22:171–94.

Koenig, Yvan 1994 *Magie et magiciens dans l'Égypte ancienne*. Paris: Pygmalion.

Kotansky, Roy 1994 *Greek Magical Amulets: The Inscribed Gold, Silver, Copper, and Bronze Lamellae*, pt. 1, *Published Texts of Known Provenance*. Papyrologica Coloniensia 22/1. Opladen: Westdeutscher.

Krause, Martin 1983 "Das Weiterleben ägyptischer Vorstellungen und Bräuche im koptischen Totenwesen." In *Das römisch-byzantinische Ägypten*. Aegyptiaca Treverensia 2, pp. 85–92. Mainz am Rhein: Von Zabern.

Kropp, Angelicus M. 1930/31 *Ausegewählte koptische Zaubertexte*. 3 vols. Brussels: Fondation égyptologique Reine Élisabeth.

Kugener, M.-A. 1907 "Sévère, patriarche d'Antioche, 512–518, Première partie: Vie de Sévère par Zacharie le scholastique." *PO* 2:3–115.

Kuhlmann, Klaus P. 1988 *Das Ammoneion: Archäologie, Geschichte und Kultpraxis des Orakels von Siwa*. Archäologische Veröffentlichungen 75. Mainz: Von Zabern.

Kuhn, K. H. 1956 *Letters and Sermons of Besa*. 2 vols. CSCO 157–58, S. coptici 21–22. Louvain: Durbecq.

Kumar, Pramod 1984 *Folk Icons and Rituals in Tribal Life*. New Delhi: Abhinav.

Łajtar, Adam 1991 "*Proskynema* Inscriptions of a Corporation of Iron-Workers from Hermonthis in the Temple of Hatshepsut in Deir El-Bahari: New Evidence for Pagan Cults in Egypt in the 4th Cent. A.D." *JJP* 21:53–70.

Lane Fox, Robin 1986 *Pagans and Christians*. New York: Knopf.

Lange, H. O. 1927 *Der magische Papyrus Harris: Herausgegeben und Erklärt*. Det Kgl. Danske Videnskabernes Selskab., Historisk-filologiske Meddelelser 14, 2. Copenhagen: Høst.

———. 1932 "Ein faijumischer Beschwörungstext." In *Studies Presented to F. Ll. Griffith*, pp. 161–66. London: Egypt Exploration Society.

Laskowska-Kusztal, Ewa 1984 *Le sanctuaire ptolémaïque de Deir el-Bahari*. Deir El-Bahari 3. Warsaw: PWN.

Lawson, E. Thomas 1985 *Religions of Africa*. San Francisco: Harper.

Leclant, J. 1951 "Fouilles et travaux en Égypte, 1950–1951.I." *Orientalia* 20:453–75.

Lefebvre, Gustave 1921 "La fête du Nil à Achôris." *BSAA* 18:47–59.

Lefort, L.-Th. 1954 "La chasse aux reliques des martyrs en Égypte au IVᵉ siè-cle." *La nouvelle Clio* 6:225–30.

———. 1955 *S. Athanase: Lettres festales et pastorales en copte.* CSCO 150, Scriptores coptici 19. Louvain: Durbecq.

———. 1958 "L'homélie de S. Athanase des papyrus de Turin." *Le muséon* 71:5–50, 209–39.

Leipoldt, Johannes 1906/13 *Sinuthii archimandritae vita et opera omnia.* 3 vols. (1–2, 4). CSCO 41–42, 73, S. coptici 1–2, 5. Paris: Imprimerie nationale.

Lenaerts, J. 1983 "Deux papyrus des Sortes Astrampsychi: *P. Iand.* 5, 71 et *P. Rain.* I, 33." *CdÉ* 58:187–99.

Lewis, Naphtali 1983 *Life in Egypt under Roman Rule.* Oxford: Clarendon.

Lexa, François 1925 *La magie dans l'Égypte antique, de l'ancien empire jusqu'à l'époque copte.* 2 vols. Paris: Paul Geuthner.

Lichtheim, Miriam 1973/80 *Ancient Egyptian Literature.* 3 vols. Berkeley: University of California Press.

Lieu, Samuel N. C. 1994 *Manichaeism in Mesopotamia and the Roman East.* RGRW 118. Leiden: Brill.

Limberis, Vasiliki 1994 *Divine Heiress: The Virgin Mary and the Creation of Christian Constantinople.* London and New York: Routledge.

Lincoln, Bruce 1989 *Discourse and the Construction of Society: Comparative Studies of Myth, Ritual, and Classification.* New York: Oxford University Press.

Lloyd, Alan B. 1976 *Herodotus Book II, Commentary 1–98.* EPRO 43. Leiden: Brill.

———. 1982 "Nationalist Propaganda in Ptolemaic Egypt." *Historia* 31:33–55.

Loprieno, Antonio (ed.) 1996 *Ancient Egyptian Literature: History and Forms.* Probleme der Ägyptologie 10. Leiden: Brill.

Loukianoff, Grégoire 1936 "Une statue parlante ou oracle du dieu Ré-Harmakhis." *ASAE* 36:187–93.

Lüddeckens, Erich 1968 "Gottesdienstliche Gemeinschaften im pharaonischen, hellenistischen und christlichen Ägypten." *Zeitschrift für Religions- und geistesgeschichte* 20:193–211.

MacCormack, Sabine 1991 *Religion in the Andes: Vision and Imagination in Early Colonial Peru.* Princeton, N.J.: Princeton University Press.

MacCoull, Leslie S. B. 1991 "Duke University Ms. C25: Dreams, Visions, and Incubation in Coptic Egypt." *OLP* 22:123–32.

MacMullen, Ramsay 1984 *Christianizing the Roman Empire, A.D. 100–400.* New Haven, Conn., and London: Yale University Press.

———. 1997 *Christianity and Paganism in the Fourth to Eighth Centuries.* New Haven, Conn., and London: Yale University Press.

Mahé, Jean-Pierre 1982 *Hermès en Haute-Égypte,* vol. 2, *Le fragment du Discours Parfait et les Définitions hermétiques arméniennes.* Bibliothèque copte de Nag Hammadi, "textes" 7. Quebec: Université Laval.

Malaise, Michel 1987 "Pèlerinages et pèlerins dans l'Égypte ancienne." *Histoire des pèlerinages non chrétiens. Entre magique et sacré: le chemin des dieux,* pp. 55–82. Ed. by Jean Chelini and Henry Branthomme. Paris: Hachette.

———. 1990 "Bes et les croyances solaires." *Studies in Egyptology Presented to Miriam Lichtheim,* vol. 2, pp. 680–729. Ed. by Sarah Israelit-Groll. Jerusalem: Magnes.

Marriott, McKim 1955 "Little Communities in an Indigenous Civilization." In *Village India: Studies in the Little Community,* pp. 171–222. Ed. by McKim Marriott. Chicago: University of Chicago Press.

Martin, Cary J. 1994 "The Child Born in Elephantine: Papyrus Dodgson Revisited." In *Acta Demotica: Acts of the Fifth International Conference for Demotists.* Egitto e vicino oriente 17, pp. 199–212. Pisa: Giardini.

Martin, Geoffrey Thorndike 1981 *The Sacred Animal Necropolis at North Saqqâra: The Southern Dependencies of the Main Temple Complex.* London: Egypt Exploration Society.

Maspero, Jean 1914 "Horapollon et la fin du paganisme égyptien." *BIFAO* 11:163–95.

McBride, Daniel R. 1989 "The Development of Coptic: Late-Pagan Language of Synthesis in Egypt." *JSSEA* 19:89–111.

McDowell, A. G. 1990 *Jurisdiction in the Workmen's Community of Deir El-Medina.* Leiden: Nederlands Instituut voor het Nabije Oosten.

Meeks, Dimitri 1971 "Génies, anges, démons en Égypte." In *Génies, anges et démons.* Sources orientales 8, pp. 17–84. Paris: Éditions du Seuil.

———. 1992 "Le nom du dieu Bès et ses implications mythologiques." In *The Intellectual Heritage of Egypt: Studies Presented to László Kákosy. . . .* Studia aegyptiaca 14, pp. 423–36. Ed. by Ulrich Luft. Budapest: La Chaire d'Égyptologie.

Mercier, Jacques 1979 *Ethiopian Magical Scrolls.* Tr. by Richard Pevear. New York: Braziller.

Merkelbach, Reinhold 1977 *Die Quellen des griechischen Alexanderromans.* Munich: Beck.

Meyer, Marvin, and Smith, Richard (eds.) 1994 *Ancient Christian Magic: Coptic Texts of Ritual Power.* San Francisco: Harper.

Meyer, Robert T. 1950 *St. Athanasius: The Life of Saint Antony.* Ancient Christian Writers 10. Westminster, Md.: Newman.

Michailidis, Georges 1950 "Vestiges du culte solaire parmi les chrétiens d'Égypte." *BSAC* 14:37–110.

———. 1960/62 "Le dieu Bes sur une stèle magique." *BIE* 42/43:65–85, pls. I–II.

———. 1963/64 "Bès aux divers aspects." *BIE* 45:53–93, pls. I–XX.

Milne, J. Grafton 1924 *A History of Egypt under Roman Rule.* 3rd ed. London: Methuen; repr. Chicago: Ares, 1992.

Morenz, Siegfried 1973 *Egyptian Religion.* Tr. by Ann E. Keep. Ithaca, N.Y., and London: Cornell University Press.

Moret, A. 1915 "Horus sauveur." *RHR* 72:213–87.

Morgan, J. R. (tr.) 1989 "Heliodorus: An Ethiopian Story." In *Collected Ancient Greek Novels,* pp. 349–588. Ed. by B. P. Reardon. Berkeley: University of California Press.

Munier, H. 1938 "Le christianisme à Philae." *BSAC* 4:37–49.

Murnane, William J. 1983 *The Penguin Guide to Ancient Egypt.* Harmondsworth: Penguin.

Muszynski, Michel 1977 "Les 'associations religieuses' en Égypte d'après les sources hiéroglyphiques, démotiques et grecques." *OLP* 8:145–74.

Nachtergael, Georges 1985 "Les terres cuites 'du Fayoum' dans les maisons de l'Égypte romaine." *CdÉ* 60:223–39.

———. 1988 "Le panthéon des terres cuites de l'Égypte hellénistique et romaine." *Le monde copte* 14/15:5–27.

Nagel, Peter (ed.) 1984 *Graeco-Coptica: Griechen und Kopten im byzantinischen Ägypten*. Martin-Luther-Universität, Halle-Wittenberg, Wissenschaftliche Beiträge 1984, 48 (1.29). Halle: Martin-Luther-Universität.

Nau, F. 1907 "Histoires des solitaires égyptiens." *ROC* 12:43–69, 171–89, 393–413.

———. 1908 "Histoires des solitaires égyptiens." *ROC* 13:47–66, 266–97.

———. 1909 "Histoires des solitaires égyptiens." *ROC* 14:357–79.

———. 1912 "Histoires des solitaires égyptiens." *ROC* 17:204–11, 294–301.

———. 1913 "Histoires des solitaires égyptiens." *ROC* 18:137–46.

Nautin, Pierre 1967 "La conversion du temple de Philae en église chrétienne." *Cahiers archéologiques* 17:1–43.

Nock, Arthur Darby 1972 *Essays on Religion and the Ancient World*. 2 vols. Ed. by Zeph Stewart. Oxford: Clarendon.

———. 1972a "A Vision of Mandulis Aion." In Nock 1972, 1:356–400.

———. 1972b "Later Egyptian Piety." In Nock 1972, 2:566–74.

O'Leary, De Lacy 1938 "The Destruction of Temples in Egypt." *BSAC* 4:51–57.

Orlandi, Tito 1982 "A Catechesis against Apocryphal Texts by Shenute and the Gnostic Texts of Nag Hammadi." *HTR* 75:85–95.

Otto, Walter 1905/8 *Priester und Tempel im hellenistischen Ägypten*. 2 vols. Leipzig and Berlin: Teubner.

Papaconstantinou, Arietta 1994 "Oracles chrétiens dans l'Égypte byzantine: Le témoignage des papyrus." *ZPE* 104:281–66.

Papini, Lucia 1985 "Biglietti oracolari in copto dalla necropoli nord di Antinoe." In *Acts of the Second International Congress of Coptic Study*, pp. 245–55. Ed. by Tito Orlandi and Frederik Wisse. Rome: C.I.M.

Parássoglou, George M. 1976 "Circular from a Prefect: Sileat omnibus perpetuo divinandi curiositas." In *Collectanea Papyrologica: Texts Published in Honor of H. C. Youtie* 1. Papyrologische Texte und Abhandlungen 19, pp. 261–74. Ed. by Ann Ellis Hanson. Bonn: Habelt.

Parker, Richard A. 1959 *A Vienna Demotic Papyrus on Eclipse- and Lunar-Omnia*. Providence, R.I.: Brown University Press.

———. 1962 *A Saite Oracle Papyrus from Thebes*. Providence, R.I.: Brown University Press.

Pearson, Birger A., and Goehring, James E. (eds.) 1986 *The Roots of Egyptian Christianity*. Philadelphia: Fortress.

Perdrizet, Paul 1921 *Les terres cuites grecques d'Égypte de la Collection Fouquet*. 2 vols. Nancy: Berger-Levrault.

Perdrizet, Paul, and Lefebvre, Gustave 1919 *Les graffites grecs du Memnonion d'Abydos*. Nancy: Berger-Levrault.

Pernigotti, Sergio 1979  "Il codice copto." *SCO* 29:19–53.

Perpillou-Thomas, Françoise 1993  *Fêtes d'Égypte ptolémaïque et romaine d'après la documentation papyrologique grecque.* Studia Hellenistica 31. Louvain: Studia Hellenistica.

Pettazzoni, Raffaele 1949  "Kronos in Egitto." In *Studi in Memoria di Ippolito Rosellini,* vol. 1, pp. 274–99. Pisa: Lischi & Figli.

Phillips, Charles Robert 1986  "The Sociology of Religious Knowledge in the Roman Empire to A.D. 284." *ANRW* II.16.3:2677–2773.

Piankoff, A. 1958/60  "The Osireion of Seti I at Abydos during the Greco-Roman Period and the Christian Occupation." *BSAC* 15:125–49.

Picard, C. 1958  "La sphinge tricéphale dite 'panthée,' d'Amphipolis et la démonologie égypto-alexandrine." *Académie des Inscriptions et Belles-Lettres, Commission de la fondation Piot, Monuments et mémoires* 50:49–84.

Pinch, Geraldine 1993  *Votive Offerings to Hathor.* Oxford: Griffith Institute.

———. 1994  *Magic in Ancient Egypt.* London: British Museum.

Podemann Sørensen, Jørgen 1992  "Native Reactions to Foreign Rule and Culture in Religious Literature." In *Ethnicity in Hellenistic Egypt.* Studies in Hellenistic Civilization 3, pp. 164–81. Ed. by Per Bilde, Troels Engberg-Pedersen, Lise Hannestad, and Jan Zahle. Aarhus: University Press.

Potter, David 1994  *Prophets and Emperors.* Revealing Antiquity 7. Cambridge, Mass.: Harvard University Press.

Poulsen, Frederik 1945  "Talking, Weeping, and Bleeding Sculptures: A Chapter of the History of Religious Fraud." *Acta Archaeologica* 16:178–95.

Préaux, Claire 1936  "Esquisse d'une histoire des révolutions égyptiennes sous les lagides." *CdÉ* 22:522–52.

Preisendanz, Karl 1973/74  *Papyri Graecae Magicae: Die griechischen Zauberpapyri.* 2 vols. 2nd ed., ed. by Albert Henrichs. Stuttgart: Teubner.

Price, Richard 1975  *Saramaka Social Structure: Analysis of a Maroon Society in Surinam.* Caribbean Monograph Series 12. Río Piedras PR: Institute of Caribbean Studies.

Quaegebeur, Jan 1975  *Le dieu égyptien Shaï dans la religion et l'onomastique.* OLA 2. Louvain: Leuven University Press.

———. 1977  "Tithoes, dieu oraculaire?" *Enchoria* 7:103–8.

———. 1983a  "Cultes égyptiens et grecs en Égypte hellénistique: L'exploitation des sources." In *Egypt and the Hellenistic World.* Studia Hellenistica 27, pp. 303–24. Ed. by E. Van 't Dack, P. Van Dessel, and W. Van Gucht. Louvain: Studia Hellenistica.

———. 1983b  "De l'origine égyptienne du griffon Némésis." In *Visages du destin dans les mythologies (Mélanges Jacqueline Duchemin).* Centre de recherches mythologiques de l'université de Paris 10, pp. 41–54. Ed. by François Jouan. Paris: Les Belles Lettres.

———. 1984  "La désignation 'Porteur(s) des dieux' et le culte des dieux-crocodiles dans les textes des époques tardives." In *Mélanges Adophe Gutbub,* pp. 161–76. Montpellier: University of Montpellier.

———. 1986  "Tithoes." *LexÄg* 6:602–6.

———. 1997 "L'Appel au Divin: Le Bonheur des hommes mis dans la main des dieux." In Heintz (ed.) 1997:15–34.

Quaegebeur, Jan; Clarysse, Willy; and Van Maele, Beatrijs 1985 "Athena, Neith and Thoeris in Greek Documents." *ZPE* 60:217–32.

Ranger, Terence 1993 "The Local and the Global in Southern African Religious History." In *Conversion to Christianity: Historical and Anthropological Perspectives on a Great Transformation,* pp. 65–98. Ed. by Robert W. Hefner. Berkeley: University of California Press.

Rassart-Debergh, Marguerite 1990 "De l'icône païenne à l'icône chrétienne." *Le monde copte* 18:39–70.

Ray, John D. 1976 *The Archive of Hor.* London: Egypt Exploration Society.

Rea, John 1977 "A New Version of P. Yale inv. 299." *ZPE* 27:151–56.

Reddé, Michel 1990 "Quinze années de recherches française à Douch." *BIFAO* 90:281–301.

———. 1992 *Le trésor de Douch (Oasis de Kharga).* Douch 4. Cairo: IFAO.

Redfield, Robert 1941 *The Folk Culture of the Yucatan.* Chicago and London: University of Chicago Press.

———. 1956 *Peasant Society and Culture: An Anthropological Approach to Civilization.* Chicago and London: University of Chicago Press.

Redmayne, Alison 1970 "Chikanga: An African Diviner with an International Reputation." In Douglas (ed.) 1970:103–28.

Reinhold, Meyer 1980 "Roman Attitudes toward Egyptians." *The Ancient World* 3:97–103.

Rémondon, Roger 1951 "A propos de deux graffiti grecs d'une tombe siwite." *CdÉ* 26:156–61.

Reymond, E. A. E. 1983 "Demotic Literary Works of Graeco-Roman Date in the Rainer Collection of Papyri in Vienna." In *Papyrus Erzherzog Rainer (P.Rainer Cent.),* vol. 1, pp. 42–60. Vienna: Hollinek.

Riedel, Wilhelm, and Crum, W. E. 1904 *The Canons of Athanasius of Alexandria.* London: Williams & Norgate.

Ritner, Robert K. 1984 "A Uterine Amulet in the Oriental Institute Collection." *JNES* 43:209–21.

———. 1989 "Horus on the Crocodiles: A Juncture of Religion and Magic in Late Dynastic Egypt." In *Religion and Philosophy in Ancient Egypt.* Yale Egyptological Studies 3, pp. 103–16. Ed. by William Kelly Simpson. New Haven, Conn.: Yale University Press.

———. 1992 "Religion vs. Magic: The Evidence of the Magical Statue Bases." In *The Intellectual Heritage of Egypt: Studies Presented to László Kákosy. . . .* Studia aegyptiaca 14, pp. 495–501. Ed. by Ulrich Luft. Budapest: La chaire d'Égyptologie.

———. 1993 *The Mechanics of Ancient Egyptian Magical Practice.* SAOC 54. Chicago: Oriental Institute.

———. 1995 "Egyptian Magical Practice under the Roman Empire: The Demotic Spells and Their Religious Context." *ANRW* II.18.5:3333–79.

Roberts, Colin H. 1934 "Two Papyri from Oxyrhynchus." *JEA* 20:20–28.

Roccati, Alessandro, and Siliotti, Alberto (eds.) 1987 *La Magia in Egitto ai*

*Tempi dei Faraoni*. Milan: Rassegna Internazionale di Cinematografia Archeologica.

Roeder, Günther 1914 *Naos*. Catalogue général des antiquités égyptiennes du Musée du Caire, ##70001–50. Leipzig: Breitkopf & Härtel.

Rondot, Vincent 1990 "Le Naos de Domitien, Toutou et les sept flèches." *BIFAO* 90:303–37.

Rubenson, Samuel 1995 *The Letters of St. Antony: Monasticism and the Making of a Saint*. Minneapolis, Minn.: Fortress.

Rübsam, Winfried J. R. 1974 *Götter und Kulte in Faijum während der griechisch-römisch-byzantinischen Zeit*. Bonn: Habelt.

Russell, Norman 1980 *The Lives of the Desert Fathers*. London and Oxford: Mowbray.

Ryholt, Kim 1993 "A Pair of Oracle Petitions Addressed to Horus-of-the-Camp." *JEA* 79:189–98.

Sadek, Ashraf Iskander 1987 *Popular Religion in Egypt during the New Kingdom*. Hildesheimer ägyptologische Beiträge 27. Hildesheim: Gerstenberg.

Satzinger, Helmut 1975 "The Old Coptic Schmidt Papyrus." *JARCE* 12:37–50.

———. 1984 "Die altkoptischen Texte als Zeugnisse der Beziehungen zwischen Ägyptern und Griechen." In Nagel (ed.) 1984:137–46.

Sauneron, Serge 1952 "Les querelles impériales vues à travers les scènes du temple d'Esné." *BIFAO* 51:111–21.

———. 1959 "Les songes et leur interprétation dans l'Égypte ancienne." In *Les songes et leur interprétation*. Sources orientales 2, pp. 17–61. Paris: Éditions du Seuil.

———. 1960a *The Priests of Ancient Egypt*. Tr. by Ann Morrissett. Evergreen Profile Book 12. New York: Grove.

———. 1960b "Le nouveau sphinx composite du Brooklyn Museum et le rôle du dieu Toutou-Tithoès." *JNES* 19:269–87.

———. 1962a *Les fêtes religieuses d'Esna aux derniers siècles du paganisme*. Esna 5. Cairo: IFAO.

———. 1962b "Les conditions d'accès à la fonction sacerdotale à l'époque gréco-romaine." *BIFAO* 61:55–57.

———. 1966 "Le monde du magicien égyptien." In *Le monde du sorcier*. Sources orientales 7, pp. 27–65. Paris: Éditions du Seuil.

———. 1970 *Le papyrus magique illustré de Brooklyn [Brooklyn Museum 47.218.156]*. Brooklyn, N.Y.: Brooklyn Museum.

Sayce, A. H. 1894 "Inscriptions et papyrus grecs d'Égypte." *Revue des études grecques* 7:284–304.

Schiffman, Lawrence H., and Swartz, Michael D. 1992 *Hebrew and Aramaic Incantation Texts from the Cairo Genizah*. Semitic Texts and Studies 1. Sheffield: JSOT.

Schoffeleers, Matthew 1994 "Christ in African Folk Theology: The *Nganga* Paradigm." In Blakely et al. (eds.) 1994:73–88.

Schubart, W. 1931 "Orakelfragen." *ZÄS* 67:110–15.

Scott, James C. 1977 "Protest and Profanation: Agrarian Revolt and the Little Tradition." *Theory and Society* 4:1–38, 211–46.

Scott, Walter 1924/36 *Hermetica*. 4 vols. Oxford: Oxford University Press; repr. Boulder, Colo.: Shambhala, 1985.

Scott-Moncrieff, Philip David 1913 *Paganism and Christianity in Egypt*. Cambridge: Cambridge University Press.

Seckel, Emil, and Schubart, Wilhelm 1919 *Der Gnomon des Idios Logos*. BGU 5. Berlin: Weidmann.

Shafer, Byron E. (ed.) 1991 *Religion in Ancient Egypt: Gods, Myths, and Personal Practice*. Ithaca, N.Y., and London: Cornell University Press.

Smallwood, E. Mary 1976 *The Jews under Roman Rule*. SJLA 20. Leiden: Brill.

Smelik, K. A. D., and Hemelrijk, E. A. 1984 " 'Who knows not what monsters demented Egypt worships?' Opinions on Egyptian Animal Worship in Antiquity as Part of the Ancient Conception of Egypt." *ANRW* II.17.4:1852–2357.

Smith, Jonathan Z. 1978 *Map Is Not Territory: Studies in the History of Religions*. SJLA 23. Leiden: Brill.

———. 1978a "The Temple and the Magician." In Smith 1978:172–89.

———. 1995 "Trading Places." In *Ancient Magic and Ritual Power*. RGRW 129, pp. 13–27. Ed. by Marvin Meyer and Paul Mirecki. Leiden: Brill.

Solmsen, Friedrich 1979 *Isis among the Greeks and Romans*. Martin Classical Lectures 25. Cambridge, Mass.: Harvard University Press.

Spiegelberg, Wilhelm 1910 *Der Sagenkreis des Königs Petubastis*. Leipzig: Hinrichs.

———. 1924 "Ägyptologische Beiträge, III. Der Falkenkultus auf der Insel Philae in christlicher Zeit." *Archiv* 7:186–89.

———. 1933 "La littérature démotique." *CdÉ* 15:44–68.

Srinivas, M. N. 1989 *The Cohesive Role of Sanskritization and Other Essays*. Delhi: Oxford.

Sternberg-El Hotabi, Heike 1994 "Der Untergang der Hieroglyphenschrift: Schriftverfall und Schrifttod im Ägypten der griechisch-römischen Zeit." *CdÉ* 69:218–45.

Stewart, Charles 1991 *Demons and the Devil: Moral Imagination in Modern Greek Culture*. Princeton, N.J.: Princeton University Press.

Stewart, Randall 1987 "Another Look at *P. Iand.* 5.71 and *P. Rain.* 1.33." *ZPE* 69:237–42.

Stewart, Susan 1993 *On Longing*. Durham, N.C., and London: Duke University Press.

Strobel, Karl 1992 "Soziale Wirklichkeit und irrationales Weltverstehen in der Kaiserzeit, I. Sortes Astrampsychi und Sortes Sangellenses." *Laverna* 3:129–41.

Tait, W. J. 1991 "P. Carlsberg 207: Two Columns of a Setna-text." In *The Carlsberg Papyri 1: Demotic Texts from the Collection*. Carsten Niebuhr Institute Publications 15, pp. 19–46. Copenhagen: Museum Tusculanum.

———. 1992 "Demotic Literature and Egyptian Society." In J. Johnson (ed.) 1992:303–10.

———. 1994a "Egyptian Fiction in Demotic and Greek." In *Greek Fiction: The Greek Novel in Context*, pp. 203–22. Ed. by J. R. Morgan and Richard Stoneman. London and New York: Routledge.

————. 1994b "Some Notes on Demotic Scribal Training in the Roman Period." In *Proceedings of the XX International Congress of Papyrologists, Copenhagen 23–29 August 1992*, pp. 188–92. Copenhagen: Museum Tusculanum.

Tcherikover, Victor A., and Fuks, Alexander 1957/64 *Corpus Papyrorum Judaicarum*. 3 vols. Cambridge, Mass.: Harvard University Press.

Te Velde, Herman 1977 *Seth, God of Confusion: A Study of His Role in Egyptian Mythology and Religion*. Probleme der Ägyptologie 6. Leiden: Brill.

Thelamon, Françoise 1981 *Païens et chrétiens au IV^e siècle: L'apport de l'"Histoire ecclésiastique" de Rufin d'Aquilée*. Paris: Études augustiniennes.

Thissen, Heinz Josef 1992 *Der verkommene Harfenspieler*. Demotische Studien 11. Sommerhausen: Zauzich. 1992/93 "Zur Begegnung von Christentum und 'Heidentum': Schenute und Gessios." *Enchoria* 19/20:155–64.

Thompson, Dorothy J. 1988 *Memphis under the Ptolemies*. Princeton, N.J.: Princeton University Press.

Till, Walter 1936 *Koptische Heiligen- und Martyrerlegenden*. Orientalia Christiana Analecta 108. Rome: Pontifical Institute for Oriental Studies.

Török, László 1989 "Notes on the Kingdom of the Blemmyes." In *Studia in honorem L. Fóti*. Studia aegyptiaca 12, pp. 397–412. Budapest: University Loránd Eötvös.

————. 1993 *Coptic Antiquities*, vol. 1. Bibliotheca Archaeologica 11. Rome: Bretschneider.

————. 1995 *Hellenistic and Roman Terracottas from Egypt*. Bibliotheca Archaeologica 15. Rome: Bretschneider.

Toutain, J. 1915 "Le culte du crocodile dans le fayoum sous l'empire romain." *RHR* 71:171–94.

Tran Tam Tinh, Vincent 1986 "L'acculturation des divinités grecques en Égypte." In *Iconographie classique et identités régionales*. BCH Supplément 14, pp. 355–63. Ed. by Lilly Kahil, Christian Augé, and Pascale Linant de Bellefonds. Athens: École française d'Athènes.

Traunecker, Claude 1979 "Manifestations de piété personnelle à Karnak." *BSFE* 85:22–31.

————. 1984 "La revanche du crocodile de Coptos." In *Mélanges Adolphe Gutbub*, pp. 219–29. Montpellier: Université de Montpellier.

————. 1987 "Une pratique de magie populaire dans les temples de Karnak." In Roccati and Siliotti (eds.) 1987:221–42.

————. 1992 *Coptos: Hommes et dieux sur le parvis de Geb*. OLA 43. Louvain: Peeters.

Treu, Kurt 1986 "Varia Christiana II." *Archiv* 32:23–31.

Trexler, Richard C. 1980 *Public Life in Renaissance Florence*. New York: Academic.

Trigger, Bruce G. 1978 "The Ballana Culture and the Coming of Christianity." In *Africa in Antiquity: The Arts of Ancient Nubia and the Sudan*, vol. 1, pp. 107–19. Brooklyn, N.Y.: Brooklyn Museum.

Trombley, Frank R. 1985 "Paganism in the Greek World at the End of Antiquity: The Case of Rural Anatolia and Greece." *HTR* 78:327–52.

————. 1993/94  *Hellenic Religion and Christianization c. 370–529.* 2 vols. RGRW 115. Leiden: Brill.

Turner, Victor 1974  *Dramas, Fields, and Metaphors.* Ithaca, N.Y., and London: Cornell University Press, 1974.

Van Dam, Raymond 1985  "From Paganism to Christianity in Late Antique Gaza." *Viator* 16:1–20.

Van der Horst, Pieter Willem 1984  *Chaeremon: Egyptian Priest and Stoic Philosopher.* EPRO 101. Leiden: Brill.

Van der Vliet, Jacques 1991  "Varia magica coptica." *Aegyptus* 71:217–42.

————. 1993  "Spätantikes Heidentum in Ägypten im Spiegel der koptischen Literatur." In *Begegnung von Heidentum und Christentum im spätantiken Ägypten.* Riggisberger Berichte 1, pp. 99–130. Riggisberg: Abegg-Stiftung.

Vanderlip, Vera Frederika 1972  *The Four Greek Hymns of Isidorus and the Cult of Isis.* ASP 12. Toronto: Hakkert.

Vandier, Jacques 1961  *Le papyrus Jumilhac.* Paris: CNRS.

Veilleux, Armand 1980  *Pachomian Koinonia,* vol. 1, *The Life of Saint Pachomius and His Disciples.* CSS 45. Kalamazoo, Mich.: Cistercian Publications.

Vergote, J. 1954  *Les noms propres du P. Bruxelles inv. E.7616: Essai d'interprétation.* P. Lugd.-Bat. 7. Leiden: Brill.

Vernus, Pascal 1979  "Douch arraché aux sables." *BSFE* 85:7–21.

Vikan, Gary 1982  *Byzantine Pilgrimage Art.* Washington, D.C.: Dumbarton Oaks.

Vivian, Tim 1993  *Histories of the Monks of Upper Egypt and the Life of Onnophrius by Paphnutius.* CSS 140. Kalamazoo, Mich.: Cisterican Publications.

Vleeming, S. P. (ed.) 1995  *Hundred-Gated Thebes: Acts of a Colloquium on Thebes and the Theban Area in the Graeco-Roman Period.* P. Lugd.-Bat. 27. Leiden: Brill.

Vogt, Evan Z. 1976  *Tortillas for the Gods: A Symbolic Analysis of Zinacanteca Rituals.* Cambridge, Mass., and London: Harvard University Press.

Wagner, Guy 1987  *Les oasis d'Égypte à l'époque grecque, romaine et byzantine d'après les documents grecs.* Bibliothèque d'Étude 100. Cairo: IFAO.

Wagner, Guy, and Quaegebeur, Jan 1973  "Une dédicace grecque au dieu égyptien Mestasytmis de la part de son synode." *BIFAO* 73:41–60.

Weill, Raymond 1918  *La fin du moyen empire égyptien.* Paris: Imprimerie nationale.

Welles, C. Bradford 1946  "The Garden of Ptolemagrius at Panopolis." *TPAPA* 77:192–206.

Wente, Edward 1990  *Letters from Ancient Egypt.* Society of Biblical Literature Writings from the Ancient World 1. Atlanta: Scholars.

Werbner, Richard P. 1989  "Regional Cult of God Above." In Richard P. Werbner, *Ritual Passage, Sacred Journey: The Process and Organization of Religious Movement,* pp. 245–98. Washington, D.C.: Smithsonian Institution; Manchester: Manchester University Press.

————. 1977  (ed.). *Regional Cults.* Association of Social Anthropologists Monographs 16. London: Academic.

Whitby, Michael 1991 "John of Ephesus and the Pagans: Pagan Survivals in the Sixth Century." In *Paganism in the Later Roman Empire and in Byzantium*. Byzantina et Slavica Cracoviensia 1, pp. 111–31. Ed. by Maciej Salamon. Cracow: BCS.

White, Geoffrey M. 1988 "Symbols of Solidarity in the Christianization of Santa Isabel, Solomon Islands." In *Culture and Christianity: The Dialectics of Transformation*. Contributions to the Study of Anthropology 2, pp. 11–31. Ed. by George R. Saunders. New York: Greenwood.

Whitehorne, John 1995 "The Pagan Cults of Roman Oxyrhynchus." *ANRW* II.18.5:3050–91.

Wilcken, Ulrich 1901 "Heidnisches und Christliches aus Ägypten." *Archiv* 1:396–436.

Willis, William H. 1978 "Two Literary Papyri in an Archive from Panopolis." *ICS* 3:140–53.

———. 1979 "The Letter of Ammon of Panopolis to His Mother." In *Actes du XV<sup>e</sup> congrès international de papyrologie*, pt. 2, *Papyrus inédits*. Papyrologica Bruxellenisa 17, pp. 98–115. Brussels: Fondation égyptologique Reine Élisabeth.

Winkler, Jack J. 1980 "Lollianos and the Desperadoes." *JHS* 100:155–81.

Winlock, Herbert E.; Evelyn White, Hugh G.; and Oliver, James H. 1941 *The Temple of Hibis in El Khargeh Oasis*. 2 vols. New York: Metropolitan Museum.

Wipszycka, Ewa 1988 "La christianisation de l'Égypte aux IV<sup>e</sup>–VI<sup>e</sup> siècles. Aspects sociaux et ethniques." *Aegyptus* 68:117–65.

———. 1992 "Le nationalisme a-t-il existé dans l'Égypte byzantine?" *JJP* 22:83–128.

Wolf, Eric R. 1966 *Peasants*. Englewood Cliffs, N.J.: Prentice-Hall.

Wormald, F. 1929 "A Fragment of Accounts Dealing with Religious Festivals." *JEA* 15:239–42.

Worp, K. A. 1989 "Marginalia on Published Documents." *ZPE* 78:133–38.

Worrell, William H. 1935 "Coptic Magical and Medical Texts." *Orientalia* 4:1–37, 184–94.

Young, Allan 1975 "Magic as a 'Quasi-Profession': The Organization of Magic and Magical Healing among Amhara." *Ethnology* 14:245–65.

Young, Dwight W. 1981 "A Monastic Invective against Egyptian Hieroglyphs." In *Studies Presented to Hans Jakob Polotsky*, pp. 348–60. Ed. by Dwight W. Young. Beacon Hill, Mass.: Pirtle & Polson.

Youtie, Herbert C. 1973 "The Heidelberg Festival Papyrus: A Reinterpretation." In *Scriptiunculae*, vol. 1, pp. 514–45. Amsterdam: Hakkert.

———. 1975 "Questions to a Christian Oracle." *ZPE* 18:253–57 + pl. VIII.

Yoyotte, Jean 1963 "L'Égypte ancienne et les origines de l'antijudaïsme." *RHR* 163:133–43.

———. 1955 "Une étude sur l'anthroponymie gréco-égyptienne du nome prosôpite." *BIFAO* 55:125–40.

———. 1969 "Bakhthis: Religion égyptienne et culture grecque à Edfou." In *Religions en Égypte hellénistique et romaine (Colloque de Strasbourg 16–18 mai 1967)*, pp. 127–41. Paris: Presses Universitaires.

Žabkar, Louis V. 1975 "A Hieracocephalous Deity from Naqa, Qustul, and Philae." *ZÄS* 102:143–53.

Zauzich, Karl-Theodor 1983 "Das Lamm des Bokchoris." In *Papyrus Erzherzog Rainer (P.Rainer Cent.)*, vol. 1, pp. 165–74. Vienna: Hollinek.

———. 1991 "Einleitung." In *The Carlsberg Papyri 1: Demotic Texts from the Collection*. Carsten Niebuhr Institute Publications 15, pp. 1–11. Copenhagen: Museum Tusculanum.

Zucker, Friedrich 1956 "Priester und Tempel in Ägypten in den Zeiten nach der decianischen Christenverfolgung." In *Akten des VIII. internationalen Kongresses für Papyrologie, Wien 1955*, pp. 167–74. Vienna: Rohrer.

# INDEX

## About the Author

David Frankfurter is Assistant Professor of History and Religious
Studies at the University of New Hampshire. He is the author of
*Elijah in Upper Egypt: The Apocalypse of Elijah
and Early Egyptian Christianiy.*